Warfare in History
ISSN 1358–779X

Editorial Board
Matthew Bennett, Royal Military Academy, Sandhurst
David Parrott, University of Oxford
Hew Strachan, University of Oxford

This series aims to provide a wide-ranging and scholarly approach to military history, offering both individual studies of topics or wars, and volumes giving a selection of contemporary and later accounts of particular battles; its scope ranges from the early medieval to the modern period.

New proposals for the series are welcomed; they should be sent to the publisher at the address below.

Boydell and Brewer Limited, PO Box 9, Woodbridge, Suffolk, IP12 3DF

*Previously published volumes in the series
are listed at the back of this book*

Warfare in History

WAR AND THE SOLDIER
IN THE FOURTEENTH CENTURY

WAR AND THE SOLDIER
IN THE FOURTEENTH CENTURY

Adrian R. Bell

THE BOYDELL PRESS

First published 2004
The Boydell Press, Woodbridge

ISBN 1 84383 103 1

The Boydell Press is an imprint of Boydell & Brewer Ltd
PO Box 9, Woodbridge, Suffolk IP12 3DF, UK
and of Boydell & Brewer Inc.
668 Mt Hope Avenue, Rochester, NY 14620, USA
website: www.boydellandbrewer.com

A catalogue record for this book is available
from the British Library

Library of Congress Cataloging-in-Publication Data
Bell, Adrian R. (Adrian Robert), 1971–
   War and the soldier in the fourteenth century / Adrian R. Bell.
     p. cm. – (Warfare in history)
   Includes bibliographical references and index.
   ISBN 1–84383–103–1 (alk. paper)
   1. Great Britain – History, Military – 1066–1485. 2. Arundel and Surrey,
Richard Fitzalan, Earl of, 1346–1397 – Military leadership. 3. Military art
and science – Great Britain – History – Medieval, 500–1500. 4. Hundred
Years' War, 1339–1453 – Participation, British. 5. Soldiers – Great Britain
– History – To 1500. I. Title. II. Series.
DA60.B45 2004
944'.02542'092242 – dc22   2004004825

This publication is printed on acid-free paper

Printed in Great Britain by
The Cromwell Press, Trowbridge, Wiltshire

Contents

Tables

General Editor's Preface

Warfare involving English armies in the last third of the fourteenth century has been relatively little studied. Traditional military historians like A.H. Burne avoided it as a period from which nothing could be learnt, because there were few 'great battles'. Instead, it featured the far more 'normal' activities of chevauchée, amphibious operations and bouts of internecine conflict. The last was directly connected to the decline of English fortunes in France, and the subsequent difficulties in profiting from ransom and plunder. Indeed, the historiography of the Hundred Years War has a decidedly nationalistic flavour, with English-speaking historians concentrating on periods of English victory. For example, Clifford Rogers' recent work on the campaigns of Edward III, focuses on the successful period of his reign, and even Jonathan Sumption provides a rather brief account; moreover, his approach is relentlessly narrative, allowing little space for the necessary analysis of trends, people and events. To find detailed studies of 1369–99 one has to go back thirty years or more to the work of J.W. Sherborne and J.J.N. Palmer, for their analysis of war and diplomacy respectively.

Adrian Bell's doctoral research, from which this book comes, bears witness to the teaching of two influential scholars in Later Medieval Studies, both of whom are published in this series. Dr Andrew Ayton of the University of Hull initially taught him the value of using computer databases, a technique which he further developed under the direction of Professor Anne Curry, then at Reading (and now at Southampton). This technique enables him to draw a detailed picture of military activity and royal and other expeditionary forces across a neglected generation of Hundred Years War Studies. The scale of this activity is striking: it involves almost 100,000 soldiers, and although five royal armies make up almost half of this total, earls and others frequently led forces of 3–6,000 men to France, Flanders and the Iberian Peninsula.

In Part I, Bell provides a survey of the war after 1369, especially in the reign of Richard II, and particularly the campaigns of 1387 and 1388, which adds a great deal to our understanding of the period. In Part II, he turns to an analysis of the military community not just in Richard's reign, but across the seeming divide into Henry IV's regime. Despite the inevitable gaps in the evidence, his tracing of relationships and obligations over time and through specific contingents is a major achievement. His study of loyalties is particularly revealing, not least in exploring how far kings were prepared to go in forgiving rebels. For example, the case of Sir William Clifford, who served both Richard II and Henry IV, but was continually rebellious against the latter (see pp. 206–7), may be exceptional, but it is clearly not extraordinary. This goes to reinforce just how dependent upon the military community and its local affiliations medieval monarchs had to be, if they hoped to rule effectively.

In sum, then, Dr Bell's attention to detail and thorough investigation of the sources make this volume an important contribution to fourteenth-century studies and to this series. His exploration of the careers of both major and minor figures tells us what it truly meant to be a soldier in the wars of a previously neglected era.

Matthew Bennett
Royal Military Academy Sandhurst
September 2004

Preface

This book started a long time ago, in the Round Room of the Public Record Office at Chancery Lane, before the medieval records were moved to the modern building at Kew. I remember looking at the lists of names on the muster rolls and thinking how am I going to manage this? However, perseverance with a laptop (very heavy then) and databases enabled me to make this information more manageable. I was very idealistic, before I grew old, and believed I was researching real people, men who actually fought and died for their king in the Hundred Years War. This was going to be history about the little people, the esquires and archers who did not appear in regular history texts. I think I have achieved some of this ambition and perhaps put a name and sometimes a face to a number of the men fighting these wars. I hope that I have managed to provide a 'class photo' or a snapshot in time detailing who these men were, and I have speculated on what motivated them to serve and risk their lives. My history has developed into an attempt to push back the boundaries of what we think of as modern. I have constantly been surprised by the levels of control achieved by the crown over expeditionary armies, and the sophistication of the administrative mechanisms that existed to enable these campaigns to succeed. These were large undertakings, even by today's standards. I hope my findings will inspire others to discover that the past is not such a dark place after all.

The thesis upon which this book is based took far longer to complete than I ever expected; that it is finally complete is in no small part due to the constant encouragement and patience of my supervisor Professor Anne Curry. I also would like to show my gratitude to my thesis examiners, Professor Brian Kemp and Professor Anthony Goodman, who gave me valuable advice and inspired me to write the book. I have also been lucky to have a work environment, at the ISMA Centre, that has enabled me to complete my research, and the Director, Professor Brian Scott-Quinn, has supported me from the very start. I am not going to list everyone who has supported me in my research (no doubt someone will be upset as a result) – they know who they are – but I would like to say that without Michelle it would never have been finished, and I dedicate this work to her.

Timeline of Major Events and Expeditions, 1386–1389

1386

1 October   Assembly of the Wonderful Parliament at Westminster. Summoned 8 August. Dissolved 28 November

19 November   Appointment of royal council

10 December   Richard, earl of Arundel, appointed Admiral of the North and West

16 December   Arundel retained to serve with 2,500 men from 1 March 1387

1387

16 February   Summons for assembly of the fleet at Sandwich on 11 March 1387

8 March   Order for the commission to muster

12 March   Arundel's arrival at Sandwich

13 March   Muster of army

23 March   Expedition put to sea

24 March   Battle joined with Flemish fleet

14 April   Fleet returns to Orwell for refit and supplies

1 May   Expedition sets out for second time

end May   Richard II sends representatives to negotiate for peace with the French

12 June   Expedition returns to Southampton

August   Richard's questions to the judges at Shrewsbury and Nottingham

13 November   Arundel, Thomas duke of Gloucester and Thomas earl of Warwick gather forces at Harringay

14 November   First appeal against five named 'traitors'

17 November   Meeting of the king with senior Appellants at Westminster. Appeal to be heard at parliament in February 1388

end November   Robert de Vere, duke of Ireland, travels to Cheshire to gain armed support for the king

12 December   Senior Appellants joined at Huntingdon by Henry earl of Derby, and Thomas earl of Nottingham and Earl Marshal

20 December   Battle of Radcot Bridge and defeat of the royal force under Robert de Vere by the combined forces of the Appellants

end December   Possible deposition of Richard II for three days by the Appellants

1388

3 February   Assembly of the Merciless Parliament at Westminster. Summoned 17 December 1387. Prorogued 20 March to 13 April. Dissolved 4 June

10 March	Parliament grants subsidy for an army
24 March	Arundel retained to serve for three months with 3,500 men from 11 May 1388
9 April	Arundel appointed captain of Brest
5 May	Army and fleet gathered at Southampton
14 May	Order for commission to muster. Muster taken between now and 1 June
10 June	Arundel joins force and expedition sets sail
2 July	Gloucester responds to proposal for peace from Philip duke of Burgundy
17 July	Arundel recalled from expedition to assist against Scottish incursions
5 August	Defeat of English forces and capture of Sir Henry Percy by Scottish at the battle of Otterburn
3 September	Arundel and his expedition return to Winchelsea
9 September	Assembly of parliament at Cambridge. Summoned 28 July. Dissolved 17 October

1389

3 May	Richard II declares himself fit to govern in person and dismisses principal officers of state

Abbreviations

CCR	*Calendar of Close Rolls*
CIPM	*Calendar of Inquisitions Post Mortem*
Complete Peerage	*The Complete Peerage*, ed. G.E. Cokayne (13 vols, London, 1910–1957)
CPR	*Calendar of Patent Rolls*
DNB	*Dictionary of National Biography* (63 vols, London, 1885–1900)
Foedera	T. Rymer, *Foedera, Conventiones, Litterae etc.*, ed. A. Clarke, F. Holbrooke and J. Caley (4 vols, London, 1816–1869)
Froissart, *Chronicles*	J. Froissart, *Chronicles*, ed. and trans. T. Johnes (2 vols, London, 1874)
Handbook of British Chronology	*Handbook of British Chronology*, ed. E.B. Fryde, D.E. Greenway, S. Porter and I. Roy, 3rd edn (London, 1961)
HOP	J.S. Roskell, L. Clark and C. Rawcliffe (eds), *The History of Parliament: The House of Commons 1386–1421* (4 vols, Stroud, 1992)
Royal Household	C. Given-Wilson, *The Royal Household and the King's Affinity: Service, Politics and Finance, 1360–1413* (New Haven and London, 1986)
RP	*Rotuli Parliamentorum* (6 vols, London, 1767–1777)
Scrope v. Grosvenor	*The Scrope and Grosvenor Controversy*, ed. N. Harris Nicolas (2 vols, London, 1832)
Two Estate Surveys	Marie Clough (ed.), *Two Estate Surveys of the Fitzalan Earls of Arundel* (Sussex Record Society, 1969)
VCH	*The Victoria History of the Counties of England*
Westminster Chronicle	*The Westminster Chronicle 1381–1394*, ed. and trans. L.C. Hector and B.F. Harvey (Oxford, 1982)

To Michelle

Introduction

In recent years there has been renewed interest in the Hundred Years War. A wander into any high street bookshop will show the 21st-century shopper a large number of publications dealing with this subject, including collections of essays emanating from specialised conferences. Much of this work has concentrated on the campaigns of Edward III in the early stages of the Hundred Years War down to the treaty of Brétigny in 1360. This emphasis is not surprising when one considers that this stage of the war was highly successful for the English in the wake of Edward III's assumption of the title King of France in 1340. English dominance was secured with the great naval battle at Sluys in 1340, the victory at Crécy in 1346, and the Black Prince's capture of the French king at the battle of Poitiers in 1356.[1] The English had to wait until 1415 at Agincourt for their next great military success, under the leadership of Henry V. Not surprisingly, a number of recent publications demonstrate a similarly great interest in the later stages of the struggle with France.[2] Historians of the Hundred Years War clearly like winners.

There has also been a renaissance of scholarly research into the reign of Richard II. Numerous books have been published which discuss the king and his reign. Rather than focus on the military events of the reign, however, these studies have mainly concentrated on the image of kingship, the royal character and events leading towards the deposition of 1399. Nigel Saul has written perhaps the definitive biography, concentrating upon Richard the monarch in the framework of the events and political machinations of the reign.[3] Saul has developed a portrait of a man obsessed by the concept of Kingship and the Divine Right of the monarch: so much so, that Richard was unable to judge the political mood in the country and let his arrogance and belief in his own concept of kingship lead to his own downfall. Saul uses his thesis to explain the decisions Richard took during his reign and especially the way that he dealt with the Appellants once he had cemented his own authority. He describes Richard as a monarch not only motivated by political expedience but also affected by changes in his own personal circumstances. My book is concerned with the Appellant period of supremacy (1386–1389) in particular, years that are also judged by Saul to be crucial in the development of Richard's particular brand of kingship which led in turn to his tyranny.

Warfare during the second phase of the Hundred Years War (1369–1399) has been relatively neglected. This is probably because these years witnessed territorial reverses compounded by the absence of any army led by the king into

---

1 The Hundred Years War up to 1369 is amply illustrated by recent texts by Sumption and Rogers: see bibliography for details.
2 In particular, the work by Curry: see bibliography.
3 Saul, *Richard II* (New Haven, 1997).

France. However, as will be shown, this was not a period of inaction. Indeed, nearly 100,000 troops were employed on English expeditions to France and campaigns led by the king to Ireland and Scotland. J.J.N. Palmer recognised the importance of campaigning in this period, especially throughout the phase of active hostilities between 1369 and 1389. He described the fighting in the Hundred Years War at this time as 'unremitting', and commented that England and France were at war with each other for all but four of these twenty years. Other historians have agreed that the last quarter of the fourteenth century was not glorious, with the English forces unable to bring the French to battle, thus failing to make a political impact on France during this stage of the Hundred Years War.[4]

Generally speaking, there has been much interest in the development of military organisation during the Hundred Years War. This has built upon the pioneering work of A.E. Prince on the indentured retinue.[5] Prince provided a detailed summation of what an indenture was and how it worked. He discussed the numbers of soldiers involved in warfare, using many documentary sources from the earlier stages of the reign of Edward III. He overlooked the last fifteen years of the reign because of what he supposed was a lack of documentation. The seminal studies by J.W. Sherborne demonstrated that a full picture of military life *was* possible for these years and beyond by using the existing indentures and by combining the data with information from other Exchequer sources. By utilising this evidence Sherborne was able to reconstruct the manpower utilised in the expeditions of 1369–1380.[6] Sherborne ended his study of expeditionary armies in 1380 since that year saw the last royal army leaving to campaign in France in the later fourteenth century. Nevertheless, Sherborne's studies have been an inspiration as they provided a methodology for working with the surviving sources in order to reconstruct the English expeditionary forces of 1387 and 1388, which will be the focus of this text.

Andrew Ayton has worked on the earlier phase of the Hundred Years War under Edward III and has demonstrated that this period is of considerable interest in military terms, for instance, regarding the Edwardian military revolution. He shows that the methods used by the English government for the organisation of warfare became standardised as the war progressed. This enabled the English crown to launch successive campaigns, many overseas, utilising this well developed military administration. Ayton's work has been further inspiration to this book as he demonstrated that much of interest is still to be discovered in the sources.

---

[4] Palmer, *England, France and Christendom, 1377–99* (London, 1972), p. 1; for commentary on this period of the war see Anne Curry, *The Hundred Years War* (London, 1993), pp. 74–88; Christopher Allmand, *The Hundred Years War* (Cambridge, 1989) p. 96; May McKisack, *The Fourteenth Century, 1307–1399* (Oxford, 1959), p. 145.

[5] A.E. Prince, 'The Indenture System under Edward III', in J.G. Edwards, V.H. Galbraith and E.F. Jacob (eds), *Historical Essays in Honour of James Tait* (Manchester, 1933), pp. 283–297, and A.E. Prince, 'The Strength of English Armies in the Reign of Edward III', *English Historical Review*, xlvi (1931), pp. 353–371.

[6] J.W. Sherborne, 'Indentured Retinues and the English Expeditions to France, 1369–1380' *English Historical Review*, lxxix (1964), pp. 718–46; and J.W. Sherborne, 'The English Navy: Shipping and Manpower, 1369–89', *Past and Present*, 37 (1967), pp. 163–175.

In his book *Knights and Warhorses: Military Service and the English Aristocracy under Edward III,*[7] Ayton turned to other uses of evidence in order to introduce more information to the subject of military organisation. He made excellent use of the horse inventories that have survived in sufficient numbers to provide additional evidence from the reign of Edward III. He utilised this information to investigate the perceived Edwardian military revolution, the method of record keeping, and how this information related to other surviving evidence. He demonstrated that the process of conducting warfare had become formalised by the English government because of the pursuit of the Hundred Years War. This led to professionalism in the mechanisms of the government which provided soldiers for service, as well as the professionalism of those fighting the wars. Major research on military organisation is also currently being undertaken by Anne Curry on field armies and garrison service in Lancastrian Normandy. For this work, Curry is utilising a computer database in order to manage the original record sources.[8]

Despite the volume of work in this area, never before has anyone looked in detail at the personnel of the specific campaigns. Ayton has argued that although the war itself has been studied, the men who actually fought in the war, the 'military community' have been neglected. He comments: 'So far, indeed, are we from a comprehensive study of those who engaged in military activity in later medieval England that we lack a full prosopographical study for even a single major royal army.'[9] By drawing together such nominal evidence as he could gather, Ayton demonstrated how a career profile of a soldier in the Hundred Years War could be built up.[10] In addition to Exchequer materials and letters of protection and attorney, Ayton also utilised the evidence provided by the cases heard at the court of chivalry in the 1380s. Ayton used the first-hand evidence provided by the deponents to provide a career framework in order to discuss the military experiences, attitudes to war, reasons for service and *mentalité* of the fourteenth-century soldier.[11] By investigating these sources together, by a process he describes as 'nominal record linkage',[12] Ayton demonstrated that men served in royal expeditions as part of their public duty. Their lifestyle was such that pursuit of service in local governance and military endeavour went hand in hand for the gentry fighting the battles of the Hundred Years War.[13] This

---

7   Ayton, *Knights and Warhorses: Military Service and the English Aristocracy under Edward III* (Woodbridge, 1994).
8   See, for instance, Anne Curry, 'English Armies in the Fifteenth Century', in Anne Curry and Michael Hughes (eds), *Arms, Armies and Fortifications in the Hundred Years War* (Woodbridge, 1994), pp. 39–68.
9   Ayton, *Knights and Warhorses*, p. 1.
10 *Ibid.*, pp. 156–169.
11 See especially Andrew Ayton, 'Knights, Esquires and Military Service: The Evidence of the Armorial Cases before the Court of Chivalry', in A. Ayton, and J.L. Price (eds), *The Medieval Military Revolution: State, Society and Military Change in Medieval and Early Modern Europe* (New York, 1995), pp. 81–104.
12 Andrew Ayton, 'Edward III and the English Aristocracy at the Beginning of the Hundred Years War', in Matthew Strickland (ed.), *Armies, Chivalry and Warfare in Medieval Britain and France* (Stamford, 1998), pp. 173–206, p. 205.
13 *Ibid.*, pp. 175–176.

work on the court of chivalry has been supplemented by research by Maurice Keen who has also looked at the literary sources and the historical evidence provided by the portrait of Chaucer's knight in the Canterbury Tales.[14]

In this book I have attempted to explore the 'military community' who were involved in the two royal naval expeditions led by Richard Fitzalan, earl of Arundel in 1387 and 1388. These campaigns are not only interesting for the wealth and concentration of materials surviving on military organisation but also because of the political background against which the expeditions were undertaken. The army personnel of the campaigns can be fully reconstructed by the unique survival of the muster rolls for both expeditions.[15] These sources are supported by the indentures of service, Arundel's accounts returned to the Exchequer after the campaigns, the enrolled accounts, the issue rolls – recording payments made, and by letters of protection and attorney.[16] In addition, the careers of those serving can be supplemented by other relevant sources, including the depositions taken for the Scrope v. Grosvenor case at the court of chivalry in 1386.[17] The sources and the campaigns will be discussed in detail in Chapter 2.

Anthony Goodman, J.J.N. Palmer and, more recently, Nigel Saul have demonstrated that these campaigns should be identified with the Appellant seizure of power from 1386 to 1389.[18] The expeditions, it is argued, were contrary to the king's own previous foreign policy of peaceful relations with France, as directed by his Chancellor, Michael de la Pole. The campaigns were also divided by a civil war, which ended in defeat of the royal forces under Robert de Vere, duke of Ireland, at Radcot Bridge on 20 December 1387. Indeed, Goodman places the campaign of Radcot Bridge firmly within the framework of expeditions undertaken by Arundel during 1387–1388. By investigating the careers of men who served in the campaigns it is possible to draw conclusions about why they may have chosen to serve. The particular circumstance of the expeditions of 1387–1388 adds a further political dimension to other motives for service.

In order to utilise fully the evidence contained within the surviving muster rolls, a computer database has been created. The use of the computer database

---

14 Maurice Keen, 'English Military Experience and the Court of Chivalry: The Case of Grey v. Hastings', in P. Contamine, C. Giry-Deloison and M. Keen (eds), *Guerre et société en France, en Angleterre et en Bourgogne, XIVe–XVe siècle* (Lille, 1992), pp. 123–142, and Maurice Keen, 'Chaucer and Chivalry Re-visited', in Matthew Strickland (ed.), *Armies, Chivalry and Warfare in Medieval Britain and France*, pp. 1–13.

15 Muster roll for 1387: Public Record Office, E101/40/33; and for 1388: E101/41/5.

16 Accounts for 1387: E101/40/35; and for 1388: E101/41/4. The accounts for 1388 contain the copy of the indenture for the campaign. The indenture for 1387 does not survive but the indenture terms are recorded on the Enrolled (Foreign) Accounts, E364/21 m. 6d. For 1388: E364/24 m. 5. For payments see Issue Rolls, for 1387: E403/515 mm. 25, 27. For 1388: E403/519 mm. 8, 12, 19, 23; E403/521 mm. 6, 7. Letters of protection and attorney, 1387: C76/71; 1388: C76/72. These sources will be discussed in detail in Chapter 2.

17 *Scrope v. Grosvenor.*

18 Anthony Goodman, *The Loyal Conspiracy: The Lords Appellant under Richard II* (London, 1971), pp. 128–133. Palmer, *England, France and Christendom*, ch. 5 for 1387 and ch. 7 for 1388. Saul, *Richard II*, pp. 166–169 for 1387 and pp. 196–198 for 1388.

has enabled more to be gained from the documentary sources than has been possible hitherto.[19] We are able to compare and contrast quickly the nominal data with other sources and also to analyse the level of continued service between the two campaigns. The computer database was planned to replicate fully the source material as presented in the muster rolls. This ensures consistency and also the integrity of the original data which is left in its abbreviated form and thus does not suffer from any errors of translation. The tables in this book deliberately preserve the spellings of names as entered in the original muster and, where necessary, abbreviated forms are highlighted with an apostrophe.

It is necessary to comment further at this stage on the problematic nature of the source material for nominal recording. The two muster rolls were compiled by royal clerks and each is mainly written in the same hand. We are therefore reliant upon the clerk's understanding of a soldier's name for the spelling that he uses on the muster roll. It is possible to speculate from some of the spellings used that names had not been regularised during the fourteenth century. It is therefore not unusual to find a soldier serving in both expeditions, but with his surname spelt differently. This makes identification of continuance of service more difficult, though not impossible. From the spelling of some names it appears that the soldiers told the clerk their name during the muster. The clerk then wrote his understanding of what the soldier had said. This has produced the variety of spellings used. One example is that of Sir Nicholas Clifton, who is recorded as 'Mons' Nich' Clifton' in the muster roll for 1387 and 'Mons' Nichol' Clyfton' for 1388.[20] The source is further complicated by the use of three languages whilst compiling the muster rolls. The clerk preparing the roll has used Latin for his comments, but has generally written the actual names in English, perhaps, as mentioned above, as pronounced at the muster. The comments made during campaign regarding dubbings, deaths and absentees have generally been recorded in French. This implies that the clerks checking the muster against Arundel's accounts at the Exchequer would have been trilingual. As mentioned, the spelling of the names and annotations, as recorded on the muster roll, will be preserved in the footnotes and the tables that appear in this book. This may seem cumbersome but is designed to ensure no pre-judgement over identification before compilation of the entire database. I have modernised and normalised the nominal material for use in the main body of the text.

The book begins with an overview of the expeditions from 1369 to 1389 and places them in the political context of the end of the reign of Edward III, the reign of Richard II, and of the latter's deposition by his cousin, Henry IV. I then discuss the sources for the campaigns of 1387–1388 in more detail before reconstructing the events of these campaigns using these original materials. I also analyse the information provided on the muster rolls for the two campaigns. The

---

[19] I was first introduced to the value of the computer database whilst studying the 'History and Computing' module as an undergraduate at the University of Hull, guided by Dr Andrew Ayton.
[20] 1387: E101/40/33 m. 12d; 1388: E101/41/5 m. 11.

second part of the book concentrates on the army personnel who can be identified serving in the two campaigns. It examines evidence for continuity of service in other earlier and later expeditions, and provides case studies of those who can be identified from within the English military community. I have looked for evidence concerning the recruitment of the two expeditionary forces and also links to the civil war that culminated at Radcot Bridge. Finally, I have attempted to look for connections that may tell us more about the loyalties demonstrated by the medieval soldier. By analysing this material, we are able to identify and discuss the careers of the individuals who served on these expeditions and to draw conclusions about their motivation for such service within the context of contemporary politics.

The scope of the present book had to be limited. It focuses on a concentrated period: the campaigns spanning 1369–1400. This period conveniently begins with the second phase of the Hundred Years War and closes following the end of the reign of Richard II. I halted my search for evidence at Henry IV's first expedition to Scotland, at the beginning of his reign. Future and earlier service has been mentioned on occasion but by no means systematically, as this would be a huge undertaking at this stage. I have not attempted to write biographies of the major figures involved in the campaigns, as this has already been done,[21] and thus I have relied on other works of scholarship for some of their career details.

I have not attempted to reassess the methods of military organisation of the later fourteenth century, but have relied upon the scholarship of those cited in the text. The study concentrates upon the service of the army personnel and makes no comment upon the many thousands of naval personnel and other ancillary personnel who would also have been involved in the expeditions. Although we know something of the shipping, including the numbers of sailors and ships supporting the expedition, no muster rolls survive for the mariners.[22] Servants and camp followers did not receive royal pay and so are missing from the records. Even without such groups of participants, however, what we have for the expeditions of 1387–1388 is a considerable amount of source material which can permit an in-depth study of two fascinating and politically important campaigns.

---

[21] For instance Goodman, *Loyal Conspiracy*, contains detailed biographies of the earl of Arundel and the Earl Marshal.

[22] Sherborne, 'The English Navy', p. 38, utilising the following sources: for 1387: E101/40/36; for accounts of payments to mariners: E403/515 mm. 25, 27, payments made for shipping; for 1388: E101/40/40 for accounts of payments to mariners, E403/515 m. 12 and E403/515 mm. 6, 7 for payments made for shipping. These sources detail the cost of the shipping to the crown and also some of the names of captains and the ships used. These sources would benefit from more systematic study.

Part One

THE EXPEDITIONS AND THEIR SOURCES

1

Military and Political Background
to the Expeditions of 1387–1388

The expeditions of 1387 and 1388 must be considered in the wider context of the Hundred Years War and the campaigns conducted in the later fourteenth century as a whole. The campaigns can be seen summarised in Table 1. The expeditions undertaken between 1369 and 1400 can be roughly divided into three separate themes. Firstly, expeditions were launched at land and sea against the French and the Scots in order to protect the rights and territories of the English crown. Secondly, further overseas expeditions reflect the growing dynastic ambitions of Richard's uncles with forays into Spain and Portugal. Thirdly, following the ending of hostilities with France, Richard II concentrated on consolidating his domains in Ireland. This coincided with renewed crusading activity that was encouraged in order to cement peace with France and to divert the military instincts of the nobility. Unlike his grandfather and father, Richard did not lead an expedition against France in person.

Table 1 demonstrates the extent of the undertaking of the English crown on its royal campaigns in the last thirty years of the fourteenth century.[1] In the years

---

[1] The table is compiled from figures provided by a number of different commentators. Many of the figures are based on the administrative records; however some of the figures are estimates based on contemporary accounts and chronicles. I have not included figures for the crusades, as these were joint campaigns with other nationalities. The figures for 1369, 1370, 1370a, 1372b, 1373 and 1375 are drawn from, Sherborne, 'Indentured Retinues' – the figures for 1369 include a number of unknown retinues and Welsh lance men. Figures for 1378 and 1380 are from Sherborne, 'The English Navy'; for 1381 from P.E. Russell, *English Intervention in Spain and Portugal* (Oxford, 1955), p. 302; for 1383 from Norman Houseley, 'The Bishop of Norwich's Crusade, May 1383', *History Today*, xxxiii (May 1983), pp. 15–20, p. 17, and Margaret Aston, 'The Impeachment of Bishop Despencer', *Bulletin of the Institute of Historical Research*, vol. xxxviii, 98 (1965), pp. 127–148, p. 137; for 1385 from Lewis, 'The Last Medieval Summons', p. 7; for 1386 from Anthony Goodman, *John of Gaunt: The Exercise of Princely Power in Fourteenth-Century Europe* (Harlow, 1992), p. 117 – Russell, *English Intervention*, p. 418, suggests a considerably larger figure of up to 7,000 men for this campaign. Figures for 1394 are from Saul, *Richard II*, p. 279 – see James L. Gillespie, 'Richard II: King of Battles?', in James L. Gillespie (ed.), *The Age of Richard II* (Stroud, 1997), pp. 139–164, p. 151 for discussion of other estimates for the size of the force: he suggests a figure of around 6,000. Figures for 1399 are from Saul, *Richard II*, p. 289, citing D.B. Johnson, 'The Interim Years: Richard II and Ireland, 1395–1399', in *England and Ireland in the Late Middle Ages: Essays in Honour of Jocelyn Otway-Ruthven*, ed. J.F. Lydon (Dublin, 1981), pp. 446–455; for 1400 from A.L. Brown, 'The English Campaign in Scotland, 1400', in *British Government and Administration: Studies presented to S.R. Chrimes*, ed. H. Hearder and H.R. Loyn (Cardiff, 1974), pp. 40–54, p. 45.

Table 1: English expeditions in the later fourteenth century

Year	Commander	To	Men-at-arms	Archers	Total	Ratio men-at-arms to archers
1369	John of Gaunt	France	1500	2758	6000	1 to 1.8
1370	Sir Robert Knolles	France	2000	2000	4000	1 to 1
1372a	Edward III	Naval expedition			6000	
1372b	John, Lord Neville	To support the duke of Brittany	480	480	960	1 to 1
1373	John of Gaunt	The Great Chevauchee across France	3032	2893	5925	1 to 1
1375	Edmund, earl of Cambridge	Brittany	1990	1985	3975	1 to 1
1378	John of Gaunt	Naval expedition	2500	2500	5000	1 to 1
1379	John de Montfort, duke of Brittany	Brittany	650	650	1300	1 to 1
1380	Thomas, earl of Buckingham	Brittany	2581	2610	5191	1 to 1
1381	Edmund of Langley	Portugal	1500	1500	3000	1 to 1
1383	Bishop Despencer of Norwich	Flanders	2500	2500	5000	1 to 1
1385	Richard II	Scotland	4590	9144	13764	1 to 2
1386	John of Gaunt	Castile	1600	2000	3600	1 to 1.3
1387	Richard, earl of Arundel	Naval expedition	1107	1390	2497	1 to 1.3
1388	Richard, earl of Arundel	Naval expedition	1578	2014	3592	1 to 1.3
1390a	Duke of Bourbon	Crusade				
1390b	Henry, earl of Derby	Crusade				
1394	Richard II	Ireland			7000	
1396	John Beaufort	Nicopolis, Crusade				
1399	Richard II	Ireland			4500	
1400	Henry IV	Scotland			13000	
Total					94304	

1369–1400 it can be estimated that very close to 100,000 soldiers were mobilised for land and naval campaigns on behalf of the crown. This is without including the numbers of soldiers included on minor campaigns, on crusade, those involved in the civil war at Radcot Bridge in 1387 and also the troops who rose in arms during the revolution of 1399. Nethertheless, it shows that a large number of men were involved in the military events of the later fourteenth century, despite the truce with France for many of these years.

The table also demonstrates the development in the ratio of men-at-arms to archers participating in royal campaigns. In his review of fourteenth century English armies, Andrew Ayton has suggested that the optimal ratio of one man-at-arms to one archer, maintained in the years 1369–1380, was eroded in the last years of the fourteenth century.[2] This move in the favour of the numbers of archers on campaign can be seen in the numbers involved in armies in the first half of the fifteenth century. Anne Curry has shown that the ratio of one man-at-arms to three archers, for instance in the army at Agincourt, was replicated throughout the English armies of 1415–1450. The ratios went as high as one man-at-arms to 19 archers for the army crossing to France in 1429.[3] It can be seen from the above table that the argument for such a change in composition occurring during the final years of the fourteenth century, is not supported by the surviving numerical evidence. The Scottish campaign of 1385 does indeed have a ratio of one man-at-arms to two archers, but this may have been unusual because of the method of recruitment, as it was raised by feudal summons. It can indeed be shown that for 1386–1388, the ratio of the armies is static at one man-at-arms to 1.3 archers. This suggests a slight shift towards a larger number of archers, but is not really a significant change. It is unfortunate that more information does not arise for the Irish campaigns of 1394 and 1399 and also the Scottish campaign of 1400, which would identify whether a change in the composition of English armies really occurred at this time.

There has been much discussion of the expeditions led against France, as they relate directly to the continuance of hostilities in the Hundred Years War. Anne Curry describes how the English efforts against the French became stunted during the later reign of Edward III and early reign of Richard II.[4] She comments that many historians are of the opinion that the English failed to bring the French to battle, even though this was their intent. Christopher Allmand is also dismissive about these French expeditions:

> On the whole these armies were a powerful force of destruction in those parts of France in which they moved; however, in terms of securing military advantage it is doubtful whether they constituted the threat which, in theory, it was in their power to pose.[5]

Both Palmer and Sherborne have done much work in this previously neglected period concerning the expeditions undertaken by the English crown.[6] This work has shown that these years constituted the most intensively fought of the Hundred Years War. Palmer comments on the truce secured by the marriage of Richard II in 1396,

> When they put their seals on this truce the rulers of England and France could look back on the longest, hardest, most bitter and wide-ranging war in the history of their two countries. By comparison, the Edwardian Phase of the war had been a comparably mild affair, and England at least was not to be involved

---

2 Andrew Ayton, 'English Armies in the Fourteenth Century', pp. 32–33.
3 Anne Curry, 'English Armies in the Fifteenth Century', pp. 39–68.
4 Anne Curry, *The Hundred Years War*, pp. 74–88.
5 Christopher Allmand, *The Hundred Years War*, p. 96.
6 Sherborne, 'Indentured Retinues' and, *idem*, 'The Cost of English Warfare with France in the Later Fourteenth Century', *Bulletin of the Institute of Historical Research*, 50 (1977), 135–50; Palmer, *England, France and Christendom*.

in so tough a struggle for another two centuries, if not longer. The Edwardian War was intermittent; the Caroline War (1369–89) unremitting.[7]

Although Palmer may be perhaps overstating the comparison somewhat, it is true that, between 1369 and 1389, England was at war for sixteen years of this twenty-year period. As we have also seen, by virtue of the numbers of soldiers mobilised in these years, the war effort would have been a great strain on the government. Historians previously neglected this section of the war, for although military activity could be demonstrated to have been intensive during this period, it was also a time of territorial reverses in France. It was during this period of hostilities that the threat of invasion was at its highest; for instance Winchelsea, a port on the south coast was allegedly completely destroyed by a French attack in 1380.[8] Indeed, one of the participants in the campaigns of 1387–88, Sir Edward Dallingridge, was injured in one such French incursion whilst defending the Sussex coast.[9] As a result of this pressure the crown felt encouraged to pursue an active policy in order to protect their interests.

Historians writing earlier on this phase of the Hundred Years War were more damning in their analysis. May McKisack commented that 'the final chapter of its history in the fourteenth century reads like a dreary tale of ineptitude and failure'.[10] She argued that under Charles V, the French had found a leader who understood the lessons of past mistakes at Crécy and Poitiers and thus formulated a strategy of refusing to be brought to battle. Therefore, although the English raids were successful in terms of booty, they failed to make a political impact. Much of the continuing warfare between the two countries was exacerbated from 1378 by the schism in the Church, resulting in the abortive crusade of 1383, led by Bishop Despencer to Flanders. This aggression with France was stemmed following the years of truce arranged with the French crown following the expedition of 1388.

The political ambitions of the sons of Edward III were demonstrated in a number of expeditions, as they attempted to make alliances and conquests in order to secure personal overseas fiefdoms. As will be shown in the discussion of the political context, Richard II was increasingly keen to secure a lasting peace with France and thus would have encouraged such diversions for his ambitious uncles. The expeditions against Ireland are also linked by Richard's wish to bring his own dominions under control, whilst pursuing a peaceful policy with France.

When Richard was born in 1367, England was at the zenith of its military domination in Europe; as Saul comments,

> Her armies had won spectacular victories in the field over the French and the Scots. Her navy assured her of superiority in the narrow seas; and commanders of English origin were active in theatres of war as far afield as the Baltic

---

7 *Ibid.*, p. 1.
8 Allmand, *The Hundred Years War*, p. 122.
9 *HOP*, vol. ii, pp. 742–744.
10 May McKisack, *The Fourteenth Century*, p. 145.

and the Mediterranean. No other power of significance could match England in the quality and effectiveness of her fighting men.[11]

However, in 1399, at the age of thirty-two, Richard was deposed by his cousin, Henry Bolingbroke, earl of Derby, son of John of Gaunt. The ease of this deposition accomplished by invasion whilst Richard was in Ireland begs the question, What had gone wrong? A closer inspection of the expeditions and the political context will help shed light upon this conundrum.

The expedition of 1369 was to be a continuation of royal policy of aggression towards France in support of Edward III's claim on the French crown. Charles V had begun to retake previous English gains in France and Edward III was not fully prepared for the resumption of hostilities. Edward III intended to lead the English force in person, however, the death of Queen Philippa on 15 August, meant that his son John of Gaunt was given command of the army. At twenty-nine years old, this was his first such command and he had taken an advance contingent of the army to Calais in July. The bulk of the expedition still comprised the royal household, including men who had served in 1359–1360, even though the king did not lead in person. Thirteen of the thirty-five lords who were summoned to Parliament crossed to France. A number of those involved in the campaign of 1387–1388 can also be identified as serving in the expedition of 1369, six of whom testify to this in the Scrope v. Grosvenor case. Sir Piers de Bokton captained a retinue in 1388 in which Sir William Chauncer served.[12] As both men also served in 1369, this perhaps is evidence of a martial relationship between these two knights which continued for nearly twenty years. We can also trace the service on both campaigns for Sir Edward Dallingridge, who was present in the retinue of the earl of Arundel in 1387;[13] John, Lord Lovel, who served in the retinue of Lord Welles in 1388;[14] Sir Gilbert Talbot, who captained a retinue in 1387 and 1388.[15] Finally, the earl of Arundel also testifies to service on campaign in 1369, thus suggesting that this is when he first became aware of these men and their military abilities.[16] The expedition took the form of a defensive action against the strategy of the French king Charles V, who was planning an invasion of England. This expedition saved England from invasion by diverting the French troops. The French threatened battle, but withdrew when the second army under the command of the earl of Warwick joined Gaunt in mid-September. The cost of the expedition was £85,000 and 70% of the army was contracted by Gaunt and the five royal earls.[17]

---

[11] Saul, *Richard II*, p. 6.

[12] Bokton: *Scrope v. Grosvenor*, vol. i, p. 195, vol. ii, p. 466; Chauncer: *Scrope v. Grosvenor*, vol. i, p. 112, vol. ii, p. 304; Public Record Office, E101/41/5 m. 12.

[13] *Scrope v. Grosvenor*, vol. i, p. 164, vol. ii, p. 370; E101/41/5 m. 1. Enrolled protection, Public Record Office, C76/71 m. 12.

[14] *Scrope v. Grosvenor*, vol. i, p. 190, vol. ii, p. 450; E101/41/5 m. 3.

[15] *Scrope v. Grosvenor*, vol. i, p. 174, vol. ii, p. 397; E101/40/33 m. 12. Enrolled protection, C76/71 m. 11, E101/41/5 m. 11d.

[16] *Scrope v. Grosvenor*, vol. i, p. 219.

[17] Sherborne, 'Indentured Retinues', pp. 721–722; see also *idem*, 'John of Gaunt, Edward III's Retinue and the French Campaign of 1369', in *Kings and Nobles in the Later Middle Ages*, ed. R.A. Griffiths and J. Sherborne (Gloucester, 1986), pp. 41–61.

In the following year, 1370, an experiment in campaigning was introduced using the skills of Sir Robert Knollys to attempt to economise on the cost of expeditions to France. The army was to serve in expectation of the profit of war, using Knollys' extensive experience as a freebooter. Sherborne points out that this was an experiment not only in leadership but also in funding. The army was only paid for thirteen weeks and for the rest of its two-year contract was expected to live off the profits of war. Knollys was an experienced soldier and commander of mercenary 'free companies', but probably because of his lack of perceived noble status and a degree of dissension amongst the young nobles in the army, the force broke up after six months in the field and was ultimately defeated by the French.[18] After this experiment, armies were generally fully paid and led by nobility, if not by the king's sons or uncles. If an army could not be commanded by the king in person, it was practicable only with a member of the royal family in command and with adequate funding arranged in advance. This expedition included Sir Thomas Trivet, the experienced soldier, who also captained a retinue in 1387.[19]

In the same year, John of Gaunt also led a small expedition into Aquitaine. Together with the forces of his brother, the Prince of Wales, they infamously laid waste to Limoges. William Plumstead, an esquire in 1388, testified in the Grey v. Hastings case that he had begun his military experience on this campaign.[20] Gaunt was made Lieutenant of Aquitaine from October 1370 to July 1371, firstly on behalf of the Black Prince and following his elder brother's return to England due to ill health, on behalf of the king. The latter's eldest son, Edward, died the night before his father left for England, leaving Richard as heir.[21]

In 1372, Edward III again prepared to lead an army into France. However, the plans were altered by 10 July and the king decided to undertake a naval expedition. It was intended to provide an effective demonstration of English sea power, in order to avert the threat of invasion. The retinues were summoned to Sandwich and during August around 6,000 troops assembled. This was the largest army raised for France between 1359 and 1415. But it never set sail due to bad weather.[22] The change from land to naval expeditions demonstrates how land and sea forces were deemed to be interchangeable. Ian Friel discusses how battles were fought at sea in his essay on ships and the Hundred Years War.[23] He describes how men-at-arms would fight a boarding action, whilst projectiles

---

[18] For Sir Robert Knollys' lively career see *DNB*, vol. xxxi, pp. 281–286. From apparently humble origins he rose to become one of the most respected commanders in England. He was also a cousin of Sir Hugh Browe, who was a retinue captain in the expedition of 1388. Knollys' successes as the leader of the 'Great Company' probably inspired Edward III to experiment with this campaign. See Sherborne, 'Indentured Retinues', pp. 723–725.

[19] *Ibid.*, p. 723; E101/40/33 m. 7. Enrolled protection, C76/71 m. 14.

[20] Keen, 'English Military Experience and the Court of Chivalry', pp. 132–133; E101/41/5 m. 8.

[21] Goodman, *John of Gaunt*, pp. 47–48, 189.

[22] Sherborne, 'Indentured Retinues', p. 725; N. Harris Nicolas, *History of the Royal Navy* (London, 1847), vol. ii, pp. 147–148; P.E. Russell, *English Intervention*, pp. 187, 189, n. 1.

[23] Ian Friel, 'Winds of Change? Ships and the Hundred Years War', in Curry and Hughes (eds), *Arms, Armies and Fortifications*, pp. 183–193, pp. 185–186.

would be thrown at the enemy ship from the topcastle. The English would also use ranks of massed archers, with the longbow, as the main offensive weapon. It is therefore clear that both the man-at-arms and archer were equally useful in a land or sea battle and so there was no real difference in the composition of armies on land or at sea.

Another expedition was also undertaken in 1372, that of John, Lord Nevill, steward of the king's household. The expedition was a result of the alliance between Edward III and John de Montfort, duke of Brittany, on 19 June 1372. The king undertook to send 480 men-at-arms and 480 archers. Although they arrived at Southampton on 10 July, they did not sail until 16 October as all ships had been pressed into service for the royal expedition.[24] Nevill's retinue was one article of his impeachment in the Good Parliament of 1376, where he was accused of defrauding the crown. It was alleged that he had sailed under strength and with men who were unfit for service.[25]

The 'Great March' of 1373 was led in person by John of Gaunt and was one of the longest chevauchées ever undertaken. One quarter of the total force of just fewer than 6,000 men was provided by Lancaster's personal retinue. The remainder of the force consisted of 13 retinues under English captains and 15 retinues under foreign command. Gaunt's force contained a number of men who can also be identified in the muster rolls for the campaigns of 1387–1388. This includes Sir Edward Dallingridge and Sir Thomas Trivet, who have been mentioned in conjunction with their service on earlier campaigns.[26] Service on both campaigns can be identified for John Bathe,[27] Sir Stephen Lescrope,[28] who served in Arundel's retinue in 1387, and Sir Payn Tiptoft, who served in Arundel's retinue in 1387 and 1388.[29] The campaign lasted 312 days as Gaunt marched his army from Calais across France to Bordeaux.[30]

The expedition of 1375 was to have comprised four large retinues making a force of 3,975. The expedition was placed under the joint command of John de Montfort, duke of Brittany and the king's fourth son, Edmund, earl of Cambridge. Although it was intended that the expedition should last for one year, it only served for three months after being cut short by the truce of Bruges on 27 June. In a similar experiment to the expedition of 1370, the crown only paid wages and regard for six months: the next six months of service were to be paid from the ransom of French territories.[31]

The death of the Black Prince, Edward, Prince of Wales, on 8 June 1376 left his second son, Richard, as heir to the throne. On 21 June 1377 Richard's grand-

---

[24] Sherborne, 'Indentured Retinues', pp. 725–727.
[25] G. Holmes, *The Good Parliament* (Oxford, 1975), p. 130.
[26] Dallingridge: *HOP*, vol. ii, pp. 738–742; Trivet: *Scrope v. Grosvenor*, vol. i, p. 179, vol. ii, p. 413.
[27] 1373: Walker, *The Lancastrian Affinity*, pp. 113, 264; 1387: E101/40/33 m. 1.
[28] 1373: *Scrope v. Grosvenor*, vol. ii, pp. 45–52; 1387: E101/40/33 m. 1.
[29] 1373: *HOP*, vol. iv, pp. 628–630; 1387: E101/40/33 m. 1; 1388: E101/41/5 m. 1; enrolled attorney, C76/73 m. 2.
[30] Sherborne, 'Indentured Retinues', pp. 727–730.
[31] *Ibid.*, p. 730; C.C. Bayley, 'The Campaign of 1375 and the Good Parliament', *English Historical Review*, lv (1940), pp. 370–383.

father, Edward III, died, thus making his ten-year-old grandson, king of England.[32] The death of the king put paid to English plans for a major expedition, which was to include the young Prince Richard as a leader of a retinue. It was planned that Richard would have been joined by a force numbering 3,940 soldiers with retinues led by John of Gaunt, the duke of Brittany, the earl of Warwick, Lord Latimer, Guy Lord Brian, Thomas of Woodstock, Sir Michael de la Pole and Sir Richard Stury and Sir Philip la Vache.[33] During 1377, the earl of Arundel had been Admiral of the Western Fleet and had managed to save Southampton from French assault. Nevertheless, a great number of south coast ports were attacked and burned by the French. Arundel, in response, attacked Harfleur but was driven to sea. The command of the channel returned to the English fleet at the end of October, and Gaunt also recorded some successes against Castilian merchant shipping.

John of Gaunt led the expedition of 1378, which was an impressive force and included his brothers, Thomas of Woodstock and Edmund of Langley, and the earls of Arundel, Stafford, Suffolk and Warwick.[34] Gaunt was in charge of 5,000 soldiers and 5,000 sailors in 150 vessels. The fleet, led by the young earl of Arundel, embarked in April and Gaunt departed from Southampton in July. The expedition was to be mainly a naval event. The aim was to counter the Franco-Castilian threat at sea and also seize and occupy French coastal ports. To this end the English force commenced the siege of St Malo in August. The defenders managed to destroy the English mine due to the negligence of the earl of Arundel, who barely escaped with his life. Froissart comments on this embarrassing episode for the earl of Arundel:

> Richard, earl of Arundel, was on guard one night with his people, but he was very inattentive to obey the orders he had received, of which the garrison were informed by their spies or otherwise. When they imagined the army (trusting to lord Arundel's want of vigilance) would be fast asleep, they sallied from the town very secretly, and advanced to where the miners were at work, who had little more to do to complete the mine. Morfonace (*Guillaume Picard, dit Morfouace, capitaine de St Malo* – a valiant man-at-arms) and his company, being prepared to accomplish their enterprise, destroyed the mine at their ease; and some of the workmen who were within were never seen afterwards, as the mine fell upon them . . . Upon this, the earl of Arundel was sent for and sharply reprimanded by the duke of Lancaster and earl of Cambridge for his neglect: he excused himself as well as he was able, but was so greatly ashamed that he had rather have lost several thousand pounds.[35]

It was too late to start another mine and as it was a naval expedition, there were no horses for a chevauchée. The siege was therefore abandoned as the English soldiers' six-month contracts ran out. Gaunt had failed in his aim to lessen the French threat by sea.

32 Saul, *Richard II*, pp. 17, 22.
33 Goodman, *John of Gaunt*, pp. 63–64.
34 Sherborne, 'The English Navy', p. 36, and Goodman, *John of Gaunt*, pp. 226–227.
35 Froissart, *Chronicles*, vol. i, pp. 551–552.

Arundel's retinue for the campaign of 1378 is detailed in the extant muster roll for the campaign, E101/36/32, and shows some continuation of service of personnel with his retinues of 1387 and 1388. Arundel's retinue consisted of at least 286 soldiers including the earl himself, 11 knights, 174 esquires, 90 archers and 10 'arblasters'. Of these soldiers, 44 men (15% of Arundel's force in 1378) can be identified as serving with Arundel in 1387–1388. The muster roll, E101/36/32, consists of twelve membranes of differing lengths and composition and written in different ink and hands. Much of the membrane has deteriorated badly and cannot be transcribed. It appears to contain details of other retinues captained by Sir Waryn del Pole, Sir William Fitz Ralf, Sir William Trussel, Lord Say, Sir Robert Pashley and Sir Guy de Briene. Some of the membranes have comments to the right of the lists of names, suggesting that this roll has been used to monitor the movement of combatants; however this writing is too faint to read. Sherborne, using this muster roll and also accounts of payments, comments that Arundel led 800 men in the first part of the campaign. He has therefore perhaps included all of the separate retinues detailed in the muster roll in his calculation of Arundel's force.[36]

The expedition of 1379 was the first attempted land expedition into France since the resumption of hostilities in 1377, and was also the first of the reign of Richard II. As we have seen, since 1377 the English efforts had been concentrated on the war at sea. This expedition was to be led by John de Montfort, duke of Brittany. The English force included Sir John Arundel, Sir Hugh Calveley and Sir Thomas Percy.[37] Sir Thomas Percy also sailed on expedition with Arundel in 1388, prior to joining John of Gaunt in Gascony.[38] In addition, the aforementioned Sir Piers Bokton, William Plumstead, esquire, and Sir Thomas Trivet can be identified as serving in both 1379 and 1387–1388 along with the archer Robert Fyshlake.[39] Both Fyshlake and Plumstead testify to this service in the Grey v. Hastings case and Bokton and Trivet in their depositions during the Scrope v. Grosvenor case.[40]

The army of 1379 sailed from Southampton around 6 December and was intended to number 2,000 men at arms and 2,000 archers. However, the financial return of the second Poll Tax had been overestimated and as a result the force had to be reduced to just 650 men at arms and 650 archers. De Montfort arrived in Brittany on 3 August with English ambassadors, in order to negotiate a treaty. The fleet was delayed at Southampton and when it did sail it was scattered by a gale. Nineteen of the ships transporting horses were wrecked in Mount's Bay, Cornwall, and others were blown into the Irish Sea, where some

[36] Sherborne, 'The English Navy', p. 172. This comparison is discussed in detail in Chapter 5.
[37] Sherborne, 'Indentured Retinues', pp. 730–731.
[38] E101/40/39, partial muster roll damaged by fire.
[39] 1388: E101/41/5 m. 3d.
[40] Fyshlake and Plumstead: Keen, 'English Military Experience and the Court of Chivalry', pp. 132–133; Bokton: *Scrope v. Grosvenor*, vol. i, p. 195, vol. ii, p. 466; Trivet: *ibid.*, vol. i, p. 179, vol. ii, p. 413.

sank off the coast of Wales. Sir John Arundel's ship ran aground off Ireland and he was drowned. Due to this disastrous start, the expedition was not continued.[41]

The following year saw another major expedition, this time under the command of Richard's youngest uncle, Thomas of Woodstock, earl of Buckingham. The expedition and the retinue captains are detailed in the study by Sherborne, where he demonstrated that the army consisted of thirteen retinues.[42] For his study, Sherborne gathered information from indentures and from wage payments.[43] He did not refer to the retinue rolls, as he was concerned more with the numbers and the command structure than with individual attendance or continuation of service.[44] However, a pouch containing retinue rolls does exist for this expedition, for the force commanded by Sir William de Windsor, who personally financed 100 men-at-arms for the first six months of the campaign. These rolls, catalogued as E101/39/7 m. 3, list a retinue of 410 soldiers, including 2 bannerets, including Sir William, 10 knights, 192 esquires 'genz armes', and 206 archers; E101/39/7 m. 4 lists a retinue of 404 soldiers, including 2 bannerets, including Sir William, 10 knights, 186 esquires and 206 archers. By comparing these muster rolls with the records for service in 1387–1388, 49 men (12% of Windsor's force) can be identified as serving in both campaigns.[45] Andrew Ayton comments that these retinue rolls are examples of mid-campaign musters, demonstrating 'a system of *periodic* manpower checks'.[46] In addition, Anthony Goodman has investigated the subcontracts of Sir Hugh Hastings for his service on this campaign with the earl of Buckingham.[47] They show that Hastings formed twenty-four separate subcontracting indentures in order to provide the force he had promised in his own indenture with the crown for service overseas, thus demonstrating the complexity of the indenture system.[48] Buckingham's army numbered approximately 5,200 soldiers, almost half of whom were contained within his own retinue, which included the earls of Devon and Oxford. The earl of Devon also served with his own retinue in both 1387 and 1388,[49] and he was joined with other soldiers who also demonstrate service in 1380 and 1387–1388. This included, Sir Edward Dallingridge, Sir Alexander

41 Sherborne, 'Indentured Retinues', pp. 730–731. Sir John Arundel was the brother of the earl of Arundel.
42 *Ibid.*, pp. 731–735.
43 E364/15, 16, 19, E403/478 m. 22, E101/39/8, 9, E101/68/8, nos 190, 191.
44 Sherborne, 'Indentured Retinues', p. 731;
45 This comparison is discussed in Chapter 4.
46 Ayton, *Knights and Warhorses*, p. 149.
47 Anthony Goodman, 'The Military Subcontracts of Sir Hugh Hastings, 1380', *English Historical Review*, 95 (1980), pp. 114–120.
48 In another example Simon Walker has described the subcontracts of Sir John Strother for his intended service with the earl of March in Brittany and France in 1374. Walker has calculated that Strother would have made a profit of £40 16s on the surviving eight subcontracts, by paying his subcontractors at below the standard rate for pay which he received from the crown: Simon Walker, 'Profit and Loss in the Hundred Years War: the Subcontracts of Sir John Strother, 1374', *Bulletin of the Institute of Historical Research*, 58 (1985), pp. 100–106.
49 1387: E101/40/33 m. 3; enrolled protection, C76/71 m. 12; enrolled attorney, C76/71 m. 4. 1388: E101/41/5 m. 4.

Goldingham,[50] John, Lord Lovel, Sir Geoffrey St Quintin[51] and Sir Thomas Trivet. All of these men, along with the earl of Devon, testified to their service in 1380 at the Scrope v. Grosvenor case during 1386.[52]

The indenture for the expedition by the earl of Buckingham was sealed on 3 May 1380 and that of the other captains between 10 and 12 May. They all undertook to serve the crown for one year. The army mustered at Sandwich in June and crossed the channel to Calais on 19 July. The army entered Brittany, but the death of Charles V on 16 September meant that they received a cooler reception than expected from the duke of Brittany. They began an unsuccessful siege of Nantes and went into winter quarters in January 1381. Secret negotiations were concluded between Charles VI and John de Montfort, duke of Brittany, on 15 January 1381. Such secret negations by England's ally, de Montfort, would become a theme of the later expeditions of 1387–1388. These negotiations were unknown in England and preparations were made to send a further 2,000 reinforcements under the command of Sir Thomas Feltham. John de Montfort ratified his peace with Charles VI on 6 April 1381 and, following the loss of his ally, Buckingham embarked for England on 28 April 1381 and reached Falmouth on 2 May. The reinforcements stayed at Dartmouth until 16 June when they were called to London because of the Peasants' Revolt stimulated by the Poll Tax of the same year.

The underlying problem of the reign would seem to be one which has been touched upon above, the failure of the English crown to maintain its dominance over France in the continuing struggle of the Hundred Years War. This was a problem that had already developed by the beginning of Richard's reign in 1377 when he ascended as a minor. Edward III's infirmity and also the deterioration in health of Richard's father and Edward's expected successor, the Black Prince, had meant that the English campaigns in France had lost their focus in royal leadership. The victories at Crécy and Poitiers were long behind them and the English experiments to find a successful solution to the leadership problem of overseas expedition, as aforementioned, were short-lived. These English problems in turn were met with an upturn in the fortunes of the French crown which managed to bring England's former allies in Brittany and Ghent under its dominance.

The Peasants' Revolt did not deter Edmund of Langley, the earl of Cambridge, from attempting to bolster his own position and English influence in Iberia. He led an expedition to Portugal that landed at Lisbon in July 1381 and returned to England by 24 November 1382.[53] During 1380, the Anglo-Portuguese alliance of 1373 had been reaffirmed. As a result of this, Fernando I,

---

50 1388: E101/41/5 m. 6d; enrolled protection, C76/72 m. 7.
51 1388: E101/40/39 m. 1.
52 *Scrope v. Grosvenor*: Devon, vol. i, p. 73, vol. ii, p. 235; Dallingridge, vol. i, p. 164, vol. ii, p. 370; Goldingham, vol. i, p. 70, vol. ii, p. 277; Lovel, vol. i, p. 190, vol. ii, p. 450; St Quintin, vol. i, p. 62, vol. ii, p. 207; Trivet, vol. i, p. 179, vol. ii, p. 413.
53 *Westminster Chronicle*, p. 31; Goodman, *John of Gaunt*, p. 113; F. Lopez, *The English in Portugal 1367–87*, ed. Lomax and Oakley (Warminster, 1988), pp. 66–151; Russell, *English Intervention*, ch. 14.

the king of Portugal, agreed to receive an army led by Langley and to wage war on Castile in pursuit of John of Gaunt's claim to the Castile crown. Fernando's daughter and heiress, Beatriz, was to marry Langley's son, Edward, to secure this lasting alliance.

Warfare between Castile and Portugal broke out in May 1381 and Langley landed with a force of 3,000 in support of Portugal in July of the same year. The force was strongly Lancastrian with Gaunt's knights, Sir Thomas FitzSimond, Sir Matthew Gourney, Marshal of the army, Sir Thomas Fichet, Sir Mauburney de Linières and Sir John Falconer, leading retinues.[54] The promised betrothal was carried out, but this did not lead to the intended marriage. The expedition itself was a fiasco. There were problems over pay, finding suitable horses, food, soldier indiscipline, a failure to get on with the hosts and bad leadership. There was some raiding over the frontier in 1382, but peace between Portugal and Spain was made in August without consultation with the English, who, as a final insult, were shipped home in Castilian ships.

The expedition undertaken during 1383 was a completely different affair being led by the bishop of Norwich and undertaken primarily for financial savings rather than for strategic gain. This 'crusade' included the retinue captains Sir Thomas Trivet, Sir William Elmham, Sir William Faringdon, Sir Hugh Calveley and Francis Ackerman of Ghent.[55] Trivet and Elmham were both also involved in the expeditions of 1387–1388.[56] In addition William, Lord Hylton, can be identified as serving in 1383 and also in the campaigns of 1387–1388.[57] The force landed at Calais on 17 May, and Bishop Despencer was back in England by October of the same year.

This expedition took its impetus from the schism in the Church. Bishop Despencer had been issued with bulls from the Roman Pontiff, Pope Urban VI, published 17 September 1382, which empowered him to preach a crusade against the Clementists, who included the French and Flemish. He was also allowed to grant indulgences in return for supporting the crusade and he interpreted these bulls as a commission to lead such a crusade in person.

At the Parliament in February 1383, Despencer proposed his action against Clement VII, the anti-pope based at Avignon, offering yearly wages from the money he had been raising from the sale of indulgences. He ran up against opposition from the ill will of the lords because of the problem of conquest on behalf of the Church rather than the crown. He prevailed against the lords, especially John of Gaunt, and won support and monetary backing from Parliament, who believed that it would prove cheaper than a royal expedition. Financing a royal expedition was a concern of Parliament at this time; following

---

[54] For the most recent discussion of Lancastrian retainers see Simon Walker, *The Lancastrian Affinity, 1361–1399* (Oxford, 1990).

[55] *Westminster Chronicle*, pp. 31–49; Palmer, *England France and Christendom*, pp. 7, 10, 49.

[56] Elmham, 1387: E101/40/33 m. 11. 1388: E101/40/39 m. 1. Trivet was late and only left on crusade after being threatened by the bishop's friends and people of London: Housley, 'The Bishop of Norwich's Crusade', p. 19.

[57] 1383: *Complete Peerage*, vol. vii, p. 26; 1388: E101/41/5 m. 5d.

the problems they had experienced collecting the previous Poll Taxes. They hoped that the bishop could stir up trouble in Flanders for the French. There is a possibility that the bishop was later recalled by Parliament, but chose to ignore the command.[58]

The campaign began successfully and the bishop was granted extra powers as a result of this early success. The English forces managed to take control of most of the Flemish coast between Gravelines and Blankenberghe. Despencer declined the assistance of the earl of Arundel, who would have represented the crown on campaign. The bishop's forces then carried out an unsuccessful siege of Ypres, which turned the whole course of the expedition. The French king approached with a large army in order to oppose the incursion. The bishop wanted to take them by surprise and to meet them in the field, but his captains could not agree on the action to be taken. The king of France attacked the town of Bourbourg where some of the English forces were sheltering and the English captains took bribes to surrender without a fight. Trivet only survived the wrath of Parliament for his actions by throwing himself upon the king's mercy.[59] Sir Hugh Calveley and Bishop Despencer took refuge in Gravelines but they were forced to surrender and return to England.[60]

The bishop was undone by his failure to control his forces during the expedition. The Monk of Westminster summarised his arraignment in Parliament by the Chancellor:

> My lord bishop, you have your sword borne before you everywhere like a temporal lord. Lay aside that sword of yours; its presence is an affront to the king, and the rest of your temporal lords are loud in their murmurs of complaint about it: and for the future conduct yourself according to what is proper for a bishop. Furthermore, my lord bishop, at the petition of the commons and in conformity with your own desire the king advanced you to the control of military operations on his behalf for one whole year, to wage vigorous war upon his enemies wherever they might chance to cross your pass, and you received from the king a large sum of money for this purpose. Lastly you undertook to carry out the project without delay. Yet now, with almost half the year gone, you leave your undertaking unfulfilled; with the country's treasure drained away and no expedition in being, you have brought the military situation to virtual ruin.[61]

This was the only English army of the entire period under discussion that the French were prepared to face, and yet this opportunity was not taken. The bishop took the blame for the failure of the expedition and as a result he was

---

58 Palmer, *England, France and Christendom*, p. 49.
59 *Westminster Chronicle*, p. 53.
60 For a recent discussion of the crusade see Housley, 'The Bishop of Norwich's Crusade, May 1383'. Housley suggests that Bishop Despencer later joined the earl of Arundel's naval expedition to the French coast in 1386–1387. However, I have not discovered any evidence to support this claim in the muster roll evidence and the statement in Housley's article is not referenced. He is probably referring to Froissart's claim that the bishop of Norwich was present on campaign: Froissart, *Chronicles*, vol. ii, pp. 215–217.
61 *Westminster Chronicle*, p. 53.

deprived of his temporalities. The young Richard II's efforts to attack the French and rescue the bishop were frustrated through lack of money.

The new Chancellor, Michael de la Pole, had realised on taking office that he had to make a settlement with France. This stance led to the creation of the circumstances that encouraged the Appellants to seize power. Parliament was becoming resistant to the constant burden of taxation to support the fighting in France. However, de la Pole was unable to follow a united peace policy because, as has been suggested by Palmer, he did not have the support of the nobility or Parliament for his aims. What is certain is that de la Pole, who had been associated with Richard's father, the Black Prince, heavily influenced the young king who was still in his minority. Together with Sir Simon Burley, another associate of the Black Prince, de la Pole pursued peace in order to rescue the crown from its continuing indebtedness to Parliament, which threatened the prerogative of the English crown.[62]

However well intentioned the peace policy was, it did, unfortunately for the young king, lead to his first serious political crisis. As a result, the Wonderful Parliament of 1386, removed Richard's councillors and imposed a 'great and continual council' to oversee the kingdom.

The other expedition of these years was led in person by Richard II in 1385 and took the form of a major campaign into Scotland. The expedition was supported by John of Gaunt and all the earls except the earl of Kent, and at least fourteen major barons who had been summoned by individual writ. Richard led his forces into Scotland in the first week of August. The army was contracted for forty days, but the actual length of service appears to have been a fortnight. However, it was possible that men served for forty days if travel to and from the muster is included. The English host was summoned to muster at Newcastle on 14 July. The method by which this force was organised has been much debated in successive articles in the *English Historical Review* by N.B. Lewis and J.J.N. Palmer.[63] The army was raised by feudal summons and the debate concerns whether it was organised in this way to ensure a large and impressive turn out, including the king's senior opponents, or as a way of raising funds for the campaign. As the army was indeed paid from a subsidy specifically granted to a royal expedition, the argument that the summons was to encourage people to turn out in support of the king's first campaign is a strong one. Palmer, counters this, by stating that such a campaign would not have to rely on such a form of persuasion as men would have readily supported this expedition.

This was the first expedition led by an English king since 1359 so, as discussed, a popular response was perhaps guaranteed. The need for an expedition had been triggered when the French sent Sir Jean de Vienne, who landed in Scotland with 2,000 men, in order to join with the Scots in an attack on English territory. Royal writs summoning a general feudal levy to muster at Newcastle

---

[62] For Richard's relationship with Burley and de la Pole see Saul, *Richard II*, pp. 112–120.
[63] Lewis, 'The Last Medieval Summons'; J.J.N. Palmer, 'The Last Summons of the Feudal Army in England (1385)', *English Historical Review*, 83 (1968), pp. 771–775; N.B. Lewis, 'The Feudal Summons of 1385', with a reply by J.J.N. Palmer, *English Historical Review*, 100 (1985) pp. 729–746; *Westminster Chronicle*, pp. 121–131.

were issued on 4 and 13 June, but the army of 14,000 that Richard led into Scotland was nevertheless recruited on a contractual basis. This expedition was intended to restore the repute of the monarchy and to establish Richard's reputation in the field. One third of the whole army consisted of Gaunt's men (he had also led a smaller raid against the Scots, in the spring of the previous year). Leaving Berwick, Richard reached and occupied Edinburgh, but he could not bring the Scots to battle. The king refused Gaunt's advice to raid into the highlands, as he was concerned that the ordinary soldier would not be able to find sufficient supplies. However, southern Scotland was laid waste so effectively that there was no danger from the north for the following three years. In hindsight, this risk of attacking Scotland was worth taking as a threatened French invasion had again not materialised.

Because of the nature of the organisation of this force, a large number of the English military community can be identified as serving in 1385 and 1387–1388.[64] This included the retinue captains: Richard, earl of Arundel; Sir John D'Arundel;[65] John, Lord Beaumont;[66] Edward, earl of Devon; Sir William Elmham; Sir Thomas Mortimer;[67] Sir Robert Mountenay;[68] the Earl Marshal;[69] Sir Thomas Percy; Sir Arnald Savage;[70] John Slegh;[71] Sir Gilbert Talbot; Sir Thomas Trivet; John, Lord Welles;[72] and Sir Thomas West.[73]

The year 1386 saw Richard's uncle again concentrating on foreign conquest and glory. An expedition heading to Spain, under the command of John of Gaunt, sailed from Portsmouth 9 July 1386, landing at La Coruna on 25 July. The expedition returned to Bayonne from Portugal at the end of September 1387.[74]

Gaunt could pursue his personal claim to the crown of Castile now that the invasion scare from Scotland and France had passed following the decisive royal expedition of the previous year. The duke had a problem in finding funding for his force, but managed to receive some from a commons subsidy and more from the king in the form of a loan. He also raised money from the sale of indulgences granted by Urban VI. Although, this was a royal expedition, undertaken for the crown by a royal uncle, there was a notable absence of leading nobles from this campaign. The actual force totalled around 3,000 men, mainly of Lancastrian

---

64 Service for all below listed as serving in 1385, taken from Lewis, 'The Last Medieval Summons', Appendix II, pp. 17–23, comparison detailed in Table 22: Military Service of Retinue Captains.
65 1387: E101/40/33 m. 5; enrolled attorney, C76/71 m. 6. 1388: E101/41/5 m. 5.
66 1387: E101/40/33 m. 4.
67 1387: E101/40/33 m. 10; enrolled attorney, C76/71 m. 10.
68 1387: E101/40/33 m. 16; enrolled protection, C76/71 m. 14.
69 1387: E101/40/33 m. 1. 1388: E101/41/5 m. 3.
70 1387: E101/40/33 m. 6d; enrolled protection, C76/71 m. 14. 1388: E101/41/5 m. 13d.
71 1387: E101/40/33 m. 18.
72 1388: E101/41/5 m. 3.
73 1387: E101/40/33 m. 1; enrolled protection, C76/71 m. 14; enrolled attorney, C76/71 m. 10. 1388: E101/41/5 m. 7; enrolled protection, C76/72 m. 6.
74 Goodman, *John of Gaunt*, pp. 115–131, 139n. See also Russell, *English Intervention*, pp. 400–494.

composition with also a few foreign mercenaries. However, it is notable that again soldiers can be identified as continuing their service with Gaunt in 1386 to service with Arundel in 1387–1388. This includes Esmon Barry, esquire;[75] Sir John de Brewes;[76] Thomas, Lord Camoys;[77] Sir Thomas Percy; William Plumstead, esquire; Sir Ralph Shelton;[78] and Sir John Wiltshire.[79] The service of these men between 1386 and 1388 demonstrates a certain professionalism and desire to participate continuously in royal expeditions.

Both Richard II and Gaunt believed that it was possible to win the crown of Castile. By supporting this expedition, Richard II was treating his uncle, John of Gaunt, as a royal equal, as, if successful, he would become king of Castile and León, a title he already bore. Gaunt certainly intended to be in Spain for the duration and therefore was accompanied by his wife and his three daughters. The English force landed in and conquered Galicia, took Compostela and La Coruña and processed to the shrine of St James at Santiago. These conquests were a considerable achievement.

However, these early successes were not sustainable. Charles VI of France was making impressive preparations to invade England, therefore Gaunt could not be reinforced. By the end of 1386, he ran out of money and his troops were suffering from peasant attacks and epidemics. Instead of returning to England at this point, Gaunt decided to stay and gamble on a further joint campaign with Portugal. However his force suffered desertions through 1387 because of inadequate wage payments. In the joint agreement with Portugal, an attack on Castile would be mounted with the Portuguese providing 5,000 men for 8 months. In return, Gaunt's daughter, Philippa, would marry Joao, the king of Portugal. This marriage was concluded in February 1387.

In the planned joint invasion of León, Gaunt only had 1,500 men to Joao's 9,000. Because the English force was so small, Gaunt did not have a strong bargaining position and was forced to make honourable terms with Castile on the recommendation of his Portuguese allies. These terms were agreed in June and July of 1387. As part of this agreement, Gaunt gave up his claim to the throne of Castile in return for a cash payment and the promise that his daughter would marry the heir of Castile. The resultant treaty of Bayonne was ratified in early 1388.

John of Gaunt's decision to lead the royally backed expedition to Castile to defend his own claim to the throne became a significant event for the political world in England. This move left a void at the centre of English politics for two years. Gaunt had previously acted to iron out the differences between the king and his critics. However, without his presence, the king's opposition began to

---

[75] 1386: Keen, 'English Military Experience and the Court of Chivalry', p. 139. 1388: E101/41/5 m. 1.

[76] 1386: *Scrope v. Grosvenor*, vol. i, p. 63, vol. ii, p. 208. 1387: E101/40/33 m. 1. Enrolled protection, C76/71 m. 12. 1388: E101/41/5 m. 12.

[77] 1386: *DNB*, vol. viii, p. 306. 1388: E101/41/5 m. 6; enrolled protection, C76/72 m. 6.

[78] 1386: *HOP*, vol. iii, pp. 355–357. 1388: E101/41/5 m. 1.

[79] 1386: Keen, 'English Military Experience and the Court of Chivalry', pp. 132–133. 1388: E101/41/5 m. 1.

move against the king and his advisors. The Wonderful Parliament impeached the Chancellor, de la Pole, and imposed their own nominees as Chancellor and Treasurer. The commons followed this up with the impeachment of the former Chancellor and he was found guilty on charges of peculation. As a result of the impeachment de la Pole was imprisoned for a short time, but was soon released and joined Richard's household on its travels around the kingdom.[80]

The second major attack on Richard's prerogative concerned the establishment of the 'great and continual council', which was appointed for a year with comprehensive powers of government on 19 November 1386.[81] This was a major blow to the young king, and he even appeared personally before Parliament to make a protestation. In reality, the government of the realm had been removed from the king and his advisors and favourites and placed in the hands of the council. The king could not now spend money without first gaining the agreement of the council. The tensions thus created by the appointment of the council, would lead to Richard attempting to reassert his authority, through process of law and force of arms.

The council was led by the king's main opponents to peace with France, namely his uncle, Thomas of Woodstock, by now duke of Gloucester, and Richard Fitzalan, earl of Arundel. Under their influence from 19 November 1386, the council now acted as an effective regency and changed domestic and foreign policy to suit their own agenda. The relationship between king and council was now untenable. The king saw the attacks upon his prerogative as unacceptable and was unable to countenance the removal of his power. It was this unbridgeable difference between the king and his council which formed the background to the Appellant-led expeditions of 1387 and 1388 and also the brief civil war culminating in the battle of Radcot Bridge in December 1387. While the king was so opposed to war against France it makes the composition of the said expeditions extremely relevant. Would the political background mean that the composition of the expeditions differed significantly from any other royal expeditions? The analysis enabled by the use of relational databases will make it possible to draw conclusions on the political make-up of an expeditionary army at the time of constitutional crisis. How far were the ordinary soldiers affected by this political turmoil and were the expeditions populated with a private army of Appellant supporters? These questions will be tackled in Part 2, though we have already shown a number of links in personnel between the campaigns since 1369 and those of 1387–1388.

This activity brings us to the expeditions central to this book, namely those led by the earl of Arundel in the years of 1387 and 1388. As we have seen, Arundel had previously been on campaign, but not very successfully. These expeditions were undertaken by the Appellant lords, who had taken over govern-

---

[80] See J.S. Roskell, *The Impeachment of Michael de la Pole, Earl of Suffolk, in 1386, in the Context of the Reign of Richard II* (Manchester, 1984). See also J.J.N. Palmer, 'The Impeachment of Michael de la Pole in 1386', *Bulletin of the Institute of Historical Resarch*, xlii (1969), pp. 96–101.

[81] The letters patent containing the commission of appointment of the continual council are repeated in *Westminster Chronicle*, pp. 167–175.

ment and who wished to reinvigorate the war with France. Full details of the expeditions will be provided in the next chapter. However it is useful to give an overview of them at this point.

The expedition of 1387 was a naval campaign commanded by the Admiral, Richard Fitzalan, earl of Arundel, and consisted of two phases. The first phase saw battle joined with the Flemish fleet with a successful outcome for the earl and his forces. After pursuing the remnants of the Flemish fleet into harbour at Sluys, the English force returned to Orwell for a brief rest and refit. The second phase saw the force sail to Brittany for the relief of Brest. Brest had been acquired from the duke of Brittany in 1378. However, de Montfort was in dispute with the English over their occupation and had been besieging Brest since 1386.[82] This expedition was hugely popular at home due to the large amount of wine captured from the enemy force.

The expeditions were divided by the brief civil war culminating in the battle of Radcot Bridge during December 1387. The king had attempted to gain a legal opinion to establish whether the Wonderful Parliament and the appointment of the council had deprived him of his prerogative. These 'questions to the judges' of August 1387, produced the answers that the council was illegal and also that the people who had directed the actions should be treated as traitors. As a result, the earls of Gloucester, Arundel and Warwick were joined by the earls of Derby and Nottingham, who went on the offensive and named five favourites of the king as traitors, who would be 'appealed' in Parliament. It is from this action that the previously mentioned senior peers received their collective description of the Lords Appellant.[83] Robert de Vere, duke of Ireland, managed to gather a force of loyal Cheshire men in defence of the king, numbering around 3,000 in strength. This force was no match for the organised force of the Lords Appellant and the actual battle was a debacle, with de Vere fleeing from the skirmish. The Appellants may have used the aftermath of the battle to briefly depose the king, although they had to restore him when they could not decide on the succession. At the Merciless Parliament of 1388 the accused were formally appealed and executed if they had not already managed to escape the country. The two principal, and now victorious Appellants, Gloucester and Arundel, then took a firmer grip on government and foreign policy.

As a result, the expedition of 1388 was planned on a more ambitious scale to build on the success of the previous year and was also commanded by the earl of Arundel. The expedition was again a naval campaign, though it was also intended to link up with John de Montfort in Brittany and Gaunt in Gascony. However, Gaunt did not want to cooperate and due to the late arrival of the force in Brittany, de Montfort had secured his own alliance with the French. Arundel failed to make any impact in France, due to the lack of mobility inland, as the horses for the campaign were to have been provided by England's ally, John de Montfort.

---

[82] Palmer, *England, France and Christendom*, pp. 62, 72.

[83] They are described as the Lords Appellant, 'les seignurs appellantz', in the transcript of the Appeal presented to the Merciless Parliament of 1388 and recorded in *Westminster Chronicle*, pp. 274–275.

Following the return of the force to England in September 1388, Richard II was able to reassert himself and the Appellants became less influential. This was demonstrated in the Cambridge Parliament which opened on 10 September 1388. The Scottish incursions into the north-west and north-east of England during July 1388, which had culminated in Scottish victory at Otterburn on 5 August 1388, and the capture of Sir Henry Percy, had increased the pressure on the Appellant government.[84] This manifested itself in an attack upon liveried retainers and Arundel was even made to explain the reasons for the delay for the departure on campaign in 1388. Richard offered to give up liveried retainers himself and then brokered a compromise deal.[85] Richard demonstrated that he was politically astute and over the next few months, as his friends and favourites who had been banished from court during the Appellant supremacy returned to the king's service. On 3 May 1389, at a council meeting at Westminster, Richard declared that he was now ready to enjoy his full rights. He dismissed the Treasurer and the Keeper of the Privy Seal and Archbishop Arundel, the Chancellor, had to surrender the great seal. Both Gloucester and Richard, earl of Arundel were removed from the council and Arundel was replaced as Admiral and Captain of Brest. By the terms of his indenture for service in 1388, Arundel had been confirmed in his post of Admiral for five years. He was therefore removed from office with four years still to run.[86]

This period, 1369–1388, of intensive but unrewarding fighting had led the English government to tax its subjects heavily, resulting in the popular revolt against the Poll Tax in 1381. The Appellants had failed to drive new impetus into the war with France in 1387–1388 and thus, when Richard pursued his peace policy, following his return to power, it was a relief in many ways from the war of attrition which had been fought for twenty years. Historical commentators often make the point that the medieval ruler who prefers peace to war will often be deposed by his now unfocused nobility. Richard lost his throne and the analysis of why and how has been intelligently discussed by other historians.[87] However, for the current book, it is necessary to frame the expeditions of 1387 and 1388 against the political events of this most calamitous of reigns.

As we have seen from the summary of the English expeditions earlier in this chapter, by the time Richard II ascended the throne in 1377, the course of the Hundred Years War had taken a downturn in terms of English dominance of France. In addition to these setbacks, Richard was just of boy of ten, with none of his late father's experiences of the successes at Crécy and Poitiers to draw upon. In fact, his late father's martial fame produced expectations in the realm

[84] Saul, *Richard II*, p. 198. For discussion of the battle of Otterburn see the collection of essays in Anthony Goodman and Anthony Tuck (eds), *War and Border Societies in the Middle Ages* (London, 1992).

[85] For a detailed discussion of this parliament see Anthony Tuck, 'The Cambridge Parliament, 1388', *English Historical Review*, lxxxiv (1969), pp. 225–243.

[86] Tuck, *Richard II and the English Nobility*, pp. 134–138. For a recent summary of Richard's return to authority in 1388–1389 see Bennett, *Richard II and the Revolution of 1399*, pp. 34–35. For indenture see E101/41/4 m. 2.

[87] Most recently by Saul, *Richard II*, pp. 405–434, and Bennett, *Richard II and the Revolution of 1399*, pp. 170–191.

that Richard was never able to live up to. The policy of the crown in the early years of the reign, was a continuance of previous policy of sustaining the war against France and thus prolonging the virtual stalemate in the positions of the two competing crowns. It is the relationship between the two crowns in the early years of the reign, that is the most important consideration in the background to the Appellant seizure of power in England and their attempts to stimulate the conflict further.

In the early years of the reign leading to the crisis of 1386, Richard had shown himself in the position of leadership on two major occasions. The first was his meetings with the Poll Tax Rebels at Mile End and Smithfield in 1381. Following the murder of Wat Tyler at Smithfield, Richard was instrumental in leading the rebels away from London and quelling any reaction to their leader's demise. This courageous action by the young king shows that Richard was willing to take on the responsibilities of his exalted position. His other major role was the leading of the expedition to Scotland in 1385 at the head of a large, mainly feudal host.[88] Contrary to Richard's subsequent image, he demonstrated very early in his reign that he was able to take a leading role in expeditions and other violent conflicts. However, Richard became allied to the idea of peace with France, and as such did not lead an expedition against the old enemy of his father and grandfather. This has counted negatively in the subsequent treatment of his reign.

The expeditions of 1387–1388 were the last royal expeditions, until those undertaken into Ireland in 1394 and 1399. Indeed they were also the last expeditions against France of the reign of Richard II. Over the next few years, royal efforts were put into securing a lasting peace with France. The martial class in England found other ways to expend their energies. As well as taking part in the organised tournaments in England and France, they also supported a number of crusades. In 1390 John Beaufort, the son of John of Gaunt and his mistress, Catherine Swynford (later duchess of Lancaster), the chamber knights, Sir William Neville, Sir John Clanvowe and the earl of Devon (who was also involved in the campaigns of 1387–1388) joined the duke of Bourbon on his Barbary crusade.[89] The course of the campaign was ineffectual; however it is of interest as it showed English and French knights acting together for the cause of Christendom against the Infidel. Henry, earl of Derby, was not able to get safe conduct from the French king for this expedition. As an alternative, he then joined the Teutonic Knights in Prussia with up to 300 followers. During the siege of Vilna in September 1390 the English archers won great glory for their prowess. Derby returned to England in 1392 and then set off on pilgrimage to Jerusalem.[90]

---

[88] Richard II's military prowess has been discussed recently in Gillespie, 'Richard II: King of Battles?', pp. 139–164.

[89] *Westminster Chronicle*, pp. 433, 451; see also G.L. Harriss, *Cardinal Beaufort* (Oxford, 1988), p. 1.

[90] L.T. Smith (ed.), *Expeditions to Prussia and the Holy Land made by Henry, earl of Derby, in the years 1390–1 and 1392–3*, Camden Society, new series, lii (London, 1894); N. Housley, *The Later Crusades, 1274–1580: From Lyons to Alcazar* (Oxford, 1992).

One further crusade in this period also deserves a mention as a recipient of a possible English contingent. There is evidence that an expedition under the command of John Beaufort, and perhaps involving Sir Ralph Percy, joined the ill-fated crusade to Nicopolis of 1396. The atmosphere of the English crown and court at this time would certainly support an argument in favour of such inclusion. However, although much supporting evidence can be found in the art and literature of the period, actual documentary evidence reinforcing this claim is not forthcoming.[91]

The last major royal expeditions in the final years of Richard's reign were undertaken in Ireland. These two expeditions of 1394 and 1399 were led in person by the king and were intended to be a demonstration of Richard's power and domination over all of his subjects and domains. They both required the mobilisation of large expeditionary armies. Little of Ireland recognised English authority, so Richard intended to gain allegiance from his rebellious subjects. In the expedition of 1394, the bulk of the force was made up of an extended household contingent and the major magnates also brought retinues, including the duke of Gloucester, the earl of March and the earl of Nottingham (the Earl Marshal). The Earl Marshal also served in the campaigns of 1387–1388. Although there was little fighting, the Irish chieftains were impressed by the show of strength and attended the king's court in Dublin and promised submission. Richard returned to England in May 1395 thinking that he had subdued his previously disloyal subjects.[92] It is possible to make a limited comparison between the campaigns of 1387–1388 with the Irish campaigns of 1394 and 1399. This identifies ninety-seven soldiers who show a continuance of service between Arundel's campaigns and the royal campaigns to Ireland. This level of continuity demonstrates that individuals of the English military community were happy to participate, treating all these campaigns as service in the royal cause.

The Irish question remained a problem for Richard, as the Irish chiefs did not honour the bonds they had made with him in 1395. To bring matters to a head, the earl of March, the king's lieutenant in Ireland, was ambushed and murdered in July 1398. Richard decided to again lead a royal expedition in 1399 in order to re-establish his authority. Richard was supported by his newly created dukes, including Aumerle, Exeter and Surrey, and also took with him the sons of his perceived enemies in order to protect against invasion in his absence. He

---

91 For support of this argument see Adrian R. Bell, 'England and the Crusade of Nicopolis', *Medieval Life*, issue 4 (Spring 1996), pp. 18–22. For the opposite view see C.L. Tipton, 'The English at Nicopolis', *Speculum*, xxxvii (1962), pp. 528–40, disputed by Palmer, *England, France and Christendom*, pp. 239–240, who also argues that an English contingent was involved in the crusade. For details of the crusade, see A.S. Atiya, *The Crusade in the Later Middle Ages* (London, 1938), and *idem*, *The Crusade of Nicopolis* (London, 1934).

92 E. Curtis, *Richard II in Ireland* (Oxford, 1927). For the Irish expeditions see the more recent studies, J.F. Lydon, 'Richard II's Expeditions to Ireland', *Journal of the Royal Society of Antiquaries of Ireland*, xciii (1963); J.F. Lydon, *Ireland in the Later Middle Ages* (Dublin, 1973), pp. 109–124; D.B. Johnson, 'Richard II and the Submissions of Gaelic Ireland', *Irish Historical Studies*, xxii (1980), pp. 1–20; Johnson, 'The Interim Years: Richard II and Ireland, 1395–1399'.

appointed his uncle, the duke of York, as keeper of England. This expedition would ultimately lead to the downfall of Richard. The campaign did not proceed to plan, with the crown being unable to bring the rebel Irish to battle. The earl of Derby used this opportunity to invade England to claim his birthright and the crown. Richard returned to England, but his forces were in disarray and following a brief attempt to rally support he was ambushed and taken into custody by his cousin and thus ended his reign as king.[93]

From 1388 to the point of Richard's deposition, England enjoyed peaceful relations with France and although a peace treaty was not signed, a lasting truce was called. This new relationship with the traditional foe was secured with tournaments, most famously at St Inglevert and Smithfield in 1390, with joint crusading activity in 1390 and 1396, Richard's marriage to Isabella, daughter of the king of France, and with court membership of Philippe de Mézières' Order of the Passion.[94] Twenty-one English knights promised to become knights of the Passion, including the king's uncle, the duke of York, the Earl Marshal, Sir Ralph Percy and Sir Lewis Clifford. The king's other uncles, the duke of Gloucester and John of Gaunt, and also the king's half-brother, the earl of Huntingdon, promised to support the order. In addition, those knights who promised to become knights of the Passion and served in 1387–1388 included: the Earl Marshal; Thomas, Lord Despencer, the future earl of Gloucester;[95] Sir Hugh le Despencer;[96] Sir Thomas West;[97] and Sir Robert Morley.[98] This demonstrates that six members of the campaigns of 1387–1388 joined with other members of the royal court in promising to join an order devoted to peace with fellow Christians. The earlier service under the earl of Arundel had not prevented them becoming influential in the royal circle. This new atmosphere promoted at court inspired writers such as Chaucer and Gower to advocate peace in Christendom and as an alternative, promoted expeditions against the infidel.[99] This new-found inspiration can be also seen in Henry, earl of Derby's expeditions with the Teutonic Knights and his pilgrimage to Jerusalem.

Although much has been written about de Mézières and Richard's support for his ideas, one piece of evidence which has not been used by historians identifies Richard's personal interest in the ideas of de Mézières. Half of the envoys whom

---

[93] J. Creton, *French Metrical History on the Deposition of Richard II*, ed. and trans. J. Webb, *Archaeologia*, xx (1824), pp. 1–441. This is an eyewitness account by a participant on the expedition. See also Steel, *Richard II*, pp. 260–263.

[94] The order is outlined in *Philip de Mézières: Letter to Richard II: A Plea made in 1395 for Peace between England and France*, ed. G.W. Coopland (Liverpool, 1975). For the list of English members of the Order of the Passion see, Atiya, *The Crusade of Nicopolis*, pp. 134–135.

[95] 1388: E101/41/5 m. 1.

[96] 1387: E101/40/33 m. 9; enrolled protection, C76/71 m. 14. 1388: E101/41/5 m. 10 and E101/40/33 m. 18; enrolled protection, C76/72 m. 7.

[97] 1387: E101/40/33 m. 1; enrolled protection, C76/71 m. 14; enrolled attorney, C76/71 m. 10. 1388: E101/41/5 m. 7; enrolled protected, C76/72 m. 6.

[98] 1388: E101/40/33 m. 3. Described as 'factus miles xxviii die Junii'.

[99] Adrian R. Bell, 'England and the Crusade of Nicopolis'. For a recent discussion on the literature of this period see Patricia J. Eberle, 'Richard II and the Literary Arts'.

Richard II sent to France to discuss his marriage plans were members of de Mézières' Order of the Passion. According to the commission, the ambassadors were: the archbishop of Dublin, the bishop of St David's, the Earl Marshal, the earl of Rutland, John Lord Beaumont and William LeScrop.[100] The bishop of St David's, the Earl Marshal and the earl of Rutland had all promised to become knights of the Passion. John, Lord Beaumont served on campaign in 1387, along with the Earl Marshal who also served in 1388.[101] The composition of this party could not have been coincidental. By making so many supporters of the Order of the Passion his envoys, Richard was surely showing his support for de Mézières' plan to bring peace between England and France.

The actual truce with France was secured in 1396 with the marriage of Richard to Isabella, the daughter of the king of France. This was cemented by the famous meeting between the two kings on 26 October 1396 near Ardres in France. It was at this meeting that the two kings agreed to work towards a final and lasting peace and also the ending of the schism in the Church. The war party in England had been marginalised and Gloucester together with John of Gaunt were Richard's lieutenants at this meeting. Richard had reached the pinnacle of his royal power and was demonstrating his authority on the international stage. He was now able to turn his attention to settling some old scores.

The chronicler Walsingham, reports that in 1397 Richard began 'to tyrannize' his subjects.[102] Richard acted ruthlessly whilst at the height of his powers to destroy his former enemies. Why did he act in such a way? The chroniclers suggested a number of reasons, from being motivated by revenge to being criticised by envoys from Germany who implied he was unable to control his subjects. It was also suggested that Richard was acting against a current conspiracy. Saul suggests an alternative modern psychological interpretation, namely that his behaviour was 'situation dependent'. He suggests that Richard was reacting as a response to a change in his personal circumstances. He had begun to be openly criticised and therefore reacted in an unpredictable way.[103]

The king had acted swiftly against the three senior Appellants, Arundel, Gloucester and Warwick, and he stage-managed the parliament that prosecuted them with great professionalism. It was possible that he had rigged the elections to Parliament as well as stationing 300 loyal Cheshire archers to intimidate the gathering. They were appealed in direct imitation of the events of the Merciless Parliament. It seems plain that a major reason for the prosecution of these three senior peers was as retaliation for his humiliation at their hands in the years 1387–1388. As a result, the earl of Arundel was executed for treason, the duke of Gloucester was murdered in Calais and the earl of Warwick was imprisoned

---

100 *Foedera*, vol. iii, part iv, p. 108; Hardy, *Syllabus, ii, 1377–1654*, p. 528. Froissart also lists Sir Henry Clifford, Lord Despencer and Sir John Robesart as ambassadors, and significantly all these men had promised to become knights of the Passion: Froissart, *Chronicles*, vol. ii, p. 597.

101 E101/40/33 m. 4.

102 *Chronicles of the Revolution, 1397–1400*, ed. C. Given-Wilson (Manchester, 1993), p. 71.

103 Saul, *Richard II*, pp. 367–368, 202.

for life on the Isle of Man. Richard's revenge did not cease with the prosecution of the senior Appellants. He also used the circumstance of an argument between the junior Appellants, Norfolk and Hereford, over a supposed plot against the king to banish them from the kingdom. In order to settle the argument they were to fight a duel. However, Richard called a halt to the challenge as they were entering the lists. Norfolk, who served on the campaigns of 1387–1388, was banished for life and Hereford for ten years. There is no doubt that there was more to the action against these two lords than the need for revenge. However, the closeness of this event to the execution of the senior Appellants is too coincidental to dismiss. Richard had now affected a powerful revenge over those who had chosen to challenge him in force and depose him from the throne in 1387–1388.

Richard's later actions as king were those of a monarch who had grown over-confident in his own powers and authority over his subjects. The action that finally sealed his eventual deposition came following the death of John of Gaunt. He extended the duke of Hereford's banishment to life and also made his Lancastrian inheritance forfeit. He then led a large expedition to Ireland and left his kingdom open to invasion from his wronged cousin. As we have seen, Henry indeed invaded and when Richard returned to challenge this force his support evaporated. Henry assumed the crown and Richard was deposed.

As stated earlier, the aim of this book is not to analyse the political events of the reign of Richard II. What is already clear from this sketch of the reign is that the events of 1387–1388 were extremely important to Richard. In 1398 he rewarded the Cheshiremen who had fought for him with de Vere at Radcot Bridge with 4,000 marks.[104] In addition another knight was prosecuted at the parliament of 1397, namely Sir Thomas Mortimer who had killed Thomas Molineux at the battle of Radcot Bridge.[105] Furthermore at the same parliament, Richard pardoned all his subjects apart from fifty who had displeased the king.[106] What this implies is that Richard was singling out men who had been heavily involved in the events of 1387–1388. As a result of this over five hundred men requested individual pardons.[107] Many of these, as we shall discover, can be seen to have been involved in the expeditions of 1387 and 1388, and by implication also the battle of Radcot Bridge. The enrolled pardons of 1398 and 1399 and their relationship with the muster rolls for the campaigns of 1387–1388 will be discussed in detail in Chapter 4.

Thus, the significance of these expeditions and the intervening civil war places much importance on the composition of Arundel's forces. Richard himself was deeply affected by the events and did not forget those that had acted against him. It is the intention of this book to discuss the nature of the composition of the expeditions of 1387 and 1388. Were men who became involved in

---

[104] *Chronicles of the Revolution*, p. 65.
[105] J.L. Gillespie, 'Thomas Mortimer and Thomas Molineaux: Radcot Bridge and the Appeal of 1397', *Albion*, vii (1975), pp. 161–173.
[106] C.M. Barron, 'The Tyranny of Richard II', *Bulletin of the Institute of Historical Research*, xli (1968), pp. 1–18, p. 7.
[107] C67/30 and C67/31.

these actions motivated by the political scene, and did they thus support the Appellants against the king? As we have noted, soldiers from the campaigns of 1387–1388 were also involved in most of the other campaigns of the later fourteenth century. Is it possible that these men were fighting in royal expeditions just as they had fought on many previous occasions. Would they therefore fight in subsequent expeditions? They may have been serving out of a sense of patriotism, defending the king's right, or indeed may have been serving in the course of a professional military career. Or can it be shown that the men who attended these expeditions fought for personal gain and supported the ascendant party whoever that may be? The survival of the muster rolls for these years has provided a unique opportunity for detailed analysis of these expeditions to be carried out. The political background as described adds depth to what we can discover about the *mentalité* of the late fourteenth-century soldier and the recruitment of an expeditionary force.

2

The Campaigns of 1387–1388 and their Sources

In order to investigate the anatomy of the campaigns I have been able draw upon a wealth of sources. Using these sources I will reconstruct the campaigns from recruitment to muster and also relate the highlights of the two expeditions. The expeditions are widely covered by the chronicles, and accounts can be found in Walsingham, the Westminster Chronicle, Froissart and Henry Knighton.[1] Most have been translated into English, making things easier for linguistically challenged medievalists as myself. I will draw on the chronicles throughout this chapter. Other information for the expeditions comes from the published *Calendar of Patent Rolls* and *Calendar of Close Rolls*, and also from unpublished documentation in the Public Record Office, namely the Treaty Rolls (C76), Issue Rolls (E403), Enrolled Accounts (E364) and Supplementary Patent Rolls (C67).

The main part of my research has involved the military sources for the period, and, in this particular case, the muster rolls catalogued in Exchequer Accounts Various as E101/40/33 and E101/40/5. These muster rolls contain the personnel of each army thus enabling the reconstruction of the composition of the two expeditions in great detail. They contain the names of all those who fought in the campaigns, and record not only how the army was divided into retinues but also how each retinue contained different numbers of men-at-arms and archers. They also show troop movements, replacements of soldiers and mortalities. The enrolled letters of protection and enrolled appointments of attorney surviving on the Treaty Rolls C76/71 and C76/72, which cover the relevant regnal years, also add much supporting material to the names contained in the muster rolls. In addition, the particulars of account drawn up after each campaign also survive in E101/40/35 (1387) and E101/41/5 (1388); the latter also includes a copy of Arundel's indenture with the crown. The particulars of account provide a record of payments which Arundel had received from the crown and the service that had actually been provided by each type of soldier in terms of service days. This

---

[1] Froissart, *Chronicles*, for 1387, vol. ii, pp. 215–217, for 1388 vol. ii, pp. 333–334, 346–350, 391; *Knighton's Chronicle 1337–1396*, ed. G.H. Martin (Oxford, 1995), for 1387 pp. 389–391; *Westminster Chronicle*, for 1387 pp. 181–185, for 1388 pp. 351–353; T. Walsingham, *Historia Anglicana*, ed. H.T. Riley (2 vols, Rolls Series, 1863–64), for 1387 vol. ii, pp. 153–156, for 1388 vol. ii, p. 175 and recently translated, *The St Albans Chronicle: the Chronica Maiora of Thomas Walsingham, Volume 1: 1376–1396*, ed. John Taylor, Wendy R. Childs and Leslie Watkiss (Oxford, 2002), for 1387 pp. 809–815, for 1388 pp. 853–855.

allows comparison between the account and the evidence from the muster roll. These sources will be discussed in greater detail later in this chapter.

The campaigns in detail

A continual council was appointed by Parliament to govern the realm on 19 November 1386. Its terms of reference were as follows:

> Commission, by assent of Parliament, appointing William, archbishop of Canterbury, Alexander, archbishop of York, Edmund, duke of York, Thomas, duke of Gloucester, William, bishop of Winchester, Thomas, bishop of Exeter, Nicholas, abbot of Waltham, Richard, earl of Arundel, John, Lord Cobeham, Richard Lescrope and John Devereux to be of the king's great and continual council for one year for surveying along with his great officers, viz. the chancellor, treasurer and keeper of the privy seal the condition and governance of his household and realm, including all his officers, and for enquiring of all his revenues and expenditure, and of all defaults and offences whereby the king is injured and the realm disturbed, with power to enter the household and realm, including all his officers, and for enquiring of all his revenues and expenditure, and of all defaults and misprisions whatever and to compel the production of all rolls, records and other evidences, correct abuses, hear complaints which cannot be redressed and terminated by course of law, and if opinions are divided to decide by that of the majority.[2]

We can see that the council was led by the king's main opponents to peace with France, namely his uncle, Thomas of Woodstock, duke of Gloucester, and Richard Fitzalan, earl of Arundel. Under their influence, the council now acted as a regency and changed domestic and foreign policy to suit its own agenda.

At this point, it would be useful to briefly discuss the term by which Richard's enemies of this period are known. The opponents to the king are referred to collectively by historians, for sake of convenience, as the Appellants, due to their later use of the legal instrument of appeal with which they attacked the king's favourites in Parliament. Technically, they only became Appellants once they had lodged their appeal in November 1387. At this time, only the three senior Appellants, the earls of Gloucester, Arundel and Warwick were attacking the king and his favourites. They lodged their appeal at Waltham Cross on 14 November 1387 and repeated it in the presence of the king at Westminster on 17 November 1387. The king offered to accept the appeal at the next Parliament, scheduled for the 3 February 1388. The two junior Appellants joined when the king decided to oppose the Appellants by force of arms and sent Robert de Vere, duke of Ireland, to gather an army of loyal Cheshire men in December 1388. The five Appellants, together as a group, defeated this force at the battle of Radcot Bridge on 20 December 1387. They are referred to as Lords Appellant in

---

2   *CPR, 1385–1389*, p. 244.

the appeal to the Merciless Parliament in 1388, documented in the Westminster Chronicle.[3]

The king's opposition to war against France makes the composition of the expeditions extremely relevant. Would the political background mean that the composition of the expeditions differed significantly from any other royal expedition? The analysis made possible by the use of relational databases makes it possible to draw conclusions on the political make-up of an expeditionary army at the time of constitutional crisis. How far were the ordinary soldiers affected by this political turmoil? Were the expeditions populated with what we might consider as a private army of Appellant supporters?

The council wasted little time in preparing their first expedition. By 10 December 1386, the earl of Arundel had been appointed Admiral of the North and West.[4] On 16 December he was retained to serve the king with 2,500 men from 1 March 1387, with the intention of leading an expedition against the French.[5] He began to assemble the fleet which he would use to prosecute this campaign from the following February 1387.[6] The issue of recruitment of such a force will be tackled later, in Part 2. The main point to note here is that although the expedition was led by the council and against the wishes of the king, it was still a royal expedition, as in theory the council was acting in the name of the crown. Indeed the king himself can be shown to have wished for a successful outcome to this expedition, as on 20 March 1387 he desired the prayers of the abbots and bishops for the success of the fleet under the command of the admiral.[7]

Arundel's strategy was to attack Flanders in order to provoke a revolt against Burgundian rule. However, before Flanders could be attacked, the enemy French and Flemish fleet, which had been assembled in the previous year for an invasion of England, had to be destroyed.[8] Luckily, an enemy ship was captured following Arundel's arrival at Sandwich on 12 March.[9] The muster of the indented force must have been on 13 March, as Arundel's own particulars of account, returned after the campaign and to be found in the Enrolled Accounts, state that Arundel was paid from this day, and this is also the date stated at the beginning of the muster roll.[10] The actual order for the commission to muster was made on 8 March.[11] It is interesting to note that the issue rolls record details

---

[3] For the text of the Appeal presented at the Merciless Parliament see, *Westminster Chronicle*, pp. 237–239, also p. 274.

[4] *Handbook of British Chronology*, p. 139.

[5] The indenture has not survived for 1387. However, the terms of the indenture are recorded on the Exchequer's enrolled copy of the accounts, E364/21 m. 6v. Arundel's accounts, E101/40/35, also state that the indenture was sealed on 16 December 1387.

[6] *CCR, 1385–89*, pp. 208–209 for a summons dated 16 February 1387 for the assembly of a fleet at Sandwich on 11 March.

[7] *Foedera*, vol. iii, part iv, p. 13; Hardy, *Syllabus, ii, 1377–1654*, p. 513.

[8] Palmer, *England, France and Christendom*, p. 92.

[9] *Westminster Chronicle*, p. 181 for Arundel's arrival at the coast and capture of the ship.

[10] E101/40/35 for Arundel's accounts, and E101/40/33 m. 1 for the muster roll. E364/21 m. 6v for enrolled accounts. E403/515 m. 27 for payment to two Exchequer clerks to compile the muster.

[11] For the order to muster see C76/71 m. 6, also printed in *Catalogue des rolles Gascons,*

of a payment to Friar Adam Samford, who was present at the muster on his journey back from Flanders. He was able to deliver news to the council and Lords, as they were at Sandwich to supervise the muster.[12] It was discovered from the captured ship when and where the French fleet would be travelling. As a result the admiral put to sea on 23 March and battle with the Flemish fleet was joined on 24 March.[13] The evidence from the muster roll confirms the date for the battle as suggested by the Monk of Westminster, as four men are knighted on 24 March, therefore prior to battle being joined. The English fleet of just 60 ships was heavily outnumbered by 250 enemy ships.[14] However, the Flemish ships were undermanned and 70 German and Dutch ships deserted to the English side. As a result, Arundel managed a decisive victory. He immediately chased the remnants of the fleet back to Sluys and anchored nearby. However, the earl failed to capitalise on the disarray he had caused, and allowed the enemy time to regroup and did not then attempt to capture Sluys. Instead, he stayed in his ships that were used as a base from which to raid the surrounding country-side for the next three weeks.[15]

The Monk of Westminster suggests that the admiral returned to England for reinforcements as many of his men had become sick by 14 April:

Indeed the earl would have accomplished more in those parts, but the water of the district round about was so bitter and unwholesome that every man he had was exhausted by a severe cough, and other maladies were attacking them; so that if he had prolonged his stay there he would undoubtedly have lost many of them for good. On 14 April, therefore, he weighed anchor and set sail, reaching Orwell Haven in safety with his forces and all his prizes.[16]

Knighton does not suggest a date for the return but comments that it was because many of the men were seriously wounded. The muster roll would support this date for the return to England, as it records that the earl of Notting-ham left the expedition on 15 April, probably once they had returned to harbour at Orwell. Arundel's messenger, John Elyngton, esquire, was attacked on

---

Normans et François, conserves dans les Archives de la Tour de Londres tire d'après celui du garde desdites archives, ed. Thomas Carte (London and Paris, 1743), *Catalogue des rolles François*, p. 155.

12 E403/515 m. 25.

13 *Westminster Chronicle*, pp. 181–183. Knighton placed the battle around the feast of the Annunciation, 25 March 1387, and therefore agrees with this diary of events: *Knighton's Chronicle*, p. 389.

14 E403/515 m. 25, cited in Palmer, *England, France and Christendom*, p. 93. The issue roll contains information regarding payments to mariners for shipping. See also E101/40/36, which details the accounts of the payments made to the mariners. Sherborne, 'The English Navy', p. 38, comments that the fleet consisted of 31 ships, 19 barges and 1 balinger and a number of victualling ships, citing E101/40/36 and E403/515 m. 27. The latter details a payment of £1,000 made to Richard Copleston for shipping.

15 Arundel is said to have been anchored off Sluys from Monday 25 March to Thursday 11 April according to *Croniques de Franche, d'Engleterre, de Flanders, de Lile et especialement de Tournai*, ed. A. Hocquet, Publications de la Société des Bibliophiles Belges, xxxviii (Mons, 1938), p. 313.

16 *Westminster Chronicle*, p. 183.

13 April whilst returning with the king's reply and orders. This would place the return of the fleet a day earlier.[17] English success was confined to the accumulation of booty, especially the wine captured from the Flemish fleet. The Monk of Westminster puts this at more than 8,000 tuns of wine on 68 captured ships, which was sold throughout England at the knockdown price of 4d a gallon. Knighton has a higher figure quoting 126 captured ships and between 12,000 and 13,000 tuns of Rochelle wine. Froissart claims the English gained great wealth capturing more than 9,000 tuns of wine. Froissart comments on the capture of wine:

> Having entered the Thames, they landed at London, where they were joyfully received for the fine wines of Poitou and Saintonge they had on board, which were intended to have been drunk in Flanders, Brabant, Hainault, Liège, and other places. They were dispersed throughout England, and the prices so much depressed from the quantity, a gallon was sold for fourpence.[18]

Whatever the correct figure, there is no doubt that this victory and its spoils made the earl of Arundel a popular figure in England. Indeed, Walsingham comments that the earl did not keep any of the spoils for himself, thus increasing his reputation.[19] The issue rolls record payments made to the royal clerks William Hugford and John Lincoln who were ordered to travel to Orwell to receive the captured wine and other goods.[20]

As a result of the reinforcement of Sluys by the French, Arundel had been forced to return to England and to rest his fleet at Orwell. The fleet remained at Orwell for around two weeks from mid April. The Monk of Westminster comments that once the earl of Arundel had regained his health, he and his men put to sea on 1 May.[21] The first part of this campaign to date had provided the Appellants with a short-term success but had not fulfilled their aims. The admiral therefore returned to Brittany as he had two months of his contract left to run. Although John de Montfort, duke of Brittany, had recently made an agreement with the English government, he had been besieging Brest since 1386, which had been under English control since 1378.[22] Arundel had hoped to

---

[17] *Knighton's Chronicle*, p. 391; E101/40/33 m. 1, 'vacat' 15 April, noted to the left of his name; *CPR, 1385–1389*, p. 323, 13 April 1387, for a report of the attack on Elyngton. Elyngton's placing in the muster roll reflects his position as Arundel's messenger, as he is listed in fifty-eighth position overall and is the twentieth esquire listed. 1387: E101/40/33 m. 1. He appears again in a senior position in the muster roll for the expedition of 1388, listed forty-fourth overall and the eleventh esquire listed. The attack he suffered in 1388 has perhaps made him more cautious. He has appointed an attorney to protect his interests whilst on the king's service. 1388: E101/41/5 m. 1; enrolled attorney, C76/72 m. 8.

[18] Froissart, *Chronicles*, vol. ii, p. 217.

[19] *Westminster Chronicle*, pp. 183–185; *Knighton's Chronicle*, p. 391; Froissart, *Chronicles*, vol. ii, p. 217; *St Albans Chronicle*, p. 813.

[20] E403/515 m. 25.

[21] *Westminster Chronicle*, p. 185. The Monk of Westminster is the only chronicler to mention Arundel becoming sick at this time.

[22] For the council's negotiations with John de Montfort during February and March 1387, see Michael Jones, *Ducal Brittany 1364–1399: Relations with England and France during the Reign of Duke John IV* (Oxford, 1970), pp. 104–105. He suggests that the duke of Brittany's

lead an Anglo-Breton attack on France. But, he had to content himself with the relief of Brest, from the siege of the duke, and even this limited objective was only partially achieved. The Monk of Westminster describes how the admiral revictualled Brest and made an armed advance ten miles inland before returning shortly before Midsummer Day, which would have been on 24 June. Knighton describes how the earl destroyed siege engines around Brest and provided the town with supplies which would last the town for two years, before returning home.[23] Walsingham also describes the destruction of French fortifications at Brest and the supplying of the garrison,[24] whilst Froissart does not reflect on these actions in his account of the events. Arundel's own accounts state that he was back from Brest by 12 June, landing at Southampton.[25] There is also evidence that John Slegh delivered twenty prisoners to the Tower of London on behalf of the earl on 7 June, suggesting an even earlier return.[26] Froissart adds weight to this event by uniquely describing the sad story of the enemy admiral, Sir John de Bucq, who remained a prisoner on his word in London for three years, where he subsequently died.[27]

The official record can confirm Arundel's success, as reported in the chronicles, during this campaign. There is evidence in the *Calendar of Patent Rolls* to suggest that a number of enemy Castilian and Flemish ships were captured during the two stages of the campaign, to the profit of the king and the admiral.[28] According to the terms of Arundel's indenture, the king would receive a quarter share of the gains of war, and the other three quarters would be shared between the earl, men-at-arms, esquires, archers and mariners.[29] On 5 May, Richard, earl of Arundel was granted the ship called *Seint Johan* of St Sebastian, which had been captured at sea. The king received a payment of £100 for his share.[30] On 12 June, the king sold a ship called *Seint Marie* of San

---

attack and capture of Oliver Clisson, constable of France, in late June was a response to English pressure. However, as we have seen, Arundel had already returned to England by 12 June 1387.

[23] *Westminster Chronicle*, p. 185 ; *Knighton's Chronicle*, p. 391. Knighton also mentions that the earl returned to Sluys, captured ships and marched inland. This would appear to be confused with the earlier encounter and also mixed up with the events around Brest

[24] Walsingham, *Historia Anglicana*, vol. ii, pp. 155–156, and *The St Albans Chronicle*, p. 813.

[25] E101/40/35, Arundel's account.

[26] *Foedera*, vol. iii, part iv, p. 13; Hardy, *Syllabus, ii, 1377–1654*, p. 513. 1387: E101/40/33 m. 18. John Slegh was also a retinue captain in the royal expedition to Scotland in 1385, where he was described as the king's butler: Lewis, 'The Last Medieval Summons', p. 20.

[27] Froissart, *Chronicles*, vol. i, p. 217.

[28] *Westminster Chronicle*, p. 183, mentions that Arundel took 'three carracks with miscellaneous cargoes, two Norman "bargettes", a fine Spanish vessel, and some Scottish ships carrying wool', during his period at Sluys in the first part of the campaign. *Knighton's Chronicle*, p. 391, mentions that Arundel 'took Flemish ships and some from Scotland' also at Sluys. However, Knighton places these captures at the end of the second part of the campaign and therefore has his narrative slightly confused.

[29] Indenture terms recorded on the issue roll E364/21 m. 6v.

[30] *CPR, 1385–1389*, p. 302, paid at the 'Receipt of the Exchequer, to the king's clerk Roger Walden'.

Sebastian to Walter Frost of Hull. This was the king's share of profits 'arising from goods and merchandise captured at seas from enemies by Richard, earl of Arundel, admiral and others in his company'.[31] Another ship, *Gracedieux* of Santander, which had been taken in war by the admiral, was granted to Robert de Parys on 20 October. He had lost his own ship and crew, which was described as 'one of the best in the realm', during a storm in the Thames. The king granted him a replacement as a reward for his past deed and in expectation of future service. However, the treasurer had already sold this ship before the grant could be made. He was therefore granted the *Seinte Marie Cogge* of Aardenburg in Flanders, another vessel which had been taken by the earl of Arundel.[32] Finally, an esquire in the retinue of Sir Thomas Trivet, James Clifford,[33] was granted the ship *Holygost*. This ship was part of the king's share of 'goods and merchandise captured at sea from the enemy by Richard, earl of Arundel, admiral, and others in his company'.[34] It is possible that James Clifford was a professional seaman, as his retinue captain, Sir Thomas Trivet had been the previous Admiral of the West, being replaced by the earl of Arundel on 10 December 1386.[35]

Richard harboured deep resentment against the powers of the council and its foreign policy. This was shown by his 'questions to the judges' at Shrewsbury and Nottingham in August 1387 that are widely documented by the Monk of Westminster and Henry Knighton.[36] These consultations were to gain a legal opinion to establish whether the Wonderful Parliament and the appointment of the council had unlawfully deprived the king of his prerogative. The answers Richard received not only supported the king by stating the appointment of the council was illegal, but also that those who had directed these measures should be treated as traitors. The judges claimed later that they had been coerced into making the answers, however, the answers they gave were fully justified in common law.[37] The king had the answers he required to challenge the limitations that had been placed upon him in the previous year. Richard felt he was now free to work towards a peace policy with France, continuing the work of the former Chancellor, de la Pole. He therefore began to plan for an Anglo-French summit between the two kings. Palmer described how negotiations were started at the end of May 1387, with the despatch of the king's personal agent, Simon Shiringham, to negotiate with Charles VI. A meeting was arranged to follow

---

[31] *CPR, 1385–1389*, p. 308.

[32] *Ibid.*, p. 364. Robert de Parys cannot be identified in the muster rolls for the army of 1387.

[33] E101/40/33 m. 7.

[34] *CPR, 1385–1389*, p. 338, grant by mainprise for the payment of £100 at the receipt of the Exchequer.

[35] Sir Thomas Trivet had been Admiral of the Western Fleet from 22 February 1386. Richard, earl of Arundel, became Admiral of the North and West on 10 December 1386, also replacing Philip Darcy, Lord Darcy, who had been Admiral of the Northern Fleet from 22 February 1386, see *Handbook of British Chronology*, p. 139.

[36] *Knighton's Chronicle*, pp. 394–398; *Westminster Chronicle*, pp. 196–202; S.B. Chrimes, 'Richard II's Questions to the Judges, 1387', *Law Quarterly Review*, lxxii (1956), pp. 365–390.

[37] *Knighton's Chronicle*, p. 394; *Westminster Chronicle*, p. 316; Saul, *Richard II*, pp. 171–175.

Richard's return to power, following the end of the council's year of authority on 20 November 1387. These plans meant that conflict with the party which wanted to prolong the war with France was now inevitable and the peace plans were halted before any meeting could be made.[38] Palmer also argues that the eighteen men who were excluded from the general pardon in the Merciless Parliament of 1388, were being punished for their involvement in the negotiations with the French in the previous year.[39] John L. Leland has looked closely at the careers of these men and has shown that, although some of the men were involved in the negotiations, the others 'seem to have constituted a close-knit clique within the royal administration'.[40] They were therefore made scapegoats because of their close ties to the royal court, rather than any particular role in the peace plans of Richard II.

The result of this brinkmanship between the king and his council led to a brief civil war which culminated in the battle of Radcot Bridge in Oxfordshire and may also have led to a period when the king was temporarily deposed. The three senior Appellants were the king's uncle, the duke of Gloucester, the earl of Warwick and the earl of Arundel. As we saw, they had first acted against the king's policy in the Wonderful Parliament of 1386 which had established the council to control the government of the realm. They were unhappy at the attempts to make peace with France and felt that England was losing its influence and was being left open to the threat of invasion. The chroniclers state that the Appellants' deep resentment over Richard's lack of patronage towards them and his 'friendship' with a select group of favourites had led to the breakdown in relationships. The Westminster Chronicler comments that the king 'was apparently better pleased to be guided by the falsest of traitors than by those of his nobles and lords who were his most loyal supporters'. Walsingham goes further and describes how Richard showed favour to the duke of Ireland above all others and believed this continued favour was due to the use of magic spells.[41]

Two junior members joined the three senior Appellants, the king's cousin Henry, earl of Derby, and Thomas, earl of Nottingham. Both probably joined in the revolt as they were motivated by self-interest. The main bone of their contention was the rise to power of the king's favourite, Robert de Vere. His rise was meteoric; he had been created marquess of Dublin in December 1385, with the lordship and dominion of Ireland for life and from October 1386 he had been created duke of Ireland.[42] This favouritism created jealously and fear amongst the higher nobility, as such largesse would normally have been more evenly

---

[38] Palmer, *England, France and Christendom*, pp. 105–121 explains these peace plans in great detail.

[39] *Ibid.*, pp. 118–119.

[40] John L. Leland, 'Unpardonable Sinners? Exclusions from the General Pardon of 1388', *Medieval Prosopography*, 17 (1996), pp. 181–195, p. 195. It is interesting to note that Leland discovers that some of these men carried on to serve and prosper under Richard II and also continued to progress under the new regime of Henry IV. This has similar resonances to the careers of some of the men involved in the campaigns of 1387 and 1388 discussed in Part 2.

[41] *Westminster Chronicle*, p. 219; Walsingham, *Historia Anglicana*, vol. ii, p. 160, and *St Albans Chronicle*, p. 823.

[42] *Complete Peerage*, vol. iv, p. 473.

spread around. They understandably resented such a significant change to the status quo.

Once knowledge of Richard's approach to the judges became known, the Appellants reacted by appealing five named advisors to the king on 14 November 1387. This prosecution named these five 'traitors' who would be 'appealed' in parliament in February 1388; they included the king's favourite, de Vere, and his former Chancellor, de la Pole. The parliament was summoned on 17 December 1387 and assembled on 3 February 1388 at Westminster.[43] Richard was isolated from his own power base in Cheshire. He therefore sent de Vere north to mobilise an army from amongst his loyal Cheshire men to come to his aid and protect his current threatened position. De Vere had gathered an army of 3,000–4,000 men ready to march south by mid-December. The three senior Appellants decided to cut off this attempt to support the king and the two junior Appellants joined them in this plan.[44]

The details of the subsequent battle of Radcot Bridge on 20 December 1387 have been reconstructed by J.N.L. Myres from the various descriptions included in the chronicles.[45] Myres demonstrates how the chroniclers give differing accounts of the battle depending upon their source materials. Thus the Westminster Chronicle gives precedence to the earl of Warwick, whilst Knighton talks about the earl of Derby having a leading role.[46] The Lords Appellant decided to cut off de Vere's route to London and thus prevent him from joining up with the king. Following a brief skirmish with the earl of Arundel, de Vere was forced to cross the Thames at Radcot Bridge, where Derby was waiting for him. Seeing the bridge blocked and the armies of the other Appellants approaching from behind, de Vere made a break and swam the Thames on his horse to escape. His army was rounded up, disarmed and sent home.[47] The result of the battle was one of defeat for the king's forces, de Vere had fled his deserting army and the only significant casualty was Sir Thomas Molineaux, his lieutenant.[48] Richard was now left without any support and was at the mercy of the Appellants. The majority of the chroniclers suggest that the Appellants and the king maintained respect for one another and the king was not deposed. The Westminster Chronicle describes how the Appellants met the king in the Tower of London and following threats from the Appellant lords, Richard agreed 'to defer to them in

---

[43] *Handbook of British Chronology*, p. 565.

[44] Saul, *Richard II*, pp. 187–189.

[45] J.N.L. Myres, 'The Campaign of Radcot Bridge in December 1387', *English Historical Review*, xlii (1927), pp. 20–33.

[46] *Westminster Chronicle*, pp. 221–225; *Knighton's Chronicle*, pp. 410–412.

[47] See Myres, 'Radcot Bridge', pp. 21–26 for a summary of chronicle accounts. Froissart has a completely different account to that of the English chroniclers. He describes the duke of Gloucester defeating a large force of 15,000 men under the duke of Ireland. He also places the king in Bristol during these events: Froissart, *Chronicles*, vol. i, pp. 277–279.

[48] J.L. Gillespie, 'Thomas Mortimer and Thomas Molineaux: Radcot Bridge and the Appeal of 1397', *Albion*, vii (1975), pp. 161–173. See also below in Chapter 4 for identification of possible other participants at Radcot Bridge who can also be identified in the muster rolls for the expeditions of 1387 and 1388.

all permissible respects and to be guided by wholesome advice from them, without prejudice to his crown and personal diginity'.[49]

However, another source paints a different story that would explain the later significance which Richard attached to his humiliation at the hands of the Appellants and also his acts of revenge against his foes for which he patiently waited ten years. This other chronicle, originally identified by Clarke and Galbraith,[50] provides this other view. The chronicle of Whalley Abbey, Lancashire, suggests that following the battle of Radcot Bridge, Richard was actually deposed by the Appellants. During the discussions mentioned above by the Monk of Westminster, the Whalley Chronicle recounts that rather than reaching a compromise, Richard was actually deposed for three days. It goes on to state that the duke of Gloucester and the earl of Derby could not decide on which of them was to take his place. They therefore restored Richard to his crown. Clarke and Galbraith also point out that this version of events is supported by the forced confession of Gloucester in Calais in 1397 where he mentions that they deposed the king for two or three days.[51] It is doubtful whether a forced confession is evidence to be relied upon regarding this event, but this story is also supported by the lack of any entries on the Close or the Patent Rolls for the last three days of December.[52] This was a significant moment in the reign and also as an event that would have repercussions throughout the rest of Richard's life and rule. Richard's later actions become more explainable once it is accepted that not only was his rule challenged by force of arms in 1387, but that he was also removed from his birthright by force for a brief period at the end of December. More recently, Nigel Saul has used this event as a part of his overall thesis to explain the later seemingly vindictive actions of Richard which ultimately led to his downfall.

Following this briefest of civil wars and with the king now restored, the five Appellants proceeded with their prosecution of the king's favourites by the process of Appeal in the Merciless Parliament of February 1388. The Westminster Chronicle devotes a long section to the description of this parliament and the editor suggests that much of it is drawn directly from the Parliamentary Roll. The five main accused were all found guilty and sentenced to death or removal of their religious offices. De la Pole and de Vere had already escaped to France and so avoided this sentence. The Commons then impeached the king's other retainers who were also sentenced to death for treason. There was a great delay over the impeachment and sentence of Sir Simon Burley who had support on both sides of the court; the duke of York, earl of Derby and the king and queen all interceded on his behalf. Nevertheless, Gloucester prevailed and Burley was executed on 5 May 1388. The Monk of Westminster comments on his end:

---

[49] *Westminster Chronicle*, pp. 227–229.
[50] This chronicle was originally described by M.V. Clarke and V.H. Galbraith, 'The Deposition of Richard II?', *Bulletin of the John Rylands Library*, 14 (1930), pp. 125–181. See especially Note B, 'Another Deposition of Richard II?', pp. 157–163.
[51] *RP*, vol. iii, p. 379, also reprinted in *Chronicles of the Revolution*, p. 81.
[52] Clarke and Galbraith, 'Deposition of Richard II', pp. 159–160.

Sir Simon Burley was condemned by parliamentary process to be drawn and hanged and finally beheaded; but since he was a knight of the Garter, the whole sentence, except only for the beheading was remitted.[53]

It is interesting to note that three of the knights arrested as retainers of the king were released under mainprise from the Tower of London to appear at the next parliament to answer any charges. It is not clear from the Monk of Westminster as to why they escaped the unfortunate fate of Richard's other retainers who had also been arrested.[54] However, it is interesting to speculate on this in the cases of two of these knights, Sir William Elmham and Sir Thomas Trivet, as they had both served as retinue captains in the expedition led by the earl of Arundel in the previous year. They may have been spared due to this recent service with the main Appellant lord. Indeed, Sir William Elmham continued this service in 1388, perhaps out of gratitude.[55] As a result of the Merciless Parliament, Richard had been humiliated and his closest councillors and friends had either been executed or forced into exile. He now had to take a back seat in politics as Gloucester and Arundel, the two leading Appellants, took control of the government and its foreign policy.

The two main Appellants decided to build upon their limited success of the previous year and made plans to launch another large-scale expedition to France in order to bring Flanders and Castile back into the war against France, and thus lessen the threat against England.[56] This put paid to all the plans for peace with France that Richard had been making in readiness for his return to power. A half-fifteenth subsidy was granted for the raising of an army on 10 March 1388.[57] This was an exceptional award as it had been granted mid-parliament and not as was usually the case at the end of the session. On 24 March Arundel contracted to serve for three months with 3,500 men from the following 11 May.[58] In preparation for the expedition, the earl of Arundel was appointed captain of Brest and the king's lieutenant in the country adjoining the town on 9 April and subsequently the king's subjects in Brest were commanded to obey the earl.[59] As mentioned the army was indented to muster at Southampton on 11 May and was actually ready to sail in good time by 5 May.[60] The actual order to take the muster was made on 14 May 1388.[61] However, the Appellants' deter-

---

[53] *Westminster Chronicle*, p. 331; for the Monk's description of the Merciless Parliament see pp. 235–343.

[54] *Ibid.*, p. 229 for their arrest and p. 339 for their release; see also *CCR, 1385–1389*, pp. 393–395 and pp. 397–398.

[55] Elmham, 1387: E101/40/33 m. 11; 1388: muster roll E101/40/39 m. 1. Attendance is confirmed by Froissart, *Chronicles*, vol. ii, p. 383. Trivet, 1387: E101/40/33 m. 7; enrolled protection, C76/71 m. 14.

[56] Palmer, *England, France and Christendom*, pp. 122–127.

[57] *Westminster Chronicle*, p. 319n.

[58] A copy of the indenture is preserved with Arundel's accounts E101/41/4 m. 2; for terms of indenture see enrolled account E364/24 m. 5.

[59] See C76/72 m. 9 and also *Foedera*, vol. iii, part iv, p. 22; Hardy, *Syllabus, ii, 1377–1654*, p. 514.

[60] *RP*, vol. iii, pp. 244–245, cited in Palmer, *England, France and Christendom*, p. 130.

[61] C76/72 m. 2, also printed in Carte, *Catalogue des rolles François*, p. 158.

mination to prosecute Sir Simon Burley and the resistance they received in Parliament delayed their timetable until June. Palmer comments that the delay thus caused proved disastrous for what was to have been a sophisticated and large-scale attack.[62]

The expedition was intended to be a lot more impressive than the actual event turned out to be. Gloucester had envisaged a two-pronged attack on France, with John of Gaunt in Gascony, supported by Sir Thomas Percy and again involving the unreliable ally, de Montfort, duke of Brittany, who would join with the forces brought by Arundel. The intended combined English force would have numbered 6,000 men. However, Gaunt preferred talks on peace to warfare and did not go along with the plans of his brother, the duke of Gloucester.[63] Gaunt had been appointed lieutenant of Aquitaine on 26 May and set out to limit the scope of the planned conflict.[64] It was planned that Gaunt receive a small retinue under Sir Thomas Percy sent by the Appellants but it is not likely that he received these reinforcements.[65] It can be shown from the sources that Sir William Elmham, who mustered as a member of the retinue of Sir Thomas Percy, was with Arundel during his campaigning around La Rochelle. It would appear, therefore, that as a result of Gaunt's reluctance to join with Arundel, the reinforcements intended for him were absorbed into Arundel's own force. Instead Gaunt successfully concluded a peace treaty on 8 July with the king of Castile and also began working on the terms of a major truce for the south of France. Because of Gaunt's refusal to take part and Arundel's late arrival in Brittany, de Montfort broke off his alliance with the English and went back over to the French.[66]

On 2 June, the earl of Arundel was confirmed in possession of the town, county and honour of Richmond,[67] and he was also given the power to treat for

---

[62] Palmer, *England, France and Christendom*, pp. 130–131.

[63] For this and Gaunt's peace plans see Palmer, *England, France and Christendom*, pp. 126–132.

[64] *Foedera*, vol. iii, part iv, p. 24; Hardy, *Syllabus, ii, 1377–1654*, p. 515.

[65] See E101/40/39 for the muster roll for the force of Thomas de Percy in 1388. The muster roll is incomplete due to damage by fire, with only the first 346 men detailed in 8 retinues surviving. For reference to Elmham see Froissart, *Chronicles*, vol. ii, p. 383. For payments to Percy see E403/519 mm. 8, 12 and 23.

[66] The loyalty of the duke of Brittany was problematic following the release for ransom by Richard II in 1386 of the rival claimant to the duchy, Jean de Blois, who was being held prisoner in Gloucester Castle. The ransom was granted to Robert de Vere for his intended military service in Ireland. For the grant see *CPR, 1385–1389*, pp. 123 and 132. For discussion see Michael Jones, 'The Ransom of Jean de Bretagne, Count of Penthièvre: An Aspect of English Foreign Policy 1386–8', *Bulletin of the Institute of Historical Reseach*, xlv (1972), pp. 7–26. Jean de Blois was held in England as hostage for his father Charles de Blois, who had been captured by Thomas Dagworth at the battle of La Roche Derrien in 1346. Jean and his brother Guy had been in custody in England since 1353. Guy died in 1385, Jean was released in 1386 after nearly thirty-five years of captivity. The ransom of Jean de Blois was one of the articles of the Appeal against the king's favourites in the Merciless Parliament of 1388.

[67] *CCR, 1341–1417*, p. 309.

peace with the duke of Brittany.[68] A great banquet had been held at Westminster on 1 June where Arundel requested permission to leave for the coast. He subsequently set sail from Southampton on 10 June.[69] Arundel did not find out about the desertion of his ally until landing in Brittany with an expeditionary force of 3,500 men and a further 2,900 men manning 97 ships.[70] He hung around north Brittany for a month, as he had lost all mobility on land until he had confirmation that de Montfort had made a reconciliation with the French.[71] He was further hampered by this turn of events as the horses for the planned campaigning were to have been provided by de Montfort. He then sailed towards La Rochelle, ignoring his recall from Westminster in the middle of July.[72] His only action on land throughout July consisted of plundering La Rochelle and the neighbouring islands. The story of the expedition is relayed in great detail by Froissart perhaps revealing that he had access to eyewitness accounts.[73] The Monk of Westminster also describes these events prior to Arundel's return to Hastings with his forces on 2 September. The actual date is one day later as confirmed by Arundel's accounts, which state that he actually landed at Winchelsea on 3 September.[74] Arundel was not satisified with the impact he had made and whilst still campaigning had made contact with de Montfort when the duke returned from Paris to Brittany in August. He hoped to reinvigorate the failed alliance, however his efforts were to end in failure.

To understand the nature of this campaign it is important to consider the evidence regarding the involvement of the duke of Brittany, John de Montfort. Froissart is the only chronicler to mention that the duke of Brittany was to provide horses for a land campaign for the forces commanded by the earl of Arundel. He also comments how 'cast down' Arundel was when he heard that de Montfort had travelled to Paris to treat with the French, in addition, he again mentions how the lack of horses hampered the campaign.[75] It would seem therefore that Froissart might have spoken to some of the combatants in order to gather his information. It is therefore pertinent to mention Froissart's visit to England in 1395, when such information may have been gathered. He was able to meet the king at Leeds Castle and presented him with a book of poems which he had prepared as a gift. But what is of particular interest is that he lodged in a house in Ospringe whilst awaiting his introduction to the king. Also lodged here at the same time was Sir William Lisle, a knight of the king's chamber.[76] Lisle

---

[68] *Foedera*, vol. iii, part iv, p. 25; Hardy, *Syllabus, ii, 1377–1654*, p. 514, and C76/72 m. 3, which gives the date as 1 June.

[69] *Westminster Chronicle*, p. 341.

[70] The fleet consisted of 53 ships, 9 barges and 35 victualling ships, see Sherborne, 'The English Navy', p. 38, drawing his numbers from E101/40/40, an account of mariners' wages; and records of payments to mariners on the issue rolls E403/519 m. 12 and E403/521 mm. 6, 7. The latter document details a payment of £1,255 13s 4d for shipping.

[71] Froissart, *Chronicles*, pp. 346–347.

[72] E403/519, m. 19.

[73] Froissart, *Chronicles*, vol. ii, pp. 348–350; *Westminster Chronicle*, pp. 352–353.

[74] *Westminster Chronicle*, p. 353, and E101/41/4 for accounts.

[75] Froissart, *Chronicles*, vol. ii, pp. 333–334, 347–348.

[76] Richard II: *Royal Household*, p. 282, life retainer, knight of the Chamber and lay officer of

had stayed behind whilst the king travelled to Canterbury because of a slight headache. However, could it be at this chance encounter that Froissart could have gleaned his eyewitness information from Sir William about the expedition of 1388, for he was indeed a participant, serving in the retinue of Sir William Brienne?[77] Froissart describes how they talked about the recent Irish expedition, on which Sir William had been involved. It is therefore likely that they also discussed other campaigns in which Sir William had seen action including the campaign of 1388. This unique identification of an actual witness for the description of the expedition is strengthened by the inclusion of Sir William Lisle in the list of names Froissart claims sailed with the earl of Arundel on campaign in 1388.[78]

So were these forces intended for a naval campaign, which would make raids inland from the coast or were they intended to undertake a fuller excursion into France, with the provision of horses by the duke of Brittany? The existing indenture for the campaign clearly states that the force was to be raised for a campaign at sea.[79] However, both Michael Jones and John Palmer, in their surveys of these campaigns, consider that the evidence from the peace plans between the council and de Montfort support the argument for a land campaign in 1388. In support of his argument, Jones utilises a document entitled, 'Articles of the wishes of the Duke of Brittany',[80] which he dates to around August 1388. In these articles, Jones describes how

> In return for help against his domestic enemies, John was prepared to release castles to the English and to take the field with them. But the general tone of the 'Articles' was apologetic. John excused his failure to help men who had been sent in the 'daraine flote' by saying that they had had no mounts. Any future force would find him ready to do his utmost to aid them, provided that they brought their own horses.[81]

It would therefore appear from this document that de Montfort is acknowledging his failure to support Arundel's force with the provision of horses. However, Jones admits that the dating of the document is tentative but makes sense when judged in the context of the campaign of 1388. Palmer also refers to the 'Articles' and also the powers granted to Arundel to treat with the duke of Brittany, as previously mentioned. The 'Articles' refer to an earlier agreement, which has not survived, and Palmer argues that this earlier agreement would have specified the details for the joint campaign in Brittany. In addition, it would appear that

the household, of Cambridgeshire/Oxfordshire, retained in 1395 (1392). Henry IV: *Royal Household*, p. 289, of Cambridgeshire/Oxfordshire, retained in 1401.

[77] E101/41/5 m. 9.

[78] For Froissart's visit to England in 1395 see Froissart, *Chronicles*, vol. ii, pp. 568–582. Froissart also had more time for discussions as he rode between Leeds Castle and Rochester in the company of Sir William Lisle and Sir John de Grailly a few days later. For the list of combatants see Froissart, *Chronicles*, vol. ii, p. 333.

[79] E101/41/4 m. 2, for a copy of the indenture. The campaign is described as 'supra mare'.

[80] Printed in Michael Jones, *Ducal Brittany*, Appendix A, pp. 212–214.

[81] *Ibid.*, p. 110.

the intention was to focus the campaign on Brittany as Arundel was made 'captain of the town and castle of Brest, and the king's lieutenant in the country adjoining' on 9 April 1388.[82] Palmer fully accepts this evidence in his description of the events and blames the inability of de Montfort to keep to his word as a major reason for the failure of the campaign.[83] The argument thus presented is persuasive and would suggest that the available evidence supports the claim by Froissart that this army would receive horses from de Montfort in order to undertake a major land campaign. This would have been a logical move for Arundel, as it would have built upon the naval success of the previous year.

The Cambridge Parliament of 1388, which followed Arundel's return, refused to raise any more funds for a continental war.[84] The parliament was summoned on 28 July and met from 9 September to 17 October in Cambridge.[85] It followed an invasion in the north of England by the Scots, who scored a famous victory at Otterburn on 5 August as well as causing major devastation in Cumberland and Westmorland.[86] Events had begun to turn against the leading Appellants. Arundel had been recalled from his expedition on 17 July to assist against the Scottish incursions. Two messengers had been sent to find Arundel, wherever he may be, and deliver a sealed letter.[87] Other letters had been sent to the northern lords in Northumberland, requesting them to await the arrival of Arundel and his fleet.[88] It would appear that Arundel never received the messages, or he did and chose to ignore them.

In addition, Gloucester was forced to open peace negotiations with the French in July, a position against which the Appellants were diametrically opposed. Gloucester is recorded as being granted indemnity on 2 July 1388, to respond to an approach from the French, for a treaty leading to a peace or truce proposed by Philip, duke of Burgundy.[89] The parliament therefore felt it was prudent to focus any subsidy on defence against the Scots rather than another overseas expedition. They agreed to a subsidy of one-tenth and one-fifteenth which was to be spent on defending the realm, safekeeping the sea and protecting the northern border.[90] Arundel was even called to account for the delay in the expedition that meant that they had only served for three months out of the four contracted, setting out on 10 June rather than 11 May as indented. Arundel also insisted on being paid for the full four months and thus made a healthy profit. Sir William Heron, a retinue captain in the campaign,[91] and John

---

[82] See C76/72 m. 9 and also *Foedera*, vol. iii, part iv, p. 22; Hardy, *Syllabus, ii, 1377–1654*, p. 514.

[83] Palmer, *England, France and Christendom*, pp. 127–133.

[84] For discussion see Tuck, 'The Cambridge Parliament, 1388', pp. 225–243.

[85] *Handbook of British Chronology*, p. 565. There is no surviving roll for this parliament.

[86] *Westminster Chronicle*, pp. 346–350; Froissart, *Chronicles*, vol. ii, pp. 361–376; Goodman and Tuck (eds), *War and Border Societies in the Middle Ages*.

[87] E403/519, m. 19: this issue roll details Robert Merkeley, sergeant at arms, paid 53s 4d to travel to Dartmouth, and Richard Hembugg, paid 40s to travel to Dover.

[88] E403/519 m. 19.

[89] *CPR, 1385–1389*, pp. 502–503.

[90] *RP*, vol. iii, p. 182; cited in Tuck, 'The Cambridge Parliament, 1388', p. 241.

[91] Heron (the future Lord Say), E101/41/5 m. 8.

Stephen[92] were brought before parliament to explain the delay. Arundel argued that himself and other senior figures were prevented by parliament itself from departing on 11 May.[93] Arundel was defending a strong position, as his indenture also stated that his force would be paid from 11 May if they were ready to set sail, but were delayed by any failure to take muster on this date.[94] Arundel escaped any further censure over this matter.

These reverses in fortune meant the king was able to resume power as the Appellants had been discredited and peace with France was seen as the only way out of the serious financial crisis that the crown now found itself in. Therefore, although the king had been defeated and his favourites executed, his policy of peace had won the day and he was now free to secure a lasting truce with the traditional enemy. The king allowed the Appellants to begin the diplomatic arrangements towards peace prior to taking government back into his control in May 1389.

Indenture, muster and review

I have discussed how English armies were raised by a system of indentured retinues. It would be sensible at this stage to briefly describe how this system worked in practice. The military contracts were called indentures, as both sides of the bargain between king and retinue captain would be written on one document. Then the two parts of the indenture would be separated by cutting in a form which enabled them to be identified as matching partners by their indented or serrated edges. The two parts of the indenture could be produced when the accounts were settled or in any future dispute. For the mobilisation of expeditions for the prosecution of the king's war in France, a paid contract between crown and subject superseded the earlier reliance on service by obligation. In his indenture, a retinue captain would contract with the king to provide a force of an agreed size at stipulated wages for a specified amount of time. Not only was the size of the force specified in the indenture, but also the number of each rank of soldier to be provided, for example the number of dukes, earls, bannerets, knights, men-at-arms (commonly called esquires in the muster rolls of the late fourteenth and early fifteenth century) and archers. The indenture also specified the wages that would be paid per day for each rank and also the amount of 'regard' that would be paid. 'Regard' was initially established as a 'payment introduced as a contribution towards the expenses of preparing for war' in the

---

92 John Stephen cannot be found in the muster roll for 1388 or 1387 and therefore must have been a non-military servant of Arundel. He is probably the 'John Stephene' who is a tenant of Richard, earl of Arundel, holding 4 acres, for 6d, in Cockyng in Sussex: *Two Estate Surveys*, p. 142.
93 E159/167 m. 51 (Brevia Baronibus, Michaelmas), cited in Tuck, 'The Cambridge Parliament, 1388', pp. 232–233, and also recorded in the enrolled accounts E364/21 m. 6v which state that William Heyron, chevalier, and John Stephene, esquire, explained the delay to parliament.
94 E101/41/4 m. 2 for the indenture.

1340s.[95] However, as the Hundred Years War progressed, the regard developed. Following the end of *restauro equorum* (horse compensation) in the 1370s, 'regard' was offered to those serving as men-at-arms as part of an improved package, and might be used to cover the purchase of a warhorse at the beginning of a campaign.[96] By 1387–1388, 'regard' was well established and *restauro equorum* had completely disappeared. The indenture would also specify the place and length of time that a soldier would be expected to serve as well as containing a formula for the division of spoils of war and any ransom gained from captured prisoners.[97]

The rates of wages to be paid would be specified in the indenture. The customary rates by this period were: 13s 4d a day for a duke, 6s 8d for an earl, 4s for a banneret, 2s for a knight, and 1 shilling for a man-at-arms (although all these ranks essentially served as men-at-arms) with sixpence a day being the daily rate for a mounted archer. In addition, the 'regard' payable would normally be 100 marks for every 30 men-at-arms for three months. The wages would generally be paid every three months in advance, although this might vary according to the length of campaign.[98]

In addition to the surviving indentures, in his study on expeditionary armies Sherborne made use of the warrants for issue (E404) and the issue rolls (E403), which contain information on the payments made by the Exchequer to captains of retinues, the size of the retinue and the expected ranks of the men-at-arms. The indenture and payment records detail how many peers, bannerets, knights and esquires that a captain should bring to muster. These payment materials are particularly valuable where indentures or muster rolls do not survive. Sherborne also used the accounts presented to the Exchequer by the retinue captains at their return as a major source for supporting information. In these accounts the captains, or no doubt their clerks, submitted a 'sanitised' version of service. The accounts would summarise the number of service days for each rank in his retinue drawing on the information annotated on the muster rolls. For instance, if two archers had only served for half a campaign, the captain might simplify his account and claim for just one archer for the whole length of service. These accounts 'give detailed information about the size and duration of service, and reveal how far a captain had been able to meet his undertaking'.[99] Muster and retinue rolls were also submitted to the Exchequer for proof of service and the Exchequer accounts refer to the information contained within them. Sherborne

---

95 Ayton, *Knights and Warhorses*, p. 110. Ayton explains that a form of bonus payment had been offered from the beginning of the Hundred Years War, but that this was standardised as 'regard' in the 1340s.

96 For discussion of the development of *restauro equorum* and regard see Ayton, *Knights and Warhorses*, pp. 84–137.

97 D. Hay, 'The Division of the Spoils of War in Fourteenth-Century England', *Transactions of the Royal Historical Society*, 5th series, iv (1954), pp. 91–109. See also Ayton, *Knights and Warhorses*, pp. 127–137, where he argues that a more favourable system for the soldier was introduced in the 1370s as part of the reviewed package of service.

98 Prince, 'The Indenture System under Edward III', pp. 291–293.

99 Sherborne, 'Indentured Retinues', p. 719.

refers to these rolls but relies on the data contained within the indentures, issue rolls and accounts for his study.

For the campaign of 1387, Arundel indented with the crown to produce a force of 2,500 men for three months of service. By the terms of his indenture, Arundel was required to provide himself, 15 bannerets, 100 knights, 884 esquires and 1,500 archers. Arundel was also allowed 12 servants and each man-at-arms was allowed 1 servant. However, the crown would not pay for these servants separately. As mentioned previously, the king was to take one quarter of any gains of war, whilst the other three quarters would be divided between the earl, men-at-arms, archers and mariners.[100] He was also permitted to recruit an additional 70 men-at-arms instead of 210 archers, if he so wished. No doubt he intended to bring his own company and for the remainder he would have contacted his fellow military captains who would in turn have made indentures with him to provide certain numbers of men-at-arms and archers for the proposed three months. This could have been done via word of mouth with reliance upon the individual prestige of the captain and especially of Arundel himself as overall commander. As mentioned above, the soldiers would be offered pay for their service at the standard rates of 12d per day for men-at-arms and 6d per day for archers. A captain could subcontract at below these standard rates and thus make a tidy personal profit. The wages alone would not make the men prosperous, they would also be hoping for the spoils of war. The captain would be paid quarterly in advance and the balance after presenting his accounts at the treasury after the campaign.[101] For this campaign, with contracted service for just three months, the wages would therefore be paid in advance at the point of muster. The captain's account would be checked with the muster roll to monitor for any indiscretions.

The organisation of a campaign was obviously a well-developed process by the 1380s and thus meant an expedition could be planned, recruited, undertaken and paid without the direct involvement of the king. The process of indenture, muster and review and presentation of account were bureaucratic processes which had become established through the reign of Edward III. And while the recruitment and control of the army was a highly personal process, the actual supporting framework was professional and based around the administrative structures of the Exchequer. Firstly the captain would seal an indenture for service with the crown. For 1387 the terms of the indenture are recorded on the enrolled accounts E364/21 m. 6v and for 1388 the indenture is attached to Arundel's accounts E101/41/4 m. 2. The force would then be subject to a muster prior to embarkation. This muster roll would also record any variations in the number of soldiers during campaign. The muster roll would then be submitted to the Exchequer with the captain's accounts for scrutiny following the campaign. For 1387 the muster roll is catalogued as E101/40/33 and Arundel's accounts as E101/40/35. For 1388 the muster roll is catalogued as E101/41/5

---

[100] E364/21 m. 6v for enrolled accounts which summarise the terms of the indenture.
[101] Prestwich, *Armies and Warfare in the Middle Ages*, p. 93; A.E. Prince, 'The Indenture System under Edward III', pp. 292–293.

and Arundel's accounts, with his copy of the indenture, as E101/41/4. These accounts would then be enrolled in the Exchequer together with a summary of the terms of indenture and any variations. For 1387 the accounts are enrolled on E364/21 m. 6v and for 1388 on E364/24 m. 5. Finally the payments would be issued by the Exchequer and a record of these payments for the army and its shipping can be found for 1387 on the issue roll E403/515 and for 1388 on E403/519 and E403/519. It is by utilising this wealth of source materials for the campaigns of 1387 and 1388 that we have been able to reconstruct the expeditions in such detail.

The muster roll, PRO, E101/40/33

The muster roll E101/40/33 would have been compiled at the beginning of the campaign, when the troops gathered to embark, and would have been checked throughout the expedition. This roll is dated 13 March, which matches the date given for the beginning of service in Arundel's accounts.[102] It is a collection of the names in all the retinues secured together in a roll. The muster rolls are long lists, up to a metre in length and around 15 centimetres in width. This particular roll is made up of 20 membranes, sewn together at the top of each membrane, rather than being sewn into one continuous document. It is written uniformly in the same hand and in the same ink, on both sides of the membranes, and was probably compiled by one of the crown's appointed clerks. Two Exchequer clerks were paid to travel to Sandwich to compile the muster.[103] Each man is 'pointed': in other words, a mark put at the side of his name to indicate his presence. His name is crossed out; a cross is marked at the side of his name and another name generally inserted if he is not present.[104] Such absentees are not pointed. It is also noted if a man has died. All such notes of deaths and replacements are accompanied by the date on which this event had occurred. Each retinue is counted into groups of fifty and totalled by each rank underneath the relevant entry on the roll. The clerk uses roman numerals to compile the totals. For instance the total following the retinue of the earl of Arundel is written, 'earls: 2, bannerets: 4, knights: 32, esquires, 127, archers and gunners 217'.[105] The muster roll thus serves as a permanent and dynamic record of the expedition.

This roll was only used for the first part of the expedition, however, and was not continued for the second part of the campaign. The last comment next to names is dated 29 April. The muster roll records that Sir Edward St John and Sir Reginald de Cobham have left the army on this day.[106] Sir Reginald de Cobham

---

102 E101/40/33 m. 1 for the muster and E101/40/35 for the accounts.
103 E403/515 m. 25.
104 A total number of 94 soldiers are removed from the muster roll by this method and have thus not mustered with the force. This includes 5 knights, 10 esquires and 79 archers.
105 Simplified from the roll E101/40/33 m. 2d, which reads: 'Countes ii, Baneretts iiii, Chivalers xxxii, Esquiers cxxvii, Alblasters et Gunners xvii [all crossed out], Archers ccx [number crossed out], et alblasters ccxvii'.

is a retinue captain, it is however clear that his retinue continued its service even if its captain did not as no comments are placed against their names on this day. These are the last such dated entries on this muster roll. This suggests that this muster roll lasts until the end of the period of rest and refitting at Orwell. The fleet sailed for France again on 1 May; there are no entries on the muster roll which cover any dates for this second period.[107] Possibly the second stage of the expedition had its own muster roll which no longer exists.

Another muster roll exists for this expedition, E101/40/34. This is described as a muster of the forces under the said earl, namely the earl of Arundel. This appears to be a collection of retinue lists in different hands and on different materials. The names are mostly written on one side of membrane suggesting that they were not compiled in one go but have been prepared separately, perhaps in advance, being submitted by captains as lists of their men. The details have not been altered except some names have been crossed out and some added in. There is also some counting but this is not uniform throughout the roll. There are also no dated comments next to the names of soldiers. The same names of soldiers appear as in the muster roll E101/40/33 although the names crossed out in E101/40/34 are not included, therefore suggesting that E101/40/33 may be a document compiled from E101/40/34 as it has taken account of these omissions. The numbers in these retinues are smaller than in the muster roll E101/40/33 and this suggests that E101/40/33 is the muster roll for the campaign, whilst E101/40/34 is probably a collection of the lists of their retinues which has been brought to the port of embarkation by the retinue captains. This additional muster roll therefore provides an important insight into the process of muster and review.

It can be seen that events noted on the muster roll E101/40/33 match events on the campaign. Just after the troops have gathered at the point of embarkation on 14 March one archer, Henry Person, in the retinue of Sir Thomas Mortimer, is noted as dead and has been replaced by John Deyer.[108] Then in prelude to the campaign on 19 March, Andrew Hake, an esquire in the retinue of the earl of Arundel is knighted whilst still at Sandwich, the point of muster, and his place amongst the esquires is taken by John Davy. Sir Andrew Hake showed his appreciation to the earl and commitment to military service, by continuing his service and captaining a retinue in the expedition of 1388.[109] On the actual day of the sea battle, 24 March, four men are knighted, namely John Harlyng, Thomas Roberyng, Piers de la Mare and Thomas Fleming. Replacements are made in the ranks of esquire to account for their promotions. Of these so honoured, Piers de

---

[106] St John, E101/40/33 m. 1. Cobham, 1387: E101/40/33 m. 6, listed as Mons' Reynold de Cobham. Cobham also served with Arundel in 1378: E101/36/32 m. 3.

[107] The period of rest at Orwell would appear to begin on 15 April according to the muster roll, as it is on this day that the Earl Marshal is noted as being absent from the force. E101/40/33 m. 1, 'vacat le xv d'april'. Knighton comments that the Earl Marshal was not present in the second part of the campaign: *Knighton's Chronicle*, p. 391.

[108] E101/40/33 m. 10, described as 'mort le xiii iour de marz'.

[109] 1387: E101/40/33 m. 1, described as 'factus chevalier le xviiii iour de marz'; enrolled protection, C76/71 m. 14; enrolled attorney, C76/71 m. 14. 1388: E101/41/5 m. 12d; enrolled protection, C76/72 m. 7.

la Mare can also be found in a senior position in the retinue of the earl of Arundel the following year. It is interesting to note that Arundel is rewarding his own supporters by these actions: three of the five knighted are present in his own retinue, and two of these men serve again in 1388.[110]

On the day of the sea battle, 24 March, nine men died and were replaced. This number of mortalities is made up of five esquires and four archers. Lord Beaumont's retinue has suffered the bulk of the losses following battle with Thomas Heham, esquire, and John Ferrour, esquire, Rys ap Jon, archer, and John Syner, archer, being recorded on the muster roll as dying on this day.[111] The other losses appear to be spread throughout the other retinues.

Do more men die or leave certain retinues more than others? If so what might this indicate? To investigate this, I have compiled Table 2 to summarise the information gathered from the muster roll.

It can be seen from the Table 2 that the retinue of Lord Beaumont suffers the most deaths, whilst the earl of Arundel has the most casualties and departures overall. This is perhaps unsurprising as the earl has the largest retinue and Lord Beaumont has the third largest retinue in the army. However, the losses suffered by Lord Beaumont directly following the sea battle do suggest that his retinue had been involved in the thick of the engagement. It is interesting to note that Lord Beaumont replaced Arundel as Admiral of the North on 20 May 1389.[112] Beaumont obviously took an active role in naval campaigns as can be seen by his losses in this battle and his later appointment as Admiral. Overall there does not appear to be a pattern as more than half of the retinues suffer a loss of some nature. In addition, the overall casualty rate is not particular high with 18 men meeting their deaths, which is a death rate of less than 1%. When other possible casualties are included by also looking at those who have left the retinues, this increases to 35 men, which is still just over 1% of the total fighting force. The deaths and other casualties are evenly spread between men-at-arms and archers, which one would expect as there are almost equal numbers of both in the expeditionary force. There are however, only a very small number of deaths at the rank of knight or above with Sir Edward Fitz Herbert being the only one recorded as meeting his end on this part of the campaign.[113] However, this small number of mortalities is proportionate with the losses suffered in the ranks of esquires and archers. From this information, it seems that all retinues and ranks were equally involved in the fighting.

It is interesting to compare the evidence noted above with the chronicle sources. Henry Knighton claimed that there had been heavy casualties in the initial battle:

---

110 Harlyng, E101/40/33 m. 11. Roberyng, E101/40/33 m. 1d. de la Mare, 1387: E101/40/33 m. 1. 1388: E101/41/5 m. 1. Fleming, E101/40/33 m. 3. All described as 'factus chevalier le xxiiii iour de marz'.
111 Heham, E101/40/33 m. 4. Ferrour, E101/40/33 m. 4. ap Jon, E101/40/33 m. 4d. Syner, E101/40/33 m. 4d. All described as 'mort le xxiiii iour de marz'.
112 *Handbook of English Chronology*, p. 139 and *Complete Peerage*, vol. ii, p. 61.
113 E101/40/33 m. 1, described as 'mort le xxviii iour d'aprill'; enrolled protection, C76/71 m. 14; enrolled attorney, C76/71 m. 10.

Table 2. Mortalities and casualties recorded on the muster roll for 1387

| | Deaths | | 'Vacat' | | |
Retinue Captain	Men-at-arms	Archers	Men-at-arms	Archers	Total
Richard, earl of Arundel	3	1	4		8
Lord Beaumont	4	2	1		7
Sir Reginald de Cobham	1		1	1	3
Sir Arnold Savage		1			1
Sir Thomas Trivet	1				1
Sir Hugh le Despencer	1				1
Sir Thomas Mortimer		1			1
Sir Nicholas Clifton		1		2	3
Sir Hugh Luterell		1	1	1	3
Sir Robert Hemenale					
John Wormyngton					
Sir John de Calverley		1			1
Sir John Haukeston				2	2
John Staple				1	1
John Slegh			1	1	2
John Trenbyn				1	1
Total	10	8	8	9	35

the admiral returned to England with his companions to refresh themselves and their crews, many of whom were seriously wounded.

As can be seen from Table 2, deaths and casualties only amounted to just over 1% of the total force. Why would Knighton describe many as being seriously wounded? As only a proportionally small number of men are noted as being dead on the muster roll, it is possible that the crews of the ships, not the army itself, were the casualties, or else Knighton's description was an early example of tabloid sensationalism. It may be that this small number of deaths was in fact seen at the time as being a high proportion for this type of campaign. Unfortunately, no evidence survives regarding the crews of the fleet and therefore further analysis cannot be undertaken.

The muster roll was an important document compiled and monitored by an officer of the crown. The order for the muster to be taken was made on 8 March. The muster in this instance was taken by the duke of York, the earl of Kent, Sir John Cobham and John Lincoln.[114] The presence of senior figures in this list of officers demonstrates the importance that was placed upon the system of muster and review. Arundel himself brought the biggest retinue and in total there were

[114] C76/71 m. 6, also printed in Carte, *Catologue des Rolles Francois*, p. 155, 'De assignando Edmundum Ducem Eborum, Thomam Holand Comitem Kantiae, Johannem Cobham, Chivaler, and Johannem Lincoln, ad monstrum hominum ad arma and sagittariorum in comitiva Ricardi Comitis de Arundel, Admiralli'. Lincoln may have been involved in the campaign, E101/40/33 m. 20.

Table 3. Expedition of 1387

Name	Retinue size	Peers	Bannerets	Knights	Esquires	Total men-at-arms	Archers	Ratio men-at-arms to archers
Arundel	382	2	4	32	127	165	217	1 to 1.3
Le Comte de Devens'	231	1		7	107	115	116	1 to 1
Le Sire de Beamount	196		1	6	77	84	112	1 to 1.3
Mons John Darundel	70		1		29	30	40	1 to 1.3
Mons Reynald de Cobham	99		1	4	40	45	54	1 to 1.2
Mons Arnald Savage	66			2	28	30	36	1 to 1.2
Mons Thomas Trevet	155		1	4	64	69	86	1 to 1.2
Mons Thomas de Ponynges	76		1	1	30	32	44	1 to 1.4
Mons Hugh le Despenser	94		1	2	39	42	52	1 to 1.2
Mons Thomas Mortemer	84			3	32	35	49	1 to 1.4
Mons William Elmham	114			6	44	50	64	1 to 1.3
Mons Gilbert Talbot	73			1	30	31	42	1 to 1.4
Mons Nich Clifton	86			3	39	42	44	1 to 1
Mons John de Wyngefeld	71			4	26	30	41	1 to 1.4
Mons Richard Craddok	70			1	28	29	41	1 to 1.4
Mons Hugh Loterell, Mons Robert Hemenale, John Haukeston	91			2	38	40	51	1 to 1.3
Mons Robert Mounteney	67			2	28	30	37	1 to 1.2
Mons John de Calverlee	50			1	19	20	30	1 to 1.5
Mons John Haukeston	62			2	28	30	32	1 to 1
John Staple	48				20	20	28	1 to 1.4
John Sly	71			1	32	33	38	1 to 1.2
John Treubyn	50				20	20	30	1 to 1.5
Richard Cryse	50				20	20	30	1 to 1.5
Richard Shynkylton	40				20	20	20	1 to 1
Pyers Vanbusth	30				15	15	15	1 to 1
Robert Gyffard	40				20	20	20	1 to 1
John Hayward	31				10	10	21	1 to 2
Total mustered	2497	3	10	86	1010	1107	1390	1 to 1.3
Total indented	2500	1	15	100	884	1000	1500	1 to 1.5

27 retinues of varying sizes. Table 3, constructed from the muster roll E101/40/33, demonstrates the constitution of each retinue as mustered at Sandwich on 13 March 1387.

Table 3 is a snapshot of the force as it put to sea on the first day of the campaign. The composition of the army would vary day-to-day throughout the campaign, as explained above, and noted on the muster roll. However, these figures show how well Arundel was able to meet the requirements of his indenture, sealed in December 1386. The intended number of soldiers, as indented, is also indicated on the table. Table 3 also shows the ratio of men-at-arms to archers throughout the retinues of the expedition.

It can be seen that Arundel almost met the required total number of soldiers as agreed in his indenture. He mustered 2,497 soldiers, which is only three short of the required number of 2,500. He would therefore seem to have used a successful recruitment strategy. However, when the actual numbers of each rank are considered, it can be shown that he has not been so successful in meeting his targets exactly. He has been able to bring three peers to the muster, himself, the Earl Marshal and the earl of Devon, which is two more than required. He has however fallen short of the number of bannerets and knights, by five and fourteen respectively. He has more than made up for this shortfall by bringing 1,010 esquires rather than the required 884, an over recruitment of 126 esquires. He has therefore recruited 107 more men-at-arms than was specified in his indenture. The number of archers he has been able to recruit was just 1,390, 110 short of the 1,500 required. The enrolled account in the Exchequer comments on the variations from the indented terms. It notes that Arundel has over-recruited peers and has been unable to recruit the required number of bannerets or knights. The account records that Arundel was therefore allowed to over-recruit esquires to make up for this shortfall, due to his good service, paying for the additional troops from the wages that would have been paid to the bannerets and knights. It also notes that the terms of his indenture allowed him to recruit 70 men-at-arms instead of 210 archers. The enrolled account confirmed that Arundel had been permitted to pay the daily wage rate for knights to the esquires who had taken the order of knighthood whilst on campaign.[115]

Arundel's accounts demonstrate that this muster roll has been checked against the payments that have been made to the army prior to their departure at the muster.[116] The enrolled account additionally comments that the account has been checked against a roll listing the names of all the soldiers.[117] This payment, of £10,743 14s 2d, was made from the Exchequer to Richard Coplestone, esquire, for the wages of the indented force, for the promised three months (ninety-one days) of service.[118] It is interesting to note that Richard Coplestone

---

[115] E364/21 m. 6v for enrolled account and terms of indenture.

[116] Muster roll E101/40/33 and particulars of account E101/40/35. The catalogue numbers demonstrate that these documents have been held together since presentation at the Exchequer following the end of the campaign in 1387.

[117] E364/21 m. 6v.

[118] Also described as Richard Sepleston, attorney, in the accounts.

is also listed in the retinues of the earl of Arundel in 1387 and 1388, listed sixty-fourth and thirty-eighth, respectively, on the muster roll.[119] This demonstrates that Coplestone served Arundel as an attorney as well as in a military capacity. The accounts list each rank of soldier and summarise the wages due in terms of 'service days'. For instance, they begin by stating the service of the peers, namely, the earl of Arundel, the earl of Devon and the Earl Marshal. The accounts confirm the details on the muster roll which show that the Earl Marshal left the army after the first stage of the campaign, as he is paid for only thirty-three days, from 13 March to 15 April. It is therefore clear that the accounts have been checked against the muster roll whilst being compiled. It does appear that the accounts are 'tidy', as they do not account for every individuals length of service. Rather, the accounts summarise the number of 'service days' for each rank.[120] Arundel's overall account was for £10,890 3s 7d and he was thus owed £146 9s 6d for the service of his army. These accounts are further summarised and repeated in the enrolled accounts in the Exchequer. It comments that Arundel's account was finally settled on 12 February 1388.[121]

The muster roll, PRO, E101/41/5

The army for 1388 was ordered to muster at Southampton on 11 May[122] and a subsidy was voted by Parliament to support the expedition financially.[123] The order for the muster to be made was dated 14 May 1388 and the commission to muster the forces was lead by Arundel's son-in-law, the Earl Marshal (who was also a retine captain),[124] Sir Bernard Brocas, Sir Nicholas Sharnesfield, Hugo Cheyne and John de Hermesthorp.[125] It is not clear when the muster of the forces actually occurred. It would appear that the date for the muster would have followed 14 May but been before the first dated entries of review, on 1 June. The muster could not have occurred as required on 11 May, as the commission for the muster had not yet been ordered.

A possible scenario for the compilation of the muster roll would be as follows. The army arrive at Southampton on 11 May as ordered in the indenture. The muster occurs soon after 14 May, when the commission for the muster is

---

[119] 1387: E101/40/33 m. 1. 1388: E101/41/5 m. 1. He did not fulfil his intention to serve this year as he is recorded as being 'vacat' on 1 June. This could be Richard Copeden, holding 1 virgate from the earl of Arundel, for 10s, in Sullyngton, Sussex: *Two Estate Surveys*, p. 135.

[120] The neatness of such accounts is discussed and explained in Ayton, *Knights and Warhorses*, pp. 138–155, especially pp. 152–155. He demonstrates that the royal clerks would use a system of simplification, where departures and arrivals would cancel out.

[121] E364/21 m. 6v.

[122] From indenture E101/41/4 m. 2.

[123] *Westminster Chronicle*, p. 319n.

[124] E101/41/5 m. 3.

[125] For commission to muster see C76/72 m. 2, also printed in Carte, *Catalogue des Rolles Francois*, p. 158, 'De assignando Thomam Marescallum, Bernardum Brocas, Nicolaum Carnesfeld, Hugonem Cheyne, and Johannem de Hermesthorp, ad monstrum hominum ad arma et sagittariorum in comitiva Ricardi Comitis de Arundel, Admiralli'.

ordered. The retinues are totalled on this date. A further review is carried out on 1 June, when it is clear that the earl of Arundel will be able to travel to the coast to join his forces. The force embarks when Arundel joins them on 10 June. The whole process has been complicated by Arundel's delay at Parliament, which meant he could not join the force on 11 May. For the previous campaign, this had not been a problem, and the force had embarked following the muster and had been paid from that day. For the expedition of 1388, the army was forced to wait at Southampton for a month for Arundel to join them. Arundel's accounts show that he insisted that they were paid from the day they had contracted to begin service, namely 11 May.

On this occasion, only one muster roll survives, covering the whole expedition from embarkation on 10 June to the return on 3 September. It has dated entries for troop movements prior to embarkation, on 1 June and also before the return of the army, on 29 August and 1 September. It also contains dated entries for knightings on 28 June, 16 July and 27 July. This roll is made up of long lists written on parchment, up to a metre in length and around 15 centimetres in width. E101/41/5 is a collection of twenty-one separate membranes, sewn together at the top at the time and rolled up together, being secured nowadays with a length of modern binding tape. The first retinue listed is that of Arundel himself and his name is written in bold at the top of the first membrane. His retinue is then listed, ranked in order of seniority – the 'man himself', baron, knight banneret, knight bachelor, esquire and archers. This rank is written above each section and is sometimes bracketed to the names. Each subsequent membrane containing Arundel's retinue has his name in bold at the top. All 41 retinues contained within the rolls follow this same format and all appear to have been compiled by the same hand.

From studying this roll, it is evident that it was again used as a working document and that it was carried on the campaign, as dated entries survive for the beginning and end of the expedition, unlike the roll for the previous campaign. The numbers of men of each rank are stated after the list of men in the retinue. As an aid to counting, each name in the list is pointed at least once (occasionally twice) and every forty men are indicated by 'xl' in the left margin. This is different from the roll for the campaign for 1387, where they are marked with an 'l' for every fifty men. The system of counting must have been peculiar to the clerk taking the muster. If a man has left prior to the muster his name is crossed out and the date that he left is indicated in the right margin. If he is replaced, the name of the replacement is written alongside. The number of men at embarkation has thus been recorded. Movement in soldiers can be seen to take place at the beginning and at the end of the expedition. If a man has left the expedition and has not been replaced, a cross is placed at the side of his name and his name is crossed out. No date is given, but generally the numbers given at the end of each retinue take account of these omissions; therefore they must have left the army prior to the first count at the muster, or they have never turned up to deliver their promised service. It is clear that the totals are drawn before the expedition embarked and not on its return. A number of men are not present on 29 August and 1 September, but they have been included in the tally, indicating that they were present at muster. Newhall, in his book, *Muster and Review*,

Table 4. Crossed-through names not included in the 1388 muster

Captain	Numbers crossed in each retinue				
	Knight	Esquire	Archer	Minstrel	Total
Earl of Arundel	1	13	28		42
Earl Marshall		1	4	7	12
Lord Welles		1	2		3
Earl of Devon		2	5		7
Sir John D'Arundell			2		2
Sir William Baron de Hylton			7		7
Sir Thomas West		1	1		2
Sir Hugh Browe			1		1
Sir William Brienne			4		4
Sir Hugh le Despenser	1	1	6		8
Sir Nicholas Clifton		1			1
Sir John Clanyng			1		1
Sir John Coupeland			1		1
Sir Andrew Hake and Sir John de Brewe			1		1
Sir Piers de Bokton			1		1
Sir John Sandes			1		1
John Staple			4		4
Robert Geffard and William Cavven			1		1
Thomas atte Lee and Richard Breton		1	3		4
Richard Waynill			1		1
Aleyn Seintjust, John Hulat and Thomas Legat			3		3
Robert Bland			3		3
Giles Weston and Davy Russel			3		3
Total	2	21	83	7	113

suggests that a cross next to a name on a muster roll indicates that a man has failed to pass muster because he has not turned up with suitable equipment.[126]

This might therefore explain why these crossed names are not included in the tally and might suggest that a thorough check of equipment was made at this preliminary stage of the expedition. One hundred and thirteen individuals are not included in the muster counts in this way, which is an increase on the ninety four crossed names, recorded for the previous campaign. These soldiers are spread throughout the retinues and are summarised in Table 4.

Not all of these men are missing from or are excluded from the muster. On a couple of occasions, the crossing out indicates an error by the official compiling the roll. If a name has been entered twice by error, this is discovered during the

---

[126] R.A. Newhall, *Muster and Review: A Problem of English Military Administration, 1420–1440* (Cambridge, Mass., 1940), p. 15.

muster and the second entry is crossed out. This is the case for Sir Michael de la Pole, who is listed twice in the retinue of the earl of Arundel.[127]

It is interesting to note that Sir Michael de la Pole serves on this expedition, as he was the eldest son of Michael de la Pole, earl of Suffolk. Suffolk had only just been prosecuted and sentenced to death for treason at the Merciless Parliament, and had previously been removed from his position of Chancellor in the Wonderful Parliament in 1386. As such, his father was a major enemy of the Appellants, and the leader of this campaign, the earl of Arundel. Suffolk had escaped to the continent, in order to escape the sentence of execution that had been passed upon him. Why was his son serving in this campaign and listed prominently in fifth position in the retinue of Arundel himself? Perhaps he was showing his allegiance to the Appellant regime by this service and to protect himself from any prosecution by association with his father. However, it is probably more likely that he was more interested in serving patriotically in a royal campaign. Sir Michael de la Pole did not suffer politically from his service in this campaign, and was restored to the earldom of Suffolk and Baron de la Pole by Richard II in 1397. This was temporarily removed by Henry IV, but restored without the Barony, shortly after the succession. He went on to serve in a military capacity under the new regime, and died of dysentery at the siege of Harfleur in 1415.[128]

Sir Baldwin Pygot is crossed out from the retinue of Sir Hugh le Despencer, as he is already serving and has been counted in the retinue of the Earl Marshal. Interestingly, Sir Baldwin had also intended to serve with Sir Hugh le Despenser in the previous campaign of 1387; however his name had again been crossed out at the time of the muster. On this previous occasion he did not serve in the retinue of any other captain and has therefore not fulfilled his intention to serve.[129] Therefore, both of the knights whose names are crossed in the muster roll for 1388 are indeed present in the army.

All other crossed names representing esquires and archers are not present in any other retinue. The vast majority of those names crossed, nearly three-quarters, represent the rank of archer. As Newhall suggests, it is therefore possible that they have turned up, but have been poorly equipped and therefore excluded from the muster, especially as the indenture obliged Arundel to provide men who were adequately equipped. As these soldiers have not been replaced, it is possible that fewer reinforcements of the rank of archer were available at the point of muster. It is also possible to identify serial exclusion or non-attendance. The esquire, John atte Welle, is crossed out prior to the muster for both 1387 and 1388.[130] He has therefore had reason not to fulfil his intention to serve for two

---

[127] E101/41/5 m. 1, listed fifth and thirty-first in the retinue of the earl of Arundel. This second listing is crossed out at the time of muster.

[128] For details of Sir Michael de la Pole, see *Complete Peerage*, vol. x, pp. 566–567, and *DNB*, vol. xlvi, pp. 33–34.

[129] 1388: E101/41/5 m. 3 and m. 18. This second listing is crossed out at the time of muster. 1387: E101/40/33 m. 9, his name is crossed and crossed out and not included in the muster count.

[130] 1388: E101/41/5 m. 18; 1387: E101/40/33 m. 9. On both occasions his name is crossed and crossed out and not included in the muster count.

years running, or perhaps he turned up twice poorly equipped. The crossed entries also provide important information upon individuals who have intended to join the campaign but who have then decided not to attend. Probably the most recognisable figure who can be identified in this way in 1388 is the future Welsh rebel leader, Owain Glyn Dwr, who fails to attend and is listed as the first esquire in the retinue of the earl of Arundel.[131] Finally it is also of interest to note that it was intended for a troop of minstrels to accompany the expedition, but that they have all been crossed out from the muster prior to embarkation on 10 June. They were all in the retinue of the Earl Marshal and were the seven listed at the very bottom of the archers in his retinue. The band would seem to have consisted of one 'claryoner', two trumpets and four pipers.[132] It is not clear whether they would have had ceremonial usage or entertainment value. However, they either did not turn up or else became surplus to requirements.

As well as containing relatively few dated entries relating to troop movements, the muster roll does not refer to any deaths on campaign. The chroniclers do not refer to any casualties for this expedition, unlike the previous campaign of 1387. It is therefore possible that this expedition was casualty free. This would be unlikely as there were a number of large scale skirmishes which were reported in the chronicles.[133] It is possible that there were deaths but that these have not been recorded on this roll.

The only other dated entries on the roll refer to knightings. There are ten of these entries, referring to seven dubbings on 28 June, one on 16 July and two further such entries on 27 July. William Barry, esquire,[134] in the retinue of the earl of Arundel is knighted on 28 June. A cluster of esquires are knighted in the retinue of the Earl Marshal on 28 June, namely Robert Morley, William Roos, Thomas Hanley and Banlyn Newmarche. They are listed first, second, fourth and fifth with the esquires of the Earl Marshal.[135] This is another indicator that the position in the retinue roll reflected the structure of the retinue itself. William Latymer, esquire,[136] in the retinue of the earl of Devon and Piers Besiles, esquire,[137] in the retinue of Sir Gilbert Talbot are also knighted on 28 June. On 16 July, John Souteren, esquire in the retinue of Sir Robert Massey is recorded as being knighted.[138] The retinue captain Benedict Cely[139] and William Wyshiam, esquire,[140] are both recorded as being knighted on 27 July. Of these

---

[131] 1388: E101/41/5 m. 1, this entry is crossed at the side and crossed out and not included in the muster tally. 1387: E101/40/33 m. 1.

[132] E101/41/5 m. 3d, described as 'Claryoner, Minstrel', 'Trumper, Minstrel' and 'Minstrel – Pyper'.

[133] Froissart, *Chronicles*, vol. ii, pp. 348–350; *Westminster Chronicle*, pp. 352–353.

[134] E101/40/33 m. 1d, described as 'factus miles xxviii die Junii'.

[135] E101/40/33 m. 3, all described as 'factus miles xxviii die Junii'.

[136] E101/40/33 m. 4, described as 'factus miles xxviii die Junii'.

[137] E101/40/33 m. 11d, described as 'factus miles xxviii die Junii'. Also served 1387: E101/40/33 m. 12.

[138] E101/41/5 m. 14, described as 'factus miles xvi dei julii'.

[139] E101/40/33 m. 15, described as 'factus miles xxvii die Julii'. Enrolled protection, C76/72 m. 7. Also served in 1387: E101/40/33 m. 1; enrolled protection, C76/71 m. 14.

[140] E101/40/33 m. 10, described as 'factus miles xxvii die Julii'.

men, only Benedict Cely and Piers Besiles served in the campaign of 1387, Cely in the retinue of the earl of Arundel, whilst Besiles served in the retinue of Sir Gilbert Talbot in both expeditions. These men may have been knighted as a reward for continued loyal service, however it is not possible to know the reason for the other knightings as further information is not provided by the muster rolls or other sources. As a number of the knightings are on the same day, it is possible they were being rewarded for military prowess. It was important that knightings were recorded on the muster roll as the rate of pay would be affected. Knights Bachelor were entitled to 2s per day, which was twice the rate of esquires. It is interesting to note that these knightings have indeed been recorded in Arundel's accounts for this campaign. The accounts also refer to seven knightings on 28 June, one on 15 July and two on 27 July. Their wages are calculated at a higher rate for their remaining days service. However, they were in for a sore disappointment, as the entry calculating their revised wages has been crossed out by the clerk checking the accounts, who explains that Arundel did not have a warrant to make such promotions: 'quia sine waranto et computantur pro armigeris per totum viagium'.[141]

So what else does this particular muster roll add to our knowledge of an expedition? Table 5 shows the numbers of peers, bannerets, esquires (non-knightly men-at-arms) and archers who actually mustered at Southampton and shows the figures after deletions were made on the muster roll whilst the count was being made. These figures show how well Arundel was able to meet the requirements of his indenture, sealed in March 1388. The intended number of soldiers, as indented, is also indicated on the table. The table also shows the ratio of men-at-arms to archer throughout the retinues of the expedition.

The surfeit of cheap wine in the country in 1387 had perhaps impressed would-be retinue leaders. One knight bachelor, Sir Hugh le Despencer has even provided two retinues. According to the muster roll, the total number of combatants was 3,592 soldiers: 3 nobles, 15 bannerets, 120 bachelors, 1,440 esquires and 2,014 archers. This demonstrates that Arundel has actually exceeded the requirements of his indenture by 92 soldiers. As can be seen in the table he has overcompensated for an under-recruitment of knight bannerets and knight bachelors by recruiting more esquires and archers. He has had problems persuading knights to join his campaign for 1388. This may be of significance when considered against the political background of this expedition. The Appellants had recently defeated the king's forces at the battle of Radcot Bridge in December 1387 and had just finished prosecuting the king's favourites in the Merciless Parliament.[142] As bannerets and bachelors were paid a higher daily rate (4s and 2s respectively, rather than 1s), he was able to pay more esquires and archers for the same amount of money and thus bring a larger force than indented for. In his original indenture, Arundel was allowed to substitute the wages of fifty archers for the wages and regard of men-at-arms, if he was able to recruit them.

---

[141] E101/41/4.
[142] The background of participants in the expeditions is discussed in detail in Part 2.

Table 5. Expedition of 1388

Captains	Retinue size	Peers	Bannerets	Knights	Esquires	Men-at-arms	Archers	Ratio men-at-arms to archers
l'Admirall, Mons le Count Arundell	363	1	4	27	138	170	193	1 to 1.1
Le Counte Mareshall	232	1	2	18	79	100	132	1 to 1.3
Le Monsers W Sire de Welles	73		1	2	28	31	42	1 to 1.4
Le Counte de Devons	279	1		9	110	120	160	1 to 1.3
Mons Johan Darundell	90		1	2	37	40	50	1 to 1.3
Mons William Baron de Hylton	112		1	3	48	52	60	1 to 1.2
Mons Thomas Camoys	135		3	8	49	60	75	1 to 1.3
Mons Thomas Ponyngs	97		1	2	38	41	56	1 to 1.4
Mons Johan Bohun	71		1	1	28	30	41	1 to 1.4
Mons Thomas West	89		1	3	35	39	50	1 to 1.3
Mons William Heron	94			4	37	41	53	1 to 1.3
Mons Hugh Browe	71			3	27	30	41	1 to 1.4
Mons William Briene	102			5	38	43	59	1 to 1.4
Mons Rauf Vernon	85			3	33	36	49	1 to 1.4
Mons Johan Wynkefeld	75			4	27	31	44	1 to 1.4
Mons Hugh le Despencer	76			4	30	34	42	1 to 1.2
Mons Johan Grymesby	71			2	28	30	41	1 to 1.4
Mons Johan Wogan	73			1	30	31	42	1 to 1.4
Mons Nicol Clyfton	70			2	28	30	40	1 to 1.3
Mons Johan Clanyng	65			1	30	31	34	1 to 1.1
Mons Gilbe Talbot	80			2	33	35	45	1 to 1.3
Mons Johan Coupeland	55			1	23	24	31	1 to 1.3

Mons Andrewe Hake	68			2	27	29	39	1 to 1.3
Mons Johan de Brewe								
Mons Piers de Bokton	70			2	28	30	40	1 to 1.3
Mons Johan Sandes	78			2	31	33	45	1 to 1.4
Mons Olyver Mauleverer	68			2	28	30	38	1 to 1.3
Mons Arnald Savage	70			2	28	30	40	1 to 1.3
Mons Robert Massey	70			1	28	29	41	1 to 1.4
Johan Staple	50				27	27	23	1 to 0.8
Wauter Merston	44				20	20	24	1 to 1.2
Benet Cely	63				28	28	35	1 to 1.3
Johan Trenbyn								
Robert Geffard	57				24	24	33	1 to 1.4
William Cavven								
Thomas atte Lee	68				32	32	36	1 to 1.3
Richard Breton								
Richard Shinkylton	50				20	20	30	1 to 1.5
Richard Waynill	53				21	21	32	1 to 1.5
Johan Hayward								
Aleyn Seintjust	43				20	20	23	1 to 1.2
Johan Hulat								
Thomas Legat								
Robert Bland	60				30	30	30	1 to 1
Johan Creghton								
Giles Weston	48				20	20	28	1 to 1.4
Davy Russell								
Esmon Randulph	38				17	17	21	1 to 1.2
Richard Cryse	42				18	18	24	1 to 1.3
Mons Hugh le Despencer	93			2	39	41	52	1 to 1.3
Total mustered	3592	3	15	120	1440	1578	2014	1 to 1.3
Total indented	3500	1	20	150	1329	1500	2000	1 to 1.3

However, as he has also over-recruited archers, it would seem that he has paid the esquires from the wages of the bannerets and knights which he has been unable to recruit.[143]

In the original indenture drawn up in March, Arundel contracted to take 3,500 men, consisting of 1,500 men-at-arms and 2,000 archers.[144] The actual number of soldiers contained in the muster roll matches this contracted number with just a few extra (3%), indicating that Arundel met his requirement in full. This suggests that plenty of men were willing to join this expedition against France, during a period when the king and his court were beginning to think seriously about peace with the French. The Monk of Westminster provides the most accurately dated account of the expedition and it is possible to compare the account to the dates provided by the muster. He has the expedition leaving Southampton on 10 June.[145]

The muster roll was checked on a number of occasions, indicating that the process of muster and review was ongoing. Firstly, the numbers are checked on 1st June when replacements are made to make up for those that are missing. Large numbers of men are noted as being not present on both 29 August and 1 September, probably indicating an advanced party leaving for England. It is also clear that Arundel's accounts have also been prepared in conjunction with the muster roll, as it is stated that they have been paid wages for service 'as in roll of names' and also the description of knightings correlates exactly with the annotations on the muster roll of the campaign.[146] As mentioned, the muster roll has few dated entries, when compared to the muster roll for the previous year. In addition, Arundel's accounts are very tidy when compared to the accounts for the previous year. However, it is not easy to compare the numbers of troops claimed for to the numbers recorded in the muster. For instance, it correctly identifies the payments for the earls; however, the accounts only claim for 12 bannerets whilst 15 appear on the muster roll, and also claim for 117 knights whilst 120 appear on the muster roll. It is not clear why these figures do not match, although the discrepancies are very small and are not so different to consider a fraudulent presentation of account.

The accounts first discuss the method of payment and it would seem that the funding of this campaign was much more involved and complex than the previous campaign, where only one payment, covering the whole amount of the wages for the campaign, was made in advance. It was agreed in the indenture for 1388 that Arundel would be paid in three instalments and in advance; one sixth of the payment before the feast of Easter; two sixths of the payment on the 'quinzaine' of the feast of Easter; and the remaining three sixths of the payment when he made the muster of his men.[147] However, it is clear that this schedule of

---

143 E101/41/4 m. 2.
144 A copy of the indenture is attached to Arundel's accounts, E101/41/4 m. 2.
145 *Westminster Chronicle*, p. 351.
146 Arundel's accounts, E101/41/4, are filed in the Exchequer with the muster roll for the campaign, E101/41/5, following the campaign. The two documents have been kept together since this time. The following section on payments is drawn from this document.
147 E101/41/4 m. 2.

payments was not met, which indicates that the funding was becoming a problem for the Appellants. The payment was made in five instalments, with the final instalment not being made until 14 September, which follows the return of the force on 3 September. The first instalment was for £6,706 13s 4d, which was further split into three payments: the first payment of cash of £6,466 13s 4d, was delivered to the earl by Robert Pobelowe, his clerk, from the Exchequer; a further payment of 'ten panni of gold forfeited by Nicolas Brembre', valued at £40,[148] also delivered by Pobelowe; the final payment of £200 cash, was made directly to Thomas Kardyngton, clerk of the earl of Devon, another retinue captain on the campaign.

These first instalments added up to £6,706 13s 4d, which is about one third of the total final payment. The second instalment, of £466 13s 4d, was again made by the hand of Robert Pobelowe on 13 April. This instalment was made up of money received from John Chirchman and John Organ.[149] The third instalment was made on 11 May of £1,133 6s 8d and was delivered by Hugh Overiche and Richard Depedale. Hugh Overiche can also be identified on the muster roll for 1388, serving as a man-at-arms in the retinue of the earl of Arundel.[150] It was on 11 May, according to the accounts, and required in the indenture, that the force gathered at Southampton, and thus this payment was probably distributed to the soldiers gathered at the port. The fourth instalment paid on 2 June, totalling £7,306 15s 2d was further split into three sections: the first was £40 delivered by Sir Edward Dallingridge and Thomas Wysbech. Dallingridge was a known associate of Arundel and had served in his retinue in 1387. He is not on the muster roll for this campaign;[151] another amount of £2,470 delivered to Southampton by John Hermesthorpe, Thomas Durant and William Huglot; the third sum of £4,796 15s 2½d was delivered by Hugh Overiche. These amounts were delivered directly to Southampton, where the force was awaiting the arrival of Arundel, prior to embarkation on 10 June. Therefore the wages had been paid in advance, and probably distributed, save around one sixth of the amount which was still outstanding. This final payment of £3,426 12s 4d was made on 14 September by John Hermesthorpe, one of the chamberlains of the receipt of the Exchequer, and Thomas Durant, one of the 'numinators' of the receipt of the Exchequer, at Southampton. This final payment is recorded as also being made

---

[148] This refers to the forfeited goods (probably gold cloths) of Sir Nicolas Brembre, Mayor of London, who was one of the five advisors of Richard II appealed in the Merciless Parliament. He was found guilty, drawn to Tyburn and hanged: *Westminster Chronicle*, pp. 282–285.

[149] The accounts do not say why this money came from Chirchman and Organ. It may have been money owed or loans that had been agreed.

[150] E101/41/5 m. 1.

[151] Sir Edward Dallingridge is described as Edward Dalyngrigg in the accounts. This reference probably accounts for the claim in the entry for Sir Edward Dallingridge in *HOP*, vol. ii, pp. 738–742, that he 'helped the earl to organise and finance his second naval expedition, that of the summer of 1388'. However, he was merely delivering a small payment of advance wages from the Exchequer. 1387: E101/40/33 m. 1; enrolled protection, C76/71 m. 12.

at Southampton, even though the accounts state that the force landed at Winchelsea on 3 September.

It is clear that it had been a real struggle to raise the funds for the campaign, and the final sum paid of £19,040 0s 10½d was finally settled after the return. The actual amount claimed for the campaign was £19,690 8s 6d, and thus Arundel was owed a surplus of just over £650. Arundel's account was not finally settled until 20 February in the ninth year of the reign of Henry IV.[152] This campaign therefore cost the Exchequer nearly twice that of the previous year.[153] The indenture and accounts also throw light upon the non-combatants in the force, who do not appear in the muster roll. Arundel is allowed 12 servants and each man-at-arms one servant. If every one of these men-at-arms had taken such a servant, this would have added over 1,400 more men to the overall force onboard ship during the campaign. The enrolled accounts confirm Arundel's figures and again summarise the payments made and also the terms of the indenture.

The evidence of letters of protection and attorney

Together with the muster rolls for Richard, earl of Arundel's expeditions of 1387 and 1388, we can also consider other sources such as the enrolled letters of protection and enrolled appointments of attorney available on the Treaty (or French) Rolls. These records can be compared against the names of those on the muster rolls to add a further dimension to the information we already have.

How many men had taken out legal protection? How many had taken out protection but did not serve? – and how widespread was such non-attendance? Who took out protections? – just captains and knights, or also esquires and archers? What can these records tell us in addition to the information found in the muster rolls? The legal instruments of protection and letters of attorney were important for soldiers serving overseas in royal expeditions. The enrolled protections provided the individual with the means of protecting property interests at home whilst serving overseas. A letter of attorney would offer additional legal protection by appointing a proxy to act on their behalf during their service overseas. Anyone who was serving abroad in the king's service was well advised to protect their property using the legal framework available.[154]

These enrolled letters of protection and enrolled appointments of attorney can be viewed on the Treaty Rolls in the Public Record Office at Kew. A summary of what is contained within each roll can be found in the *Catalogue des Rolles Gasçons, Normans et Francois*.[155] For the reign of Richard II the rolls

---

[152] E364/24 m. 5. The length of time taken to settle the account may be accounting practice, or it may reflect Arundel's fall from grace after Richard II's return to authority.

[153] The previous account for the campaign of 1387 had been for £10,890 3s 7d.

[154] For the background to protections see Prestwich, *Armies and Warfare in the Middle Ages*, pp. 109–110, and Ayton, *Knights and Warhorses*, pp. 157–159. For the background to letters of attorney see *ibid.*, p. 182.

[155] Thomas Carte, *Catalogue des Rolles Gasçons, Normans et Francois*, vol. xx (London and Paris, 1743).

were known at the time as *Rotuli Francie*, and contained enrolments concerning diplomatic relations with France, the administration of the king's lands in France and documents of military and commercial importance.[156] They actually consist of a number of large membranes sewn together in a large roll. Each membrane measures about 25 by 50 centimetres and each membrane has then been sewn into one continuous length to make up the rolls which can be many metres in length. The actual enrolments are dispersed throughout the treaty roll and therefore careful study must be made of the whole roll to ensure that all the enrolments are found. The roll is mostly ordered in date order, with the earliest entries first. Once a scribe has entered one enrolment in full, the entries of protection directly following are normally shortened, presumably to save time in the documenting process. Entries are usually found together in batches. However, occasionally they are also entered singularly. This may indicate that a retinue captain has brought a number of protections together on behalf of those who have contracted with him and that also sometimes individuals have made the arrangements in person.

The treaty roll C76/71, which covers the tenth year of Richard's reign, 22 June 1386–21 June 1387, contains the enrolled protections and letters of attorney that had been taken out in order to accompany the earl of Arundel on his overseas campaign in 1387. The membranes are dated with the earliest membranes on the inside of the roll. It is therefore necessary to begin by unrolling the treaty roll and then work from the inside to the outside. The first protection, that of Arundel himself is recorded on membrane 14 of the roll, dated 26 January 1387, just over one month following his commission of 16 December. Each entry follows the same formula: the name of the person for whom the protection has been gained, his alias; rank (for example knight, esquire or archer); description of his occupation; description of locality; the place of enrolment and finally the date.[157] Each enrolment consists of some of the above list, some entries contain information on all the above; however, others will only contain one or two items of information. One such example of a protection for the expedition in 1387 can be transcribed as,

> William Pygot of London, Fishmonger, at Westminster on 20 February.[158]

Each enrolment is written across one line; occasionally if a person has a long name, the entry may run to two lines. The first fifty-two protections are listed together on membrane 14, following the protection for Arundel. The dates on this membrane run from 26 January until 15 February. The protections do not seem to run in date order on the membrane, although they mostly do so.

---

[156] *Guide to the Contents of the Public Record Office, Volume 1* (London, 1963) pp. 25–26.

[157] For rank the following descriptions are used: chivaler, miles, armiger, scutifer. Some of the occupational titles used include: Fishmonger; Carpenter, Tailor. All of the enrolments on this treaty roll are enrolled at Westminster, i.e. at the Chancery.

[158] C76/71 m. 12, listed on the roll as follows, 'Willelmus Pygot de London Ffisshmonger west xx Feb'. William Pygot fulfilled his intention to serve in this expedition and is listed on the muster roll as an esquire in the retinue of Edward, earl of Devon, E101/40/33 m. 3.

Table 6. Dated enrolled protections for 1387

Name	26 Jan	28 Jan	30 Jan	1 Feb	2 Feb	4 Feb	5 Feb	6 Feb	7 Feb	8 Feb	9 Feb	10 Feb	11 Feb	12 Feb	13 Feb	14 Feb	15 Feb	16 Feb	20 Feb	21 Feb	22 Feb	23 Feb	24 Feb	25 Feb	26 Feb	27 Feb	28 Feb	1 Mar	2 Mar	3 Mar	4 Mar	5 Mar	6 Mar	10 Mar	15 Mar	18 Mar	21 Mar	Total
Arundel	2			1		1	1		1	1	1		2		1	1	4	1		1		1			1	1		1			1				1			24
Le Comte de Devens'																			1			1								1	1			2	1	1		7
Le Sire de Beamount													2														1										1	4
Mons John Darundel																																						0
Mons Reynald de Cobham							1		1											1															1			4
Mons Arnald Savage		1														1					1		1						1							1		6
Mons Thomas Trevet							1							1	1						2																	5
Mons Thomas de Ponynges					1				1																				1									3
Mons Hugh le Despenser																1			1			1										1						4
Mons Thomas Mortemer																		1																				1
Mons William Elmham																														1			1					2
Mons Gilbert Talbot																																2						2
Mons Nich Clifton																																						0
Mons John de Wyngefeld	1						2																															3
Mons Richard Craddok																						1																1
Mons Hugh Loterell								1																														1
Mons Robert Hemenale																																						
John Wormyngton																																						
Mons Robert Mounteney									1																1													2
Mons John de Calverlee										1																												1
Mons John Haukeston												1												1														2
John Staple																								3														3
John Sly																																						0
John Treubyn											1																		2									3
Richard Cryse			1																					2														3
Richard Shynkylton												1																										1
Pyers Vanbusth																																						0
Robert Gyffard																										1												1
John Hayward															1																							1
Totals	3	1	1	1	1	1	5	1	4	2	2	2	4	1	3	3	4	2	2	2	3	4	1	6	2	2	1	1	4	2	2	3	1	2	2	2	1	84

Membrane 13 does not contain any protections. The next membrane, membrane 12 contains eighty-seven enrolled protections dated from 16 February until 16 March. Four more protections can be found on membrane 11 dated 5, 17 and 18 March. The final protections are written on membrane 5 dated 17 and 21 March.

Table 6 shows that protections are sought evenly throughout the three months prior to the expedition disembarking. The majority of the protections are enrolled in February, with entries being recorded on all but four days of this month. There are no major clusters by date, with the largest number of six enrolments being recorded on 25 February. The largest number of protections for the 1387 campaign can seen to have been taken out by participants in the earl of Arundel's retinue and the other protections are spread throughout the other constituent retinues. Four of the retinues have no enrolled protections relating to mustered troops.[159] It could be assumed that men who have taken protections on the same day and who serve in the same retinue may have sought their protections together. This can be shown to indeed be the case for Sir Thomas West and Sir Edward Dallingridge who have both received protections on the 15 February and who are serving in the earl of Arundel's retinue. These men have other connections that suggest that the protections have been gained in tandem.[160] Other evidence does not survive linking others who have taken protections on the same day. However, it would seem likely that some of these men would have other local connections.

The letters of attorney are also found interspersed between the protections and other items on the treaty rolls. They have also been entered in batches or individually. The attorneys are identified by the words 'General' Attorn' ' written in the left hand margin of the membrane. The first two enrolled attorneys appear on membrane 14. The actual formation of the attorney entry is more longwinded than that for a protection. It names the combatant and their two nominee attorneys. It also has a date for the enrolment. The two attorneys on membrane 14 are dated 1 February and 4 March.[161] Other letters of attorney are spread throughout subsequent membranes namely: membrane 10 with thirteen attorneys grouped together; membrane 8 with one; membrane 6 with four and membrane 4 with one. They are dated throughout February and March, the latest being that of Edward, earl of Devon, dated 28 March.[162] This final date follows the beginning of the expedition.

The protections and attorneys for the expedition in the following year are listed in a similar way on the treaty roll C76/72 for Richard II's eleventh regnal year, 22 June 1387 – 21 June 1388. The protections begin on membrane 7 and are generally grouped together under the heading 'Arundel', which is a slightly different format from the previous year. The first 120 protections are thus listed in bulk over membrane 7 and onto membrane 6. Other protections also appear

---

159 The retinues were captained by Sir John Darundel, Sir Nicholas Clifton, John Sly and Pyers Vanbusth.
160 This will be discussed in Part 2.
161 The letters of attorney are dated at Westminster.
162 C76/71 m. 4.

Table 7. Dated enrolled protectons for 1388

Captain	4 Apr	7 Apr	8 Apr	9 Apr	11 Apr	12 Apr	13 Apr	15 Apr	17 Apr	18 Apr	19 Apr	20 Apr	21 Apr	22 Apr	23 Apr	24 Apr	26 Apr	28 Apr	2 May	3 May	4 May	5 May	6 May	7 May	9 May	10 May	12 May	13 May	14 May	15 May	16 May	21 May	30 May	11 Jun	Total
l'Admirall, Mons le Count Arundell	1		1							2					2					1				1	2	1	1	1		3			1	1	18
Le Counte Mareshall			1											2	1				1	1															6
Le Monsers W Sire de Welles																													2		1				3
Le Counte de Devons												1									1														2
Mons Johan Darundell																														1					1
Mons William Baron de Hylton																							1	1											2
Mons Thomas Camoys												2	1	1													1	1	1						7
Mons Thomas Ponyngs										1																									1
Mons Johan Bohun			1				1			1																									3
Mons Thomas West							1				1											1													3
Mons William Heron																															3				3
Mons Hugh Browe									2	2																									4
Mons William Briene									2																										2
Mons Rauf Vernon											1																								1
Mons Johan Wynkefeld																																			0
Mons Hugh le Despencer		1																			1														2
Mons Johan Grymesby												1				1			1													1			4
Mons Johan Wogan												2			1																				3
Mons Nicol Clyfton				1																						1									2
Mons Johan Clanyng																										1		1							2
Mons Gilbe Talbot																																			0
Mons Johan Coupeland																											1								1
Mons Andrewe Hake								1													1														2
Mons Johan de Brewe																																			0
Mons Piers de Bokton																																			0

Name	Total
Mons Johan Sandes	2
Mons Olyner Mauleverer	2
Mons Arnald Savage	1
Mons Robert Massey	3
Johan Staple	0
Wauter Merston	0
Benet Cely	2
Johan Trenbyn	0
Robert Geffard	2
William Cavven	0
Thomas atte Lee	0
Richard Breton	0
Richard Shinkvlton	1
Richard Waynill	1
Johan Hayward	0
Aleyn Seintiust	0
Johan Hulat	0
Thomas Legat	0
Robert Bland	1
Johan Creghton	0
Giles Weston	3
Davy Russell	0
Esmon Randulph	2
Richard Cryse	1
Mons Hugh le Despencer	0
Total	93

Column totals (left to right): 2 1 4 2 1 1 1 3 1 7 1 6 1 7 2 1 1 5 2 1 3 2 5 2 3 2 6 4 4 1 1 1

on membrane 5 and membrane 2. They follow the exact format as for the previous treaty roll and are dated from 4 April until 11 June, again therefore over a three month period. This expedition left England on or around 10 June.

Table 7 shows that the protections were sought evenly throughout April and May and only one protection was taken during June. Protections have not been as evenly recorded as in the previous year with the protections being clustered around fewer days. The most protections are again taken in the retinue of the earl of Arundel and are then distributed throughout the retinues. Seventeen of the constituent retinues do not have any soldiers with a protection. Most protections are enrolled on 23 April, with seven protections being recorded. It is again noticeable that the most number of protections taken on the same day in any retinue is only three. This suggests that protections were not sought in bulk by retinue captains. It can be shown on occasion that relationships exist and thus protections have been taken out jointly. For instance, it is unique amongst this set of protections for both campaigns, that the description following the protection for Sir John de Roos[163] mentions the retinue in which he is serving. It is thus possible that on this occasion his retinue captain, Lord Welles, has organised this protection. In addition, two esquires with the same surname, Richard Pemberton and John Pemberton,[164] have enrolled protections for the same day and both serve in the retinue of Sir Robert Massey. This shows that these two men must have been related and must have gained their protections together. These identifications are only possible for a handful of the total protections that are taken out for this expedition. The letters of attorney for this campaign begin on membrane 8 and continue to membrane 1, with the bulk being listed on membrane 8. They date from 26 April until 8 June.

It should be possible to test how popular the use of protections was during Arundel's expeditions. By comparing against the database of the muster rolls for the same expedition those individuals who felt it necessary to take out a protection can be cross referenced. It can then be confirmed whether an individual actually performed the service implied in his taking out of a protection or letters of attorney.

Table 8 shows the numbers of individuals who had enrolled letters of protection and attorney and who also appear on the muster roll for Arundel's expedition in 1387. This number is also expressed as a percentage of the total number of each rank on the expedition. The total number of enrolled protections and letters of attorney on the Treaty rolls is also shown.

From this Table 8 can be demonstrated that only 84 of the 143 individuals who have taken out protections for the campaign can be found on the muster roll. This suggests that 41% of those individuals who intended to participate in this particular expedition did not attend muster and so therefore did not fulfil this intention, or else are non-combatants. The earlier evidence produced by Ayton suggested that fraud could be highly prevalent amongst the enrolled

---

163 E101/40/33 m. 3; enrolled protection, C76/72 m. 5, as 'Johannes de Roos miles cum Johannes de Welle'.
164 E101/40/33 m. 14; enrolled protections dated 10 May 1388, C76/72 m. 7.

Table 8. Enrolled letters of protection and attorney for the expedition of 1387[1]

	Total no. mustered	Protections mustered	Attorney mustered
Captains	29[2]	15 (52%)	4 (14%)
Knights	68[3]	19 (28%)	13 (19%)
Esquires	1010	44 (3.17%)	2 (0.02%)
Archers	1390	6 (0.43%)	1 (0.07%)
Total	2497	84 (3.36%) Enrolled 143	20(0.8%) Enrolled 22

[1]   Protections and attorney enrolled in the Public Record Office, C76/71.
[2]   Including joint captains – 26 retinues on campaign.
[3]   Not including captains, but including other nobles and bannerets.

protections. By comparing the evidence of the muster roll with the treaty roll it can be seen that large scale fraud is a possibility. However, as Saul pointed out, it is also possible that many of the men taking out protections may have been non-combatants. When considering the number of enrolled letters of attorney it can be seen that 91% of the individuals who have taken this precaution are also on the muster roll. It therefore appears that the appointing of an attorney would be a more certain indicator of a real intention to serve. It is also pertinent to note that 14 of the 20 individuals who have taken the trouble of appointing an attorney have also secured a letter of protection and have mustered for the expedition. It is interesting that nine of the individuals who have taken protections to serve with Arundel in 1387, have had their protections revoked in the *Calendar of Patent Rolls*, through February to May 1388.[165] This demonstrates that these

[165] The nine individuals are: enrolled protection, C76/71 m. 14, Richard, fitz William del crooke de Whithull, at Westminster on 30 January 1387; revocation, *CPR, 1385–1389*, p. 280, Richard, son of William del Crook of Whithull, at Westminster on 26 February 1387 (this is dated incorrectly as 1378 in *CPR*); enrolled protection, C76/71 m. 12, Nicholus Tryte de London, Pelliparius, at Westminster on 24 February 1387; revocation, *CPR, 1385–1389*, p. 285, Nicholas Tryce of London, skinner, at Westminster on 4 March 1387, 'as obtained fraudulently'; enrolled protection, C76/71 m. 12, Thomas Nuttyng de Kyketon, at Westminster on 2 March 1387; revocation, *CPR, 1385–1389*, p. 289, Thomas Nuttyng of Kirketon, at Westminster on 26 April 1387, 'as not preparing to go'; enrolled protection, C76/71 m. 12, William atte Heyerst de Okestede, at Westminster on 6 March 1387; revocation, *CPR, 1385–1389*, p. 292, William atte Heyerst of Okestede, at Westminster on 26 April, 'because it is credibly testified in Chancery that he is not preparing to go'; enrolled protection, C76/71 m. 14, Richard de Byngham, *miles*, at Westminster (unclear) February 1387; revocation, *CPR, 1385–1389*, p. 297, Richard de Bymgham, knight, at Westminster on 14 May 1387, 'because he tarries in the county of Chester on his own affairs'; enrolled protection, C76/71 m. 12, Thomas de Heryngton, at Westminster on 28 February 1387; revocation, *CPR, 1385–1389*, p. 302, Thomas de Heryngton, on 20 May 1387, 'because he tarries in Newcastle-upon-Tyne on this own affairs'; enrolled protection, C76/71 m. 14, John Henley Junior, at Westminster on 13 February 1387; revocation, *CPR, 1385–1389*, p. 303, John Henley the younger, at Westminster on 15 May 1387, 'because he tarries in the county of Warwick on his own affairs'; enrolled protection, C76/71 m. 14, Hugo Martin de Walden Regis com' Herts. Valet camere Regis, at Westminster on 6 February 1387; revocation, *CPR,*

individuals have had their own reasons for not attending this campaign, but this still leaves fifty protections taken and unaccounted for. Most of these revocations are dated whilst the campaign was being fought, and therefore it has been noticed that they were not participating as promised. One of the revocations is because the individual concerned was busy on the king's business and another one is revoked because it was obtained fraudulently.

Table 8 also reinforces the point made earlier that the evidence is mainly indicative of only the higher echelons of society. More than half the retinue captains and nearly a third of knights secured a letter of protection for the expedition of 1387. However, the numbers of esquires and archers making use of this legal cover are negligible. This information implies that only the retinue captains and knights felt that it was necessary to protect their landed interests whilst overseas in the king's service.

The total numbers securing protections on this expedition appear small compared to numbers suggested by Ayton for the expeditions of Edward III. Of the 1,107 men-at-arms serving in the expedition of 1387 only 78 (7%) have taken out enrolled protections. Ayton showed that numbers of protections could vary from two-thirds to one-fifth of the men-at-arms serving overseas. He also commented that overseas expeditions were likely to have a higher proportion of enrolled protections than those in the British Isles.[166]

For the expedition of 1387 the proportion of men-at-arms with protections is unexpectedly smaller than the figures for expeditions earlier in the century, with less than a tenth feeling the need for such a protection. Does this suggest a fall in the importance or perceived effectiveness of the legal cover provided by the letter of protection? As I have noted, this expedition shows a fall in the numbers of knights compared to earlier expeditions. This could therefore account for the drop in numbers of protections in this expedition as fewer of the men-at-arms were of knightly status. It may also be that the relative shortness of the planned expedition, at three months, also made combatants less concerned about legal threats whilst they were overseas. The speed at which the expedition was recruited may have also had an effect on an individual's ability to petition beforehand for protections and letters of attorney. The politics of this particular expedition and the fact that it was led by the earl of Arundel, and not the king, may have attracted a different kind of participant. This participant may not have been landed and wealthy but may have been wishing to improve their fortunes with the spoils of war.

Table 9 shows the numbers of individuals who had enrolled letters of protection and attorney and who also appear on the muster roll for Arundel's expedition in 1388. This number is also expressed as a percentage of the total number of each rank on the expedition. The total number of enrolled protections and attorney on the treaty rolls is also shown.

1385–1389, p. 305, Hugh Martin of Walden Regis, co. Hertford, yeoman of the chamber, 'because he tarries in the king's household and elsewhere in England on his own affairs'.
[166] Ayton, *Knights and Warhorses*, p. 159.

Table 9. Enrolled letters of protection and attorney for the expedition of 1388[1]

	Total no. mustered	Protections mustered	Attorney mustered
Captains	51	16 (31%)	3 (6%)
Knights	87	16 (18%)	10 (11.49%)
Esquires	1430	50 (3.49%)	
Archers	2014	11 (0.55%)	
Total	3582	93 Enrolled 134	13 Enrolled 21

[1] Protections and attorney enrolled in the Public Record Office, C76/72.

From Table 9 it can be demonstrated that only 93 of the 134 individuals who had taken out protections can be found on the muster roll. Thus 31% of those individuals who intended to participate in this particular expedition have not attended muster and so therefore did not fulfil this intention. Alternatively, as suggested earlier, these entries in the treaty rolls could represent non-combatants or sailors. This shows a smaller number of non-attendances than the expedition a year earlier. Of these non-attendees, only four are to be found revoked in the *Calendar of Patent Rolls* in May, July and November 1388, and thus 37 protections are left unaccounted for.[167] These men are not going as other matters have diverted them. One individual, John Peyntour, is a chaplain, the only man described as such within all the protections for both expeditions. He would have been a non-combatant if he had attended the campaign, and thus would not have appeared on the muster roll anyway. When considering the number of enrolled letters of attorney it can be seen that 62% of the individuals who have taken this precaution are also on the muster roll. This percentage had fallen from the previous year. It is also pertinent to note that eight of the thirteen individuals who had taken the trouble of appointing an attorney have also secured a letter of protection and have mustered for the expedition.

The total numbers securing protections on this expedition again appear small compared to the numbers seen in the expeditions of Edward III. Of the 1,568 men-at-arms serving in this expedition only 82 (5%) had taken out enrolled

[167] These four individuals are: enrolled protection, C76/72 m. 7, John Peyntour Capellanus (chaplain), at Westminster on 2 May 1388; revocation, *CPR, 1385–1389*, p. 444, John Peyntour, chaplain, at Westminster on 14 May 1388, 'because he is not going, as is testified by earl of Arundel'; enrolled protection, C76/72 m. 7, Roger Goswold, at Westminster on 3 May; revocation, *CPR, 1385–1389*, p. 446, Roger Goswold, merchant, at Westminster on 10 May 1388, 'because he tarries in England'; enrolled protection, C76/72 m. 7, John Bronn, armiger, de com' Devon', at Westminster on 2 May; revocation, *CPR, 1385–1389*, p. 480, John Broun, esquire, of the county of Devon, at Westminster on 6ᵗʰ July 1388, 'on certificate by the sheriffs of London that he tarries in London on his own affairs'; enrolled protection, C76/72 m. 5, Richard atte Revere de Kyngeston in com' Surrey, at Westminster on 8 May; revocation, *CPR, 1385–1389*, p. 530, Richard atte Revere of Kyngeston, co. Surrey, at Westminster on 20 November 1388, 'because he is not preparing to go'.

protections. This proportion had fallen from the level of 7% recorded for the previous year.

For the expedition of 1388, the proportion of men-at-arms who had protections, at around a twentieth, is again unexpectedly smaller than the figures for expeditions earlier in the century. These figures can again be partially explained by the numbers of non-knightly men-at-arms present in this expeditionary army. Indeed the financial success of the expedition of 1387 perhaps attracted more of the 'soldier of fortune' types to the expedition, whilst the numbers of knights has fallen. Also, the length of time available to take out letters of protection and attorney may have been restrictive on the total numbers requested. These expeditions were quickly organised, the earl of Arundel contracted to serve for three months with 3,500 men on 23 March 1388.[168] The army mustered around the beginning of June and embarked on 10 June of the same year. The participants would have had just over two months to secure their necessary legal arrangements prior to joining the expedition. The actual enrolments were made between 4 April and 11 June.

Letters of protection and attorney can also provide information regarding the occupation and residence of those who sought them. Unfortunately, for the campaigns under discussion, the treaty rolls do not provide us with a great deal of information. For 1387 an occupation is provided for five soldiers and place of residence for twenty-six soldiers. The occupations represented comprise three fishmongers, one tailor and one carpenter,[169] thus contradicting Walsingham, who stated that Arundel was careful not to conscript cobblers and tailors.[170] The counties of residence are widespread, with ten counties shown, although mainly concentrated in the south of England, with representation from the Welsh marcher counties. There are seven soldiers from London, four soldiers each from Kent and Yorkshire, two soldiers each from Cornwall, Devon, Surrey and Sussex, and one soldier from Herefordshire, Hertfordshire and Shropshire. For 1388 an occupation is provided for just one individual who is described as a mariner and merchant[171] and place of residence for twelve soldiers. The soldiers are again widely distributed, representing eleven counties, again mainly in the south of England. There are two soldiers from Kent, and one each from Cambridgeshire, Cornwall, Derbyshire, Devon, London, Shropshire, Somerset, Surrey, Sussex, and Yorkshire.

The campaigns led by the earl of Arundel in 1387 and 1388 have much potential significance in the political context of the reign of Richard II. They were held against the background of the crisis facing Richard, following the

---

[168] E101/41/4 m. 2 for the indenture.

[169] John Berforde, E101/40/33 m. 3; enrolled protection, C76/71 m. 12, as 'Johannes Bereford Carpenter de Hertford'. Richard Galeys, E101/40/33 m. 3; enrolled protection, C76/71 m. 12, as 'Ricardus Galeys de London, Ffishmonger'. William Pygot, E101/40/33 m. 3; enrolled protection, C76/71 m. 12, as 'Willelmus Pygot de London, Ffisshmonger'. William Snowball, E101/40/33 m. 3; enrolled protection, C76/71 m. 12, as 'Willelmus Snowe Tailuer et Suus, London'. John Weller, E101/40/33 m. 20d; enrolled protection, C76/71 m. 14, as 'Johannes Welles de London Ffelmonger'.

[170] *St Albans Chronicle*, p. 809.

[171] John Hayward, E101/41/5 m. 16; enrolled protection, C76/72 m. 8.

Appellant moves to control his government of the realm. This tension was heightened during 1387 and led to the Appellants raising arms and defeating the king's favourite, de Vere, who came to the defence of the king with a force of loyal Cheshire men at Radcot Bridge. The positioning of this civil war between the two overseas campaigns adds an additional significance to the soldiers who decided to support the earl of Arundel in his endeavours. Following the campaigns Richard reasserted his authority; it is therefore interesting to trace the careers of these soldiers following the campaign and for the rest of the reign. These careers will be discussed in detail in Part 2 to investigate whether such politicised motives for service are discernible from the source material.

Part Two

ANALYSIS OF THE ARMY PERSONNEL

3

Continuity of Service and the Military Career

Major figures

The remainder of the book concentrates on linking information from different sources to build case studies of participants in the campaigns of 1387–1388. This method enables us to discuss the careers of knights, and especially of esquires and archers who do not generally appear in other studies. Much more detailed information is available for the careers of the nobles who attended these campaigns, including biographies from the *Complete Peerage* and *Dictionary of National Biography*. It is therefore relatively easy to summarise the careers of the major figures who participated in the campaigns of 1387–1388 utilising the printed sources.

The leader of the expeditions and also a man who features throughout this account, is Richard Fitzalan, earl of Arundel.[1] The fullest biography of this senior Appellant is featured in Anthony Goodman's *The Loyal Conspiracy*.[2] Born in 1346, the earl was the bearer of the crown at the coronation of Richard II. Arundel was very well connected; his brother was Thomas Arundel, archbishop of Canterbury; his sisters were the countesses of Hereford and Kent; his niece, the duchess of Gloucester, had married Thomas of Woodstock, youngest son of Edward III, thus making Arundel the uncle of his fellow senior Appellant. Arundel had three sons-in-law, the Earl Marshal, one of the junior Appellants, Lord Charlton of Powys, and the brother of the earl of Warwick, Sir William Beauchamp. His other brother, Sir John Arundel, was a senior member of the military community and drowned following a storm at sea that wrecked the expedition he was leading in 1379.[3] By his second marriage to Phillippa Hastings in 1390, the earl increased his landholding and became brother-in-law to the young Roger Mortimer, earl of March.

As well as being influential Arundel was also a very wealthy man and was the greatest landholder in Sussex. His wealth probably contributed to his ability to help raise the force to oppose the earl of Oxford in December 1387. Although his main holdings were in Sussex, he also held lands in Surrey, Hampshire,

---

[1] 1387: E101/40/33 m. 1; enrolled protection, C67/71 m. 14; enrolled attorney, C67/71 m. 11. 1388: E101/41/5 m. 1; enrolled protection, C76/72 m. 2.
[2] Goodman, *Loyal Conspiracy*, ch. 6. See also *Complete Peerage*, vol. i, pp. 244–245; *DNB*, vol. xix, pp. 98–100.
[3] Walsingham describes the death of Sir John Arundel following the wrecking of his ship, *Chronicon Angliae*, ed. E.M. Thompson (Rolls Series, 1874), p. 252.

Wiltshire, Buckinghamshire, Middlesex, Essex and Norfolk. His other major landholding was in the March of Wales including lands in Shropshire and Cheshire, and these holdings were strengthened by his second marriage. Goodman calculates that his landholding, together with his activity in the wool trade would have made Arundel the richest Appellant. He had a large network of men who served with him both in peace and war. These men were mainly based in Sussex and Shropshire, and case studies of some of these individuals will be developed later in this section.

As a member of the military community, Arundel made a deposition at the court of chivalry in the case of Scrope v. Grosvenor. In his own words, aged thirty-eight, he had been in arms for 18 years.[4] He described how he served on the expedition of John of Gaunt in 1369 and also on the royal expedition to Scotland in 1385.[5] His main military achievements were naval in undertaking. He had already served as Admiral of the West between 5 December 1377 and 10 September 1378.[6] His performance as admiral was mixed: he saved Southampton from French assault; led an unsuccessful assault on Harfleur; was defeated by a Spanish fleet, but compelled Cherbourg to surrender. His next military service was during John of Gaunt's expedition in 1378. Froissart describes how Arundel's negligence led to the siege of St Malo being raised, an event which was to prove embarrassing for the earl.[7] His main military achievement was during his second appointment as Admiral of the West and north between 10 December 1386 and 18 May 1389. His defeat of the Flemish fleet in 1387, during his first campaign, resulted in the capture of a large amount of wine, the distribution of which made the earl a popular figure. The campaign of the following year 1388, did not reach the heights of 1387, and the earl returned to England without having achieved much of substance. This was his last military enterprise.

Arundel had been a member of the royal council since the coronation, but his years of prominence were during 1386–1389. Arundel was a leading member of the council appointed to reform and govern the realm. This brought him into direct conflict with Richard II which led to Arundel, Gloucester, Warwick, Derby and Nottingham rising in arms and defeating the royal force commanded by the duke of Ireland at Radcot Bridge in December 1387. This alliance then prosecuted and executed the king's favourites at the Merciless Parliament using the process of appeal. Following Richard's return to authority in 1389, Arundel played less of a role in national affairs. He was involved in a dispute with Gaunt in parliament in 1394, and offended Richard II by arriving late at the king's first wife's funeral in the same year. The three senior Appellants were finally called

---

4 *Complete Peerage*, vol. i, p. 244, suggests that Arundel was born in 1346. He would therefore have been forty at the time of his deposition in 1386, and was perhaps being slightly coy about his age.
5 *Scrope v. Grosvenor*, vol. i, p. 219. He led a retinue of 249 men into Scotland in 1385, consisting of 6 bannerets, 24 knights, 69 esquires and 10 archers, Lewis, 'The Last Medieval Summons', Appendix II, p. 17.
6 *Handbook of British Chronology*, p. 139.
7 Froissart, *Chronicles*, vol. i, pp. 551–552.

to account for their actions in 1387–1388 ten years later at parliament in 1397. Richard used the process of appeal to enact his revenge, and the earl of Arundel was executed for treason, the duke of Gloucester was murdered in Calais, and the earl of Warwick was imprisoned for life on the Isle of Man.[8]

Arundel was accompanied by another future Appellant on campaign in 1387 and 1388. Thomas Mowbray was the son-in-law of the earl of Arundel following his marriage to Elizabeth Montague in 1384, and thus supported his father-in-law both in the campaigns of 1387–1388 and in the attack upon the king. Mowbray was created earl of Nottingham in 1383, Earl Marshal in 1385 and duke of Norfolk in 1397, following Richard's prosecution of the senior Appellants. On the muster rolls for the campaigns for 1387–1388 he is indeed 'Le Counte Mareshal'.[9] The fullest biography is again to be found in the study by Goodman.[10] Born on 22 March 1366, Mowbray was thus only twenty when created Earl Marshal and twenty-one when he accompanied the earl of Arundel in 1387. Thomas had inherited the earldom of Nottingham from his elder brother, John, who died on 8 February 1383. In his youth he was a favourite companion of Richard II, and it has been suggested that it was mainly due to the king's transfer of favour to Robert de Vere which led the Earl Marshal to joining with the Appellants.[11] However, according to Goodman, the Earl Marshal was constantly scheming. He comments:

> Thomas seems to have been an intensely ambitious young man with a taste for intrigue. According to Froissart, he was notable among the courtiers of the 1390s for his pride and presumption. He plotted against Lancaster in 1385, against Richard in 1387, probably against the senior Appellants in 1389 and 1397, and in December 1397 he may have been trying to involve Hereford in manoeuvres against rivals at court. When Norfolk was imprisoned in the Wardrobe in London in April 1398, pending proceedings on Hereford's accusations, elaborate precautions were taken to prevent him from escaping.[12]

The Earl Marshal had a wide landholding mainly in the counties of Lincolnshire and Sussex. He also held lands in Bedfordshire, Buckinghamshire, Leicestershire, Cambridgeshire, Yorkshire, Wiltshire, Warwickshire, Northampton, Huntingdonshire and Norfolk. His marriage to Arundel's daughter also brought him other lands in Buckinghamshire, Essex and Norfolk. He had an Irish lordship granted in 1394 and also lands from the earl of Warwick in 1397. Despite these lands, Goodman comments that he was not particularly well-endowed for a magnate, and thus relied heavily upon royal patronage. His scheming may therefore have been aimed at ensuring a continuance of royal favour.[13]

---

8 *DNB*, vol. ii, pp. 98–100.
9 1387: E101/40/33 m. 1. 1388: E101/41/5 m. 3.
10 Goodman, *Loyal Conspiracy*, ch. 9, pp. 156–164. See also *Complete Peerage*, vol. ix, pp. 601–604 and *DNB*, vol. xxxix, pp. 230–236.
11 Saul, *Richard II*, p. 123.
12 Goodman, *Loyal Conspiracy*, p. 157.
13 *Ibid.*, pp. 159–160.

The Earl Marshal's military career probably began aged 19, on the royal expedition to Scotland, which followed closely upon his creation as Marshal of England.[14] He then served with his father-in-law on the campaigns of 1387–1388 and also joined with the Appellants in their battle against the forces of the earl of Oxford, culminating in the skirmish at Radcot Bridge.[15] He managed to regain the favour of Richard II and accompanied him on campaign to Ireland in 1394.[16] He was an accomplished knight, and was famous for his performance at international tournaments in 1390.[17] He was also interested in crusading as can be seen by his promise to become a Knight of the Passion, an order of chivalry developed by Philippe de Mézières in the 1390s.[18]

It is, however, for his political machinations that the Earl Marshal will be remembered. Along with Henry, earl of Derby, he joined with the senior Appellants on 12 December 1387. This move strengthened the Appellants and ensured they won the brief civil war.[19] Mowbray was quickly accepted back into the court circle of Richard II. He was given a number of appointments including the captaining of Calais for 5 years from 1391, and was also the king's lieutenant in Calais, Picardy, Flanders and Artois. He was also one of the commissioners who contracted the marriage of Richard to Isabella of France.[20] He was one of the Appellants who prosecuted Arundel, Gloucester and Warwick, the senior Appellants from 1387–1388, in the parliament of 1397, and had thus turned upon his former allies.[21] The two junior Appellants from 1387–1388, were rewarded at this time, Mowbray becoming duke of Norfolk, and Henry, earl of Derby, being created duke of Hereford.

It was not long before Richard's attention turned to their fate and it would be Mowbray's love of intrigue that would finally be his downfall. The series of events that led to both Norfolk's and Hereford's banishment have been well documented in other studies.[22] The quarrel centred on a reported conversation between the two junior Appellants whilst riding to London during December 1397. Hereford informed the king that Norfolk had told him that they were also about to be undone because of their actions at Radcot Bridge. Hereford famously replied that 'it was a funny old world'. This story was repeated at the parliament at Shrewsbury in January 1398. Norfolk denied the story and a parliamentary committee decided that the quarrel would be decided by duel. However, the tournament was halted by Richard who decided to settle the argument himself. Hereford was banished for 10 years whilst Norfolk was banished

---

14 He led a retinue of 249 soldiers, including 5 bannerets, 19 knights, 75 esquires and 150 archers, Lewis, 'The Last Medieval Summons', Appendix II, p. 17.
15 *DNB*, vol. xxxix, p. 231, incorrectly records that he served in 1387 but did not serve in 1388.
16 *CPR, 1391–1396*, p. 506 (attorney).
17 Goodman, *Loyal Conspiracy*, p. 158.
18 Atiya, *The Crusade of Nicopolis*, Appendix II, pp. 134–135.
19 Goodman, *Loyal Conspiracy*, pp. 28–29.
20 *Complete Peerage*, vol. ix, p. 602.
21 *The Chronicle of Adam Usk*, ed. and trans. C. Given-Wilson (Oxford, 1997), p. 27, and Michael Bennett, *Richard II and the Revolution of 1399*, p. 96.
22 Most recently in Saul, *Richard II*, pp. 395–402.

for life.[23] Hereford's banishment led to his return in the following year and deposition of Richard II. Norfolk never returned to England. He died of the plague in Venice on 22 September 1399, following his return from a pilgrimage to the Holy Land.[24]

The only other peer to accompany Arundel on campaign in 1387–1388 was Edward Courtenay, the earl of Devon, later called 'the blind earl'.[25] He was born in 1357 and thus was 30 years of age when he served with the earl of Arundel. He captained a force of 231 soldiers in 1387 and 279 soldiers in 1388.[26] Therefore in both years he captained the largest retinues apart from those of the earl of Arundel. As a senior member of the military community, the earl of Devon was a deponent at the court of chivalry in the Scrope v. Grosvenor case. In his testimony he only referred to his recent experience in the royal expedition of 1385. However Harris Nicolas provided a biography of his career which supplements the information in the *Complete Peerage*.[27] From this portrait it can be seen that Devon had a distinguished military career. His first service appears to have been aged 18, when he accompanied the duke of Lancaster in 1378. He subsequently served with the earl of Buckingham in 1380 and was made Admiral of the West from 13 November 1383 until 29 January 1385.[28] As mentioned in his testimony to the Scrope v. Grosvenor case, Devon served in the royal expedition to Scotland in 1385 leading a retinue of 220 soldiers.[29]

Apart from serving with Arundel on campaign, Devon does not appear to have been involved in the Appellant attack on the king of those years. Neither does he suffer or benefit in the later years of Richard's reign. He would seem to have taken a low profile in the 1390s and does not serve in either of the expeditions to Ireland. It is therefore possible that his blindness had already begun to affect his ability to campaign. A.L. Brown also notes that he did not attend the Scottish expedition with Henry IV in 1400 and comments that this was probably due to his blindness.[30] He managed to survive the transition to the reign of Henry IV and was indeed the High Steward for the trial of the peers who had supported Richard II in 1400. Devon was connected to Thomas, Lord Camoys, who also served in 1387, by his marriage to Lord Camoys' daughter Alice. This family connection is demonstrated with a Hugh Camoys serving in Devon's retinue in 1387.[31] It is also interesting to note a further family connection with a

---

23 *RP*, vol. iii, p. 360, translation in Given-Wilson, *Chronicles of the Revolution*, pp. 86–87, 89–93.

24 *Complete Peerage*, vol. ix, p. 604.

25 *Complete Peerage*, vol. iv, pp. 325–326.

26 1387: E101/40/33 m. 3; enrolled protection, C76/71 m. 12; enrolled attorney, C76/71 m. 4. 1388: E101/41/5 m. 4.

27 *Scrope v. Grosvenor*, vol. i, p. 73 for deposition and vol. ii, p. 235 for career and translation.

28 *Handbook of British Chronology*, p. 139. Harris Nicolas incorrectly states that Devon was appointed Admiral of the West on 12 November 1384, *Scrope v. Grosvenor*, vol. ii, p. 236.

29 Devon led a retinue of 220 soldiers, consisting of 100 esquires and 120 archers, Lewis, 'The Last Medieval Summons', Appendix II, p. 17.

30 *Complete Peerage*, vol. iv, p. 326, states that he was blind for many years before his death in 1419. A.L. Brown, 'The English Campaign in Scotland, 1400', p. 46.

31 E101/40/33 m. 3.

Sir Hugh Courtenay being listed second in the retinue of the earl of Devon in both 1387 and 1388.[32] This cannot be his son, as he was only born in 1389; therefore it may have been his brother or other relation.[33] Devon's lack of involvement in the politics of the reign suggests that he served in 1387–1388 as part of his continued military career. It is clear from his background and experience that Arundel would have benefited from his input to his campaigns. It is also clear that Richard II did not treat such service by the earl of Devon as a political act.

The future earl of Gloucester, Thomas Despencer, was present on expedition with Arundel in 1388. The career of Thomas, Lord Despencer is one that became interweaved with the deposition of Richard II and indeed led to his own execution in 1400.[34] Despencer was born on 22 September 1373 and thus was only twelve years of age when, according to Froissart, 'the young lord de Spencer', served with Richard II on his Scottish expedition in 1385.[35] As we shall see from the evidence from the court of chivalry, service at such an age was not uncommon. Lord Despencer was still only fifteen years of age, when he was listed second in the retinue of the earl of Arundel in 1388.[36] Thomas progressed to lead his own retinue to Ireland in the company of the king in 1394 and 1399.[37] His service under Arundel in 1388 must have been overlooked as he rose to prominence as one of Richard II's favourites in the later years of his reign. He was one of the Appellants who prosecuted Arundel, Gloucester and Warwick in parliament in 1397.[38] As a result, he was raised to the peerage as earl of Gloucester, and granted lands forfeited by the duke of Gloucester and earl of Arundel at the very same parliament.[39] He accompanied Richard II on his return from Ireland and the king obtained a guarantee for his safety. He was sent to the Tower and he was degraded from the peerage. The lands awarded to him in 1397 were forfeited.

Richard's faith in Despencer was not entirely lost as the latter joined in the Epiphany Plot in 1400 in an attempt to restore his former king to the throne. The rising led by Richard's other favourites and relatives, the earls of Salisbury, Huntingdon, Rutland and Kent, ended in dismal failure. The events of this conspiracy have been much discussed in other studies and thus will not be dissected here.[40] However, it is worthwhile commenting upon the final movements of Despencer, which have still not been convincingly stated. Many sources follow the description of the rising in the contemporary French account, *Chronique de la Traison et Mort de Richart II*.[41] This describes how Despencer

---

[32] 1387: E101/40/33 m. 3. 1388: E101/41/5 m. 4.

[33] *Complete Peerage*, vol. iv, p. 326.

[34] *Complete Peerage*, vol. iv, pp. 278–282; *DNB*, vol. xiv. p. 417.

[35] Froissart, *Chronicles*, vol. ii, p. 50.

[36] E101/41/5 m. 1.

[37] 1394: *CPR, 1391–1396*, p. 483 (protection), p. 506 (attorney). 1399: *CPR, 1396–1399*, p. 520 (attorney), p. 522 (protection).

[38] *The Chronicle of Adam Usk*, p. 27.

[39] *Complete Peerage*, vol. iv, pp. 278–279.

[40] See, for instance, Wylie, *Henry the Fourth*, vol. i, pp. 92–111.

[41] *Chronique de la Traison et Mort de Richart II*, ed. and trans. Benjamin Williams (London,

was trapped with the other conspirators in Cirencester, before making good his escape to Wales. J.J.N. Palmer has convincingly questioned the value of the *Traison et Mort*, and has demonstrated that much of the chronicle is based on another source and many sections are fabricated. He came to this conclusion whilst preparing a modern critical edition. He states that Despencer could not have been in Cirencester as he was gathering support for the rising in South Wales. In addition, he even disputes the inclusion of the earl of Rutland in the plot.[42] Despite Palmer's assertions, Rutland is still credited in modern studies with betraying the conspiracy, as described in colourful detail in the *Traison et Mort*.[43] How Despencer met his end is quite clear. On attempting to sail to the continent from Cardiff, he was landed at Bristol, where he was taken into custody and beheaded by a lynch mob. His head was sent to the king.[44] We have seen that Despencer had a meteoric rise to the peerage and royal favour and a similar steep descent to his undoing. He was probably too young in 1387–1388 to have been involved in the actions of the Appellants and therefore was able to become an important supporter of Richard II in his final years. His appearance in the retinue of Arundel in 1388 probably represents an example of a young lord gaining valuable martial experience in a royal expedition.

It has also been suggested by Anthony Goodman that a future duke may also have been present on the campaign in 1387.[45] Thomas de Holand is listed as the first esquire in the retinue of the earl of Arundel. If this is Thomas Holland, nephew of the earl of Arundel, and also nephew of Richard II, he would have only been seventeen years of age in 1387. It would appear sensible that a nephew would indeed campaign with his uncle and other such family relation-ships have discovered within the muster rolls. To support this particular identifi-cation, he is also knighted prior to battle on 24 March 1387.[46] This service did not prevent Thomas from later showing his support to his royal uncle, and he was created earl of Kent following his father's death in 1397 and subsequently created duke of Surrey following the downfall of the elder Appellants in the same year. He was indeed one of the new Appellants who Richard used to prose-cute his old foes from 1386–1389. The possibility that he supported the Appel-lants on campaign in 1387 did not prevent him from showing his vociferous support for Richard's aggressive prosecution of his enemies. Following the deposition of Richard, Thomas was removed from the dukedom of Surrey and the lands he had been granted as a result were forfeit. He did not entirely desert his uncle and was a part of the Epiphany Plot against Henry IV in 1400 along with his uncle, John Holland, duke of Exeter. As a result of this unsuccessful

---

1846), pp. 229–258. I am grateful to Professor Brian Kemp for his advice regarding this source. See *Complete Peerage*, vol. iv, p. 280, which follows this account.

[42] J.J.N. Palmer, 'The Authorship, Date and Historical Value of the French Chronicles on the Lancastrian Revolution', *Bulletin of the John Rylands Library*, 61 (1978–79), part 1, pp. 145–181, part 2, pp. 398–421, pp. 405–409.

[43] For instance, Saul, *Richard II*, pp. 424–425.

[44] *Complete Peerage*, vol. iv, p. 280.

[45] Goodman, *Loyal Conspiracy*, p. 171, n. 4.

[46] E101/40/33 m. 1, 'fait chivaler le xxiiii iour de marz' is noted next to his name.

rising he was executed by the mob at Cirencester. His career is therefore very similar to that of Lord Despencer, future earl of Gloucester, and demonstrates a young man gaining experience on royal campaign, before progressing in the king's service. The support of Arundel, his uncle, in 1387, did not hinder his later progress under his other generous uncle, Richard II.[47]

Sir Thomas Percy, who served with Arundel in the campaign of 1388, was also to prosper in the later years of the reign of Richard II. He was created earl of Worcester in 1397, following the prosecution of the senior Appellants of 1387–1388. Sir Thomas was the younger brother of the earl of Northumberland and the uncle of Sir Henry Percy (Hotspur). Percy was an active member of the military community and as such had probably as much experience as anybody on campaign in 1388.[48] He was a deponent at the Scrope v. Grosvenor case in 1386, at which time he was around 43 years old, having been born in 1343. His deposition does not do him justice and he only specifically mentions service in the recent Scottish expedition of 1385.[49] His military service began in 1369, when he served with Sir John Chandos in France. Percy seems to have served continuously in France until he was captured on 23 August 1372. He was ransomed in the following year. He was appointed Admiral of the North from 5 November 1378 until 8 April 1380.[50] In his position as admiral he accompanied the ill-fated expedition of Sir John Arundel in 1379, but in the storm that took the life of Sir John, Percy did not lose any men or horses. Percy led a retinue in the expedition of the earl of Buckingham in 1380. He was again made Admiral of the North from 29 January 1385 until 22 February 1386.[51] As mentioned in his testimony at the Scrope v. Grosvenor case, he served in Scotland in 1385, leading a retinue of 119 soldiers.[52] He immediately followed this service with John of Gaunt in Spain in 1386, and on his return to England sailed with the earl of Arundel on his expedition in 1388.[53] Percy also served with Richard II in Ireland in 1394 and 1399.[54] As we can see from this impressive list of expeditions, Percy was a leading example of the military community.

Whilst not campaigning, he also managed to gain influence in the royal party of the king. He was appointed vice-chamberlain of the king in 1390 and in the same year was made chief justice of South Wales. He was an ambassador to France in 1392 and was subsequently appointed Steward of the Royal House-

---

[47] For Thomas' career see *Complete Peerage*, vol. vii, pp. 156–159, and *DNB*, vol. xxvii, pp. 157–158.

[48] *Complete Peerage*, vol. xii, part ii. pp. 838–842; *DNB*, vol. xliv, pp. 429–433.

[49] *Scrope v. Grosvenor*, vol. i, p. 50, vol. ii, p. 167. Harris Nicholas states that he was about forty-five years of age when he made his deposition.

[50] *Handbook of British Chronology*, p. 139.

[51] *Ibid.*, p. 130.

[52] Lewis, 'The Last Medieval Summons', p. 20; retinue consisted of 119 soldiers, including 13 knights, 66 esquires and 40 archers.

[53] See E101/40/39 for muster roll for the force of Sir Thomas de Percy in 1388. The muster roll is incomplete due to damage by fire with only the first 346 men detailed in 8 retinues surviving.

[54] 1394: Mitchell, 'Some Aspects of the Knightly Household of Richard II', Appendix III, p. 306, citing E101/402/20 m. 33. 1399: *CPR, 1396–1399*, p. 531 (attorney).

hold in 1393.[55] He was therefore a loyal and close supporter of the king and rose quickly in his service. Following Richard's prosecution of the Appellants in September 1397, he was created earl of Worcester. He seems to have supported Richard following his return from Ireland, and following Richard's decision to make a dash for North Wales, Walsingham describes how Percy disbanded the royal household and then, 'breaking his rod of office, he wept bitterly, for he had never wished to perform such an unwelcome task'.[56]

Percy did not suffer despite his position in the household of Richard II and he was not degraded from his peerage following the deposition. In fact he was re-appointed Admiral of the North and west until 20 April 1401, a position he had held since 16 January 1399.[57] He was made steward of the household and also a knight of the chamber.[58] He received a number of appointments under Henry IV, including being made lieutenant of South Wales and also following Sir Hugh le Despencer as tutor to the Prince of Wales. Worcester's fatal act was to join with his brother, the earl of Northumberland, and his nephew Sir Henry Percy in open rebellion against Henry IV in 1403. Sir Henry Percy was killed in the battle of Shrewsbury and Sir Thomas was captured and executed two days later on 23 July 1403. His head was sent to London, and was displayed on London bridge until 18 December.[59] It would seem surprising that Percy decided to rebel in 1403 and it would appear that Henry IV was also shocked by his treachery. He was a most experienced commander and Henry was able to use his considerable military ability against the revolt in Wales. However, it would seem that although Percy did not risk his life in support of Richard II, he was willing to put his life on the line for his brother and nephew.

The inclusion of Sir Michael de la Pole in the retinue of the earl of Arundel in 1388, is perhaps surprising considering that his father had been a recipient of the Appellants' prosecution of treason. His father, also Sir Michael de la Pole, had been Chancellor from 1383 until his impeachment at the Wonderful Parliament of 1386. He had been created earl of Suffolk on the Scottish expedition in 1385, was impeached and removed from office in 1386 and a subject of the Appeal of Treason in 1388. He died in exile in 1389.[60] It is therefore against this background that his son chose to serve with Arundel, the senior Appellant, immediately following the Appeal against his father for treason. Indeed, following the forfeiture of his father's estate, Sir Michael was granted some manors at the petition of the earl of Warwick and other lords. Sir Michael's wife was the daughter of Hugh, late earl of Stafford, and the earl of Warwick's niece. Thus perhaps it was due to this association with a senior Appellant that led to de la

---

55 *Royal Household*, p. 283 (under-chamberlain 1390–1393; steward 1393–1399), knight of the chamber and lay officer of the household, of Yorkshire/diverse counties, retained in 1390 (1398).

56 Walsingham, cited in Given-Wilson, *Chronicles of the Revolution*, p. 122.

57 *Handbook of British Chronology*, p. 140.

58 *Royal Household*, p. 287 (steward 1401–1402), knight of the chamber and lay officer of the household, of Yorkshire/diverse counties, retained in 1401.

59 *DNB*, vol. xliv, p. 432.

60 J.S. Roskell, *The Impeachment of Michael de la Pole, Earl of Suffolk in 1386, in the Context of the Reign of Richard II* (Manchester, 1984).

Pole serving in 1388. Sir Michael was also restored to other lands following his father's death. The restoration of the title of earl of Suffolk did not occur until 28 January 1398, following the prosecution of the senior Appellants and annulment of the proceedings of the Merciless Parliament. This first restoration was very temporary and was again removed as a result of the annulment of Richard's last acts on the accession of Henry IV. However, Sir Michael was restored to the earldom of Suffolk, although not the barony of de la Pole, on 15 November 1399, because of his services to the new king.[61]

Sir Michael was born around 1361 and his first service would appear to be leading a retinue of men-at-arms and archers to Calais in 1386, where his uncle Sir Edmund de la Pole was captain. He served in the retinue of the earl of Arundel in 1388, listed fifth on the muster roll and described as banneret.[62] This service was despite his being made a king's knight in 1386.[63] He does not appear to have served in a military capacity in the rest of Richard II's reign, although he was preparing to go on the abandoned crusade to Prussia with the duke of Gloucester in 1391.[64] He did not regain his position of favour with Richard II and this is perhaps due to his actions in 1387–1388 in support of the Appellants. This is demonstrated by Sir Michael securing a royal pardon in 1398, following Richard's prosecution of his enemies of ten years earlier.[65] It is perhaps also pertinent to note that Sir Michael had to wait until 1398 for the estates of his father to be restored, perhaps demonstrating Richard's displeasure with his actions during the Appellant supremacy. Sir Michael decided to support the duke of York against the invasion by Henry in 1399 with a retinue of 138 soldiers.[66] His immediate favour from Henry IV would suggest that alongside York, de la Pole did not put up any actual resistance. He immediately supported Henry IV in his campaign into Scotland in 1400, jointly leading with the earl of Westmorland a retinue of 1200 soldiers.[67] His royal appointments multiplied under the reigns of Henry IV and Henry V, perhaps demonstrating how Richard II had denied him such service and he was not involved in any of the conspiracies against his new king. He died of dysentery on 18 September 1415 whilst serving with Henry V at the siege of Harfleur. His elder son Michael had also accompanied him on campaign and was to be killed at the battle of Agincourt shortly after.[68]

As mentioned before, the father-in-law of the earl of Devon, Thomas, Lord

---

61 Roskell, *The Impeachment of Michael de la Pole*, pp. 200–201; *Complete Peerage*, vol. x, pp. 566–567, vol. xii, i, pp. 441–442, and vol. xii, ii, p. 441; *DNB*, vol. xlvi, pp. 33–34.

62 E101/41/5 m. 1, listed fifth and thirty-first; the second entry has been crossed out subsequently, probably at the muster.

63 *Royal Household*, p. 285, king's knight, of Yorkshire/Suffolk/diverse counties, retained 1386.

64 *DNB*, vol. xlvi, p. 33.

65 C67/30 m. 9.

66 Given-Wilson, *Chronicles of the Revolution*, p. 250, Michael de la Pole, earl of Suffolk, 29 men-at-arms, 109 archers, paid 5–31 July.

67 Brown, 'The English Campaign in Scotland, 1400', p. 47n, the earl of Suffolk (with the earl of Westmorland), led a retinue of 200 men-at-arms and 1,000 archers.

68 *DNB*, vol. xlvi. p. 34.

Camoys, served in the expedition of 1388 as a retinue captain. He had an extensive military career and led the left wing of the army at the battle of Agincourt in 1415. Camoys' career and relationship with Richard II will be discussed in a later section; however, it would be useful to briefly sketch his career now.[69] Camoys inherited his family estates in 1372, although it is not known when he was born. His cousin was William, Lord Latimer and it may have been that his first military experience was gained under his leadership. He may have also served with John of Gaunt in Scotland in 1385 and Castile in 1386.[70] By 1388 he was sufficiently experienced to captain the fourth largest retinue in Arundel's campaign.[71] His relationship with Arundel seems to have been based upon a landholding in Sussex,[72] and perhaps explains his service with the earl despite being attacked and abjured from court by the Appellants, as a favourite of the king in 1388.[73] He did not regain his position of favour in the royal court of Richard II and this is perhaps explained by his actions in support of the Appellants in 1388. His suing for a royal pardon in 1398, when Richard II was attacking those who had opposed him ten years earlier perhaps supports this argument.[74]

He would appear to have regained his influence after the accession of Henry IV and served at the beginning of the reign in Scotland and in Wales. He was also given the responsibility for conducting Henry IV's future bride from Brittany in 1403.[75] His military career continued under Henry V and his great experience meant that he led the rearguard of the army, which was placed on the left wing at the battle of Agincourt in 1415.[76] Perhaps as a result of this service he was made a knight of the Garter on 23 April 1416.[77] Camoys died on 28 March 1421 and had been married twice, secondly to the widow of Henry 'Hotspur' Percy.[78] The biography of Camoys demonstrates the career of a lord who served militarily three kings in succession. Although he appears to have lost ground in the later years of Richard II, his military experience has brought him

---

[69] *Complete Peerage*, vol. ii, pp. 507–508; *DNB*, vol. viii, pp. 306–307.

[70] *DNB*, vol. viii, p. 306.

[71] E101/41/5 m. 6. Enrolled protection, C76/72 m. 6.

[72] *Two Estate Surveys*, p. 140, Thomas Camays: land called Donekeston 3s 0d in Wollavyngton.

[73] John L. Leland, 'The Abjuration of 1388', *Medieval Prosopography*, 15:1 (1994), pp. 115–138, p. 134.

[74] C67/31 m. 11.

[75] *DNB*, vol. viii, p. 307.

[76] For service at Agincourt see *Gesta Henrici Quinti. The Deeds of Henry the Fifth*, ed. and trans. Frank Taylor and John S. Roskell (Oxford, 1975), p. 83, also reprinted in Anne Curry, *The Battle of Agincourt. Sources and Interpretations* (Woodbridge, 2000), p. 34. Camoys led his own retinue in the Agincourt campaign. For sources see: E101/47/13 for muster; E404/31/357 for warrant for issue; E101/45/5 m. 5 for issue roll. He served with a retinue of 90 soldiers including himself as baron, 2 knights, 27 men-at-arms and 60 archers. Protection dated 16 August 1415, *Annual Report of the Deputy Keeper of the Public Records, 44* (London, 1883), p. 571. His brass can be seen at Trotton (Sussex). I am grateful to Professor Curry for all of these references.

[77] N. Harris Nicolas, *History of the Battle of Agincourt* (London, 1833 edn), p. 174.

[78] *Complete Peerage*, vol. ii, p. 508.

to the fore under Henry IV and especially with Henry V on his Agincourt campaign.

A number of other barons are discussed later and therefore a brief sketch will suffice at this stage. Lord Bardolf served in the retinue of the Earl Marshal in 1388 and later joined with the earl of Northumberland in rebellion and was killed at the battle of Bramham Moor in 1408.[79] Reginald, Lord Grey served in the retinue of the earl of Arundel in 1387. Grey is remembered for his part in sparking the revolt of Owain Glyn Dwr in the early years of the reign of Henry IV, and his dispute with Sir Edward Hastings at the court of chivalry. He served in a military capacity for three kings in succession and died at the grand old age of 78 in 1440.[80] John, Lord Lovel can also be identified as serving in the retinue of Lord Welles in the expedition of 1388. He contested another well-known case against Sir Robert Morley in the 1380s at the court of chivalry. He was an active member of the military community and survived the transition to the reign of Henry IV, serving loyally until his death in 1408.[81] Richard, Lord Talbot also served in the retinue of the earl of Arundel in 1387. He was an active member of the military community but died young at the age of just thirty-six in 1396.[82]

It is pertinent to note that two future Lord Says also appear in the muster rolls for 1387–1388. Firstly, Sir John Fawsley married John de Say's sister and heir Elizabeth in 1382. Fawsley served in the retinue of Arundel in 1387 and 1388, and in the later case is described as Lord Say on the muster roll.[83] Following Fawsley's death in 1392, Elizabeth then married Sir William Heron. Heron served in the retinue of Sir Nicolas Clifton in 1387 and captained a retinue in 1388. He was additionally required to explain the reasons for the delay of the expedition in 1388 to parliament on behalf of the earl of Arundel.[84] He was described as *Le Souz Admirall* on the muster roll for 1388, and thus was probably reporting to parliament as part of his official duties.[85] Fawsley was born around 1335 and was thus in his early fifties during the campaigns of the earl of Arundel. He was an active member of the military community and had served in France, Ireland and Scotland.[86] Heron married Fawsley's widow in 1393 and rose to prominence under Henry IV being appointed steward of the household. He fought with Henry against the Percy rebellion in 1403 and died in the following year.[87]

The remaining barons who served in 1387–1388 but who are not featured in the following discussion also deserve a brief mention. John, Lord Beaumont served in the expedition in 1387. Beaumont led the retinue listed third on the

---

[79] *Complete Peerage.*, vol. i, pp. 419–420.

[80] *Ibid.*, vol. vi, pp. 155–158; *DNB*, vol. xxiii, pp. 107–199.

[81] *Ibid.*, vol. viii, pp. 219–221.

[82] *Ibid.*, vol. xii, ii, pp. 616–617.

[83] 1387: E101/40/33 m. 1; enrolled protected, C76/71 m. 12; enrolled attorney, C76/71 m. 10. 1388: E101/41/5 m. 1; enrolled protection, C76/72 m. 7.

[84] E159/167 m. 51 (Brevia Baronibus Michaelmas) and E364/24 m. 5.

[85] 1387: E101/40/33 m. 12d. 1388: E101/41/5 m. 8.

[86] *Complete Peerage*, vol. xi, p. 478 for Elizabeth and vol. v, pp. 250–252 for Fawsley.

[87] *Ibid.*, vol. vi, pp. 492–493. See also the entry for his brother Sir Gerard Heron in *HOP*, vol. iii, pp. 353–356.

muster roll and captained 196 soldiers.[88] He was born in 1361 and was twenty-six years of age when he served with the earl of Arundel. It is interesting to note that he replaced the earl of Arundel as Admiral of the North on 20 May 1389 and held this appointment until 22 March 1391.[89] He also served on other royal appointments and was one of the ambassadors who negotiated for the marriage of Richard II to Isabella of France. Beaumont died in 1396 and therefore was not involved in the revolution of 1399.[90] William, Lord Hylton served in the expedition of 1388 as a retinue captain, leading a force of 112 soldiers.[91] Hylton was born in 1355 and was thus aged 32 when serving with the earl of Arundel. He served with Bishop Despencer in the 'crusade' of 1383 and was retained to serve the king in peace and war with 20 men-at-arms and 20 archers in 1386. He was loyal to Henry IV following the deposition in 1399 and served overseas in 1404. He lived to the ripe old age of seventy-nine, dying in 1435.[92] John, Lord Welles captained a retinue of 73 soldiers in the expedition of 1388.[93] He was also listed second in the retinue of the Earl Marshal on the same expedition. Welles was born in 1352 and first served overseas aged seventeen in the retinue of John of Gaunt in 1369. He was a retainer of the duke of Lancaster from 1372, but became linked with the Earl Marshal in the 1380s following his marriage to his sister in 1386. He was also involved in a famous dispute with Sir David Lyndsay from Scotland, the resulting meeting on London Bridge in 1390 led to Lord Welles becoming unhorsed on the third pass.[94] He was loyal to Henry IV following his seizure of the throne and died aged sixty-nine in 1421.

These brief portraits of the peers involved in the campaigns of Arundel in 1387–1388 have demonstrated a shared background of participation in the English military community. In general therefore, these earls and barons have served in the campaigns of the earl of Arundel because they were royal expeditions. The campaigns were supported by three earls, one future duke, three future earls, nine barons and one future baron. Thus the total of just 17 nobles serving over the two years of the campaign, demonstrate that Arundel had not been able to attract a large number of the higher reaches of society to his campaign. However, a number of those he had recruited later became instrumental in the events of the deposition and its aftermath. Arundel himself was executed in 1397, the Earl Marshal was banished and died in Venice in 1399, Despencer was executed for his part in the Epiphany Plot in 1400, Percy for his revolt in 1403 and Bardolf for his revolt in 1408. Others survived the changeover

---

[88] E101/40/33 m. 4.
[89] *Handbook of British Chronology*, pp. 139–140.
[90] *Complete Peerage*, vol. i, p. 61.
[91] E101/41/5 m. 5d.
[92] *Complete Peerage*, vol. vii, pp. 25–27.
[93] E101/41/5 m. 3. It is also noted that he has already been listed second in the retinue of the Earl Marshal. Lord Welles' muster roll is appended to that of the Earl Marshal, and it may well have been that they served together as one retinue. Enrolled protection, C76/72 m. 7; enrolled attorney, C76/72 m. 8.
[94] Walker, *The Lancastrian Affinity*, p. 284, retained in 1372, served overseas in 1369, 1372 and 1373. See also Goodman, *John of Gaunt*, pp. 290–291 and *Complete Peerage*, vol. xii, ii, pp. 441–443.

to the new regime and prospered. De la Pole met his end after years of service at the siege of Harfleur, Camoys commanded the left wing of the English army at Agincourt and Heron became steward of Henry IV. It is therefore difficult to note any major consistent themes from judging the actions of these men during the revolution of 1399. It will be interesting to discover whether the same is true about those who served as the bulk of the army in 1387–1388. One point of note is that only four of the 16 nobles chose to serve with Arundel in both campaigns, in addition to Arundel himself. Of the others, four serve in 1387 and eight serve in 1388. This perhaps suggests that the barons were more convinced of Arundel's supremacy following the Merciless Parliament and thus served with him on campaign in 1388 when they thought they were joining a winning team. The spectacular success of the expedition of 1387 may well have also attracted a larger number of nobles who were looking for similar gains in the following year. They may have also have been keen to keep the war against France going, as they were apprehensive about potential royal plans for peace. Whatever the reason for service, participation does not predict a lack of royal favour or indeed the inability to loyally serve Richard II or Henry IV. Judgements on loyalty must be made individually as can be seen from the varied portraits of the major figures collected in this section.

Patterns of service between the two campaigns

As I have mentioned, the use of a relational database allows us to compare the two campaigns and investigate the continuity of service by the rank of soldier. The results enable us to analyse the choices being made by these soldiers concerning royal service. How many retinue leaders took part in both expeditions? It is apparent that Arundel knew a large proportion of the retinue captains from the previous expedition as 28 of the 50 retinue captains (other than Arundel himself) in 1388 also served with Arundel in 1387. This includes the service of the Earl Marshal, the earl of Devon and Sir William Heron as previously discussed. This demonstrates that 66% of the retinue captains serving in 1388 had also served in 1387. This high level of re-service by retinue captains who were known to the commander would have provided Arundel with a loyal chain of command. Not all the men served as captains in both expeditions. Fourteen had served previously as either knights or esquires in another captain's retinue in 1387. This high percentage of continuity of service at the level of retinue leader certainly indicates a willingness to risk one's life on two successive campaigns and also that a certain professionalism is evident amongst retinue captains. It also suggests that Arundel would look to the same men to provide the manpower for his expeditions, perhaps suggesting ties that may not be apparent from the other surviving source material.

An expedition commander would indent with the crown to provide a promised number of troops for future specified service. This captain would then sub-contract with a number of other captains, who would each recruit their own retinue, in order to satisfy the requirements of his indenture. It has been shown that a sub-contracting retinue captain could make a tidy profit by paying less than the standard rate to the soldiers he recruited. This profit motive could therefore explain the high proportion of men who serve in both campaigns at the level of retinue captain. Goodman suggests that one possible reason for service as a retinue captain in 1388 may have been the success of the campaign in 1387.[95] However, if the expedition commander did not know a man already, it would seem, from the evidence of the muster rolls, to have been a consideration that he had served and proved himself in another retinue before being 'promoted' to retinue captain.

The biggest retinue captained by a lone esquire is that of John Sly (also written as John Slegh) in 1387 which totals 71 soldiers, and includes one knight, the only time that this occurs in either expedition.[96] The knight is even listed above his captain in the muster roll. To have a knight in his retinue and to be able to command a retinue of this size indicates that John Sly must have had a repute of some magnitude or have been well known to Arundel himself. In fact, John Sly also captained a retinue in the royal expedition to Scotland in 1385, and is described as 'king's butler'.[97] This would therefore explain his ability to captain such a large retinue. Other retinues captained by esquires are of no more than 50 soldiers in size, unless the esquire captains jointly with another esquire or knight. This seems to suggest that in general, esquires were only trusted individually to recruit and control a retinue of less than 50 soldiers. Indeed the average size of retinue captained by esquires was 45 men in 1387, rising to 55 men in 1388. This rise in average size reflects the wider use of joint retinue captains in the campaign on 1388. The prestige and rank of an esquire does not seem to have been considered adequate to recruit, command and maintain discipline in a larger body of men.

Together with the 14 captains who serve again as captains in 1388, 33 more men of knightly status and above serve in both campaigns. Out of 100 knights and peers who served in 1387, 47 served again in 1388. This shows nearly half of the higher ranks involved in the expedition of 1387 agreed to serve again the following year. This kind of continued service that is evident from the muster rolls supports the idea that these men were serving as professional soldiers.

Do any patterns emerge about the service of these individual knights and peers? The evidence suggests that men would serve in the same retinue in the following year unless their previous retinue captain was not campaigning (see Table 10). On only two occasions do knights choose to serve under a different captain. This suggests that loyalty, or at least familiarity, was a factor and that

---

95 Goodman, *Loyal Conspiracy*, p. 131.
96 1387: E101/40/33 m. 18, listed as John Sly or Slegh'. 1385: listed as Slegh, John, king's butler, retinue consisted of 12 men, including 2 esquires and 10 archers, Lewis, 'The Last Medieval Summons', p. 20.
97 The knight was Sir William Dangle, 1387: E101/40/33 m. 18, listed above John Sly. He also served in 1388: E101/41/5 m. 11d. Sir William Dangle can probably be identified as Sir William d'Angle, king's knight of Richard II, retained in 1386 and described as a foreigner, *Royal Household*, p. 284. He also served in Ireland in 1394 in the retinue of Richard II: for protection see *CPR, 1391–1396*, p. 474, and pay roll E101/402/20 mm. 33ff, listed in Mitchell, 'Some Aspects of the Knightly Household of Richard II', Appendix III, pp. 306–309. It was perhaps this connection to Richard II that led to his service with the king's butler in 1387.

ties existed between the captain and his retinue that continued beyond one campaign. However, we can also show that a third of the men were willing to serve again even though the retinue they had been a member of no longer existed. Therefore, these men seem to have been serving either professionally, from loyalty to the commander, loyalty to the crown and patriotism, as part of their professional military career or indeed for personal profit and not just through any sense of loyalty to the individual retinue captain.

Table 10. Loyalty figures for knights and peers

Continuity	No.	%
Continue as retinue captains	14	30
Become retinue captains in 1388	7	15
With same retinue captain in both campaigns	14	30
Serve with different retinue captains: previous captains not serving	9	19
Serve with different retinue captains: previous captain is serving	2	4
Joins a retinue in 1388 after being a captain in 1387	1	2
Total	47	100

Are similar patterns to be discovered amongst the service of the esquires? Of the 1,010 esquires who serve in 1387, 156 esquires also serve in 1388. This means that 15% of the esquires serving in 1387 served again in 1388. The larger force of esquires recruited for service in 1388 had 11% of its number constituted from soldiers who had also served in 1387. This is a smaller proportion than that indicated for the higher ranks, but still a significant core remained at the rank of esquire, which perhaps suggests an element of professionalism. It can be shown, in Table 11, that esquires who choose to serve in the same retinue account for 38% of the esquires who serve in both expeditions. A larger percentage of esquires, 23% compared to 4% in the case of knights, have changed retinues in the second expedition even though their previous retinue captain is also serving. It is difficult to know whether these men have personally decided to change retinue, or indeed the retinue captain has refused to allow them to campaign with him in the following expedition. However, a more comparable number of esquires, 39% against 19% of knights, choose to serve even though they have to join a new retinue. A large percentage of these esquires (62%), therefore campaign in different retinues across the two campaigns. This type of cross-retinue movement again corresponds with the evidence from the court of chivalry in the 1380s used by Ayton, who comments, 'it should occasion no surprise to find regular soldiers, whether knights or esquires, being prepared to look much further afield when choosing a captain'.[98] These men are demonstrating that the business of campaigning was an undertaking which could exist outside the boundaries of tenure and relationships. From this

---

[98] Andrew Ayton, 'Knights, Esquires and Military Service', p. 94.

evidence there seems to emerge a core of men who were serving for their own reasons, be it monetary, glory or a sense of adventure.[99]

Table 11. Loyalty figures for esquires

Continuity	No.	%
Serve with same retinue captain	59	38
Serve under different captain: previous captain is not serving	61	39
Serve under a different captain: previous captain is serving	36	23
Total	156	100

Other interesting comparisons can be found when we look at the men who are knighted during the two campaigns. Both Piers de la Mare[100] and Andrew Hake,[101] knighted in 1387, serve respectively as knight in the retinue of the earl of Arundel and retinue captain in 1388. Piers Besiles[102] and Benedict Cely,[103] knighted on campaign in 1388 had served as esquires in 1387. Here, service has been rewarded. It might suggest that these men were known to Arundel and had proved themselves loyal followers. Indeed it can be shown that Andrew Hake is described as being from Sussex in his letters of protection and appointment of attorney, thus suggesting that Arundel might have known him from county associations. These examples serve to show that relationships were important to some of the men who served in these expeditions and that their reasons for continued service are easily explained. It is not clear on the whole from the muster roll evidence alone whether the men who served in both campaigns did so out of loyalty or for personal gain. They may have served in both years because they enjoyed being on campaign or indeed because they felt that they had a patriotic duty to serve. The motives behind service may remain speculative; however more themes will emerge when case studies of individuals are constructed later in Part 2.

As shown in Table 12, 270 archers have campaigned in both expeditions and can be identified in the muster rolls. This accounts for 19% of the archers in 1387 and just over 13% of the archers in the force of 1388. This is a slightly higher level of continuity than is seen for the rank of esquire. Again a high

---

99 See Andrew Ayton, 'War and the English Gentry under Edward III', *History Today*, xlii, 3 (March 1992), pp. 34–40.
100 E101/40/33 m. 1, described as 'factus chevalier le xxiiii iour de marz'. 1388: E101/41/5 m. 1.
101 1387: E101/40/33 m. 1, described as 'factus chevalier le xviiii iour de marz'; enrolled protection, C76/71 m. 14, as 'Andreas Hake Armiger de com' Sussex' '; enrolled attorney, C76/71 m. 14, as 'Andreas Hake Armiger com' Sussex' '. 1388: E101/41/5 m. 12d; enrolled protection, C76/72 m. 7.
102 1387: E101/40/33 m. 12. 1388: E101/41/5 m. 11d, described as 'factus miles xxviii die Junii'.
103 1387: E101/40/33 m. 1; enrolled protection, C76/71 m. 14. 1388: E101/40/33 m. 15, described as 'factus miles xxvii die Julii'; enrolled protection, C76/72 m. 7.

Table 12. Loyalty figures for archers

Continuity	No.	%
Serve with same retinue captain	78	29
Serve under different captain: previous captain is not serving	91	34
Serve under a different captain: previous captain is serving	101	37
Total	270	100

proportion of archers, over a third at 37%, choose to serve under a different captain, even though their captain from 1387 is serving. However, the majority of archers, 63%, serve either with the same captain in both years, or only serve under a different captain because their earlier captain did not participate. These figures therefore show that a significant number of archers were willing to serve in both campaigns. It is also evident that choice of captain was not important for the archer in many cases as over a third were willing to serve in different retinues over the two campaigns. It is interesting to note that 30 of the 78 archers who serve under the same captain in both campaigns are serving with Sir Hugh le Despencer. These archers account for a third of the 94 archers which he has recruited in his two retinues in 1388. Sir Hugh's is the only retinue which shows such a high level of continuity and suggests that these archers may have had a special relationship with their retinue captain which explains this unusually high level of loyalty.

Table 13 demonstrates the continuity of service across the ranks for the campaigns of 1387 and 1388. The continuity is shown in terms of numbers of each rank, and then as a percentage of the force for each year. It can be shown that in total, across the ranks in the expeditions, 473 individuals have chosen to serve in both campaigns. The percentage of continuity of service for both campaigns drops from 100% for the peers, to just under half for knights and then just 13% and 16% for esquires and archers respectively. This continuation of service accounts for 19% of the total force in 1387 and 13% of the larger force in 1388. This demonstrates that a core of soldiers representing 16% of the two expeditionary armies consisted of men who were willing to risk their lives on an overseas expedition twice in two years.

This information has been gained by careful analysis of the existing muster rolls and has thrown additional light on the potential existence of 'professional' soldiers who were involved in these campaigns. By studying the muster rolls it can be shown that a significant number of men have campaigned across both expeditions. A certain professionalism is suggested at the level of retinue captain, where 66% of the captains in 1388 had previously served in 1387. This is perhaps unsurprising considering that it is through these subcontractors that Arundel would have raised his expeditionary force. Arundel would have known these captains, some of whom were serving as men-at-arms in 1387. He would have seen their abilities in war and in managing groups of soldiers in the battle situation and would have used these skills in the recruitment and management of the larger force in 1388.

Table 13. Comparative continuity of service

	no.	Continuity of service 1387 %	1388 %	overall %
Peers	3	100	100	100
Knights	44	51	37	43
Esquires	156	15	11	13
Archers	270	16	13	16
Total	473	19	13	16

It is also evident that the knights who campaigned on both these expeditions were professional in their outlook to service on royal expeditions. A higher percentage of these men, nearly a half of the total number of the force over both years, serve on both campaigns. The continuity of service of esquires and archers whilst still of significance only accounts for around 15% of the total force. So why did men serve on both campaigns? Was it because they were professional soldiers with a career in the king's service? Perhaps they served for profit or as a result of a successful experience in 1387. They may have served out of a sense of patriotism or because they enjoyed the camaraderie of an over-seas campaign. We will attempt to answer this question by looking in detail at the background, relationships and future actions of some of the individuals whom we can trace in the sources. It will also be interesting to test the positive spin of Walsingham who commented that Arundel,

> made every effort to get good, reputable men. He therefore avoided conscript-ing cobblers and tailors from London and other cities, such as some had con-scripted previously on low pay in order to put more money in their own purse. . .The earl on the other hand, as we have said, spared no expense, and chose men of valour whom he knew, in order that he could achieve something great for his country.[104]

Case studies drawn from the evidence provided by letters of protection

It can be shown that twelve men served in both of the expeditions of 1387 and 1388 and also secured protections for both campaigns. These include Sir Hugh Browe, who served in Arundel's retinue in 1387,[105] and who had been promoted to retinue captain in 1388.[106] This promotion can probably be assigned to his success in the previous expedition when he was a prominent member of Arundel's own retinue. It is possible to build on this information and to create a

---

[104] *The St Albans Chronicle*, p. 809.
[105] E101/40/33 m. 1; enrolled protection, C76/71 m. 12.
[106] E101/41/5 m. 8d, described along with retinue captain Sir William Heron as *Le Souz Admiralls* – the under-admiral in this campaign. Enrolled protection, C76/72 m. 8.

fuller picture of a member of the military community. The fact that Browe took out enrolled letters of protection for both campaigns suggests that he was a man with substantial landholding that required protection whilst he was abroad. However, his name is one that is mentioned in many of the discussions of the military community from this period, and we can therefore make a substantial attempt to outline what kind of man he was.

Sir Hugh Browe can more precisely be described as Sir Hugh Browe of Teigh and Woodhead (Rutland) and Tushingham (Cheshire).[107] Andrew Ayton has identified him as being a witness at the Scrope-Grosvenor trial in 1386–87, where he testified that his twenty years in arms had been spent 'in the garrisons of France, and never on great expeditions'.[108] Therefore the information provided for the 1387 -88 campaigns in this present study gives additional information showing that he had decided to join in the expeditions of these years. Sir Hugh Browe appeared in Parliament as member for Rutland in 1388 (February), the Merciless Parliament, and 1390 (November).[109] It is interesting to note that his first attendance at parliament is at the Merciless Parliament. This could indicate evidence of the Appellants trying to control Parliament through their supporters. His attendance in both expeditions would support such a supposition. It is also of interest to note that one of his circle of friends, Sir Oliver Mauleverer, also appears at the Merciless Parliament and serves in the expedition of 1388.[110] Although the *History of Parliament* discusses Sir Hugh's military career it fails to mention his involvement in the expedition of 1388.

Sir Hugh Browe was born in 1346 and died in 1403. He was married three times and was knighted by March 1376.[111] Browe claimed kinship with Sir Robert Grosvenor, whom he supported in 1386, during his dispute, with Lord Scrope. On his own evidence, Sir Hugh had by then spent more than twenty years on active service, mostly in France, where he took part in several campaigns as well as being employed on garrison duty. In 1369, he and Grosvenor fought together at the siege of La Roche-sur-Yon under the banner of James, Lord Audley. The two men also served in the army that Richard II took to Scotland much later in 1385.[112] His connection with Sir Robert Knollys involved him in the struggle of John Montfort, duke of Brittany, against the French. He was entrusted to the custody of Derval castle during Knollys' capacity as lieutenant of Brittany. Browe denied taking part in any major continental expeditions in the Scrope v. Grosvenor case. However he was in Edmund, earl of March's planned retinue in 1374 and he was with Knollys and John of Gaunt on the expedition to Gascony in 1378.[113] His military fame was such that

---

107 *HOP*, vol. ii, *1386 – 1421*, pp. 384–386.
108 Ayton, *Knights and Warhorses*, p. 188, n. 264. *Scrope v. Grosvenor*, vol. i, p. 82, vol. ii, p. 266.
109 *HOP*, vol. ii, *1386 – 1421*, p. 384.
110 E101/41/5 m. 13d. Enrolled protection, C76/72 m. 7.
111 *VCH: Rutland*, vol. ii, pp. 153, 232–233.
112 *Scrope v. Grosvenor*, vol. i, pp. 82, 256–257, vol. ii, p. 266.
113 Muster roll for the expedition of 1378: E101/36/32 m. 3.

Froissart mentions him by name in his description of the siege of St Malo during the campaign of 1378.

> The siege of St. Malo was directly commenced, for they were in sufficient numbers to undertake it: they overran the country, and did much damage. Those who were most active in this business were sir Robert Knolles, and sir Hugh Broc his nephew, who were well acquainted with those parts. These two made excursions daily, and the canon de Robesart in company with them. Some days they lost, and at others gained: they, however, burnt and destroyed all round St. Malo.[114]

In 1380 he took out letters of protection as he intended to accompany Thomas of Woodstock on his Breton expedition. The *History of Parliament* comments that Browe again took up arms in March 1387 as a member of the highly successful naval expedition mounted by Richard, earl of Arundel, against the allied French, Spanish and Flemish fleets. It is not noted there that he also served in 1388. He went on to also serve in the king's expeditions to Ireland in 1394[115] and in April 1399 he was instructed to raise a force of Cheshire archers for the king's expedition to Ireland. Following Richard's deposition he appeared loyal to Henry IV. However, this was to end with his support of the Percy rebellion in 1403. This was surprising, as he was serving in the company of Prince Henry against the Welsh rebellion[116] when he decided to desert from the royal cause and join the Percies. If he did not die at the battle of Shrewsbury on 21 July 1403, he was dead by 16 August of that year.[117] His son, Robert, was pardoned for his part in the rebellion.[118]

It can be seen from the entry in the *History of Parliament* and also other sources that Browe's relationship with Arundel was well secured. His position in the retinue of 1387, listed twentieth, would suggest some seniority has already been established by this time, and that a relationship may have already existed. Goodman identifies Browe as a retainer of Arundel. He suggests that Arundel retained Browe because of his great military experience.[119] Philip Morgan provides an insight into the dangers of campaigning overseas as even though Browe has taken out an enrolled protection, 'in 1387 Sir Hugh Browe's manor house at Christleton was robbed of clothes and silver objects during his absence with the earl of Arundel'.[120]

This relationship can indeed be traced back to as early as 1378 when Browe can be shown to have served in Arundel's retinue in Gascony on the campaign led by John of Gaunt.[121] At this stage he is listed third in Arundel's retinue,

---

114 Froissart, *Chronicles*, vol. i, pp. 544–545.
115 1394: *CPR, 1391–1396*, p. 489 (protection).
116 W.R.H. Griffiths, 'The Military Career and Affinity of Henry, Prince of Wales, 1399–1413' (M.Litt. thesis, Oxford University, 1980), p. 22.
117 Morgan, *War and Society in Medieval Cheshire*, pp. 82–83; Browe forfeited 39 horses as a result.
118 *CPR, 1401–1405*, p. 265.
119 Goodman, *Loyal Conspiracy*, p. 120.
120 Morgan, *War and Society in Medieval Cheshire*, p. 155, citing Chester 25/8 m. 23.
121 E101/36/32 m. 3.

which would suggest a relationship had already been established at this early part of his career. The *History of Parliament* suggests that the expedition of 1387 marks the beginning of a long association that proved to be of crucial importance in furthering his career. However, from the evidence in the muster roll for the expedition of 1378 it can be seen that he had already served in Arundel's retinue prior to the campaign of 1387 and thus had a relationship at least of eight years.

The entry in the *History of Parliament* suggests that it was quite possibly through Arundel's influence that Sir Hugh first entered parliament in 1388 to help the Lords Appellant impeach the king's chief ministers. It suggests that Browe played an active and willing part in this scheme as he was given a grant of land for his services. The *Calendar of Patent Rolls* lists the following award during the Appellants' control of government:

> Licence with the assent of the Council, for Richard, earl of Arundel, to demise his manors of Trofford and Dunham, co. Chester, with the appurtenances (except knight's fees and advowson), held in chief, to Hugh Browe, knight, for life.[122]

This generous gift of land is dated 16 March 1388 between the two expeditions and can be seen to be a reward for Browe's past service and continuing loyalty. Is this relationship with Arundel something that tainted his relationship with the crown? It may be expected that Browe, as a loyal retainer of Arundel, would therefore find this loyalty questioned when Arundel was executed in 1397. This is indeed the case and Browe had to secure a royal pardon at this time.[123] The necessity for a pardon at this time may also suggest that Browe was involved in the battle of Radcot Bridge, although this cannot be known for certain. Browe however proved to be something of a survivor and a man with a long and interesting career, ending at the battle of Shrewsbury in 1403.

From the evidence provided by the muster rolls and the enrolled protections, we have identified a man who had a long career, much of it in the service of the earl of Arundel. Nethertheless, he managed to survive the fall of his mentor and to rebel against Henry IV. How typical is such a man of the military community represented in the expeditions of these years? Was his relationship with Arundel unusual or were the expeditions populated with retainers like him?

As I mentioned earlier it is possible to draw information on colleagues with whom Browe was involved during his life from sources such as the *History of Parliament*. It is interesting to note that some of these men can also be identified on the muster rolls for 1387 and 1388. Of the land that Browe received from Arundel, it is stated that he subsequently farmed out this property to Sir Ralph Vernon and others at an annual rent of £51.[124] Sir Ralph Vernon, like Sir Hugh

---

[122] *CPR, 1385–1389*, p. 433.
[123] C67/30 mm. 3 and 4. These pardons state that those listed joined with Arundel and Gloucester in their treasonable acts against the king in the tenth year of his reign. They do not mention specifically that the pardons are for fighting at Radcot Bridge.
[124] *HOP*, vol. ii, p. 384.

Browe, was also a retine captain in 1388, although he did not serve in 1387.[125] Vernon was also a local Cheshireman and may have been connected with Arundel because of this. Also, it is of note that Sir Ralph Vernon was sent by the king to muster his forces against the Appellants prior to the battle of Radcot Bridge.[126] This suggests therefore that an appearance in the campaigns of these years did not depend on previous loyalties: Vernon had been in the royal army at Radcot Bridge, yet served on campaign under Arundel.

Another colleague of Browe from Cheshire, Sir John Calveley, was also a representative in the Parliament of 1390. Sir John Calveley can be identified as serving as a retine captain in 1387 and in the retinue of the Earl Marshal in 1388. He also took out a letter of protection for his service in 1387.[127] In the *History of Parliament*, the relationship is shown to be close, as Sir John Calveley married Sir Hugh's widowed mother-in-law, Margaret Folville. Sir John is described as also being from a Cheshire family related in some way to Sir Robert Knollys.[128] As Sir John Calveley was also an MP he has an entry in the *History of Parliament*. He is described as Sir John Calveley of Stapleford (Leics.) and Teigh (Rutland). It is interesting to note that Browe is also described as being from Teigh (Rutland), demonstrating that Browe and Calveley were indeed neighbours. Calveley served as MP for Rutland in 1383 (October), Leicestershire in 1385, Rutland in 1390 (November) and Leicestershire in 1397 (September). Although there is not a date for his birth, he died in 1403 and was probably knighted between October 1383 and November 1384.[129] As the nephew of Sir Hugh Calveley, it is not surprising to find that he was involved in military matters. In 1384 he served in the garrison of Berwick upon Tweed for one year under the command of the earl of Northumberland. He is also identified as taking part in the expedition of 1387, but not that of 1388. Although closely connected with Sir Hugh Browe, his son-in-law, their loyalties can be seen to be otherwise divided. Although Sir John also needed a royal pardon in 1398,[130] taken on the same day as Sir Hugh Browe, he was also a king's knight of Richard II.[131] He was later a loyal supporter of Thomas, duke of Norfolk, the Earl Marshal who also campaigned in 1387 and 1388. The *History of Parliament* comments on this relationship:

> When the duke left England as an exile in October 1398, Calveley was among the band of 80 well-wishers who accompanied him to Lowestoft, and although other evidence of their association has so far not appeared, we may justifiably assume that it had by then grown fairly strong.[132]

---

[125] E101/41/5 m. 9, described as being 'vacat' on 29 August 1388, and had left the expedition early.
[126] *Knighton's Chronicle*, p. 419.
[127] 1387: E101/40/33 m. 17; enrolled protection, C76/71 m. 14. 1388: E101/41/5 m. 3.
[128] *HOP*, vol. ii, p. 385.
[129] *HOP*, vol. ii, p. 467–469.
[130] C67/30 m. 3.
[131] *Royal Household*, p. 284, retained for life, of Cheshire/Leicestershire, in 1394.
[132] *HOP*, vol. ii, p. 469.

The *History of Parliament* has not found any other information linking Calveley to the Earl Marshal, but from the evidence provided by the muster roll for 1388, we can see that this relationship was established ten years earlier, when he is listed eighth in the Earl Marshal's retinue.[133] It is also noteworthy that although a retinue captain in 1387, Calveley has chosen to serve in the retinue of the Earl Marshal in 1388. He is the only retinue captain in 1387 who chooses to continue his service under another captain in the subsequent campaign.

Even though a king's knight he did not find it unseemly to join with Henry IV. As noted in the *History of Parliament*:

> Calveley clearly did not scruple to throw in his lot with the newly-crowned Henry IV, who, in December 1400, gave his 'dear bachelor' custody of the manor of Stapleford with rents to the value of £40 a year. Our member was one of the six persons summoned in the following July to represent Leicestershire at a great council. He did not, however, live long enough to improve upon his fortunes as a supporter of the house of Lancaster, for he was killed (and died intestate) while fighting for the king, on 21st July 1403, at the battle of Shrewsbury.[134]

Philip Morgan comments that he in fact died fighting as a rebel, as a keeper of his estate was appointed in 1404 'by reason of his forfeiture and outlawry'.[135] However, it is not clear that his estate was lost because he was a rebel, as it would seem that his lands were forfeit because he had offered sureties of £200 for another rebel Sir Richard Vernon. Indeed, the *Calendar of Patent Rolls* clearly records that this was indeed the reason for his goods being declared forfeit.[136] It would appear that he had been fighting for the king, but had ironically been tainted because of his relationship with one of the rebels.

Another interesting point to note is that Calveley leaves the country in 1396, as he appointed attorneys for the supervision of his affairs in England. He had returned by the second parliament of 1397. It is not clear what purpose he travelled overseas for.[137] Could it be possible that he had gone on expedition to the crusade of Nicopolis in 1396? Another possible participant at Nicopolis is Sir Ralph Percy, and Calveley had indeed previously served with the Percies at Berwick-upon-Tweed. Various European chroniclers place an English contingent at the final battle of the crusade,[138] but modern historians have disagreed

---

133 E101/41/5 m. 3.

134 *HOP*, vol. ii, p. 469.

135 Morgan, *War and Society*, p. 216, with reference to: DL28/15 m. 17d, m. 185; *Annales Richard Secundi et Henrici Quarti*, p. 369.

136 *CPR, 1401–1405*, p. 353, 'Grant to John Calveley and John Swerston, administrators of the goods of John Calveley, "chivaler", who died intestate, of all his goods, taken into the kings hands on his death on account of an outlawry against him in a foreign country, because he was mainpernor of Richard Vernon "chivaler", to the value of £200, that they may pay his debts and execute his will for the safety of his soul.'

137 *HOP*, vol. ii, p. 469.

138 This paragraph on Nicopolis draws upon Adrian R. Bell, 'England and the Crusade of Nicopolis', *Medieval Life*, issue 4 (Spring 1996), pp. 18–22, p. 19. For the chroniclers see Froissart, *Chronicles*, p. 618; Antonio Fiorentino in L. Muratori (ed.), 'Antonio Fiorentino – Chronica Volgare', *Rerum Italicarum Scriptores*, xxvii, part ii (Cita de Castella, 1900–23);

over the accuracy of such remarks. The question of English involvement was addressed in an article by Charles L. Tipton.[139] Tipton argued that the English were not involved in the expedition on the grounds that he could not identify any individual leaving England in order to be at Nicopolis. As we have seen Sir John Calveley has left the country and has been unaccounted for long enough to have served in the crusade. Tipton also provided evidence to show that the suggested participants could be placed elsewhere at the time of the crusade. Palmer argued against Tipton's conclusions and provided other evidence to support his opposing case.[140] Neither work has answered the question of English participation satisfactorily, but recently other historians have stated that John Beaufort, the son of John of Gaunt, was present at Nicopolis.[141] The participation of an English contingent at Nicopolis is perhaps a subject that deserves further study.

The careers of these three men, Browe, Vernon and Calveley, connected as they are by service in the campaigns of 1387 and 1388 and their Cheshire links, give an interesting insight into the military community. Even though they have ties of kinship, they have still had varied careers and show several links with different masters. This is demonstrated in the experience of 1403 where Sir John Calveley died fighting for the king at the battle of Shrewsbury and Sir Hugh Browe died fighting for the rebels. What becomes clear is that personal and local relationships were as important to these men as loyalty to the Crown. In addition although they serve in the expeditions of 1387 and 1388, their actual relationships within national politics can be seen to be slightly different. Whilst it is not clear from the sources whether Vernon had a direct relationship with the earl of Arundel, Sir Hugh Browe was a close colleague, and according to Goodman, a retainer of the Appellant earl, whereas Calveley was a king's knight and a close supporter of the Earl Marshal, who was also an Appellant and was present on the expeditions. Both these men however found it necessary to secure pardons on the same date in 1398; therefore they were seeking immunity from prosecution by the Crown for something they had been involved in. It may be fair to suggest that during the years of Appellant supremacy, both men had shown disloyalty to the king, and so, following the king's attack on the Appellants, protected themselves against further troubles.

Can we elucidate the careers of other participants who have also taken protections and served in both expeditions? Do they also reveal such complex ties of loyalty? John Chesterfield serves in both campaigns at the rank of esquire.[142] However, although he serves in Arundel's retinue in the first expedition, he serves in the retinue of Sir John Grymesby in 1388. Sir John de Brewes serves in Arundel's retinue in 1387 and has been promoted to retinue captain in

Schiltberger in *The Bondage and Travels of Johann Schiltberger*, ed. J.B. Telfer, Hakluyt Series, 58 (London, 1879).

[139] Charles L. Tipton, 'The English at Nicopolis', *Speculum*, 37 (1962), pp. 528–40.

[140] Palmer, *England, France and Christendom*, Appendix (o), pp. 239–240.

[141] Goodman, *John of Gaunt*, p. 203; N. Housley, *The Later Crusades, 1274–1580: From Lyons to Alcazar* (Oxford, 1992), p. 75.

[142] 1387: E101/40/33 m. 1d; enrolled protection, C76/71 m. 12. 1388: E101/41/5 m. 10d; enrolled protection, C76/72 m. 7.

1388, commanding jointly with Sir Andrew Hake.[143] Andrew Hake is an esquire in the retinue of Arundel in 1387, is knighted on campaign on 19 March 1387 and has been promoted to retinue captain in 1388.[144] Hake was also a king's knight of Richard II and was executed for his support of the Epiphany Plot in 1400.[145] John Fort is an archer in the retinue of Sir Hugh Le Despencer in 1387 and an esquire in the retinue of Sir John Wogan in 1388.[146]

Sir Hugh le Despencer is captain of a retinue in 1387 and of two retinues in 1388.[147] Knighton mentions that the French captured him in 1387,[148] but he had obviously been released in time to serve in the following campaign. It is not likely that Sir Hugh le Despencer was related to Thomas, Lord Despencer, the future earl of Gloucester, who also serves in the campaign of 1388 in the retinue of the earl of Arundel.[149] He can be identified as the Sir Hugh le Despencer, who was the governor of the young Henry, Prince of Wales, and in charge of his household force in 1401 at the siege of Conway Castle. W.R.H. Griffiths, in the study of Henry IV's military career and affinity, describes how Sir Hugh le Despencer of Colly Weston (Nhants) was the nephew of Bishop Despencer. The description of this career does not mention his service in 1387–1388, but describes how Sir Hugh was responsible for teaching the young prince martial arts. He had served at Brest in 1389 and was in Aquitaine between April 1400 – January 1401 to receive the duchy for the king. He died in October 1401.[150] He can also be shown to be a king's knight for Richard II from 1391[151] and subsequently served in the king's retinue in Ireland in 1394 and on the royal expedition to Ireland in 1399.[152] His transition to the new regime was swift and Henry IV retained him in 1399,[153] and as mentioned he was also appointed to the governership of Prince Henry. His previous loyalty to Richard II was not a problem and did not halt his advancement under Henry IV.

Sir Edmund Missenden is a knight in Arundel's retinue in 1387 and 1388.[154] He was also a MP as knight of the shire of Buckinghamshire in 1393.[155] From

---

[143] 1387: E101/40/33 m. 1; enrolled protection, C76/71 m. 12. 1388: E101/41/5 m. 12d; enrolled protection, C76/72 m. 7.

[144] 1387: E101/40/33 m. 1. Knighted on campaign and described as, 'factus chevalier le xviiii iour de marz'; enrolled protection, C76/71 m. 14; enrolled attorney, C76/71 m. 14. 1388: E101/41/5 m. 12d; enrolled protection, C76/72 m. 7.

[145] *Royal Household*, p. 285, from 'Gloucestershire/Sussex', retained in 1397, also pp. 224–225 for reference to execution for support of the Epiphany Plot.

[146] 1387: E101/40/33 m. 9; enrolled protection, C76/71 m. 12. 1388: E101/41/5 m. 18; enrolled protection, C76/72 m. 7.

[147] 1387: E101/40/33 m. 9; enrolled protection, C76/71 m. 14. 1388: E101/41/5 m. 10 and 18; enrolled protection, C76/72 m. 7.

[148] *Knighton's Chronicle*, p. 391

[149] *Complete Peerage*, vol. iv, pp. 278–282. E101/41/5 m. 1.

[150] Griffiths, 'The Military Career and Affinity of Henry, Prince of Wales', pp. 9, 167–168.

[151] *Royal Household*, p. 284, retained for life, of Northants, in 1391.

[152] 1394: *CPR, 1391–1396*, p. 483 (protection), p. 498 (attorney). 1399: *CPR, 1396–1399*, p. 541 (attorney).

[153] *Royal Household*, p. 288, retained for life, of Northants, in 1399.

[154] 1387: E101/40/33 m. 1; enrolled protection, C76/71 m. 12. 1388: E101/41/5 m. 1; enrolled protection, C76/72 m. 6.

[155] *HOP*, vol. iii, p. 740. Again his participation in 1387 is noted but his participation in 1388

his entry in the *History of Parliament*, it can be shown that he was born in 1355 and died in 1394 and was knighted before June 1369. In the expedition of 1387 he was thirty-two years old, and had probably served in other overseas expeditions, thus gaining his knighthood. The *History of Parliament* mentions his relationship with Arundel on the expedition of 1387 but does not mention his service in 1388. Sir William Swalewe is the only knight in the retinue of Sir Arnold Savage in 1387 and the only knight in the retinue of Sir Nicholas Clifton in 1388.[156]

Sir Thomas West was in the retinue of Arundel in 1387 and had been promoted to retinue captain in 1388.[157] He has also been identified as a king's knight.[158] More light is shed on this individual's career with a few references to a Sir Thomas West in the *Calendar of Patent Rolls*. His father appears to have died in 1386[159] and is also pardoned for his acquisition of land in the same year.[160] This reference is important as also in the same pardon a John Dauntesey is mentioned. This provides valuable insight into the relationships within the retinues as Sir John Dauntesey is also in Arundel's retinue in 1387.[161] Therefore, West is serving with an associate of his father. This shows that the relationships within the retinues, when identifiable, are strong and sometimes lengthy. Local relationships can be seen to be continuing into service together in military expeditions. Thomas West himself is also pardoned for acquisition of land and is described as 'Thomas West son and heir of Thomas West'.[162] It is also possible to gain information from the Inquisition Post Mortem for the Sir Thomas West who died in 1386.[163] He is recorded as dying on 3 September 1386 (9 Richard II). The age of his son, the Sir Thomas West who serves with Arundel, is given as twenty-one years on 2 July 1386. He was therefore twenty-two when serving in Arundel's retinue in 1387, and twenty-three years old when he captained a retinue in 1388, although it should be noted that it was common to say that an heir was twenty-one (the age of knightly majority) even if the heir was over twenty-one years of age. Inquisitions were conducted on the elder Sir Thomas West's possessions in Somerset, Dorset, Warwick, Gloucester, Devon, Southampton and Wiltshire. Sir John Dauntesey is also mentioned in two of the inquisitions, showing that the relationship with West's father was close.[164]

Sir Thomas West's father held land from Sir Edmund Fitz Herbert, who also

---

is missed. His most important connection was with his uncle, Sir Bernard Brocas. Otherwise, no significant connections have been found, apart from this service with the earl of Arundel.

[156] 1387: E101/40/33 m. 6d; enrolled protection, C76/71 m. 14. 1388: E101/41/5 m. 11; enrolled protection, C76/72 m. 7.

[157] E101/40/33 m. 1; enrolled protection, C76/71 m. 14. 1388: E101/41/5 m. 7; enrolled protection, C76/72 m. 6.

[158] Mitchell, 'Some Aspects of the Knightly Household of Richard II', p. 237.

[159] *CPR, 1385–1388*, p. 289, described as late citizen of London.

[160] *Ibid.*, p. 249.

[161] E101/40/33 m. 1.

[162] *CPR, 1385–1388*, p. 242.

[163] *CIPM*, xvi, 7–15 Richard II, nos 490–496.

[164] *CIPM*, xvi, nos 495 and 496.

served with Arundel in 1387.[165] Fitz Herbert also took out an enrolled protection and attorney for this expedition. Fitz Herbert is listed eleventh in Arundel's retinue and West is listed sixteenth in the same retinue. This implies a local land relationship continuing in a military expedition. Fitz Herbert is especially of interest because he is a victim of war, recorded as being killed on expedition on 28 April 1387.[166] This unfortunate incident is confirmed by the entries in the Inquisitions Post Mortem. Here he is recorded as dying on 20 April 1387 and his heir is recorded as Alice West.[167] Alice West was in fact Thomas West's mother. Thus Fitz Herbert's and Thomas West's proximity in the retinue list can be shown to be representative of their actual relationship. This indeed is evidence of an uncle and nephew serving together in an expedition overseas. Thomas West was perhaps only twenty-two; therefore his uncle has taken him with him on expedition to give him the benefit of his experience. Unfortunately, this did not work out as expected.

The *History of Parliament* outlines Fitz Herbert's military experience. Born in 1338, he went on expedition with Gaunt in 1372 and then in the retinue of the earl of Salisbury in 1377. He campaigned in Scotland in 1385, before meeting his death with Arundel in 1387. He was an MP on six occasions, and his association with Arundel probably began with his friendship with Sir Edward Dallingridge. He stood surety at the Exchequer in 1380 for Dallingridge and mainpernor for Arundel in 1381 whilst at Westminister. From the *History of Parliament*:

> FitzHerbert was also recorded as a witness to a grant made early in 1385 by the earl of Arundel to the chapel of St. Laurence, Putney, and that summer he rode north in Arundel's company to join the king's army, which was about to invade Scotland. There can be little doubt that in the Parliament of 1386 FitzHerbert and Dallingridge, who was his fellow shire knight (of Sussex), were well disposed to support the policies of the earl and his colleague, the duke of Gloucester, when they attacked the court party and took control of the government.[168]

The *History of Parliament* therefore places Fitz Herbert, with Dallingridge, clearly in the circle of Arundel. Fitz Herbert was a follower of Arundel and therefore, when required, supported him in his retinue for campaigning overseas. Fitz Herbert's link with Sir Thomas West shows how a member of the retinue could in turn bring along a member of his family to introduce him to the military community. It is these links which can be identified from different sources that provide much illumination about the makeup of a retinue and thus provide important information about the military community. One could serve, such as Fitz Herbert, because of a relationship with the commander, or one

---

165 *Ibid.*, no. 495. E101/40/33 m. 1; enrolled protected, C76/71 m. 14; enrolled attorney, C76/71 m. 10.
166 E101/40/33 m. 1, described as 'mort le xxviii iour d'aprill'.
167 *CIPM*, xvi, nos 400–403. This is different from the date recorded on the muster roll which records his death as 28 April: see previous note.
168 *HOP*, vol. iii, p. 79.

could serve, as in the case of West, because of a relationship with his uncle. Unfortunately, for Fitz Herbert, this was a relationship which brought death, and for West a lesson in the perils of warfare.

Another combatant who has secured protections for both expeditions and who is present in the muster rolls is Gyles Weston. Weston was an esquire in the retinue of Sir Thomas de Poynings in 1387 and has been promoted to a retinue captain in 1388, commanding jointly with David Russel.[169] This advancement could be explained by his description in the enrolled protection as being from Herefordshire, as Arundel was a large landowner in this region. Also his retinue captain in 1387, Sir Thomas de Poynings, seems to have had a close relationship with Arundel, which resulted in his eventually marrying his widow.[170] Like Sir Hugh Browe, Poynings had also served in 1378 in Arundel's retinue on Gaunt's expedition to France. Thus, Poynings can be seen to have had a long military relationship with Arundel.[171] The fact that he actually married his widow, implies this relationship was extremely close.

One further example of a man who has taken out protections and also served in both years is Sir Ralph Whithors, who was in Arundel's retinue in 1387 and 1388.[172] No further information has been discovered to throw more light on his career; however from his prominent position within Arundel's retinue for both expeditions, it could be assumed that he was a close supporter of the earl.

Another name that has appeared in the previous discussion is that of Sir Edward Dallingridge, who has a close relationship with a number of other combatants in the muster rolls. From the available evidence, he also appears to have been a close supporter of Arundel.[173] There is also a wealth of secondary evidence concerning this individual. From the *History of Parliament* it can be seen that he was a member of parliament for his county of Sussex on no fewer than eleven occasions. He also held a great number of administrative positions within Sussex at various times during his lifetime. His relationship with the earl of Arundel began at a young age, when he accompanied the earl's father in the royal army that invaded France in 1359–60 at the age of only 13.[174] However, he also served for other commanders. He accompanied Lionel, duke of Clarence to Milan in 1367, and he was also in trouble for failing to join the expedition of Sir Robert Knollys in 1371 after receiving an advance payment of wages. In 1371, he again accompanied Arundel on the naval expedition led by Humphrey, earl of

---

[169] 1387: E101/40/33 m. 8; enrolled protection, C76/71 m. 14, as 'Egidius Weston de Weston in com' Herford' Scutifer'. 1388: E101/41/5 m. 16d; enrolled protection, C76/72 m. 7.

[170] Listed seventh in Arundel's retinue in 1378, E101/36/32 m. 3. For his marriage to Arundel's widow see Goodman, *Loyal Conspiracy*, p. 118.

[171] 1387: E101/40/33 m. 8; enrolled protection, C76/71 m. 12. 1388: E101/41/5 m. 6d.

[172] 1387: E101/40/33 m. 1; enrolled protection, C76/71 m. 14. 1388: E101/41/5 m. 1; enrolled protection, C76/72 m. 6.

[173] Sir Edward Dallingridge had taken a protection for 1387 and attorney for 1388 but only served in 1387. He was, however, serving as captain of Brest in 1388. 1387: E101/41/5 m. 1; enrolled protection, C76/71 m. 12. 1388: enrolled attorney, C76/72 m. 8 (his son-in-law Thomas Sackville is named as attorney; see *HOP*, vol. ii, p. 740 for their relationship).

[174] *Scrope v. Grosvenor*, vol. i, p. 164.

Hereford, and in 1373 he was with John of Gaunt on his great chevauchée from Calais to Bordeaux. In 1374 he also received a lifetime annuity from John, duke of Brittany, of £40 per year to be paid from the duke's Sussex estates. In 1374 he went on naval expedition with Edward, Lord Despenser, and again in 1375 in support of the duke of Brittany. He became attached to Richard, earl of Arundel, following the death of the earl's father, and it was this relationship that would prove the strongest throughout the rest of his career. He accompanied Thomas of Woodstock on his Brittany expedition of 1380, and assisted Arundel in 1381 in the quelling of the Peasants Revolt in Sussex. He was also involved in the protection of the Sussex coast from French attack and indeed was seriously wounded in one such incursion. He was granted a licence to crenellate his castle at Bodiam on 21 October 1385, in order to defend against such French incursions.[175] He ran into conflict with John of Gaunt over his Sussex holdings and was indeed imprisoned because of his actions, only to be freed due to the influence of this patron, Arundel. In 1385 he attended the royal expedition to Scotland in the retinue of the earl of Arundel.[176]

The *History of Parliament* claims that he was a major supporter of Arundel in his move to take over the administration of the realm with the duke of Gloucester. It also comments that he was involved in the organisation of the fleet in 1387, and took a prominent place on the flagship. It suggests that he would have been a member of Arundel's retinue who fought at Radcot Bridge. He was even appointed in Sussex to take the oaths pledging support for the Lords Appellant. He helped organise and finance the second expedition in 1388, and supplied his own ship, *The Trinite* of Winchelsea, for service. The reference to Dallingridge helping finance the expedition is probably referring to the inclusion of Dallingridge in the accounts for the campaign. It is stated that he collected £40 of the advance payment for the campaign and brought it to Southampton where the army was mustering. Although this implies a close relationship, this does not mean that he financed the expedition as suggested in the *History of Parliament*.[177] As was pointed out, he did not serve in this expedition, even though he had taken out a protection. This was probably because Arundel made him his lieutenant as captain of Brest, where he spent the winter.[178] It would appear that Dallingridge served with the Appellant forces who opposed the duke of Ireland in 1387, as his tenants and son were required to pay 500 marks in 1398 for a pardon, remission and quitclaim resulting from his disloyalty.[179] Despite this, following the dismissal of the Appellants, Dallingridge was able to make himself indispensable to Richard II and was appointed to the Council on 4 May

---

[175] *VCH Sussex*, vol. ix (London, 1937), pp. 258–262. *CPR, 1385–1389*, p. 42.

[176] *CCR,1385–1389*, p. 6, Richard, earl of Arundel, Edward Dalyngrugge, Edmund Fitz Herberd and William Waleys, in the king's company to Scotland.

[177] For advanced payment see E101/41/4, Arundel's accounts for the expedition of 1388. *HOP* references this source and therefore this is perhaps a misunderstanding of the account. It is not clear where *HOP* has sourced the information regarding his involvement in the campaigns of 1387–1388.

[178] *CPR, 1388–1392*, p. 118, Edward Dalyngrugge, supplying the place of the captain of Brest castle.

[179] *CPR, 1396–1399*, p. 341.

1389. He evidently made a good impression and was created king's knight in the same year.[180] For the rest of his career he was a prominent member of the king's council. His association with Arundel did not affect him politically. Dallingridge died in 1393 before the tumultuous occurrences later in the reign and before his new loyalty to the king was tested.[181] His only son, Sir John, who also served on both expeditions, succeeded him.[182]

Saul suggests that following the Appellant crisis, Richard II had a deliberate policy of recruiting men of local influence in order to be able to use them to secure royal will in the shires. One such retainer was indeed Sir Edward Dallingridge, who had much influence in the county of Sussex. Saul does not claim that this was a deliberate policy to attract retainers of the Appellants in order to undermine their local influence. However, men such as Dallingridge with their connections would have empowered Richard against his former opponents within their circle of influence. The example of Dallingridge demonstrates that ties of loyalty were certainly fluid and those who had been previously loyal to the Appellants were able to later gain much influence within the royal circle. Saul mentions that the level of fee paid by the king would also influence these ties. Dallingridge was retained for 100 marks per annum, whereas the average fee paid by the king was 40 marks or £40 per annum. Knights in the service of private lords would have received an average of £20 per annum. The king therefore was able to pay above the market in order to attract the retainers he wanted.[183]

We can again find friendships identified within the secondary sources that are mirrored in the retinue membership from the muster rolls. Saul comments that Sir Edward Dallingridge was a friend of Sir Phillip Medsted.[184] Medsted also served as a knight in the retinue of Arundel, both in 1387 and 1388.[185] From what we have seen, such a level of service within Arundel's personal retinues would be expected to reflect other connections with the earl. Medsted was close to Arundel in his own right as a Sussex landowner. Indeed, it can be seen that he successfully petitioned the council at the Cambridge Parliament of 1388,[186]

---

[180] *Royal Household*, p. 284, of Sussex, retained for life, 1389.

[181] The summary of his career is taken from his entry in *HOP*, vol. ii, pp. 738–742.

[182] Sir John Dallingridge also served in both expeditions as an esquire, but did not take out protections or attorney for either expedition. *HOP* mentions the expedition of 1387 but not that of 1388: *HOP*, vol. ii, pp. 742–744. 1387: E101/40/33 m. 1d. 1388: E101/41/5 m. 8. He later served with Henry, earl of Derby, in Prussia and prospered under his reign as Henry IV.

[183] Saul, *Richard II*, pp. 265–268.

[184] Nigel Saul, *Scenes from Provincial Life: Knightly Families in Sussex, 1280–1400* (Oxford, 1986), citing S. Walker, 'Lancaster v. Dallingridge: A Franchisal Dispute in Fourteenth Century Sussex', *Sussex Archaelogical Collections*, 121 (1983), p. 89. On 25 July 1384, at Arundel's request, Philip Medsted obtained from the king a pardon for a felony (PRO, KB27/502 Rex m. 11).

[185] 1387: E101/40/33 m. 1. 1388: E101/41/5 m. 1.

[186] *CPR, 1385–1389*, p. 517. Also, J.A. Tuck 'The Cambridge Parliament', *English Historical Review*, lxxxiv (1969), p. 241, citing a petition to the Cambridge Parliament of 1388, where 'Philip Mestede presented a petition in which he alleged that the former chief justice of king's bench, Sir Robert Tresilian, had corruptly obtained from him the manor of Clawton in Devon, and he successfully sought restitution'.

which followed the return of the expedition of that year, for the restitution of a manor from the former chief justice of the King's Bench. Such loyal service to Arundel has therefore been rewarded in real terms by the Appellants towards the end of their period of authority. It is also interesting to note the following entry in the *Calendar of Patent Rolls*:

> Revocation of protection for one year granted 28th January last to Philip de Mestede, knight, as going to Brittany on the king's service in the company of Edward Dallyngryge, supplying the place of the captain of Brest castle, because he tarries in England on his own affairs.[187]

It would seem that he had not fulfilled his obligation to serve with Dallingridge in Brest during 1389. This does show that he had a relationship with another of Arundel's retainers; however on this occasion he has not served as promised.

The initial conclusion from this survey of the available evidence is that many of these individuals who have taken protections for both expeditions and also appear on the muster rolls have strong links with Arundel. This implies that there was at the very least a hard core of participants who already had a relationship with the earl and who were therefore trusted allies and supporters. The expedition would have therefore been peopled with at least a minority of Arundel's supporters that meant that these particular campaigns might have been different in composition to that of a regular overseas expeditionary army in the service of the crown. In addition these case studies have shown that a number of these individuals have family or local ties with one another and are campaigning together within a retinue. This demonstrates that men would serve because of a relationship with the commander or because of ties of kinship and local relationships as a shared experience. These case studies and the personal links demonstrated within them have emerged from the study of those who served and took out protections for both campaigns. More themes regarding motives for service will emerge when we investigate other ties of loyalty.

---

[187] *CPR, 1388–1392*, p. 118.

4

Recruitment and the Military Community

Recruitment

Arundel must have recruited captains who he knew would be able to provide him with the troops he required in order to prosecute his campaigns. The earl would probably know some of these men but there also may have been a pool of professionals from which the earl could have drawn.[1] The captains themselves would have then to sub-contract with the men who would serve in their own retinues. A retinue captain could contract with knights or esquires who would then also bring archers to the retinue, or indeed other men-at-arms. This can be seen in the retinue roll for 1387, E101/40/34, where some soldiers are linked to individual knights within each retinue, showing an earlier connection prior to muster, that is not apparent in the later muster roll for 1387, E101/40/33. For instance Sir Richard Seymour has brought Sir John Rodeney and Sir Richard Talbot has brought Sir Homan Vaghn to the retinue of the earl of Arundel for the expedition of 1387.[2] In the joint retinue of Sir Hugh Lutterel, Sir Robert Hemenale and John Wormyngton, esquire, in 1387, each member of the retinue has a note next to his name indicating to which retinue captain he had come to the muster with. It would therefore appear that each of these captains has brought his own independent retinue to the muster and they have been merged into one retinue for the purposes of the campaign.[3]

It is evident that captains would also have drawn upon their own personal retainers. The retinue captain, the earl of Nottingham, Earl Marshal,[4] in the expedition of 1388, has three men in his retinue, namely Sir Thomas Clinton, Sir Richard Basset and Richard Burgh,[5] who later would take out private indentures

---

[1] Walsingham states that Arundel recruited, 'men of valour whom he knew', *St Albans Chronicle*, p. 809.
[2] Seymour, E101/40/33 m. 1. Rodeney is not listed on this muster roll and has therefore not been present in the muster undertaken prior to embarkation. E101/40/34 m. 1 lists Mons' John Rodeney and it is noted 'with Seymour' next to his name. Talbot and Vaghan, E101/40/33 m. 1 and E101/40/34 m. 1; the latter roll lists Mons' Hamon' Vaghan and notes 'with Talbot' next to his name.
[3] E101/40/33 m. 15, Lutterel's force consisted of 1 knight, 14 esquires and 23 archers; Hemenale's force consisted of 1 knight, 14 esquires and 20 archers; Wormington's force consisted of 10 esquires and 8 archers. Wormington, although a joint retinue captain, is only listed with the esquires on the muster roll.
[4] E101/41/4 m. 3.
[5] *Ibid.*, listed fourth, eighteenth and twenty-eighth in the retinue of the Earl Marshal.

for life service in peace and war with the Earl Marshal.[6] According to Jones and Walker, only around 150 of these indentures have survived. The survival of three such indentures for one retinue would suggest that this practice was prevalent. It may also suggest that it was the service in 1388 that led to the men later being retained by the earl. Whichever way these existing indentures are interpreted, the evidence shows just how strong the links could be between captain and his retinue.

The question of recruitment was tackled in an article by Neil Jamieson, 'The Recruitment of Northerners for service in English Armies in France, 1415–50'.[7] Although covering a slightly later period, I believe that the same principles of recruitment would apply. Jamieson claimed that a captain's retinue would come from his locality and would have a regional character. He showed this through evidence from muster rolls and sub-contracts. Men who were friends would serve together, as would men from the same family. This can also be seen from my own research on the expeditions of 1387 and 1388.

The most obvious relationship would be that between the retinue captain and his retinue. It would not be a surprise that such a leader would bring members of his family along for moral support and companionship. If retinue captains are considered, the following have men with the same surname in their own retinue (see Table 14). Family ties were undoubtedly important in the recruitment of retinues, and this is further reinforced by the muster roll for 1388. Here cross-retinue links can be identified which show that family relationships were important in the constituent parts of the expedition. The earl of Devon's father-in-law was Lord Camoys,[8] who is a retinue captain in his own right, and the earl of Devon has a Hugh Camoys in his personal retinue.[9] This pattern of family service can be seen when the individual members of a retinue are also considered. There are esquires and archers in the same retinue with the same surnames, suggesting members of families would decide to go on expeditions together.[10] This has also been demonstrated in the earlier case study of Sir Edmund Fitz Herbert, who served in the same retinue as his nephew, Sir Thomas West, in 1387.

Those listed in the table above would therefore appear to be serving because of family links with the retinue captain. But were soldiers within the constituent retinues bound by other formal loyalties to the captain?

6   Michael Jones and Simon Walker (eds), 'Private Indentures for Life Service in Peace and War 1278–1476', *Camden Miscellany XXXII*, Camden Society, Fifth Series, vol. 3 (London, 1994), Indentures 76, 79 and 80.
7   Neil Jamieson, 'The Recruitment of Northeners for Service in English Armies in France, 1415–50', in Dorothy L. Clayton, Richard G. Davies and Peter McNiven (eds), *Trade, Devotion and Governance: Papers in Later Medieval History* (Stroud, 1994), pp. 102–115.
8   E101/41/5 m. 6; enrolled protection, C76/72 m. 6.
9   E101/41/5 m. 4.
10   For instance E101/41/5 m. 6. Sir Thomas Camoys' retinue has the esquire Johan Algode, listed fourteenth in the retinue, and the archer William Algode, listed ninety-sixth in the retinue. This pattern is repeated throughout the constituent retinues.

Table 14. Family links with Retinue Captains

Retinue captain	Likely family members in retinue
1387	
earl of Arundel	earl Marshall (son in law)[1]
earl of Devon, Edward Courtenay	Sir Hugh Courtenay and Sir John Grenville (his cousin)[2]
Sir Reginald de Cobham	Raynold Cobham and Banlyn Cobham (esquires)[3]
Richard Cryse	Henry Cryse and Geffray Cryse (esquires)[4]
1388	
earl of Devon	Sir Hugh Courtenay[5]
Sir Ralph Vernon	Thomas Vernon and James Vernon (esquires)[6]
Sir John Coupeland	Thomas Coupeland (esquire)[7]
Sir John de Brewe	Richard Brewe (esquire)[8]
Sir Robert Massey	Banlyn Massey and John Massey (esquires)[9]
John Staple	John Staple (esquire)[10]
Aleyn Seintjust	Martin Seintjust (esquire)[11]
Giles Weston	Stacy Weston (archer)[12]
Richard Cryse	Henry Cryse (esquire)[13]

[1] E101/40/33 m. 1, listed first and second in the muster.
[2] E101/40/33 m. 3, listed first, second and sixth in the retinue.
[3] E101/40/33 m. 6, listed first, thirty-sixth and forty-seventh in the retinue. Raynold Cobham, enrolled protection, C76/71 m. 14.
[4] E101/40/33 m. 19, listed first, third and fourth in the retinue. Richard Cryse, enrolled protection, C76/71 m. 19.
[5] E101/41/5 m. 4, listed first and second in the retinue.
[6] E101/41/5 m. 9, listed first, fifth and twenty-fourth in the retinue.
[7] E101/41/5 m. 12, listed first and second in the retinue. Thomas Coupeland, enrolled protection, C76/72 m. 7.
[8] E101/41/5 m. 12d, listed first and second in the retinue. Sir John de Brewe, enrolled protection, C76/72 m. 7.
[9] E101/41/5 m. 14, listed first, fifth and sixth in the retinue. Sir Robert Massey, enrolled protection, C76/72 m. 7.
[10] E101/41/5 m. 14d, listed first and fourteenth in the retinue.
[11] E101/41/5 m. 16, listed first and seventh in the retinue.
[12] E101/41/5 m. 16d, listed first and forty-second in the retinue. Giles Weston, enrolled protection, C76/72 m. 7.
[13] E101/41/5 m. 17, listed first and third in the retinue.

Arundel's estates

The question of whether Arundel recruited from his own lands can be tackled partially by comparing the names on the muster rolls with those contained within two estate surveys of the Fitzalan earls of Arundel compiled by Marie Clough.[11] The two surveys have been recorded at different times throughout the fourteenth century. The author dates the first, survey books A and C, to 1301

[11] *Two Estate Surveys*. In this section I have kept the medieval placenames in the footnotes and used the modern placename in the text. For the modern placenames I have used the glossary in *Two Estate Surveys*, pp. 175–183.

Table 15. Comparison of landholding against military service

Captain	1387			1388			Total
	Knight	Esquire	Archer	Knight	Esquire	Archer	
Arundel, Richard, earl of	4	6	13	1	8	12	44
Le Counte de Devens	1	4		1	4	7	17
Le Counte Marshall				1	1	3	5
Richard Cryse		1	4		1		6
Mons Gilbe Talbot		2	3		1		6
Thomas atte Lee			1		1	3	5
Mons Johan Darundell			3			2	5
Mons Hugh le Despencer		1	2		2		5
Mons Thomas Ponynges				1	3	1	5
Mons Hugh Browe			1		1	2	4
Le Sire de Beaumount		2	2				4
Johan Staple		1	2		1		4
Mons Reynold de Cobham		1	3				4
Robert Geffard		1			1	1	3
Mons William Elmham		1	2				3
Mons Johan Bohun				1	1	1	3
Mons Hugh Loterell			3				3
Aleyn Seintjust					2	1	3
Mons Thomas Trevet		2				1	3
Mons Johan Sandes					2		2
Benet Cely						2	2
John Slegh			2				2
Mons William Briene					1	1	2
Mons Johan Wynkefeld			1			1	2
Mons William Briene					1	1	2
Mons Andrewe Hake					2		2
Mons William Heron						2	2
Mons Henry Jugloos					1	1	2
Mons Thomas Camoys				1			1
Richard Waynill						1	1
Mons Robert Massey					1		1
Mons Johan Coupeland					1		1
Mons Thomas Percy					1		1
Esmon Randulph					1		1
Mons Robert Mounteney			1				1
Mons Nichol Clyfton			1				1
Mons Thomas Mortemer		1					1
Pyers Vanbusth		1					1
Mons Rauf Vernon						1	1
David Lacy						1	1
Richard Shingulton		1					1
Esmon Randulph						1	1

John Hayward		1					1
Mons Johan Grymesby						1	1
Mons Richard Craddok		1					1
Mons Piers de Bokton						1	1
Le Monser W Sire de Welles						1	1
Total	5	27	44	6	38	49	169

and the second, survey book B to around 1400, at the time that Earl Thomas Arundel recovered his late father's estates following Henry IV's assumption of power. It is the second survey that has most relevance to the current research. It is therefore of interest to investigate the number of tenants of the earl of Arundel who can also be identified as taking up arms with their lord in his overseas expeditions. The tenants described in survey book B hold lands mainly for rent, although in some manors they also hold lands for work and rent.

The second survey is limited in its geographical extent and contains information regarding landholding in the honour of Arundel and thus only covers those who were wholly or partially resident in Sussex. The survey does not detail the earl of Arundel's other landholdings in the Welsh Marches, Shropshire, Wiltshire, Norfolk and Surrey. Nevertheless, a high level of correlation can be found between those listed in the survey and those appearing in the muster rolls for 1387 and 1388. In Sussex there is no mention of any type of military service in return for holding the land. Therefore these men are serving perhaps out of loyalty to their lord and king, because their fellow tenants were also serving, or because they were hoping to gain financially by serving in the expedition. It is evident that Arundel has recruited from his own lands and has utilised people whom he knew and could trust.

Table 15 summarises the pattern of landholding within the retinues. The numbers of Arundel's tenants in each of the constituent retinues is indicated by rank and totals are given for each retinue captain. It can be seen that Arundel's tenants in Sussex are spread throughout the constituent retinues in both expeditions. In addition the tenants are found throughout all the ranks of the expeditionary army, from archer through to retinue captain. In total 169 individuals hold land and also serve with Arundel in his expeditions. The largest number of tenants can be found in Arundel's own retinues with 44 tenants serving in his retinue in both years. Most interestingly however, Arundel's tenants are spread throughout 46 different retinues over the two expeditions. It would therefore appear that Arundel has somehow publicised his expedition and actively recruited from his tenantry. They have taken up this invitation in large numbers, and not just to serve in his retinue. This spread throughout the retinues would provide Arundel with a number of key supporters throughout the army. As mentioned above this survey is concentrated upon Arundel's lands in Sussex, it would likely follow that many more men from Arundel's other holdings would have also taken part in the expeditions. It may also be that many of these tenants, drawn as they are from Sussex; would be interested in joining these campaigns, leaving from a southern port. They are geographically close to the point of embarkation, Sandwich in 1387 and Southampton in 1388, and this may also account for the large number of tenants found to be serving on the campaigns.

The information provided by the survey enables us to provide insights into the backgrounds of the soldiers who are fighting in these expeditions. It is possible to identify the land holdings of senior figures and also the archers in the muster rolls for whom other significant evidence does not survive. The most senior figure who can be found to be a tenant of Arundel is his son-in-law, the Earl Marshal.[12] The Earl Marshal serves in both years, firstly in the retinue of Arundel and secondly with his own retinue. He can be shown to be holding two pieces of land in Sussex within the demesne of Bourne. In addition to homage, he owes rent and also must provide a sparrowhawk and one pound of pepper for the land.

In addition to the Earl Marshal, three other retinue captains can be identified as holding land as a tenant of Arundel. Sir John Bohun holds separate pieces of land in three different areas of Sussex.[13] Bohun serves in both expeditions, firstly in the retinue of Arundel and secondly captaining his own retinue.[14] It is significant that two other members of Bohun's retinue in 1388 also hold land of Arundel. Firstly, Bartholomew Boditon holds a quarter of a knight's fee and a virgate of land for rent.[15] Boditon serves as an esquire in the retinue of Sir John Bohun in 1388 following his service as an esquire in the retinue of the earl of Arundel in 1387.[16] Boditon also has to secure a royal pardon in 1398,[17] thus indicating that he was probably involved in the events supporting the Appellants in 1387–1388. Secondly, Richard Tanner holds land and a cottage in two manors for rent, goods and services.[18] Tanner serves as archer in the retinue of Sir John Bohun in 1388.[19] Tanner has also gone to the trouble of securing a royal pardon in 1398.[20] From this information it can be shown that all three men hold land from Arundel; further, Bohun and Boditon both hold land in the manor of Woolbeding. It is evident that these men would have known each other and had local ties that were cemented by serving together in the overseas expedition. It is also of interest to note that the rank of soldier is reflected in their social land-

---

[12] *Two Estate Surveys*, p. 157, 'Stoghton Manor for homage & 1 soar sparrowhawk or 6*s* 8*d*; Also the land "Hurst" for 1 lb. pepper in Bourne'.

[13] *Ibid.*, p. 140, 'Taillardeslond for homage and fealty in Wollavyngton'; p. 144, '1 virgate 1*s* 0*d* in Wolbedyng'; p. 169, 'land 7*s* 8*d* in Estden'.

[14] 1387: E101/40/33 m. 1; enrolled attorney, C76/71 m. 10. 1388: E101/41/5 m. 7.

[15] *Two Estate Surveys*, p. 136, Batholomew Boditon: '¼ knights fee as free tenant of Bygenenore'; p. 144, '1 virgate 14s 0d, in Wolbedyng'.

[16] 1387: E101/40/33 m. 1d. 1388: E101/41/5 m. 7.

[17] C67/30 m. 3.

[18] *Two Estate Surveys*, p. 138, 'Messuage 4s 0d in Westeburton'; p. 158, 'Messuage & 5a for 1 hen, 5 eggs and 3s 6d. He owes 2 boonworks, stooks oats ½ a day, hoes for a ½ a day, packs once on foot, makes a hurdle of the lord's withies, reaps 2½a wheat and barley, and carries the lord's fold. Also 1a in Aylond 3s 0d. Also Clipan's cottage 10½d. He owes 2 boonworks, stooks and hoes as above; and pays ½d for Swellemede in Bourne'.

[19] E101/41/5 m. 7.

[20] C67/30 m. 15, 14 June 1398, of Cheltenham, Gloucs. The description of his location does not match the information we have about him owning land in Sussex. This may therefore not have been his principle residence.

holding status. The archer, Richard Tanner, is required to perform a long list of services for the land he holds from Arundel unlike his colleagues Bohun and Boditon.

Sir Thomas Camoys also holds land for rent in the manor of Woolavington.[21] Sir Thomas serves as a retinue captain in the expedition of 1388.[22] Even though he holds land from Arundel and also served in 1388, he shows mixed alliances and was forced to withdraw from the court as a result of his support of the king in 1388.[23] In addition, it is interesting to note that Camoys was discharged from parliament as knight of the shire for Surrey in 1383. This was because he was a banneret, and Richard II claimed that bannerets were not eligible for election.[24] Although he was attacked for being a favourite in 1388, his subsequent service with Arundel, and other actions in the years of Appellant supremacy, resulted in him having to secure a pardon in 1398.[25]

Sir Thomas de Poynings is detailed as a tenant of Arundel.[26] Poynings can be linked militarily with Arundel from 1378 when he serves in his retinue on expedition with John of Gaunt. He then serves as retinue captain in the expeditions of 1387 and 1388.[27] This additional link found in the estate survey demonstrates the close relationship between Poynings and Arundel, which is cemented when Poynings marries Arundel's widow after the death of the earl. In addition to Poynings himself, three other tenants of Arundel can be identified in Poyning's retinue in 1387 and 1388. Richard Wodeland, esquire, seems to be a major landholder in Sussex.[28] He is obviously a man of some local status as the last two of this list are held as a free tenant. With this amount of land held from Arundel, it is no surprise to find him in the expedition of 1388.[29] However, without the evidence from the survey, his appearance in the muster rolls would have gone unnoticed as a supporter of Arundel. Robert Frye, esquire, also appears to be a major landholder.[30] Frye serves in Poynings' retinue in the expedition of 1388.[31] Finally, the archer Thomas Fletcher, who serves with Poynings in 1388,[32] also

21 *Two Estate Surveys*, p. 140, 'land called Donekeston 3s 0d in Wollavyngton'.

22 E101/41/5 m. 6; enrolled protection, C76/72 m. 6.

23 John L. Leland, 'The Abjuration of 1388', *Medieval Prosopography*, 15:1 (1994), pp. 115–138.

24 D. Crouch, *The Image of Aristocracy in Britain, 1000–1300* (London, 1992), p. 118.

25 C67/31 m. 11.

26 *Two Estate Surveys*, p. 115, 'free suitor to the court of the honour of Arundel for Westerton'.

27 1378: E101/36/32 m. 3. 1387: E101/40/33 m. 8; enrolled protection, C76/71 m. 12. 1388: E101/41/5 m. 11d.

28 *Two Estate Surveys*, p. 118, 'The tenement he lives in 1s 2d; Tenement in the corner 7d; Roper's tenement 7d; 3a on Le Ligher 1s 9d; Total 4s 1d in Arundell'; p. 119, 'Caryas' tenement 1s 0d; 1 Chanell 7d; House in Chupyng 7d in Arundell'; p. 125, '5 roods 1½d (listed beneath John Wilteshire) in Polyng'; p. 126, 'Messuage & 4a 2s 0d as Free Tenant in Lunemenstr' '. p. 131, '6a. meadow for 1½lb cummin and 1d. as Free Tenant in Offham'.

29 E101/41/5 m. 6d.

30 *Two Estate Surveys*, p. 114, 'free suitor to the Hundred court of Bourne'; p. 155 '(blank) for 1 lb. of pepper and 3s 0d; Also 2 virgates 10s 0d; 4a. 2s 0d in Oupmerdon'; p. 156, 'with Edith Carpenter, 6a 5s 4d in Compton; 8a. 3s 5d in Bymthe; part of Bourne manor'.

31 E101/41/5, m. 6d.

32 *Ibid.*

holds land. This evidence shows that Arundel was able to use his tenants to captain retinues, which were in turn populated by more tenants. It is also significant that the three retinues of Bohun, Camoys and Poynings are all listed in sequence on the muster roll in seventh, eighth and ninth position. This shows that these retinues have been given a prominent position at the muster and that the listing of these retinues in order, reflects their position as tenants of Arundel.

When looking at the retinues of Arundel himself, it can be seen that he has three knights who hold land and serve in his retinue in 1387, and one knight who holds land and serves in his retinue in 1388. Accompanying Bohun in 1387 were Sir Henry Hussey[33] and Sir Edward St John.[34] Hussey owns two separate parcels of land, one as a free tenant and the other for one pound of cummin.[35] Clough suggests that such rental in kind could be seen as a token and therefore perhaps suggests a strong link between tenant and lord.[36] This can indeed be shown from the other surviving evidence which shows that Hussey was a close and loyal supporter of Arundel.[37] St John held three parcels of land throughout Sussex, for rental and for one pound of pepper. This payment in kind again suggests a close relationship with Arundel. It is interesting to note that St John leaves Arundel's retinue during the period of rest at Orwell following the initial sea battle in 1387.[38]

In 1388 only one knight in Arundel's retinue, namely Sir John Wiltshire,[39] can be identified as holding lands in Arundel, including a 'garden beneath the castle', land in Poling for payment of one arrow and land in Offham.[40] It is evident from the amount of lands that Wiltshire holds as a tenant of Arundel that they had a close relationship, although other direct evidence of this does not survive. However, he can be identified as securing a royal pardon in 1398, which states that it was for the support that he gave the Appellants in 1387–1388.[41] Perhaps to cement this newly found support for Richard II, he can be found on campaign in Ireland with the king in 1399.[42]

There are also a good number of esquires serving in 1387 and 1388 who can also be identified as holding land in Sussex. Of these, of special interest are

---

[33] E101/40/33 m. 1.

[34] *Ibid.*, described as 'Vacat de xxix iour d'aprill'.

[35] *Two Estate Surveys*, p. 123, 'Messuage & croft for 4s 0d as free tenant in the Manor of Angemeryngg.' Page 149, 'Knighteslond, otherwise Wodeslond, for 1 lb. Cummin (margin: Note for Garton) in Lygh'.

[36] *Ibid.*, p. xxx.

[37] *HOP*, vol. iii, pp. 462–464.

[38] Goodman, *Loyal Conspiracy*, p. 110.

[39] E101/41/5 m. 1.

[40] *Two Estate Surveys*, p. 117, 'Garden, lately Somdon (?) 9d; p. 118, 2 messuages, 'Leante's' 2s 0d; Half of Hernys tenement 6d; Botiller's tenement 1s 7d; The tenement beside it 1s 0d; 1½a meadow 5¼d; 'Schopp' in mid-street 3½d; Nicholas Kyng's former tenement 6d; Atheryngton's tenement 2d; Garden un Didestrete 9d; 1a formerly Hereward's 1s 0d; 2a in the field 2s 0d; 2a on Le Ligher 6d; Garden beneath the castle 6d; Croft by Mary's Gate 3d; Plot formerly Bovat's 1d; half of Sewale's croft 5d; Total 12s 7¾d in Arundell'. Page 125, '¹⁄₆ of a fee 1 arrow in Polyng; & Thomas Warnecamp, 2a meadow 3d as free tenant in Offham'.

[41] C67/30 m. 3.

[42] *CPR, 1396–1399*, p. 541 (attorney), p. 545 (protection).

Wauter Haket, esquire, and Richard Romyn, esquire, listed next to each other on the muster roll in Arundel's retinue in both 1387 and 1388.[43] These men can also be identified as holding neighbouring land in the same hundred of Bourne in Sussex.[44] This is evidence of men holding land from the earl of Arundel, deciding to serve under him in both of these expeditions and presumably also deciding to accompany their neighbour, and perhaps friend, to the expedition. The close identification of these two men on the muster rolls suggests that the order of names could be a significant source of information on retinue connections. These men are serving together in the spirit of shared experience from the position of shared background. Further to this, Haket also required a pardon in 1398 for his earlier adherence to the Appellants.[45] Another esquire who can be found serving in both expeditions and also who is a tenant of Arundel is John Babelake.[46] Babelake is a free suitor to the hundred-court of Rutherebrugge and also jointly holds land in Pallingham.[47] Babelake can also be shown to be a loyal supporter of Arundel from other evidence and thus his appearance in the muster rolls demonstrates the earl's reliance upon his tenants for building his expeditions. Babelake also had to secure a pardon in 1398.[48]

It is possible to investigate whether other tenants of Arundel holding land in the same locality also serve together in a retinue within the expeditions. In this way it is possible to throw light on the behaviour of men who served as archers as it may show that they chose deliberately to serve with people whom they knew. It can be shown that John Kyng, archer,[49] and William Cok, esquire,[50] who both serve in the retinue of Sir William Briene in 1388 have holdings within Pallingham in the hundred of Bury.[51] John Kyng can be shown to have secured a royal pardon in 1398 and also to be serving in the retinue of Arundel on Gaunt's expedition in 1378.[52] This archer has therefore a long-standing relationship with Arundel, which meant he needed a pardon after Arundel's prosecution in 1397. William Cok also demonstrates a wider military experience and served with Sir William de Windsor in Buckingham's army in France and

---

[43] 1387: E101/40/33 m. 1, listed sixty-ninth and seventieth in retinue. 1388: E101/41/5 m. 1, listed forty-eighth and forty-ninth in retinue.

[44] *Two Estate Surveys*, p. 142, Haket: '2 virgates, 'Mynstede' 4s 0d in Cockyng'; p. 154, Haket, 'Aldewineslond 10s 0d in Aldesworth in the hundred of Bourne'. Page 154, Romyn: 'Tenement formerly Marcolf's 16s 0d in Northewode in the hundred of Bourne'.

[45] C67/30 m. 3.

[46] 1387: E101/40/33 m. 1. 1388: E101/41/5 m. 1.

[47] *Two Estate Surveys*, p. 100, 'free suitor to the Hundred-court of Rutherebrugge, for lands in Keredeforde.' Page 149, 'jointly with William Steghere: holds the demense and 1a in Palynghame'.

[48] C67/30, m. 2.

[49] E101/41/5 m. 9.

[50] *Ibid.*

[51] *Two Estate Surveys*, p. 142, Kyng: 'Messuage 2s 0d in Wollavyngton'; p. 142, 'Messuage 5s 0d in Wonneworthe'; p. 150, '1 virgate 9s 10d. Also a cottage in Bournehou 6d in Palynghame'. Page 151, Cok: '1 virgate, 3s 4d in Palynghame'.

[52] C67/30 m. 2.

Brittany in 1380–1381.[53] John Leche, archer,[54] and Simon Godefrey, esquire,[55] who both serve in the retinue of Sir William Elmham in 1387 also have holdings in Bourne.[56] It is therefore likely that these men knew each other and probably discussed their intended service prior to joining the expedition. John Leche may also have taken a royal pardon in 1398.[57]

Another such example is that of John atte Hall, Richard Mareschall and John Fuller,[58] archers in the retinue of the Earl Marshal. These men are listed within 25 men of each other amongst the archers serving with the Earl Marshal in 1388. Without the evidence from the estate survey they would have remained simply names within the muster roll. However, from the survey we can see that they all hold land within the demesne of Storrington within the hundred of Bourne in Sussex.[59] These men who are serving together also held lands within the same area and were therefore serving in the expedition with a sense of shared experience. John Fuller may also have secured a royal pardon in 1398.[60] Further to these ties, it is also possible to identify the relative of John atte Hall, namely Thomas atte Hall, with whom he holds his land jointly in Storrington within the muster rolls. Thomas atte Hall served in the retinue of Thomas atte Lee, esquire in the same expedition.[61] Another such example can be identified in the retinue of Sir William Heron in 1388, where two of Arundel's tenants are listed next to each other in the list of archers. The tenants, Robert Kyng and Wauter Smyth, both hold lands within Sussex but not within the same hundred.[62] This demonstrates that bands of loyalties would have stretched beyond the tenant's most immediate neighbours. Smyth also can be found on campaign with Sir William de Windsor in 1380–1381.[63] Both of these men may also have taken royal protections in 1398.[64]

---

53 E101/39/7 m. 3.

54 E101/40/33 m. 11d.

55 *Ibid.*, m. 11.

56 *Two Estate Surveys*, p. 158, 'Cottage for services like Clipan's and 1s 0d, he owes 2 boonworks, stooks oats ½ a day, hoes for a ½-day, packs once on foot, makes a hurdle of the lord's withies, reaps 2½a. wheat and barley, and carries the lord's fold; and Also 1a. in Aylond 3s 0d; Also a plot of land 9d; Also 1½a. in Wodecroft 1s 6d; Also ½a. in Tounfeld 1d. in Bourne. Page 160, Simon Godefray: 5a. for services like Fauconer and 3s 0d. He packs once with a horse, hoes, harrows, carts corn and performs 3 boonworks; pays 2d. towards the Arundel mowing and 2d. for nuts; and harvests corn for half a day in Bourne'.

57 C67/30 m. 9, 'of Gamlingay, Cambs'. However, this location does not match his landholding in Sussex, thus suggesting that Sussex was not his primary residence.

58 E101/41/5 m. 3d, listed 129th, 145th and 153rd in the retinue.

59 *Two Estate Surveys*, p. 133, atte Halle: 'with Thomas atte Halle, 20a. (blank) in Storgheton.' Marchall: p. 133, 'Cottage 1s 0d in Storgheton'; p. 150, 'Twelfponylond 1s 0d in Palynghame'; p. 151, 'cottage 2s 0d, also Gryg's tenement 6d in Palynghame.' Fuller: p. 132, 'Cottage 1d in Storgheton'.

60 C67/30 m. 23, 'of Banbury (Oxon)'. Again John Fuller is described as of Banbury rather than Sussex, suggesting that this was not his primary residence.

61 E101/41/5 m. 15d.

62 E101/41/5 m. 8, listed eighty-eighth and eighty-ninth in the retinue of Sir William Heron. *Two Estate Surveys*, p. 151, King or atte Forde: '1 virgate 14s 0d in Palynghame'; p. 142, Smith: '6a (margin: Nativus domini) 3s 4d in Cockyng'.

63 E101/39/7 m. 3.

64 Kyng, C67/31 m. 9, 'of Thunscoe, Yorks WR'; Smyth, C67/30 m. 11, 'of Chastleton,

The existence of these sets of relationships within the ranks of archers demonstrated in the estate survey, does suggest that this kind of shared service may not have been uncommon. The insights available from the comparison of these two sources enable us to look at the *mentalité* of the archer and conclude that their local landholding ties were a major reason for serving in this particular royal expedition. This insight provides us with valuable information regarding the activities of the lower orders of society that are perhaps sometimes over-looked because of lack of evidence. It is also significant that, of this selection of tenants taken from Arundel's estate surveys, so many have also taken royal pardons in 1398. It can be shown that 12 of these tenants have probably taken out royal pardons in 1398, following Arundel's execution for treason during the years 1386–1388. This includes 4 knights, 2 esquires and 6 archers. This demonstrates that all levels of society felt at risk because of their association with Arundel during these years. It may well have been that, as tenants of Arundel, these men had joined with the Appellant earl in the short campaign against de Vere, which culminated with the defeat of the king's forces at Radcot Bridge in 1387.

The evidence from Radcot Bridge

To measure the strength of the relationships within retinues and loyalties within the expeditions of 1387 and 1388 to the Appellants, the membership of the Radcot Bridge campaign should be investigated. Both Arundel himself and Nottingham, the Earl Marshal, were involved in all three campaigns. Notting-ham probably served under Arundel at Radcot Bridge as he is not identified in the chronicle sources as being a retinue leader. The main forces opposed to de Vere and his Cheshiremen were under the command of Arundel, Gloucester, Warwick and Derby.[65] The Appellants' campaign is well documented in the contemporary chronicles but sources, such as muster rolls, documenting the actual retinues do not survive. Service in a civil war was a different proposition to service in the king's pay. As the organisation would be less formal and men would probably not be serving for pay, it is not surprising that such records do not exist. Goodman suggests that the men serving would have required payment in advance, and that the Appellants would have used the £20,000 granted in the Merciless Parliament to cover the debts so incurred.[66] However, the evidence for any payments or debts resulting from the civil war have not been discovered.

The one man who does appear by name in the narrative sources is Sir Thomas Mortimer. Sir Thomas was the uncle of the earl of March. March had been placed in the wardship of a number of peers including Arundel and Warwick. Sir Thomas had been appointed to look after the young earl's estates in the

Oxon, alias of Evenlode, Worcs'. Again neither of these pardons lists Sussex as the primary location of these individuals.

65 Myres, 'The Campaign of Radcot Bridge in December 1387', pp. 20–33.

66 Goodman, *Loyal Conspiracy*, p. 34.

Marches.[67] It is also interesting to note that Mortimer married the recently widowed mother of Lord Bardolf in 1386.[68] Lord Bardolf served on campaign in 1388, in the retinue of the Earl Marshal.[69] Mortimer is remembered for the ignominious murder of Sir Thomas Molyneaux following a parley between the opposing forces. The Westminster Chronicle describes it thus: 'Despite the parley, however, one Molyneaux, a leading henchman of the duke, was attacked by Sir Thomas Mortimer, who killed him on the spot.'[70] The career of Mortimer is extremely relevant to this discussion. He was closely related to the Appellants and is described by Saul as 'Arundel's chief steward'.[71] His appearance in the chronicles also provides a snapshot into the continuity of service throughout the expeditions of these years.

Mortimer's retinue of 89 soldiers on the 1387 expedition consisted of 3 knights, 32 esquires and 49 archers.[72] He had previously served on Richard II's Scottish expedition of 1385 but with a less powerful following of just one esquire.[73] Mortimer can therefore be identified as a strong supporter of Arundel and he was indeed appealed for treason in the parliament of 1397. The career of Mortimer and his appearance in the sources suggests that the expedition of 1387 and also the campaign of Radcot Bridge could have consisted of Arundel's supporters and these were therefore men who possibly did not support the king. Mortimer did not partake in the expedition of 1388, perhaps suggesting that Arundel had managed to gain further support and could afford to leave some of his more loyal supporters in England.

Only one other name has been firmly presented as a candidate for inclusion at Radcot Bridge and this is a close associate of Sir Thomas Mortimer, the esquire William Curtis. Saul has suggested that Curtis assisted Mortimer when he despatched Molyneaux.[74] Gillespie also refers to this event but makes it only a probability, whilst pointing out that Curtis, a man who had been associated with the Mortimers for some time, also served with Mortimer on the 1387 expedition.[75] William Curtis can be identified on the muster as William Carteys, listed fourth in Mortimer's retinue and second of his esquires.[76] Gillespie shows that Curtis served Mortimer continuously throughout the 1390s and he can also be shown as serving on the royal expedition to Ireland of 1394, in the company

---

[67] Goodman, *Loyal Conspiracy*, pp. 34–35.

[68] *Complete Peerage*, vol. i, p. 419.

[69] E101/41/5 m. 3.

[70] *Westminster Chronicle*, p. 223. Mortimer's association with Arundel would support the account of the Monk of Westminster, who places the murder at an earlier skirmish before de Vere's flight from the earl of Derby. *Knighton's Chronicle*, p. 423, 'Thomas Molyneaux, trying to follow him [de Vere], was held back by Sir Thomas Mortimer, by whom he was slain.' For Walsingham see *St Alban's Chronicle*, p. 839.

[71] Saul, *Richard II*, p. 188.

[72] E101/40/33 m.10; enrolled attorney, C76/71 m. 10.

[73] Lewis, 'Last Medieval Summons', p. 18.

[74] Saul, *Richard II*, p. 188. Could William Curtis be the one esquire accompanying Mortimer to Scotland in 1385?

[75] James L. Gillespie, 'Thomas Mortimer and Thomas Molineaux: Radcot Bridge and the Appeal of 1397', *Albion*, 7 (1975), pp. 161–173, 171.

[76] E101/40/33 m. 10.

of the earl of March.[77] Gillespie quotes a writ found in the Chester gaol delivery file linking Curtis with the murder of Molineaux. Curtis managed to survive this attempt to bring him to justice and went on to serve the Mortimers in the reign of Henry IV.[78] It is also interesting to note that Curtis secured a royal pardon in 1398.[79]

Goodman suggests other names for inclusion in the battle of Radcot Bridge using information gained from the pardon rolls for 1397–1398.[80] Of these men, a William Barry from Northampton, who he suggests joins the Appellants following their proclamation at Northampton, is also involved in Arundel's expedition of 1388. Barry served under Arundel himself and is placed ninety-seventh in the list of esquires. More interestingly it is noted on the muster roll that he was made a knight on 28 June.[81] The information provided by Goodman, linked with the information on the roll indicates that it is not a coincidence that he is knighted during this campaign as he was probably being rewarded for his previous loyal service at Radcot Bridge. It was not unusual for men to be knighted on the eve of battle. However, the choice of recipient is of significance.

Do we have any evidence for those who fought for the king at Radcot Bridge? The chronicler, Knighton, mentions that Sir Ralph Vernon and Sir Ralph Radcliffe were sent by the king to muster his forces in Cheshire prior to Radcot Bridge.[82] It is surprising perhaps to note that Vernon then serves under Arundel in his 1388 expedition.[83] This could suggest that Vernon was a professional soldier, who would serve whoever was paying his wages. Alternatively, he could be still showing his allegiance to the king by serving on what was officially a royal expedition. What is evident is that allegiances were fluid during these years and an actual solid partisanship is hard to pin down. For instance, as discussed earlier, he may have served in this expedition because of his links to Sir Hugh Browe and other Cheshire landowners. Therefore local connections may have also played a major role in the motivation for attending such an expedition.

Continuity of service between the expedition of 1387 and the campaign of Radcot Bridge is a question that is not supported by the evidence of surviving military records. Only a few combatants can realistically be identified. However, it is feasible that Arundel would have held together the hardcore of his personal retinue for this campaign and also that men such as Mortimer would have done likewise. It is not possible to state whether the men who had accompanied Arundel on his expeditions also served at Radcot Bridge. To have

---

77 *CPR, 1391–1396*, p. 481 (protection).

78 Gillespie, 'Thomas Mortimer', pp. 171–172.

79 C67/30 m. 3.

80 Goodman, *Loyal Conspiracy*, pp. 31–32, citing C67/30, mm. 2, 3, 19.

81 E101/41/5 m. 1d, described as 'factus miles xxviii Junii'.

82 *Knighton's Chronicle*, p. 419.

83 E101/41/5 m. 9. This could also be the same Sir Ralph Vernon whom Andrew Ayton identifies as having fought on the Breton campaign of 1342–1343 as captain of a retinue consisting of 1 knight and 3 esquires, Ayton, *Knights and Warhorses*, p. 264.

fought de Vere would have meant opposing the king and the men who took part would have to have been loyal supporters of Arundel and his fellow appellants. It is not clear that involvement in the expeditions against France would lead directly to action against the supporters of the crown. The evidence from the pardon rolls of 1398 may add more to this discussion. We have already referred to the pardon roll evidence in the section discussing Arundel's tenants; this evidence will now be discussed in more detail.

The evidence from the pardon rolls

Historians have utilised the pardon rolls of 1397–1399 as evidence for an individual's support of the Appellants, and especially service at Radcot Bridge, ten years earlier. The pardon evidence was originally discussed in detail by Caroline Barron and was developed by Anthony Goodman and more recently Nigel Saul.[84] Richard II first announced a general pardon for all, except fifty unnamed persons, at the beginning of the parliament on 17 September 1397.[85] The monk of Evesham records that these pardons were to be obtained before the feast of St Hilary (13 January 1398).[86] This statement preceded the appeal in parliament of Gloucester, Arundel and Warwick. These excepted persons were those who had risen against the king with the Appellants in 1387–1388; thus the identity of those obtaining these pardons is of relevance to this research. Barron comments that pardons had already begun to be secured by October 1397 and that a proclamation was made on 1 January 1398 reasserting the need for pardons, but extending the time limit to 24 June 1398.[87] This statement was repeated at the close of the subsequent parliament at Shrewsbury on 31 January 1398. From the rolls of parliament:

> And provided always that none of those who rose up forcibly and rode against the king, in the company of the lords who have now been adjudged and convicted, in the eleventh year of his reign, may claim pardon for that deed done at that time unless they sue out charters of pardon for it between now and the feast of John the Baptist next.[88]

Such men were again given until 24 June 1398 to secure a royal pardon for their actions in 1387–1388. On 18 June 1398 another proclamation was made reminding those who had served the Appellants that they should appear before

---

[84] C. M. Barron, 'The Tyranny of Richard II', *Bulletin of the Institute of Historical Research*, xli (1968), pp. 1–18, pp. 7–9, who identifies 596 pardons. Goodman, *Loyal Conspiracy*, pp. 35–41. Saul, *Richard II*, p. 377. Saul cites C67/30 for the enrolled pardons. However, as Barron and Goodman point out, relevant pardons are also enrolled on C67/31.

[85] Barron, 'Tyranny of Richard II', p. 7, citing *RP*, vol. iii, p. 347.

[86] *Historia Vitae et Regni Ricardi Secundi*, ed. G.B. Stow (1977), p. 138, translation in *Chronicles of the Revolution*, pp. 55–56.

[87] For pardons, C67/30 m. 3, 18 October 1397; for proclamation, C81/517/11819, writ under the privy seal sent from Coventry, 1 January 1398, both cited in Barron, 'Tyranny of Richard II', p. 7.

[88] *RP*, vol. iii, pp. 368–369, translation in *Chronicles of the Revolution*, p. 88.

the council and sue for pardons.[89] The deadline was, however, further extended, as can be seen in an order to the sheriff of Staffordshire recorded in the *Calendar of Close Rolls* on 25 June 1398. This makes reference to all those who joined with Gloucester and Arundel in their rising against the king in 1387–1388, and due to the king's 'tender love for the said lieges the king has extended the time of grace to the feast of Allhallows next'.[90] Thus those requiring pardons would now have until 31 October 1398. It is not even clear that this would be the final deadline, for Barron comments that Richard subsequently announced that the general pardon itself would only last until Martinmass 1399.[91] Many may have still felt it would be safer to gain an individual pardon even after this date.

It is clear from the number of statements in parliament and supporting royal proclamations that Richard was serious about ensuring that all those involved in the Appellant rising in 1387–1388 secured pardons for their actions. This method of forcing his subjects to claim royal pardons has been identified as an instrument of Richard's tyranny. Barron has suggested that Richard had a number of motives for requiring pardons. One of these was to collect money from the fines that would be levied when a pardon was sued for. Barron gives the example of John Moor, a London mercer, who had to pay 100 marks, 'for having ridden with the condemned lords, contrary to his allegiance'.[92] This fine is therefore probably due to Moor serving at Radcot Bridge with the Appellants. He would also appear to have continued this service with Arundel, as he appears in the retinue of the earl in the expedition of 1388 as an esquire.[93] How many other such men can also be identified as showing continuance of service? In addition, Barron suggests that Richard wanted to know who his enemies were. By forcing them to take pardons in this way, Richard was provided with a list of names of those who had assisted the Appellants in 1387–1388. It is with this list of names that we can compare the muster rolls for the expeditions of 1387–1388 and look for any correlations.

A small number of pardons survive in the *Calendar of Patent Rolls*, which explicity state that they are for supporting the Appellants in their revolt against the king. Two of these are for Sir John Bussy and Sir Henry Green, neither of whom appears in the muster rolls.

> Pardon to John Bussy, knight, for adhering to Thomas, duke of Gloucester, and Richard, earl of Arundel, when they assumed the royal authority in the tenth year of the king's reign by commission under the great seal in derogations of the king and his crown, drew after them Thomas then earl of Warwick, and others, into insurrection at Haringhey and elsewhere, came to the king in his palace at Westminster, and plundered, imprisoned and killed

---

[89] Bennet, *Richard II and the Revolution of 1399*, p. 130, citing E403/559 m. 10.

[90] *CCR, 1396–1399*, p. 392.

[91] Barron, 'Tyranny of Richard II', p. 7, citing *CCR, 1396–1399*, p. 438, 27 February 1399.

[92] Barron, 'Tyranny of Richard II', p. 8, citing C81/573/12038, writ under the privy seal from Windsor dated 24 April 1398. He was pardoned from paying the fine. Royal pardon: C67/30 m. 19, described as 'mercer', of London.

[93] E101/41/5 m. 1d.

many lieges in divers parts of the realm, which commission was declared by
Parliament to be high treason, and for any offences connected therewith.
The like, under the same date, to Henry Grene, knight.[94]

It is interesting to speculate about why only a few pardons, from the many
enrolled, are to be found in the patent rolls.[95] It can probably be explained by the
fact that both Bussy and Green were in 1398 favourites of the king, members of
his council, and seen by contemporaries as the proponents of Richard's tyranny.
As a result they were both executed in Bristol by Henry IV in 1399 and together
with Richard II were the most senior casualties of the deposition.[96] They had
been prime movers, together with Sir William Scrope, earl of Wiltshire, in the
prosecution of the Appellants in the parliament of 1397, Bussy as speaker of the
commons and Green as a member of parliament. Steel also comments that
Bussy protested against Richard's proclamation regarding the need for pardons
for those who had supported the Appellants in 1387–1388, and as he himself
secures such a pardon, his difficulty with this seems to have been personal.[97]
Roskell suggests that Bussy may have needed the pardon due to his taking the
oath of allegiance to the Appellants in 1388.[98] This demonstrates that even men
who had become very close to Richard required pardons for their actions in
1387–1388. Neither man served in the campaigns of those years; therefore their
support for the Appellants must have been concerning service against de Vere at
Radcot Bridge. As both men were retainers of John of Gaunt, it may have been
that they had served with Henry of Derby and therefore assisted in the defeat of
the king's forces.[99] Perhaps a previous relationship is evident in the famous
exchange between Bussy and Arundel in the Parliament of 1397 and reported by
Adam Usk.

> Then Sir John Bussy said, 'That pardon is revoked by the king, the lords, and
> us, the faithful commons'. 'Where are those faithful commons?' retorted the

---

[94] *CPR, 1396–1399*, p. 331, cited in Goodman, *Loyal Conspiracy*, p. 36. Other pardons can
be found in *CPR* for Sir Richard LeScrope, who cannot be identified in the muster rolls, *CPR,
1396–1399*, p. 272, with similar wording as that for Bussy; Sir William Bagot, *CPR,
1396–1399*, p. 317, 'William Bagot, knight for all treasons, felonies, trespasses and
misprisions perpetrated before 6 Jan last' – this pardon does not specifically mention service
with the Appellants.

[95] See Barron, 'Tyranny of Richard II', p. 9, for discussion.

[96] Green, *HOP*, vol. iii, pp. 225–228; Bussy, *HOP*, vol. ii, pp. 449–454. Bussy is also sometimes referred to as Sir John Bushy. For his career see, J.S. Roskell, 'Two Medieval
Lincolnshire Speakers, Part 1: Sir John Bussy of Hougham', *Lincolnshire Architectural and
Archaelogical Society, Reports and Papers*, vol. 7, part 1 (1957), pp. 27–45. As previously
mentioned, a pardon can also be found for Sir William Bagot, the third member of this infa-
mous triumvirate.

[97] Steel, *Richard II*, p. 242, citing *Chronicon Adae de Usk, 1377–1421*, ed. E.M. Thompson
(1904), p. 152.

[98] Roskell, 'Sir John Bussy', p. 33, citing *RP*, vol. iii, p. 401a.

[99] Walker, *The Lancastrian Affinity*: Bussy, p. 266, retainer of John of Gaunt, 1382–97,
served overseas 1378, and p. 286, member of the household of John of Gaunt, Chief Steward
– North Parts, 1396–1397; Green, p. 270, retained 1379–1399, served overseas 1372, 1373
and 1386.

earl, 'I know you and your crew well enough, and why you have gathered here – not to act in good faith, for the faithful commons of the realm are not here. They, I know, are grieving greatly for me. But you, as I know only too well, have always been false.'[100]

This does seem to hint at former dealings between Bussy and Arundel; however no real evidence survives to link Bussy, Bagot and Green to the Appellants. Their subsequent rise to favour demonstrates that such men who had served against Richard II were able to later prosper under his patronage. Any previous service, perhaps indeed with Henry himself in 1387, unfortunately did not do them any favours in 1399.

A pardon, remission and quitclaim was also granted to a group of men in custody of the lands of Sir Edward Dallingridge, including Bodiam Castle, and his son Sir John Dallingridge for the payment of 500 marks. This, however, was due to the service of the late Sir Edward Dallingridge, 'an adherent of Thomas, duke of Gloucester, in the tenth year'.[101] Therefore, although Sir Edward had died in 1393, these men and his son had to pay for his deeds in 1387–1388.[102] This was despite the fact that Sir Edward had subsequently served as a member of the royal council and had been retained as a king's knight. Of those men named in this pardon, Sir John Dallingridge served with the earl of Arundel in 1387 and Sir William Heron in 1388; John Brook, archer, served in the retinue of Sir William Elmham in 1387; Richard Prat, archer, served in the retinue of Sir Hugh le Despencer in 1387 and 1388.[103] Indeed, Richard Prat had also secured an individual pardon on 12 June 1398.[104] Therefore, although some of these men were militarily active in years 1387–1388, and one had secured an individual pardon, this fine is for the 'adherence' of Sir Edward to the Appellants in their opposition to the king.

It is possible to compare the pardon roll evidence against the muster rolls for 1387 and 1388 to discover the number of names who appear in both sources. A high correlation would suggest that these individuals were taking out the pardons because of their service in the overseas expeditions in support of Arundel. As it would be unusual for someone to have to secure a pardon for serving on what was in effect a royal expedition, it may be surmised that these men had continued this service into action against the king at Radcot Bridge. Alternatively, these expeditions may have achieved the status of an expression

---

[100] *The Chronicle of Adam Usk, 1377–1421*, ed. and trans. C. Given-Wilson (Oxford, 1997), p. 29.

[101] *CPR, 1396–1399*, p. 341, listing John Scarle, clerk, Thomas Sakeville, knight, Thomas Wysbeche, clerk, Robert Echyngham, Robert Oxenbregg, John Brook, Richard Prat and Sir John Dallingridge.

[102] Sir Edward Dallingridge had taken a protection for 1387 and attorney for 1388 but only served in 1387. He was, however, serving as Captain of Brest in 1388. 1387: E101/41/5 m. 1; enrolled protection, C76/71 m. 12. 1388: enrolled attorney, C76/72 m. 8.

[103] Sir John Dallingridge, 1387: E101/40/33 m. 1d. 1388: E101/41/5 m. 8; Brook, E101/40/33 m. 11; Prat, 1387: E101/40/33 m. 9. 1388: E101/41/5 m. 18.

[104] Prat, C67/30 m. 1, 12 June 1398; Brook: C67/30 m. 25, 8 May 1398, listed 'of Barking, Essex or Suffolk'. From the locality described it is possible that Sussex was not his principal residence.

**Table 16. C67/30 and C67/31 pardon rolls, spread of enrolments
of those serving on campaigns of 1387-1388**

Membrane	No. of pardons	Membrane	No. of pardons	Membrane	No. of pardons
30 m 1	14	30 m 18	23	31 m 1	0
30 m 2	21	30 m 19	7	31 m 2	6
30 m 3	20	30 m 20	6	31 m 3	0
30 m 4	6	30 m 21	16	31 m 4	0
30 m 5	15	30 m 22	2	31 m 5	0
30 m 6	16	30 m 23	14	31 m 6	0
30 m 7	22	30 m 24	10	31 m 7	9
30 m 8	15	30 m 25	12	31 m 8	4
30 m 9	16	30 m 26	0	31 m 9	14
30 m 10	12	30 m 27	18	31 m 10	15
30 m 11	14	30 m 28	13	31 m 11	15
30 m 12	22	30 m 29	12	31 m 12	15
30 m 13	24	30 m 30	12	31 m 13	4
30 m 14	18	30 m 31	0		
30 m 15	19	30 m 32	22		
30 m 16	26	30 m 33	0		
30 m 17	18	30 m 34	12		

of disloyalty to the king, led as they were by the Appellant lord, Arundel. Before we discuss the results of the correlation, it is necessary to discuss the source material, the actual pardon rolls in more detail.

The pardons are enrolled on two supplementary pardon rolls held in the Public Record Office, namely C67/30 and C67/31. All the names included on these rolls can be found in a typewritten alphabetical listing in the index to the class C67. Barron identified specific pardons which refer to service with the Appellants on C67/30 mm. 19, 4, 3 and C67/31 mm. 13, 13d, 12, 4, 2. She calculated that 596 people between October 1397 and September 1398 had enrolled pardons on these membranes alone.[105] The general pardons on other membranes on the two rolls were discounted. When looking at the rolls it can be seen that the men named on these membranes are listed after a pardon worded as that quoted above for Sir John Bussy. It is therefore clear that these men have specifically sought pardons for service with the Appellants. The pardon states that the insurrection began at Harringay Park, north of London,[106] but does not mention service against the earl of Oxford at Radcot Bridge. Therefore, even if a man has secured one of these pardons, it does not prove that they fought at

[105] Barron, 'Tyranny of Richard II', p. 9.
[106] The reference to Harringay Park, refers to the point when the three senior Appellants first rose to arms on 13 November 1387, following their discovery of Richard's questions to the judges, *Westminster Chronicle*, p. 211.

Radcot Bridge, even though this is perhaps likely. From careful reading of the pardon roll, in addition to those identified by Barron, further pardons referring to service with the Appellants can also be found on C67/30 mm. 1, 2, and, contrary to Barron, no pardons are recorded on C67/30 m. 13d.

Due to the proximity of the other general pardons recorded on the rolls, we have also extended our correlation to all of the names recorded as having taken a pardon between 1397–1399 and recorded on these rolls. This follows the line taken by the editors of *History of Parliament* who refer to inclusion on these pardon rolls as evidence of an individual demonstrating loyalty to the Appellants in 1387–1388, noting pardons on other membranes and not simply those containing specific reference to service with Gloucester, Arundel and Warwick. John Chamberlain of Arundel, Sussex, was a known associate of Arundel and serves in the retinue of Lord Welles in 1388.[107] He can be identified as securing a pardon on 14 June 1398, recorded on C67/30 m. 17, thus not one of the pardons referring to service with the Appellants.[108] *History of Parliament* suggests that the pardon was secured because of his association with Arundel. Therefore, it may well be that all of the pardons recorded on these two supplementary pardon rolls were secured by those who were concerned about how their actions in 1387–1388 might perhaps lead to prosecution from Richard following his successful attack on the senior Appellants.

Table 16 demonstrates the spread of men on each membrane throughout the two pardons rolls who can also be identified on the muster rolls for the expeditions of 1387–1388. The table demonstrates the extraordinary results of the correlation between the two sources. In total, 559 of the force of 6,000 men mobilised in 1387–1388 have secured a pardon during the period of uncertainty following the prosecution of the senior Appellants. This accounts for 10% of the actual total number of men who served in the campaigns of Arundel.[109] This is a significant result and it would appear that a large number of men demonstrated continued service from the campaigns of 1387–1388 to the military action which resulted in the defeat of the duke of Ireland at Radcot Bridge in December 1387. This is strong supporting evidence for the suggestion that men who served with Arundel in his overseas campaign would also have been willing to fight for him against the forces raised in support of Richard II. However, this evidence is tempered by the fact that only a proportion of these pardons are recorded on the membranes specifically mentioning support for the Appellants. The actual number of soldiers with pardons found on such membranes is just 93 and thus a smaller proportion of the total force mustered for the expeditions in 1387–1388. However, these men account for 16% of the 596 pardons enrolled specifically for service with the Appellants. Thus a reasonable number of the men who are recorded as specifically supporting Arundel, Gloucester and Warwick also served on campaign.

---

[107] John Chamberlain, *HOP*, vol. ii, pp. 511–512, MP for Arundel in 1383 (February), 1383 (October), 1385 and 1393; 1388: E101/41/5 m. 3.

[108] C67/30 m. 17.

[109] The total force campaigning in 1387–1388 totals 6,089. However, 473 men served in both expeditions, therefore the total number of men serving was 5,616.

Table 17. Distribution of pardons by county

County	No. of pardons	County	No. of pardons	County	No. of pardons
Bedfordshire	8	Herefordshire	9	Rutland	1
Berkshire	1	Hertfordshire	1	Shropshire	9
Buckinghamshire	8	Huntington	2	Somerset	4
Cambridgeshire	7	Kent	6	Staffordshire	10
Cheshire	2	Lancashire	5	Suffolk	7
Cornwall	1	Leicestershire	14	Surrey	12
Cumberland	6	Lincolnshire	24	Sussex	34
Derbyshire	5	London	8	Warwickshire	33
Devon	5	Middlesex	2	Wiltshire	3
Dorset	3	Norfolk	10	Worcestshire	7
Essex	16	Northampton	20	Yorkshire	15
Farnham	1	Northumberland	6	Yorkshire E.R	7
Gloucestshire	6	Nottinghamshire	5	Yorkshire W.R.	11
Hampshire	2	Oxfordshire	21		

Goodman uses the information contained within the pardon rolls for the 596 individuals enrolled specifically for supporting the Appellants in order to discuss the county of origin of those securing royal pardons. A number of counties were forced to obtain pardons for their actions prior to 1397. Goodman compared the number of individual pardons against these counties to see if there was any correlation to demonstrate where the men who fought at Radcot Bridge were drawn from. He discovered that apart from Sussex, with 57 individual pardons, there was no significant correlation which would suggest a bias of recruitment from any particular county. The significance of Sussex as a major recruitment ground for this force, reflects the role of the earl of Arundel as a senior Appellant. Goodman also found that a similar number of individual pardons were drawn from counties not included in the forced pardons. His analysis demonstrated that support for the Appellants came from throughout England and was not concentrated upon those counties singled out for pardons by Richard II in 1398–1399. In total he demonstrated that men suing for pardons came from thirty-four separate counties.[110]

Although many of the pardons are very detailed, giving name, alias, father's name and occupation, a good number only mention the name of the claimant. Table 17 demonstrates the geographical spread of 357 men who have taken pardons in 1398–1399, who mention their place of domicile and who also served with Arundel in 1387–1388. The table demonstrates that the men securing pardons were drawn from thirty-nine different counties, thus five more than those described by Goodman from the selected membranes. This demonstrates that men serving on Arundel's campaigns were drawn from the four

---

[110] Goodman, *Loyal Conspiracy*, pp. 36–41.

corners of England with representatives from Cumberland, Northumberland, Cornwall and Kent.

It is also possible to analyse the evidence provided by the pardon rolls by date of enrolment. We have discussed the timetable laid down by Richard II for the suing of pardons. Three different dates were given as deadlines for taking pardons: 13 January 1398, 24 June 1398, and finally 31 August 1398. In addition, as mentioned earlier, many individuals may have still secured pardons after the final deadline as a result of Richard deciding that the General Pardon might also expire in 1399. Table 18 shows the dates on which the 559 men who are found on the pardon rolls and also served in 1387–1388 enrolled their royal pardons. The table demonstrates that none of the combatants had secured their pardon prior to the first deadline of 13 January 1398. This suggests that either the need for pardons was not widely known or, as suggested by Barron, they were waiting for the Shrewsbury Parliament in January 1398 to see if Richard would temper his demand.[111]

The evidence presented in Table 18, suggests that those requiring pardons were indeed staying their hand and awaiting another statement from the king. It can be seen that the majority of those securing pardons were now enrolled through February to June, prior to the revised deadline of 24 June 1398. In fact 481 of the 559 pardons, or 86%, were enrolled before this deadline. It is enlightening to see that 303 pardons, or 54%, of the pardons were enrolled between 1 and 24 June, demonstrating that the medieval soldier was also prone to the modern practice of leaving things to the last possible moment. The largest peak of enrolments was on 12 June when 92, 16%, of the enrolments are made. A further 59 enrolments, 11%, were made between 25 June and 31 October, the extended deadline for receipt. Thus only 19 other pardons, 3%, are recorded on the rolls for the participants in 1387–1388 after this final deadline. This pattern of enrolments suggests that all of the pardons, which can be identified on the rolls, can be treated as indicative of a link with support for the Appellants against Richard in 1387–1388. The evidence provided by the pardon rolls can be used to provide additional evidence regarding the careers of the individuals who participated in the campaigns of 1387–1388.

Service in other campaigns

The pattern of service of the retinue captain is of great interest to the historian of military organisation in this period. How many of the retinue captains from 1387–1388 involved themselves in multiple expeditions? It is possible to look for service of these retinue captains in the surrounding years as some of these retinue captains have been identified in other sources. This includes the Reims campaign of Edward III in 1359–60,[112] the expedition to northern France led by

---

111 Barron, 'Tyranny of Richard II', p. 7.
112 Clifford J. Rogers, *War Cruel and Sharp. English Strategy under Edward III, 1327–1360* (Woodbridge, 2000), pp. 385–422.

Table 18. Pardon analysis by date enrolled

	1398											1399					
	Feb	March	April	May	June	July	Aug	Sept	Oct	Nov	Dec	Jan	Feb	March	April	May	June
1		3		5	2	1	1		1								
2			1	4				2						1			
3	2	4		6	3									1			
4	5	1	1	1	4				1								
5	5			3	6	1		1									
6	2		1	2	1	3											
7				5	2				2								
8				3	14	1		3	1								1
9			1	1	2	1										1	
10			1	3	35	2			3						1		1
11					6												
12	2			10	92	4		2	2					2	1		1
13			2	3	9												
14	1	1			29				1								
15		2	4	2	22										1		
16	7	1	2	2	44			1									
17	2			2	5			1									
18	2	3	2	3	4		2		3						1		
19	1	1	1	1	4												
20	2		6	8	16	1	1	2							1	1	
21	1			4		1	1	1	1								
22			1	1	3												
23	4																
24	1		7	2													
25	1	1	2		2			1	1						2		
26	1	2	1	2				1	1						1		
27	1		3					1							1		
28		1	4	1	1					1							
29		1	1					1	1								
30			1						1								
31																	
Total	41	21	42	74	306	15	5	17	19	1	0	0	0	4	9	2	3

John of Gaunt in 1369,[113] the mainly naval expedition led against northern France by John of Gaunt in 1378,[114] the discontinued expedition that was to be launched into Brittany under the duke of Brittany in 1379,[115] the expedition of 1380 against northern France led by the earl of Buckingham,[116] the 'crusade' of Bishop Despencer in 1383,[117] the expedition led by the king to Scotland in 1385,[118] John of Gaunt's expedition to Castile in 1386,[119] the crusade with the duke of Bourbon in 1390,[120] and the expeditions under the king to Ireland in 1394[121] and 1399.[122] Such continued service across these royal expeditions would show that these captains were serving in the expeditions of 1387 and 1388 as a further example of continuation of their service in other royal expeditions throughout this period.

Sixteen men can be seen to have served in multiple expeditions throughout this period, in addition to those of 1387–1388. This is shown on Table 19. This accounts for 26% of the total number of 61 captains serving in the campaigns of 1387 and 1388. This shows that just over one quarter of these captains served on other expeditions, indicating that their reasons for serving with Arundel during this period could not have been completely politically driven. They may have served in these campaigns as part of their military career as a professional soldier, out of patriotic duty or even because they wished to serve alongside their friends and colleagues.

It is also evident that a number of the leading figures in the expeditions, the retinue captains, have been involved in other campaigns and therefore a relationship with Arundel would not have been the sole factor in their choosing to campaign. The retinue captains, John Slegh,[123] Sir Robert Mounteney,[124] Sir Thomas Mortimer,[125] John, Lord Beaumont,[126] Sir Arnold Savage,[127] Sir

---

[113] Goodman, *John of Gaunt*, pp. 229–232.

[114] Sherborne, 'The English Navy', p. 36, and Goodman, *John of Gaunt*, pp. 226–227.

[115] Sherborne, 'Indentured Retinues', pp. 730–731.

[116] *Ibid.*, pp. 731–735.

[117] *Westminster Chronicle*, pp. 31–49; Palmer, *England France and Christendom*, pp. 7,10, 49.

[118] Lewis, 'The Last Medieval Summons' (App. II, list of 142 retinues and leaders).

[119] Goodman, *John of Gaunt*, pp. 115–131, 139n.

[120] *Westminster Chronicle*, pp. 433 and 451; see also G.L. Harriss, *Cardinal Beaufort* (Oxford, 1988), p. 1.

[121] E. Curtis, *Richard II in Ireland* (Oxford, 1927).

[122] J. Creton, 'French Metrical History on the Deposition of Richard II', ed. and trans. J. Webb, *Archaeologia*, xx (1824), pp. 1–441. This is an eyewitness account by a participant on the expedition. See also Steel, *Richard II*, pp. 260–263.

[123] 1387: E101/40/33 m. 18. Also delivering 20 prisoners of the earl of Arundel to the Tower of London 7 June 1387, *Foedera*, vol. iii, part iv, p. 13; Hardy, *Syllabus, 1377–1654*, p. 513. 1385: Lewis, 'Last Medieval Summons', p. 20.

[124] 1387: E101/40/33 m. 16; enrolled protection, C76/71 m. 14. 1385: Lewis, 'Last Medieval Summons', p. 18.

[125] 1387: E101/40/33 m. 10; enrolled attorney, C76/71 m. 10. 1385: Lewis, 'Last Medieval Summons', p. 18.

[126] 1387: E101/40/33 m. 4. 1385: Lewis, 'Last Medieval Summons', p. 19.

[127] 1387: E101/40/33 m. 6d; enrolled protection, C76/71 m. 14. 1388: E101/41/5 m. 13d. 1385: Lewis, 'Last Medieval Summons', p. 18.

Table 19. Military service of retinue captains

Year	Captain name	Also known as	Retinue size
1369	Richard, earl of Arundel		
1378			
1385			249
1387		Fitzalan	382
1388		Fitzalan	361
1379	Sir John d'Arundel		
1385		John de Arundel, Knight	5
1387		Sir John Darundel	70
1388		Sir Johan Darundell	90
1385	John, Lord Beaumont	Banneret	69
1387		Le Sire de Beaumont	196
1380	Edward, earl of Devon		
1385		Edward Courtenay	220
1387		Le Comte de Devens	231
1388		Le Counte de Devens	279
1390a			
1383	Sir William Elmham		
1385		Knight	44
1387			114
1385	Sir Thomas Mortimer	Knight	1
1387		Mons Thomas Mortemer	84
1385	Sir Robert Mounteney	Knight	3
1387			67
1385	Thomas, earl of Nottingham	Marshal of England	249
1388		Le Counte Marshal	228
1394			200
1379	Percy, Sir Thomas		
1380		Knight	
1385		Knight Banneret	119
1386			
1386			
1388		Sir Thomas Percy	152
1399		earl of Worcester	
1385	Arnold Savage		1
1387		Sir Arnald Savage	66
1388		Sir Arnald Savage	70
1385	John Slegh	king's butler	12
1387		John Sly	71
1359	Sir Gilbert Talbot		
1369			
1383			
1385		Talbot, Gilbert, knight	17
1387		Mons Gilbert Talbot	73

1388		Mons Gilbe Talbot	80
1394			
1370	Sir Thomas Trivet		
1373			
1378			
1379			
1380			
1383			
1385		Trivet, Thomas, knight banneret	39
1387		Sir Thomas Trevet	155
1385	John, Lord Welles		69
1388		Le Monsers W. Sire de Welle	71
1385	Thomas West	Knight	5
1388		Sir Thomas West	89

Thomas West,[128] and John, Lord Welles[129] were all also involved in Richard II's expedition into Scotland in 1385. However, it should be noted that the high correlation with 1385 is probably because of the nature of the expedition of that year. This was the first expedition led by Richard II in person and it was probably raised by feudal levy. This campaign would therefore have included most of the military community in England.

Sir William Elmham[130] was involved in Bishop Despencer's campaign of 1383 and the expedition into Scotland in 1385. Edward, earl of Devon[131] was involved in the Duke of Bourbon's crusade into North Africa in 1390. Sir Nicholas Clifton was a veteran of the French war and led a rebellion in Cheshire in 1393 with Sir Thomas Talbot against the proposed peace with France.[132] Thomas, earl of Nottingham,[133] was involved in Richard II's first expedition to Ireland in 1394. In addition to the retinue captains, other combatants can be seen to have had full careers as a part of the military community. For example, John Bathe, an esquire in Arundel's retinue in 1387, had a long career as an esquire of John of Gaunt.[134] Sir John Sandes, was a retinue captain in 1388 and also had a long career with the Black Prince and probably fought alongside him at Najera

[128] 1387: E101/40/33 m. 1; Enrolled protection, C76/71 m. 14; Enrolled attorney, C76/71 m. 10. 1388: E101/41/5 m. 7; Enrolled protected, C76/72 m. 6. 1385: Lewis, 'The Last Medieval Summons', p. 18.
[129] 1388: E101/41/5 m. 3. 1385: Lewis, 'Last Medieval Summons', p. 18.
[130] 1387: E101/40/33 m. 11. 1388: E101/40/39 m. 1. 1383: *Westminster Chronicle*, p. 45, as advisor to Bishop Despencer. 1385: Lewis, 'Last Medieval Summons', p. 20.
[131] 1387: E101/40/33 m. 3. 1388: E101/41/5 m. 4. 1390: *Westminster Chronicle*, p. 433.
[132] Saul, *Richard II*, pp. 219–220. Morgan, *War and Society in Medieval Cheshire*, p. 196, comments that Clifton served in the earl's retinue in 1387 and 1388, though it is clear that he actually captained his own retinues on campaign. 1387: E101/40/33 m. 12d, the retinue consisted of 86 soldiers, including 3 knights, 39 esquires and 44 archers. 1388: E101/40/33 m. 11, the retinue consisted of 70 soldiers, including 2 knights, 28 esquires and 40 archers.
[133] 1387: E101/40/33 m. 1. 1388: E101/41/5 m. 3. 1394: *CPR, 1391–1396*, p. 506 (attorney), see also Curtis, *Richard II in Ireland*, p. 27.
[134] *HOP*, vol. ii, p. 145. 1387: E101/40/33 m. 1.

as well as serving in France and Spain.[135] Sir Ralph Shelton, knight with Arundel in 1388, also had a long career. He served the crown in expeditions in 1378, 1383, 1385, 1386, 1388.[136] The presence of this selection of individuals within the makeup of the retinues in the expeditions suggests that this campaign was accepted within the military community of England as being a legitimate attack upon France, and was not purely a whim of the Appellants, populated by Appellant supporters. The actions of these individuals could also show that the campaigns were still *royal* in name, even if Arundel commanded them, and service could be construed as showing loyalty to the king.

The court of chivalry

Much has been made of the cases contested in the court of chivalry in the later fourteenth century. Detailed depositions were delivered by the supporters of either side of the contesting parties, usually to prove a case of heraldry. Witnesses would be called to testify where they had seen the heraldry in use. On many occasions therefore this would be on the field of battle, and hence we are provided with first hand evidence of a deponent's military career. This evidence will not contain every campaign a man would have attended as one would only have to testify where he had seen the arms in question, and not list every expedition he had been on. However, a witness would often begin his deposition with his age and also the number of years he had been in arms, thus indicating the possible length of military service.

The case that has been discussed the most is that of Scrope v. Grosvenor, contested in 1386, and thus almost contemporaneous with the campaigns of 1387–1388. A full transcript of the case was published by Sir N. Harris Nicolas in 1832. The first volume contains the surviving depositions and the second volume contains a history of the house of Scrope and also biographies of the Scrope deponents. A third volume, containing a history of the house of Grosvenor and biographies of the Grosvenor deponents was sadly never delivered.[137] The Scrope v. Grosvenor case was a dispute over the right to bear the arms *azure bend or*. This was brought to a head when Sir Robert Grosvenor and Sir Richard Scrope had borne these arms on the royal expedition to Scotland in 1385. The ensuing case records over 300 depositions taken at various locations throughout England during 1386 supporting both claims to the arms. A number of historians have referred to the case in their discussions of the military community in England, most recently Michael Bennett and Philip Morgan, using the Grosvenor depositions in their discussions of military service amongst Cheshire men.[138] The case is also famous for featuring the testimony of the poet Geoffrey Chaucer, when he claimed he was aged 'forty and upwards' and 'had been

135 *HOP*, vol. iv, pp. 301–302. 1388: E101/41/5 m. 13.
136 *HOP*, vol. iii, pp. 355–357. 1388: E101/41/5 m. 1.
137 *Scrope v. Grosvenor.*
138 Bennett, *Community, Class and Careerism*, pp. 82–83, 166; Philip Morgan, *War and Society in Medieval Cheshire*, pp. 128–130.

armed twenty-seven years'. Chaucer gave support to the case of Sir Richard Scrope and stated that he had first served with Edward III in France in 1359. Chaucer, by his own account, was unlucky on this, his first campaign, and was taken prisoner by the French.[139]

Table 20 summarises the deponents in the Scrope v. Grosvenor case who also can be identified as serving in the campaigns of 1387–1388. It shows the details of their service in 1387–1388; their age as stated in the deposition; their years of active service as stated in their deposition; the campaigns at which they claim to have seen the disputed arms. The table also shows an estimate of their age at their first campaign, calculated from the information given about current age and years of service. The age of these men at the depositions is pertinent to this discussion, as they were given just one year before the campaigns of 1387–1388.

Table 20 demonstrates that 40 deponents can be identified as serving on the campaigns of 1387–1388. This includes the earl of Arundel and the earl of Devon, 22 knights, 15 esquires and 1 archer. It also includes 10 men who captain a retinue on at least one of the expeditions led by the earl of Arundel and eight men who serve in both 1387 and 1388. It is possible to calculate the average age of those testifying and also the years of service that they have shown. The youngest man testifying was Ralph Bulmer, who stated that he was twenty-one years old and had been in arms for just three years since 1383. He had therefore first served with John of Gaunt in Scotland in 1383 at the age of eighteen. He had then served on the royal expedition to Scotland in 1385. He also serves in the retinue of Sir William, Baron of Hylton in 1388, and has thus served in three campaigns by the age of twenty-three.[140] Sir Ralph also secured a royal pardon in 1398 thus indicating that his actions in support of the Appellants may have later appeared treasonous to Richard II.[141] Two soldiers appear to be serving in their seventies, namely John Boteler, esquire, intending to serve with Sir Thomas Percy in 1388[142] and Sir Andrew Lutterell, also serving with Sir Thomas Percy in 1388.[143] John Boteler can also be identified as serving with Sir William de Windsor in 1380, thus supporting his position in the military community.[144]

The average age of those testifying and serving in 1387–1388 is forty-three years old. It is also interesting to note that 11 of the men testifying have over twenty years of service by the time of the case in 1386. Many of these men began campaigning at a young age. Sir James Chudlegh's deposition demonstrated that he first served aged eleven[145] and 9 men in total had gained military experience before the age of twenty. Chudlegh served with the earl of Devon in

---

[139] *Scrope v. Grosvenor*, vol. i, p. 178, vol. ii, p. 404.

[140] *Scrope v. Grosvenor*, vol. i, p. 65, vol. ii, p. 216. 1388: E101/41/5 m. 5d.

[141] C67/30 m. 21.

[142] *Scrope v. Grosvenor*, vol. i, p. 300. 1388: E101/40/39 m. 1. His name has been marked with a 'cross', indicating that he has not passed muster and has therefore not travelled with the expedition. It is possible to speculate that he was not accepted due to his age.

[143] *Scrope v. Grosvenor*, vol. i, p. 243. 1388: E101/40/39 m. 1.

[144] E101/39/7 m. 3 and 4.

[145] *Scrope v. Grosvenor*, vol. i, p. 75, vol. ii, p. 244. These figures assume that the witnesses stated their correct age in 1386.

Table 20. Deponents in the Scrope v. Grosvenor case who can be identified in the campaigns of 1387–1388

Title	First name	Surname	Position	Captain	Year	Age in 1386	Years of service	Campaigns	Age at first campaign
Earl	Richard	Arundel, earl of	Captain	Arundel, Richard, earl of	1387	38	18		20
Earl	Richard	Arundel, earl of	Captain	Arundel, Richard, earl of	1388				
	John	Bache	Esquire	Arundel, Richard, earl of	1387	24			
Mons	Piers	Bokton, de	Captain	Mons Piers de Bokton	1388	36	17	1369, 1379, 1383, 1390	19
	John	Bolton	Esquire	Richard Shingulton	1387	51		1386	
	Johes	Boteler	Esquire	Mons Thomas Percy	1388	72			
	William	Brerton	Esquire	Mons Johan Bohun	1388				
Mons	Johan	Brewe, de	Captain	Mons Andrewe Hake	1388	54	39	1347, 1352, 1383, 1386	15
Mons	John	Brewes, de	Knight	Arundel, Richard, earl of	1387				
Mons	Hugh	Browe	Knight	Arundel, Richard, earl of	1387	40	20+		
Mons	Hugh	Browe	Captain	Mons Hugh Browe	1388				
Mons	Rauf	Bulmer	Knight	Mons William Baron de Hylton	1388	21		1383, 1385	18
Mons	John	Burgh, de	Knight	Arundel, Richard, earl of	1387	41			
Mons	William	Chauncer	Knight	Mons Piers de Bokton	1388	44	30	1359, 1369	14
	William	Chetewynd	Esquire	Arundel, Richard, earl of	1388			1386	
Mons	James	Chuddelegh	Knight	Le Counte de Devens	1388	50	39	1367	11
Mons	James	Chydeleye	Knight	Le Counte de Devens	1387				
Mons	Thomas	Clynton	Knight	Le Counte Marshall	1388	26		1386	
Mons	Edward	Dalyngrigg	Knight	Arundel, Richard, earl of	1387	40		1359, 1369, 1380, 1385	
	Robert	Danyell	Esquire	Mons John Haukeston	1387	45	25	1383, 1385	20
Earl	Edward	Devon, earl of	Captain	Le Counte de Devens	1387	29		1377, 1380, 1385	20
Earl	Edward	Devon, earl of	Captain	Le Counte de Devens	1388				
	Tudor	Glyndors, de	Esquire	Arundel, Richard, earl of	1387	24			
	Oweyn	Glyndoudy	Esquire	Arundel, Richard, earl of	1387	27			

	Oweyn	Glynoverdy	Esquire	Arundel, Richard, earl of	1388				
Mons	Alisandre	Goldyngham	Knight	Mons Thomas Ponynges	1388			1374, 1380, 1386	
Mons	Robert	Greneage	Knight	Le Counte de Devens	1387	51			
Mons	Robert	Grenenaw	Knight	Mons Rauf Vernon	1388				
Mons	Renand	Grey, de	Knight	Arundel, Richard, earl of	1387	47			
	William	Halle	Esquire	Mons Arnald Savage	1387	60	45		15
	William	Halle	Esquire	Mons Arnald Savage	1388				
	Richard	Hampton	Esquire	Arundel, Richard, earl of	1388	60	43	1367, 1385	17
Mons	John	Hastyng	Knight	Mons Thomas Percy	1388	41			
	Johan	Holand	Esquire	Arundel, Richard, earl of	1388	40			
Mons	William	Hylton, Baron de	Captain	Mons William Baron de Hylton	1388	40			
	Johan	Juse	Esquire	Mons Hugh Browe	1388				
Mons	John	Lovell	Knight	Le Monsers W Sire de Welles	1388	45	28	1358, 1369, 1371, 1374, 1380, 1385, 1394	17
Mons	Andrewe	Lutterell	Knight	Mons William Heron	1388	70			
	Davy	Malpas	Archer	Le Sire de Beaumount	1387	41			
	Johan	Massy	Esquire	Mons Robert Massey	1388				
Mons	Thomas	Percy	Captain	Mons Thomas Percy	1388	45		1386	
	Johan	Pygot	Esquire	Mons Johan Sandes	1388	30			
	Nicholas	Reymes	Esquire	Mons Johan Wynkefeld	1387	50	30+		20
Mons	Geffray	Seintvyntyn	Knight	Mons Thomas Percy	1388			1380	
Mons	Gilbert	Talbot	Captain	Mons Gilbe Talbot	1387	46	27	1359, 1369, 1383, 1385	19
Mons	Gilbe	Talbot	Captain	Mons Gilbe Talbot	1388				
Mons	Richard	Talbot	Banneret	Arundel, Richard, earl of	1387	40			
Mons	Thomas	Trevet	Captain	Mons Thomas Trenet	1387	36		1373, 1378, 1379, 1380, 1383, 1385	23
Mons	Rauf	Vernon	Captain	Mons Rauf Vernon	1388	50	20		30

1387 and 1388.[146] The average age and levels of experience demonstrated indicate that those on campaign would have consisted of well-experienced soldiers. However, it should be noted that the sample included in the Scrope v. Grosvenor case is selected and is therefore naturally skewed. The deponents were chosen because they had a lot of experience and were able to testify that they had seen the arms on a number of occasions throughout the shared English military experience. Therefore one man remembers the siege of Calais in 1347, three men served with Edward III in France in 1359 and five men had served with the Black Prince in 1369. Therefore, although the experience demonstrated by those at the Scrope v. Grosvenor case is extensive, it should be remembered that not all of our participants would be able to claim such a pedigree of service.

The list of deponents includes Sir John de Brewes, who served as a knight in the retinue of the earl of Arundel in 1387 and jointly captains a retinue in 1388 with Sir Andrew Hake.[147] He testified that he was fifty-four years old and that his service had begun at the siege of Calais in 1347, therefore when he was just fifteen years old. He also mentions that he was present at the battle of Mauron in Brittany in 1352 and he also served in 1383 and with John of Gaunt in Spain in 1386.[148] He had therefore returned from Spain, just prior to joining the campaign in 1387. Sir Edward Dallingridge stated that he was forty years of age and had been in arms for twenty-seven years, since aged thirteen when he participated in Edward III's expedition of 1359. He also stated that he had seen the arms displayed by Scrope on four separate expeditions.[149] Sir Thomas Trivet had seen the arms of Scrope at six expeditions, despite only being at arms for thirteen years and aged thirty-six at his testimony.[150] Sir Gilbert Talbot was forty-six at his deposition and had served since aged nineteen, thus had demonstrated twenty-seven years in arms. Sir Gilbert testified that he had seen the Scrope arms on four occasions since 1359.[151] John, Lord Lovell, who served with Lord Welles in 1388,[152] also testifies in the case. Despite stating that he was only forty-five in 1386, he had seen the arms of Scrope displayed on six different expeditions since 1358. He had thus served for twenty-eight years since the age of seventeen. Lovell was also a king's knight, retained by Richard II in 1386 and also served on the royal expeditions to Ireland in the retinue of the king. Despite this service in the royal household he still required a royal pardon in 1398.[153]

---

[146] 1387: E101/40/33 m. 3; enrolled protection, C76/71 m. 12; enrolled attorney, C76/71 m. 8. 1388: E101/41/5 m. 4.

[147] 1387: E101/40/33 m. 1; enrolled protection, C76/71 m. 12. 1388: E101/41/5 m. 12d.

[148] *Scrope v. Grosvenor*, vol. i, p. 63, vol. ii, p. 208.

[149] *Ibid.*, vol. i, p. 164, vol. ii, p. 370.

[150] *Ibid.*, vol. i, p. 179, vol. ii, p. 413.

[151] *Ibid.*, vol. i, p. 174, vol. ii, p. 397.

[152] E101/41/5 m. 3.

[153] *Scrope v. Grosvenor*, vol. i, p. 190, vol. ii, p. 450; king's knight under Richard II: *Royal Household*, p. 285, retained for life, of Wiltshire/Oxfordshire, in 1386; 1394: *CPR, 1391–1396*, p. 486 (attorney), p. 493 (protection); 1399: *CPR, 1396–1399*, pp. 541, 552 and 558 (attorney), pp. 545 and 563 (protection); royal pardon: C67/30 m. 17, 12 June 1398. For his biography see *Complete Peerage*, vol. viii, pp. 219–221. This individual could possibly

These few examples drawn from the table, demonstrate that these men have been almost constantly in military service and thus are examples of 'professional' soldiers. This evidence demonstrates that these men would have served in the campaigns of 1387–1388, because that is what they did. They were professional soldiers with military careers stretching back into the reign of Edward III. The earl of Arundel would have appreciated the experience of the men whose careers are illustrated in the Scrope v. Grosvenor case, when he was recruiting his forces. This is demonstrated by the significant number of soldiers who campaign in 1387–1388 and also make depositions at the court of chivalry.

Two other cases have also been discussed by historians to further illustrate the late fourteenth century military community. Maurice Keen has analysed the records from the Grey v. Hastings case in the early years of the reign of Henry IV.[154] Keen identified similar patterns of service to that shown in the analysis above. He noted that of his selection of examples, four men had served by the time they were twelve years old.[155] The Grey v. Hastings dispute was different to the case of Scrope v. Grosvenor, as it also concerned the inheritance of the earl of Pembroke, who had been killed in a tournament in 1389, without heir of the body. The man who dealt the fatal blow was Sir John St John, who also served in 1388.[156] Sir Reginald Grey of Ruthin had inherited the Pembroke estate and Sir Edward Hastings was challenging the inheritance. Both men had used the arms of the earl of Pembroke, *or a manche gules*, in the Scottish expedition of Henry IV in 1400. The case, which was brought by Grey, therefore had a wider remit than the right to bear these arms. Indeed, Hastings was using these arms[157] in an attempt to provoke such a challenge. The case is of interest because Sir Reginald Grey had also served in the retinue of the earl of Arundel in 1387.[158] Grey himself had been a deponent at the Scrope v. Grosvenor case.[159] Keen provides nominal evidence for those who supported Sir Reginald Grey. I have been unable to find any continuance with those who served in 1387–1388. However, Keen also describes the careers of 42 witnesses who testified for Hastings, and of these, 13 men can be found to have also served in the campaigns of the earl of Arundel. Table 21 summarises those who demonstrate this continuance of service.

These men have colourful careers in the military community, and it was clear that Hastings had found witnesses who could add strength to his case, due to their military experience. Robert Fyshlake is a particular relevant example, as it allows us to demonstrate the career of an archer in the English armies. Fyshlake can be identified as serving in the retinue of the Earl Marshal in 1388.[160] His

---

also be his son who also served in Ireland in 1399, *CPR, 1396–1399*, p. 563 (protection), 'as John, son of John, Lord de Lovell'.

[154] Keen, 'English Military Experience and the Court of Chivalry', pp. 123–142.

[155] *Ibid.*, p. 131.

[156] E101/41/5 m. 3.

[157] Keen, 'English Military Experience and the Court of Chivalry', pp. 125–128.

[158] E101/40/33 m. 1.

[159] *Scrope v. Grosvenor*, vol. i, p. 207.

[160] E101/41/5 m. 3d.

Table 21. Hastings' deponents

Name	Title	First name	Surname	Rank	Captain	Year
E. Barry		Esmon	Barry	Esquire	Arundel, Richard, earl of	1388
J. Bere		John	Bere	Esquire	Arundel, Richard, earl of	1387
		Johan	Bere	Esquire	Esmon Randulph	1388
Sir W. Calsthorp	Mons	William	Calthorp	Knight	Mons Thomas Camoys	1388
R. Fyshlake		Robert	Fysshlake	Archer	Le Counte Marshall	1388
Sir R. Morley		Robert	Morlee	Esquire	Le Counte Marshall	1388
C. Mortimer		Constantyn	Mortunere	Esquire	Arundel, Richard, earl of	1388
J. Parker		John	Parker	Esquire	Mons Johan Darundell	1387
		Johan	Parker	Esquire	Mons Johan Darundell	1388
J. Payn		Johan	Payn	Esquire	Arundel, Richard, earl of	1388
W. Plumstead		William	Plumstede	Esquire	Mons William Heron	1388
J. Roger		Johan	Roger	Esquire	Benet Cely	1388
T. Stanton		Thomas	Stanton	Archer	Robert Geffard	1387
Sir J. Wiltshire	Mons	Johan	Wylteshyre	Knight	Arundel, Richard, earl of	1388
Sir W. Wisham		William	Wyshiam	Esquire	Mons Hugh le Despencer	1388

deposition does not feature this service, as Hastings did not serve in these campaigns. His testimony states that he accompanied Edward's father, Hugh Hastings III to Jerusalem and the Eastern Mediterranean; he had been on expedition with John of Gaunt in 1378; he had served on the ill-fated expedition of Sir John Arundel in 1379; in 1380 he had served with the earl of Buckingham in Britanny; and he had served in Scotland in 1385.[161] Therefore, together with the campaign of 1388, Fyshlake had served in five major expeditions and demonstrates that archers could also show a professional level of service in the royal armies. William Plumstead, an esquire with Sir William Heron in 1388,[162] also shows an extensive career in the English expeditions. He had served in Guienne in 1370; with Gaunt in 1378; with Sir John Arundel in 1379; with Buckingham in 1380; and in Portugal with Gaunt in 1386.[163] He had therefore continued this service swiftly by joining Arundel's expedition in 1388. Sir John Wiltshire, who served in the retinue of the earl of Arundel in 1388,[164] also demonstrates an impressive military career. He testified that he served in the sea fight off La Rochelle in 1372; in Scotland in 1385; and with Gaunt in 1386.[165] Wiltshire also served with Richard II in Ireland in 1399.[166] These three men, archer, esquire and knight respectively, demonstrate extensive careers and this is mainly utilising their first hand evidence when they had seen a Hastings bearing arms. This supports the evidence provided by the Scrope v. Grosvenor case, which demonstrates that many professional soldiers served in 1387–1388, regardless of the political implications. As far as they were concerned they treated the

---

161 Keen, 'English Military Experience and the Court of Chivalry', pp. 132–133.
162 E101/41/5 m. 8.
163 Keen, 'English Military Experience and the Court of Chivalry', pp. 132–133.
164 E101/41/5 m. 1.
165 Keen, 'English Military Experience and the Court of Chivalry', pp. 132–133.
166 *CPR, 1396–1399*, pp. 541 and 551 (attorney), p. 545 (protection).

campaign as another part of their military career. However, Plumstead and Wiltshire both secured a royal pardon in 1398, perhaps because of their actions during the period of Appellant supremacy.[167] It has not all been plain sailing for them in the later years of Richard II's reign, as the earlier adherence to the Appellants had taken on a treasonous undertone. Perhaps men who served in such a professional manner would have been drawn to the Appellants' company in opposing the royal force of de Vere in December 1387. Wiltshire's service in 1399 suggests that the pardon had provided him with the ability to serve in the royal expedition.

Andrew Ayton has worked on the rolls for the case between John, Lord Lovel, and Thomas, Lord Morley, in the mid-1380s, which again followed a dispute over the right to bear arms, this time *argent a lion rampant sable crowned and armed or*, triggered by service in Scotland in 1385.[168] Sir John Lovell served in the retinue of Lord Welles in 1388 and as we have discussed above was also a deponent in the Scrope v. Grosvenor case. It is interesting that he decided to serve in 1388 for the Appellants despite being abjured from the royal court in the same year for his loyalty to the king.[169] It could be Lord Lovel's son, Sir John who served in 1388; however this is not clear. Leland, in his article on the abjuration admits that it is difficult to tie Lord Lovel down, because of the preponderance of Sir John Lovels in the family. He points out, for instance, it may well be that Lord Lovel died in 1391; however *Complete Peerage* does not acknowledge this.[170] It could be possible that the career of Lord Lovel as discussed above may be an amalgam of the careers of father and son.[171]

We are not able to make any further comparisons with the Lovel v. Morley case and the campaigns of 1387–1388, as only a small number of the deponents are mentioned in the article. Ayton is able to make a number of generalisations from the evidence, which demonstrates that the gentry of the later fourteenth century were actively involved in the military community. He comments:

> In short, the active warrior aristocracy extended well down the social hierarchy, beyond the knightly community, to rest squarely in the ranks of the lesser gentry.[172]

The preponderance of esquires in the comparisons made with the Scrope v. Grosvenor evidence and also Grey v. Hastings evidence supports this claim. It can be seen that those men who testified and served in 1387–1388 had extensive military careers and they came from the ranks of esquires and archers, as well as the knights as one would expect.

---

[167] Plumstead: C67/30 m. 15; Wiltshire: *ibid.*, m. 3.
[168] Ayton, 'Knights, Esquires and Military Service', pp. 81–104.
[169] John L. Leland, 'The Abjuration of 1388', *Medieval Prosopography*, 15:1 (1994), pp. 115–138, see pp. 115, 135–137. Thomas, Lord Camoys, was also abjured and served in the campaigns of 1387–1388.
[170] *Complete Peerage*, vol. viii, pp. 219–221 for father and p. 221 for son.
[171] Leland, 'The Abjuration of 1388', p. 136, citing *CPR, 1388–1392*, pp. 520 and 512 for reference to him as dead and replaced by Sir John Lovel as heir.
[172] Ayton, 'Knights, Esquires and Military Service', p. 96.

Table 22. Comparison with Windsor, 1380

Year	Title	First name	Surname	Position	Captain name
1380		John	Apulton	Archer	Sir William de Windsor
1388		Johan	Appulton	Archer	Mons Olyner Mauleverer
1380		Roger	atte Wode	Esquire	Sir William de Windsor
1387		Roger	atte Wode	Esquire	Mons Thomas Trevet
1380		John	Barton	Esquire	Sir William de Windsor
1388		Johan	Barton	Esquire	Mons Thomas Camoys
1380		John	Blakeburne	Archer	Sir William de Windsor
1388		Johan	Blakburn	Archer	Mons Hugh Browe
1380		John	Boteler	Esquire	Sir William de Windsor
1388		Johes	Boteler	Esquire	Mons Thomas Percy
1380		Lucas	Botellier	Archer	Sir William de Windsor
1388		Lucas	Boteler	Archer	Giles Weston
1380		John	Bron	Esquire	Sir William de Windsor
1387		John	Bronn	Esquire	Mons Hugh le Despencer
1388		Johan	Bron	Esquire	Mons Hugh le Despencer
1380		John	Bron	Archer	Sir William de Windsor
1387		John	Bronn	Archer	Mons Johan Wynkefeld
1388		John	Bronn	Archer	Le Monsers W Sire de Welles
1380		Richard	Bron	Archer	Sir William de Windsor
1387		Richard	Bronn	Archer	John Slegh
1380		William	Burhull	Esquire	Sir William de Windsor
1387		William	Burghull	Esquire	Mons Gilbe Talbot
1380		William	Chambleyn	Esquire	Sir William de Windsor
1388		William	Chambleyn	Esquire	Mons William Baron de Hylton
1380		Thomas	Chambelen	Archer	Sir William de Windsor
1388		Thomas	Chambleyn	Archer	Mons Thomas Camoys
1380		John	Chaundeler	Archer	Sir William de Windsor
1388		Johan	Chaundeller	Archer	Mons Gilbe Talbot
1380		Wauter	Clement	Esquire	Sir William de Windsor
1387		Wauter	Clement	Esquire	Arundel, Richard, earl of
1380		William	Clerc	Esquire	Sir William de Windsor
1388		William	Clerc	Esquire	Mons Olyner Manlenerer
1380		John	Clere	Archer	Sir William de Windsor
1388		Johan	Clere	Archer	Mons Hugh le Despencer
1380		William	Cok	Esquire	Sir William de Windsor
1388		William	Cok	Esquire	Mons William Briene
1380		John	Cok	Archer	Sir William de Windsor
1388		Johan	Cok	Archer	Johan Staple
1380		John	Cok le Pisune	Esquire	Sir William de Windsor
1387		John	Cok	Esquire	Arundel, Richard, earl of
1380		Henry	le Cook	Archer	Sir William de Windsor
1388		Henry	Cook	Archer	Mons William Briene
1380		William	Cook	Archer	Sir William de Windsor
1387		William	Cook	Archer	Le Sire de Beaumount
1388		William	Cook	Archer	Mons Gilbe Talbot

1380	Thomas	Fferrour	Archer	Sir William de Windsor
1388	Thomas	Ferowr	Archer	Mons Thomas Percy
1380	William	Fferrour	Archer	Sir William de Windsor
1387	William	Fferrour	Archer	Mons Hugh le Despencer
1388	William	Ferrour	Archer	Mons Hugh le Despencer
1380	John	Ffere	Archer	Sir William de Windsor
1387	John	Ffere	Archer	Le Counte de Devens
1388	Johan	Frere	Archer	Thomas atte Lee
1380	William	Fflemyng	Archer	Sir William de Windsor
1388	William	Flemyng	Archer	Richard Waynill
1380	John	Ffrenssh	Archer	Sir William de Windsor
1388	Johan	Frenssh	Archer	Mons Johan Darundell
1380	Richard	Hampton	Esquire	Sir William de Windsor
1388	Richard	Hampton	Esquire	Arundel, Richard, earl of
1380	Robert	Horn	Archer	Sir William de Windsor
1388	Robert	Horn	Archer	Mons Andrewe Hake
1380	John	Howell	Archer	Sir William de Windsor
1387	John	Howell	Archer	Le Counte de Devens
1380	John	Hunte	Archer	Sir William de Windsor
1388	Johan	Hunte	Archer	Mons William Briene
1380	John	Kent	Archer	Sir William de Windsor
1387	John	Kent	Archer	Mons Hugh Loterell
1388	Johan	Kent	Archer	Mons William Heron
1380	John	Lancastr	Esquire	Sir William de Windsor
1388	Johan	Lancastre	Esquire	Richard Waynill
1380	Lucas	Ludegard	Archer	Sir William de Windsor
1387	Lucas	Ludegaas	Archer	Mons Thomas Trevet
1388	Lucas	Ludegard	Esquire	Mons Arnald Savage
1380	William	Marshall	Esquire	Sir William de Windsor
1388	William	Mareschall	Esquire	Mons William Heron
1380	John	Merton, de	Esquire	Sir William de Windsor
1387	John	Merton	Esquire	Mons Hugh le Despencer
1388	Johan	Merton	Esquire	Mons Hugh le Despencer
1380	John	North, de	Archer	Sir William de Windsor
1387	John	North	Archer	Le Sire de Beaumount
1380	John	Nowell	Esquire	Sir William de Windsor
1388	Johan	Nowell	Esquire	Mons Robert Massey
1380	John	Parker	Archer	Sir William de Windsor
1387	John	Parker	Archer	Arundel, Richard, earl of
1388	Johan	Parker	Archer	Arundel, Richard, earl of
1380	John	Preston	Esquire	Sir William de Windsor
1387	John	Preston	Esquire	Mons Reynold de Cobham
1380	John	Roos de Tilbury	Esquire	Sir William de Windsor
1388	John	Roos	Esquire	Le Monsers W Sire de Welles
1380	Richard	Smith	Archer	Sir William de Windsor
1387	Richard	Smyth	Archer	Mons Johan Darundell
1388	Richard	Smyth	Archer	Mons Johan Clanyng

Year	Title	First name	Surname	Position	Captain name
1380		Robert	Smith	Archer	Sir William de Windsor
1387		Robert	Smyth	Archer	Arundel, Richard, earl of
1388		Robert	Smyth	Archer	Robert Geffard
1380		Wauter	Smith	Archer	Sir William de Windsor
1388		Wauter	Smyth	Archer	Mons William Heron
1380		John	Spaldyng	Archer	Sir William de Windsor
1388		Johan	Spaldyng	Archer	Robert Geffard
1380		John	Stone	Archer	Sir William de Windsor
1387		John	Stone	Archer	Mons Richard Craddok
1380		Thomas	Talbot	Esquire	Sir William de Windsor
1388		Thomas	Talbot	Esquire	Aleyn Seintjust
1380		John	Walssh	Esquire	Sir William de Windsor
1387	Mons	John	Walssch	Knight	Le Sire de Beaumount
1380		William	Ware	Esquire	Sir William de Windsor
1387		William	Ware	Esquire	Mons Thomas Mortemer
1388		William	Ware	Esquire	Mons Johan Darundell
1380		John	West	Archer	Sir William de Windsor
1388		Johan	West	Archer	Mons Hugh le Despencer

Keen suggested that the evidence of the Grey v. Hastings case seems to infer that, in the last quarter of the fourteenth century, men were less interested in campaigning in the king's service, thus accounting for the relative lack of experiences described in the depositions.[173] Ayton, however, suggested that in fact the gentry had not become demilitarised. He comments:

> Decades of campaigning, requiring heavy, if intermittent, recruitment, and a decidedly more intensive phase of warfare after 1369, had focused the attention of the gentry on the wars in France and in Scotland – wars in which esquires and other men of subknightly status played an important if too rarely recognised part.[174]

The evidence of the court of chivalry has also demonstrated that a good number of the men who appeared as witnesses were also involved in the campaigns of 1387–1388. This demonstrates that these campaigns were not fought as a one-off experience, but for many contributed to their overall experience of warfare in the service of the English crown.

[173] Keen, 'English Military Experience and the Court of Chivalry', pp. 133–136.
[174] Ayton, 'Knights, Esquires and Military Service', pp. 96–97.

Service in 1380

It is possible to look for continued service between the campaigns of 1387–1388 and the retinue captained by Sir William de Windsor in 1380. This provides the opportunity to look below the rank of retinue captain and man-at-arms and allows us to investigate the continuity of service for archers. The muster rolls surviving for this campaign, as well as being a rare survival during the later fourteenth century, are of interest as they are from an expedition just seven years prior to the campaigns of 1387 and 1388. Windsor captained a retinue on the expedition led by the earl of Buckingham (the future duke of Gloucester) in 1380. The retinue was between 404 and 410 soldiers in strength.[175] The troops on this expedition contracted to serve for one year and campaigned through Brittany and France from 19 July 1380, returning on 2 May 1381. A number of muster rolls have survived for the force captained by Sir William de Windsor and it has been possible to conduct a comparison with the soldiers who served in the campaigns of 1387–1388.

The results of this are summarised in Table 22. From this it can be seen that 49 men serving in 1380 can be identified as continuing service in the campaigns of 1387–1388. This represents 12% of the force serving with Windsor in 1380. Of these men: 11 soldiers serve both in 1387 and 1388; 10 soldiers serve in 1387; and 28 soldiers serve in 1388. These men are spread throughout the constituent parts of the ranks of the army, though there is only one knight. The other soldiers represent 19 esquires and 29 archers. This service is spread throughout thirty-one different retinues in 1387–1388, mainly with one or two soldiers in each. The largest concentration occurs in the retinues of the earl of Arundel and Sir Hugh le Despencer, who have six men in their retinues who have also served in 1380. It is also interesting to note the service of Lucas Ludegard in 1380, 1387 and 1388.[176] If all three entries are for the same person, which seems likely, it is unusual that he is described as archer in 1378 and 1387 and as esquire in 1388. It would not be easy to progress from the position of archer to esquire and such a transition between ranks has not been noticed elsewhere in the records under consideration in this study. A man-at-arms would require a warhorse and perhaps multiple mounts in addition to arms and armour. An archer would need a horse that was suitable for travel and would have lighter armour.[177] This difference in requirements would have made it difficult for men to advance from archer to man-at-arms in terms of expense alone. However, it would seem in this particular case that Ludegard has indeed advanced through the ranks, perhaps because of his previous military experience. One other such example is the famous soldier Sir Robert Knollys, who advanced from bowman to commanding the expedition to France of 1370. Walsingham described him as

---

[175] E101/39/7, mm. 3, 4; m. 3 shows a retinue of 410 soldiers, including 2 bannerets including Sir William de Windsor, 10 knights, 192 esquires 'genz armes', and 206 archers; m. 4 shows a retinue of 404 retinues, including 2 bannerets including Sir William de Windsor, 10 knights, 186 esquires and 206 archers.

[176] 1380: E101/39/7, mm. 3 and 4; 1387: E101/40/33 m. 7. 1388: E101/41/5 m. 13d.

[177] For average costs see Ayton, *Knights and Warhorses*, pp. 224–229.

a 'pauper mediocrisque valletus' and it was perhaps his perceived lack of status which contributed to the break-up of this army in the field.[178]

This comparison has demonstrated that soldiers in the general ranks of the army may also have served on other royal expeditions. Whilst it is possible to describe the careers of more well known participants in the royal expeditions, information on those forming the largest part of the army is not always available. However, this comparison suggests that a group of other soldiers who campaigned in 1387–1388 also campaigned in further expeditions. These men were probably serving as part of a continuing military career and in support of the king's right in France.

[178] Walsingham, *Historia Anglicana*, vol. i, p. 286, and for Sir Robert Knollys see *DNB*, vol. xxxi, pp. 281–286. For comment see Prestwich, *Armies and Warfare in the Middle Ages*, p. 166. For the expedition of 1370 see Sherborne, 'Indentured Retinues', pp. 723–725.

5

Loyalties and Connections

Attendance on either of the two expeditions alone is not proof that these men were anything other than professional soldiers or indeed were part of the English military community fighting the continued campaign against the French. What other evidence survives to link the participants with the senior Appellants?

The Arundel Connection: case studies

John Mendham, an esquire of Sir Thomas Trivet in 1387 and an esquire of Arundel in 1388,[1] would appear to have a relationship with Arundel from this progression of service as shown in the muster rolls. *History of Parliament* records that he was from Canterbury, Kent, but detailed information about his life is not recorded. The biography does not record his inclusion in these expeditions.[2] It does, however, record that he was only once a member of parliament for Canterbury in February 1388, which happened to be the Merciless Parliament where the Appellants prosecuted their enemies. Although other links with Arundel are not evident, this appearance at this particular parliament does hold much significance. This could be an example of Arundel packing parliament in his favour to support his attack on the king's favourites. The appearance at the Merciless Parliament together with the service in both expeditions and indeed in the retinue of Arundel in 1388, shows that Mendham had become involved with Arundel during this period and had been able to advance his position. These small pieces of information analysed together shed light on an otherwise unknown individual. Another interesting relationship emerges from an entry in the *Calendar of Close Rolls*. He is noted as acting as a surety in Chancery for Sir Richard Hoo in May 1393.[3] Sir Richard Hoo also serves in both expeditions and is in addition present in the retinue of Sir Thomas Trivet in 1387.[4] Thus again, this is an example of men serving because of kinship; they have a bond that continues into their service in an overseas campaign. Alternatively, they

---

1   1387: E101/40/33 m. 7. 1388: E101/41/5 m. 1.
2   *HOP*, vol. iii, p. 716.
3   *CCR, 1392–1396*, p. 148.
4   1387: E101/40/33 m. 7. 1388: E101/41/5 m. 13d. I have not discovered any other information linking Sir Richard Hoo with the Appellants. Professor Anne Curry has suggested that he could be from Sussex and an ancestor of Thomas, Lord Hoo. This would place him within Arundel's sphere of influence.

may have formed a bond in the expedition of 1387 that has carried on following the campaign. It is evident that personal kinship was an important element in the *mentalité* of those who served in these expeditions.

Another combatant has a more unusual connection with Arundel. Sir Thomas de Ponynges married Arundel's widow, Philippa, after the death of the earl – an example of extreme loyalty to one's master.[5] Sir Thomas served on the expeditions of both 1387 and 1388 as a retinue captain.[6] He also can be identified as serving in Arundel's retinue in the expedition to France with John of Gaunt in 1378.[7] He has therefore had a relationship with Arundel for many years, and the expeditions of 1387–1388 are not the first time they have campaigned together overseas. In addition, Ponynges can be identified as being a tenant of Arundel[8] and three other tenants of Arundel serve under his captaincy in 1388.[9] These tenancy relationships would also suggest a strong relationship with the admiral. To be in the position to marry Arundel's widow, Ponynges relationship with the earl (or the countess!) may have been very close. Ponynges also secures a royal pardon in 1398 following the prosecution of the earl of Arundel.[10] However, it appears that Ponynges has not been damaged by the fall of the earl for he leads a royal commission in 1399:

> Commission to Thomas Ponynges, William de Hoo, William Fienles, sheriff of Sussex, William Percy, William Burcestre, William Echyngham, John Halsham and Richard Hurst, on information that certain enemies of the king in no small number, armed and unarmed, have assembled in parts beyond the sea to invade the realm during his absence in Ireland, and that others have landed and taken the castle of Pevensey, co. Sussex, and hold it as in war – to besiege the said castle with all the *posse comitatus*, to take order for its recovery (*recuperacione*), as well as guard the coasts against invasion.[11]

He has been given responsibility for defence against a possible invasion that suggests that he has gained a position of trust with the king. His close relationship with Arundel, which has included captaining a retinue in both expeditions

---

5   Goodman, *Loyal Conspiracy*, p. 118, citing *Complete Peerage*, vol. xi, pp. 328–329, Thomas de Poynings, Lord St John. See also *ibid.*, vol. x, pp. 667–668; his identification as Thomas, Lord Poynings is possibly because of a mistake in a summons to Parliament.
6   1387: E101/40/33 m. 8; enrolled protection, C76/71 m. 12. 1388: E101/41/5 m. 11d.
7   E101/36/32 m. 3.
8   *Two Estate Surveys*, p. 115.
9   Thomas Fletcher: E101/41/5 m. 6d; *Two Estate Surveys*, p. 139, '1 virgate 3s 3d in Rogate'. Robert Frye, 1388: E101/41/5 m. 6d; *Two Estate Surveys*, p. 114, 'free suitor to the Hundred court of Bourne'; p. 155 '(blank) for 1 lb. of pepper and 3s 0d; Also 2 virgates 10s 0d; 4a. 2s 0d in Oupmerdon'; p. 156, 'with Edith Carpenter, 6a 5s 4d in Compton; 8a. 3s 5d in Bymthe; part of Bourne manor.' Richard Wodeland, 1388: E101/41/5 m. 6d; *Two Estate Surveys*, p. 118, 'The tenement he lives in 1s 2d; Tenement in the corner 7d; Roper's tenement 7d; 3a on Le Ligher 1s 9d; Total 4s 1d in Arundell'; p. 119, 'Caryas' tenement 1s 0d; 1 Chanell 7d; House in Chupyng 7d in Arundell'; p. 125, '5 roods 1½d (listed beneath John Wilteshire) in Polyng'; p. 126, 'Messuage & 4a 2s 0d as Free Tenant in Lunemenstr' '; p. 131, '6a. meadow for ½ lb cummin and 1d. as Free Tenant in Offham.'
10 C67/30 m. 17.
11 *CPR, 1396–1399*, p. 596.

of 1387 and 1388, has not prevented him from such advancement with the crown. Following the deposition, he gained a licence to go on Pilgrimage to Jerusalem for three years.[12] It is of note that two of the men serving with Ponynges on the above commission can also be identified within the muster rolls. William Echyngham is listed as the first esquire in the retinue of Sir Arnold Savage in 1387[13] and Richard Hurst is listed as an esquire in the retinue of Sir William Briene in 1388.[14]

One participant who can be firmly identified as a supporter of Arundel is Sir William Heron, a knight with Sir Nicholas Clifton in 1387 and a retinue captain in 1388.[15] He was a loyal servant of Arundel and explained to Parliament in 1388, on the earl's behalf, the reasons for the delay in the departure of the naval expedition that year.[16] Although he appeared twice for Northumberland at Parliament in 1382 and 1385, this representation is not covered by *History of Parliament*, which does not begin until 1386. However, some information can be gained by viewing the entry for his brother, Sir Gerard Heron.[17] This entry describes Sir Gerard as the younger brother of Sir William, Lord Say (d.s.p. 30 October 1404), steward of the household to Henry IV (1402–4).[18] It also mentions that, from the beginning of Henry's reign, Sir William was despatched on a number of important missions overseas. Both Sir William and his brother supported Henry IV during the rebellion mounted in the summer of 1403 by the earl of Northumberland.

Goodman constructs a brief biography of Sir William Heron in *Loyal Conspiracy*, and refers to him as a 'landowner connected with Arundel'.[19] He comments that Heron married the widow of another Arundel loyalist who also served in 1387 and 1388, namely John, Lord Fawsley of Fawsley (Northants).[20] The lady both of these men marry was Elizabeth, sister and heir of John, Lord Say. Fawsley is described as Lord Say in Arundel's retinue in 1388.[21] Fawsley was a long standing colleague of Arundel and also held land in Sussex. He also can be identified as serving in Arundel's retinue in the earlier expedition of 1378.[22] Heron was already a staunch supporter of Arundel and marries the widow of another staunch supporter. Goodman mentions that Heron was to be

---

12 *Complete Peerage*, vol. xi, p. 329.

13 E101/40/33 m. 6d.

14 E101/41/5 m. 9.

15 1387: E101/40/33 m. 12d. 1388: E101/41/5 m. 8. Also described as *Le Souz Admiralls*, along with Sir Hugh Browe.

16 E159/167 m. 51 (Brevia Baronibus Michaelmas) cited in Tuck, 'Cambridge Parliament', p. 233, with John Stephens, and also E354/24 m. 5, described as William Heyron, chevaler.

17 *HOP*, vol. ii, pp. 353–357.

18 *Royal Household*, p. 287 (steward 1402–1404), knight of the chamber and lay officer of the household, of Northumberland/Sussex, retained in 1402.

19 Goodman, *Loyal Conspiracy*, pp. 117–118.

20 1387: E101/40/33 m. 1; enrolled protection, C76/71 m. 12; enrolled attorney, C76/71 m. 10.

21 Goodman, *Loyal Conspiracy*, p. 117; 1388: E101/41/5 m. 1; enrolled protection, C76/72 m. 7. *Complete Peerage*, vol. xi, p. 478 for Elizabeth, Baroness Say and v, pp. 250–252 for Sir John Falvesle.

22 1378: E101/36/32, m. 3.

pardoned in 1398 for his earlier adherence to the Appellants.[23] Heron also owned a ship, the *la Marie* of Sandwich, which was to be used in the expedition of 1388.[24] It seems that he later sought military service with Richard II in Ireland, as he is mentioned in a letter from the earl of Rutland 'as having received the submission of a captain of Munster'.[25] He may also have served earlier in Ireland as can be seen from a reference in the *Calendar of Patent Rolls* in 1386, when he took out a protection to accompany Sir John Stanley on expedition to Ireland.[26] Therefore, although associated with Arundel, Heron also served Richard II and later was a close supporter of Henry IV. His career shows how an individual could advance by making sure that he changed loyalties with the changing political mood. It also shows how the people he served with on expedition were also people he had relationships with in his non-military life. However, at the time of the expedition, we can see that he was an Arundel man and thus was involved in the expedition because of the support he had shown to the earl.

John Elyngton is listed on the muster rolls for both expeditions of 1387 and 1388 in the retinue of the earl of Arundel.[27] His position on the muster roll as the twentieth esquire listed in 1387 is reflected by his position as Arundel's messenger. He was attacked on his return to England in 1387 and this event is recorded in the *Calendar of Patent Rolls*.[28] This has provided us with the ability to identify an esquire holding a position within the household of the earl of Arundel and thus serving with his earl in a military capacity. In 1388, Elyngton has found it pertinent to appoint an attorney to protect his interests whilst on service overseas. Elyngton can also be shown to have secured a royal pardon in 1398, to protect against his actions in support of Arundel in 1387–1388.[29]

Another esquire in both expeditions who also has strong connections to Arundel is John Babelake.[30] He has an entry in *History of Parliament* where he is described as an 'obscure esquire'. He was a member of parliament only once in November 1414 as representative for Sussex. It describes his career as being spent in the service of the earls of Arundel – Richard Fitzalan and his son, Thomas. It mentions that he served in Arundel's retinue in 1387, however, it misses his service also in Arundel's retinue in 1388.[31] In both retinues he is listed high amongst the esquires, eighteenth in 1387 and ninth in 1388, which

---

23 Goodman, *Loyal Conspiracy*, p. 117; C67/30 m. 3. See *Complete Peerage*, vol. vi, pp. 492–493.
24 Goodman, *Loyal Conspiracy*, p. 117; *CPR, 1385–1389*, p. 449, 5 June 1388, 'appointment of John atte Mede and Richard Hille to repair his ship la Marie of Sandwich'. A Johannes atte Meede is also in the expedition of 1388 in Arnold Savage's retinue as an archer, this could be the same carpenter who has decided to join the expedition. E101/41/5 m. 14.
25 E. Curtis, *Richard II in Ireland* (Oxford, 1927), p. 123; *CPR, 1391–1396*, p. 483 (protection).
26 *CPR, 1385–1389*, p. 125.
27 1387: E101/40/33 m. 1. 1388: E101/41/5 m. 1; enrolled attorney, C76/72 m. 8.
28 *CPR, 1385–1389*, p. 323.
29 C67/30 m. 16.
30 1387: E101/40/33 m. 1. 1388: E101/41/5 m. 1.
31 *HOP*, vol. i, p. 93.

further represents this close relationship. In addition, Babelake was rewarded for his support of the Appellants, by being awarded a share in the Exchequer lease of the alien priory of Deerhurst. However, this reward was quickly removed in 1389 when Richard regained control of crown patronage and the share was awarded to a king's knight.[32] It is also pertinent to note that he took the precaution of purchasing a royal pardon in June 1398, following the execution of Arundel, which specifically related to the support he had given to the Appellants.[33] This involvement with Arundel during these years of Appellant supremacy, and also the fact that he took out a royal pardon, could point to his being involved at Radcot Bridge. As has been noted above he held lands in Sussex as a result of the patronage of the earls of Arundel[34] and he was quick to support Thomas, earl of Arundel[35] on his return from exile in support of Bolingbroke in 1399. His career blossomed under the young earl of Arundel and the new regime.

Babelake was involved in the suppression of the revolt of Owain Glyn Dwr during 1404–1405. This would have been an ironic turn of events, for he would probably have known Glyn Dwr well from the expedition of 1387. They are listed eleventh and eighteenth respectively in the muster roll of esquires of the retinue of the earl of Arundel.[36] Following this, he represented Thomas, earl of Arundel in negotiations for the hand of Beatrice, the illegitimate daughter of King João I of Portugal, and then escorted her to England. He is also then connected with another supporter of Arundel, Sir Peter Besiles, to whom he conveys his holdings in Oxfordshire in 1411.[37] His appearance at Parliament was during his patron, the earl of Arundel's height of influence, as treasurer of the Exchequer and friend of Henry V. Thomas, earl of Arundel died in October 1415, shortly after the siege of Harfleur, and after this date Babelake disappears from the records.[38] Babelake's presence in both expeditions in a prominent position in the retinues, has thrown extra light on this 'obscure' and 'enigmatic' figure. It also shows that Arundel's retinue contained many trusted retainers, which was not unusual for a figure of such authority.

Peter Besiles[39] serves in the expedition of 1387 and 1388. His allegiance to Arundel is suggested by his attendance for both years and also the fact that Arundel dubs him as a knight on campaign on 28 June 1388.[40] He serves in the

---

[32] *CPR, 1388–1392*, p. 71.

[33] C67/30, m. 2.

[34] *Two Estate Surveys*, p. 100, free suitor to the Hundred-court of Rutherebrugge, for lands in Keredeforde; p. 149, with William Steghere: hold the demense and 1a in Palynghame.

[35] The son and heir of Richard Fitzalan, earl of Arundel.

[36] E101/40/33 m. 1.

[37] *CCR, 1409–1413*, p. 300.

[38] *HOP*, vol. i, p. 93n, mentions that J.H. Wylie and W.T. Waugh, *The Reign of Henry the Fifth* (3 vols, Cambridge, 1914–29), vol. ii, p. 68, thought that John Bartlot, executor of the will of Earl Thomas, was 'probably the enigmatic "Vabelate" or Bablake of the Portuguese negotiations', but no evidence has been found to confirm this identification.

[39] *HOP*, vol. ii, pp. 216–217, identifies the variants on the name Bessels, as Beselles, Besiles and Besyles. He is described in the muster rolls as Piers Besiles and Piers Besilles.

[40] E101/41/5 m. 11d, described as 'factus miles xxviii die Junii'. Interestingly, *HOP* has the correct reference for this occurrence but places the event in the previous year, 1387.

retinue of Sir Gilbert Talbot in both years,[41] who is in turn identifiable as a strong supporter of the king in the years following the Appellant supremacy. Besiles served in Parliament for Oxfordshire in January 1404 and for Berkshire in March 1416 and 1423. His entry in *History of Parliament* identifies him as a substantial landholder in the upper Thames valley.[42] He can also be shown to have taken a protection in order to accompany the king and Sir Gilbert Talbot on the Irish expedition of 1394.[43] No other relationships with either Talbot or Arundel are evident from the sources. The muster roll entries, and especially the evidence of his knighting in 1388, suggest such a relationship and indeed would intimate that he was being rewarded for loyal service to the Appellants. It would not be such a leap of imagination to suggest that Besiles may have been involved in the skirmish at Radcot Bridge, considering his landholding was in that area. However, he did not feel that it was necessary to secure a royal pardon in 1398.

John Leland, in his article on the 'Oxford Trial of 1400', discusses those involved as jurors and those prosecuted.[44] He describes how many of these men on opposing sides had similar backgrounds and shared values and thus it is difficult to draw conclusions about why such decisions about supporting or opposing Henry IV had been taken at this point. One such man was indeed Sir Peter Besiles whose loyalty swiftly switched to the new regime in 1400 so that he acted as a juror on the trial of Sir Thomas Blount and other traitors at Oxford castle on 12 January 1400. Leland describes how Besiles had a full and active career under Henry IV and how he had not had such recognition under Richard II. Following the support given by Bessels to the Appellants in 1387 and 1388, he served under Richard II in Ireland in 1394.[45] However, in his support for the new regime of Henry IV, Bessels can perhaps be seen to be returning to the loyalties he had shown in the years of Appellant supremacy.

Another combatant who would appear to have a relationship with Arundel is Sir Benedict Cely. This could be assumed as, like Besiles, he serves as an esquire in the retinue of Arundel in 1387 and is knighted on campaign on 27 June 1388.[46] Cely also served with Richard II in Ireland in 1394 in the company of the earl of Huntingdon.[47] An interesting contrast is highlighted when his later involvement in the Epiphany Plot uprising of 1400 in support of Richard II is noted. He was brought before the court at Oxford for which Besiles was serving as a juror.[48] These two former colleagues in arms would later oppose each other in a court room, since Cely decided to rebel against the new

---

41 1387: E101/40/33 m. 12. 1388: E101/41/5 m. 11d.
42 *HOP*, vol. ii, pp. 216–217.
43 *CPR, 1391–1396*, p. 498 (protection).
44 J.L. Leland, 'The Oxford Trial of 1400: Royal Politics and the County Gentry', in *The Age of Richard II*, ed. J.L. Gillespie (Stroud, 1997), pp. 165–189. Leland describes him as Sir Peter Besiles.
45 *Ibid.*, p. 172.
46 1388: E101/40/33 m. 15, described as 'factus miles xxvii die Julii'; enrolled protection, C76/72 m. 7. 1387: E101/40/33 m. 1; enrolled protection, C76/71 m. 14.
47 *CPR, 1391–1396*, p. 535 (protection).
48 Leland, 'Oxford Trial', p. 170.

regime established by Henry IV. Sir Benedict's allegiance has therefore swung to Richard II in the intervening years. He can indeed be found to have served with the king on his Irish expedition of 1399, and was one of the few followers to retain their loyalty after the deposition.[49]

Supporters of Arundel can be identified from land holdings within the areas of his influence. It would be normal for men with such connections to serve their local lord in expeditions and one such man would appear to be the esquire, John Chamberlain. In 1388 he served in the expedition in the retinue of Lord Welles.[50] He is listed in *History of Parliament* as being from Arundel, Sussex, and represented the borough of Arundel as a Member of Parliament in February 1383, October 1383, 1385 and 1393.[51] This biography is short, but interestingly shows that he held land in the hundred of Arundel, as well as the house in which he lived as a tenant of Richard, earl of Arundel. This landholding is confirmed in the estate surveys discussed above.[52] He was well informed about the earl's property holdings and following Arundel's execution was required to provide evidence about his possessions, then declared forfeit. He also found it prudent to secure a royal pardon for his previous relationship with the Appellants in 1398.[53]

Another supporter of Arundel who can be identified from the sources is John Daras. He appeared as a member of parliament for Shropshire in 1393 and 1404. The entry in *History of Parliament* describes his significant enlistment in the retinue of Arundel in the expedition of 1387 (from whom he held a knight's fee in Gretton).[54] It does not, however, mention his continued service in the following year. Daras served as an esquire in Arundel's retinue in the expedition of 1387, but had only entered this retinue as a replacement for Thomas de Holand, the future duke of Surrey, after Holand was knighted on the 24 March 1387, the day of the naval battle.[55] Prior to this, he was an esquire in the retinue of Robert Gyffard. In 1388 he served in the retinue of Sir William Baron of Hylton.[56] He was summoned before the king's council in June 1390 over violence regarding a land dispute with his niece.[57] In this dispute he had amassed an impressive array of supporters including Sir Richard Ludlowe, another man who had connections with the earl of Arundel.

A further connection can be identified with Thomas Whitton, for whom he acted in business transactions relating to land, and who also served in the expe-

---

[49] *CPR, 1396–1399*, p. 494 (protection). Cited in Leland, 'Oxford Trial', who points out that his protection is immediately preceded by a protection for Sir William Lisle, who is also a juror at the trial.

[50] E101/41/5 m. 3.

[51] *HOP*, vol. ii, pp. 511–512.

[52] *Two Estate Surveys*, p. 116, 1 house by Marie gate 8d; 2 tofts by the cemetery (occupied by the lord) 1s 8d; The house he lives in 9d; total 3s 1d. in Arundell.

[53] C67/30 m. 17.

[54] *HOP*, vol. ii, pp. 755–756.

[55] E101/40/33 m. 1, described as 'factus chivaler, le xxiiii iour de March'. Holand also serves in the company of Richard II in 1394 on his expedition to Ireland: *CPR, 1391–1396*, p. 554 (attorney).

[56] 1387: E101/40/33 m. 20, and subsequently m. 1. 1388: E101/41/5 m. 5d.

[57] *CPR, 1388–1392*, p. 340.

dition of 1388.[58] Whitton also served as a member of parliament in November 1390 and 1406 and he therefore has an entry in *History of Parliament*. This incorrectly claims that he enrolled in the expedition of 1387 and not 1388. As a Shropshire landholder, he was a neighbour of Daras and is identified as being amongst his closest associates. It is probably through his landholding that he became involved with Arundel, who was a leading landowner in Shropshire. He appears to survive both the prosecution of the Appellants and their supporters in 1398 and also the transition to the new regime of Henry IV as his appearances at Parliament span this period of time.[59] Whitton also did not have the need to secure a pardon in 1398.

By 1389, Daras was acting in association with Fulk Sprenghose and John Burley, as a trustee of estates in Shropshire belonging to Richard, Lord Talbot, who had married Arundel's niece. Fulk Sprenghose also served in the expedition of 1387 in Arundel's retinue.[60] Interestingly, Fulk is also present in the retinue as a replacement. Daras is used as a replacement following the knighting of a colleague and is already present on campaign in another retinue. Fulk is used as a replacement whilst the expedition was back in England after the naval battle prior to sailing for Brest on 1 May 1387. As he has entered the retinue at short notice, it is probable that Arundel knew Fulk personally. More information about his relationship with Arundel is not forthcoming from *History of Parliament*, although it does identify his service in 1387. It mentions that he holds land in Shropshire and thus it is probably through this and his local connections as described that led to his involvement in this expedition.[61]

John Burley also served in the expedition of 1388 in the retinue of Sir Gilbert Talbot.[62] Thus he has a connection with both Sir Gilbert Talbot and as aforementioned Richard, Lord Talbot. Burley is another man with a detailed entry in *History of Parliament*. This entry identifies Burley as an associate of the Corbets and Sir John Cornwall, who are in turn associates of Daras.[63] *History of Parliament* describes how Burley, who was a lawyer by profession, served a number of the nobility who were landholders in Shropshire. His closest relationship was with the earl of Arundel, with whom he joined on expedition on 1388. Burley did not suffer when Arundel's supporters were persecuted following the earl's execution. However, he did find it necessary to secure a pardon in 1398[64] and immediately renewed his service for the Arundel earls following the return of Earl Thomas with Henry IV in 1399. Indeed, the first Lancastrian parliament was also his first as a member of parliament. Burley played an important role in the suppression of the rebellion of Owain Glyn Dwr, alongside Sir John

---

58 E101/41/5 m. 18.
59 *HOP*, vol. iv, pp. 851–852. Served in two parliaments, 1390 (November) and 1406, as the representative for Shropshire.
60 E101/40/33 m. 1, replacing Rusty, who is described as 'vacat' on 28 April 1387.
61 *HOP*, vol. iv, p. 431. Served in one parliament, that of 1397 (January) as the representative for Shropshire.
62 E101/41/5 m. 12.
63 *HOP*, vol. ii, pp. 430–432. Was returned as member of parliament for Shropshire on seven occasions from 1399 to 1411.
64 C67/30 m. 16.

Cornwall, who had also served in Arundel's expeditions. He probably died of dysentery caught at the siege of Harfleur on Henry V's first expedition to Normandy, from which he returned early, along with his retinue captain, the earl of Arundel.[65] Therefore, Burley was able to prosper under the regime of Henry IV and his own local influence increased under the patronage of Earl Thomas.

Returning to the career of Daras, he gained increased importance in Shropshire under Henry IV possibly due to his relationship with the Fitzalans. He was granted for life the stewardship of Morfe and Shirlet and two years later he was appointed sheriff.[66] He was occupied in the suppression of Glyn Dwr's revolt in Wales, and it was in consideration of these services that in 1407, described as 'king's esquire', he was granted for life the keepership of Morfe and Shirlet, with permission to nominate a ranger to carry out his duties during further absence in the marches.[67] This is again of interest as Daras had served as an esquire with Glyn Dwr in Arundel's retinue in 1387 and was now involved in action against him. His association with the earls of Arundel continued, as is clear from his participation, along with his wife's nephews, Robert and Roger Corbet (both of whom were esquires in the earl's service), and another Fitzalan retainer William Ryman of Sussex, in a grant made in 1407 to Shrewsbury abbey.[68] Neither of the Corbets or Ryman served in the expeditions of 1387 and 1388. *History of Parliament* describes Daras's death as follows: 'The most unusual feature of Daras's life was his way of ending it, for shortly before 30 March 1408 he hanged himself at Neenton.'[69] Both Burley and Daras can be seen to be associated with Sir John Cornwall, for whom, it was claimed, Daras fixed a panel of jurors whilst sheriff in 1402. Cornwall served as an esquire in both expeditions of 1387 and 1388.[70] He also served as a member of parliament, but *History of Parliament* does not list his service in these years, or indeed any connections to Arundel.[71] It would therefore seem that his service was in support of his local circle of associates. He was retained to serve John of Gaunt in peace and war in 1395[72] and he soon found favour with the new regime of Henry IV, even though he had been retained as king's knight in 1397 and was serving with Richard II in Ireland in 1399.[73] He was knighted by the new king and was a king's knight by 1400.[74] As mentioned, he was a leading figure in the

---

65 E101/47/1, particulars of the account of Thomas, earl of Arundel with retinue roll for this expedition, also cited in *HOP*, vol. ii, p. 432. According to the issue roll E101/45/5 m. 3d, the earl of Arundel served with 400 solders, including 1 peer, 1 banneret, 3 knights, 95 men-at-arms and 300 archers. I am grateful to Professor Curry for this reference.

66 *CPR, 1399–1401*, p. 64.

67 *CPR, 1405–1408*, p. 296.

68 *Ibid.*, p. 339.

69 *HOP*, vol. ii, p. 756.

70 1387: E101/40/33, m. 1. 1388; E101/41/5, m. 6.

71 *HOP*, vol. ii, pp. 661–663. He was returned to parliament as representative for Shropshire in 1402 and 1407.

72 Walker, *Lancastrian Affinity*, p. 267, retained 1395–1399, served overseas 1394.

73 *Royal Household*, p. 284. 1399: *CPR, 1396–1399*, pp. 550 (protection), 559 (attorney).

74 *Royal Household*, p. 288.

fight against the Welsh rebellion led by Owain Gyn Dwr and thus gained much influence under Henry IV.

History of Parliament points out that it is difficult to separate the career of Sir John Cornwall, member of parliament, from that of his more famous namesake, Sir John Cornwall, who was later created Lord Fanhope by Henry VI on 17 July 1432.[75] The future Lord Fanhope married Elizabeth, the sister of Henry IV, before 12 December 1400. He was created knight of the Garter in 1409 and was present at the battle of Agincourt in 1415. *History of Parliament* comments that it was this Sir John Cornwall who served with Richard in Ireland in 1399. It is therefore not entirely clear which individual served with Arundel in 1387 and 1388. However, because of his connections within Shropshire it seems likely that the Sir John Cornwall who was member of parliament for Shropshire fought on the campaigns of 1387–1388.

All the circle described above can be seen to have served for Arundel in 1387 or 1388 under a sense of shared experience. They were also very close in local matters and all served as members of parliament for Shropshire. This demonstrates how the muster rolls are full of relationships that can be identified by careful study.

A known supporter of Arundel was among his knights mustered in 1387.[76] As noted earlier, Sir Henry Hussey held land in Sussex from the earl.[77] Hussey was therefore a man closely linked to Arundel during the years of Appellant supremacy, and according to *History of Parliament*, even participated in the short civil war culminating in the battle of Radcot Bridge with the defeat of the king's forces under the duke of Ireland.[78] From this evidence, it would seem that Arundel's own retinue was peopled with men on whom he could rely, even in a battle against the king. Because of the closeness of this relationship, Hussey required a royal pardon in 1398 following the execution of the earl and perhaps even because of his suggested involvement at Radcot Bridge. Following this setback, Hussey showed his political acumen by allying himself with the king's half brother, John Holland, duke of Exeter, who had secured possession of the forfeited Arundel estates. He managed to survive successfully the transition to the new regime and under Henry IV, prospered after the return of earl Thomas, the son of the earl of Arundel. He did not represent Sussex in Parliament until he was returned as member in 1401 and 1402. As with many of the men in the expeditions of 1387 and 1388, Hussey was able to move with the changing political circumstances and adjust to the political upheavals of these years without losing lands or influence.

A knight of some military experience, Sir John Dauntsey also serves in the

---

[75] *Complete Peerage*, vol. v, pp. 253–254 for details of Lord Fanhope. This source also uses aspects of the careers of both individuals. I am grateful to Professor Curry for drawing my attention to the career of Lord Fanhope.

[76] E101/40/33 m. 1.

[77] *Two Estate Surveys*, p. 123, 'Messuage & croft for 4s 0d as free tenant in the Manor of Angmering', p. 149, 'Knighteslond, otherwise Wodeslond, for 1 lb. Cummin [margin: Note for Garton] in Lygh'.

[78] *HOP*, vol. iii, pp. 462–464.

expeditions of 1387 and 1388.[79] He already had at least twenty-five years in arms by this date and would have been in his forties during these campaigns.[80] He began his military career by 1361 when he took out letters of protection to serve overseas.[81] He then entered the service of Edward, Lord Despenser and probably fought for him in his campaigns abroad. Following the death of Lord Despencer in November 1375, he was engaged in putting his affairs in order. This relationship may have continued with his son, as both Dauntsey and Thomas, Lord Despencer serve in Arundel's retinue in 1388.[82] *History of Parliament* claims that he had entered the service of the earl of Arundel by 1381 when he was named as one of his feoffees of the marcher lordships of Chirk and Chirksland.[83] However, it can be shown that his relationship with the earl had begun much earlier than this. He is in fact named fourth in the ill-fated retinue of Arundel in the expedition of John of Gaunt in 1378.[84] Sir John is a good example of a father serving with his son in order to introduce him to military campaigns. His son serves in the retinue of Arundel in both 1378 and 1388, listed in five and three places respectively, below his father on the muster rolls.[85] This relationship with Arundel can be seen to have grown closer when in 1386, Dauntsey was granted a yearly rent of £20 from Arundel's manor of Keevil in Wiltshire for life.[86]

This grant also exposes another link in the relationships of Arundel as the like is also granted to John Chisleden.[87] John Chisleden served in Arundel's retinue in 1387 and 1388.[88] In addition to this, Chisleden also served with Arundel in 1378.[89] This is a fleeting and accidental reference that tells us much more about how the relationships within the retinues continued in everyday life. These men, Dauntsey and Chisleden, are rewarded in the same royal licence. It can be seen from the muster rolls that they served Arundel on three separate occasions prior to and during the period of Appellant supremacy. It would not take a great leap of the imagination to suppose that these men would have known each other and that their purpose on this expedition was in support of their lord. As both men serve in Arundel's retinue, it can be suggested that the retinue is made up of loyal followers who have been previously rewarded for their support.

History of Parliament fails to mention Dauntsey's inclusion in Arundel's retinues in either 1388 or 1378. However, it does speculate that his six elections to

---

[79] 1387: E101/40/33 m. 1. 1388: E101/41/5 m. 1.
[80] *HOP,* vol. ii, pp. 758–759.
[81] *CPR, 1361–1364,* p. 12.
[82] E101/41/5 m. 1.
[83] *CPR, 1377–1381,* p. 35.
[84] E101/36/32 m. 3. Arundel and his retinue were blamed for letting their guard drop over a mine intended to attack the walls of St Malo. The failure of the mine led to the abandonment of the expedition, Froissart, *Chronicles,* pp. 551–552.
[85] 1378: E101/36/32 m. 1, listed as Mons' John Daundeseye le fitz. 1388: E101/41/5 m. 1, listed as Mons' Johannes Daundesey le fitz.
[86] *CPR, 1385–1389,* p. 91.
[87] *Ibid.*
[88] 1387: E101/40/33 m. 1. 1388: E101/41/5 m. 1.
[89] E101/36/32 m. 3.

Parliament for Wiltshire may have been connected to Arundel's support, especially the election to the Merciless Parliament of 1388. His loyalty to the new regime can be seen in his appointment to administer the general oaths of allegiance to the Lords Appellant in Wiltshire in March 1388.[90] Dauntsey died in 1391, so his likely career following the fall of Arundel cannot be assessed. It can be seen that Dauntsey participated fully in both the military and political affairs in the years under discussion.

Sir Richard Ludlowe is another retainer of Arundel who also seems to have begun his association with the earl in the expedition of 1378 when only sixteen years of age.[91] He also later served in Arundel's retinue in both 1387 and 1388.[92] Ludlowe served in Parliament on three occasions, including the Merciless Parliament. *History of Parliament* suggests that this may have been due to the earl's influence at this time and determination to prosecute the king's favourites. It comments that he served under Arundel in 1387, but does not identify the previous service of 1378 or later service in 1388. It does, however, point out that his only appointment as justice of the peace in Shropshire was during the years of Appellant supremacy and that he was promptly removed when Richard regained influence.[93] The biographical entry in this text describes his career in arms beginning with service in 1380–1381 in the retinue of Sir David Holgrave, in the expedition led by the then Thomas of Woodstock, later Appellant, duke of Gloucester. It also shows that he was knighted by September 1386, when he accompanied his overlord Hugh, earl of Stafford, on pilgrimage to Jerusalem. He can also be shown to be connected with John Daras another loyal supporter of Arundel.[94] Ludlowe can be seen to have been a retainer of Arundel's from a very young age and also had served on expedition with Gloucester. It is no surprise that he serves in the expeditions of 1387 and 1388 or that he also appears to be rewarded for this service. In fact his only appearance as justice of the peace is during this period. This was a man who used his position of closeness to the Appellants to advance his local position. This advancement was, however, to be short lived and he did not suffer from this association having died at the age of thirty in 1390 before his masters had lost their heads.

From his entry in *History of Parliament*, another knight, Sir William Hugford, can be seen to have been associated with Arundel and coincidentally can also be seen to have been associated with the previously mentioned Sir Richard Ludlow.[95] Sir William Hugford took part in the expedition of 1388 as a knight in the retinue of Arundel.[96] His career in Parliament spanned four representations as member for Shropshire and included the Merciless Parliament. *History of Parliament* describes Sir William as a landowner of substance and shows that he had tenure from the earl of Arundel of knights' fees valued at 40

---

90 *CCR, 1385–1389*, p. 462.
91 E101/36/32 m. 3.
92 1387: E101/40/33 m. 1. 1388: E101/41/5 m. 1.
93 *HOP*, vol. iii, pp. 650–651.
94 *CCR, 1389–1392*, p. 143; *CPR, 1388–1392*, p. 340.
95 *HOP*, vol. iii, pp. 438–439.
96 E101/41/5 m. 1.

marks a year. With such a connection, it is therefore no surprise that Hugford partakes in this expedition. *History of Parliament* speculates about his relationship with Arundel:

> Quite how much importance should be attached to Hugford's service at sea in the retinue of his feudal overlord Richard, earl of Arundel, in the year before that Parliament was to meet, is difficult to ascertain. It should be noted, however, that Hugford's career with regard to royal employment was neither favourably affected when Arundel came to power, nor, apparently, adversely affected by his fall and execution in 1397.

The reference to his service at sea, in the year before the Merciless Parliament, dates this to 1387. This has been confused with Hugford's actual service in 1388 that has been correctly referenced in the footnotes. His service in the expedition following the Merciless Parliament, at which the king's favourites were prosecuted, shows that Hugford fully supported the earl in his actions against the king. He had not been adversely affected by his association and demonstrates that the king could ill afford to alienate too many men in positions of local authority following the fall of the Appellants as his official appointments continued under Richard II and indeed Henry IV.[97] He did feel the need to take out a royal pardon following Arundel's execution in May 1398.[98]

Another interesting relationship within the retinue can be seen from information contained in *History of Parliament*. In the muster roll for 1388, Hugford is listed seven places below the previously mentioned Sir Richard Ludlowe. It can be assumed that these knights would be aware of one another. In fact they had other relationships that show that their proximity on the muster roll was not accidental. Both men had relationships with another third party, Sir David Holgrave, and Hugford acted as a trustee of the Shropshire estates of Ludlowe. Thus both men shared a common background in landowning and in their relationship to the earl. Both men also supported the earl in the expeditions of the years 1387 and 1388 and it can be seen that proximity in the muster rolls could be reflected in close relationships in other walks of life.

Further evidence for those with a prominent position in the muster rolls being in positions of influence can be seen in the case of the esquire, Richard Alderton. Alderton is a member of Arundel's retinue in both 1387 and 1388.[99] He seems to have achieved some prominence having been listed in twenty-first position amongst Arundel's esquires in 1387 rising to third in Arundel's esquires in 1388. This position rose to second when Owain Glyn Dwr did not fulfil his intention to serve. Is this prominence in the muster rolls significant, or are placings merely accidental, perhaps a reflection of the order in which soldiers confirmed their attendance to their captain? In Alderton's case, his position is not an accident. From the *Calendar of Patent Rolls*[100] it can be shown that Arundel secured a royal licence for the granting of the manor of

97 Summarised in *HOP*, vol. iii, p. 438.
98 C67/30 m. 24.
99 1387: E101/40/33 m. 1. 1388: E101/41/5 m. 1.
100 *CPR, 1385–1389*, p. 359.

Margaretting, Essex, from himself to Alderton for life. This licence is dated 1 August 1387. This grant therefore follows the return to England of Arundel and Alderton in June. Alderton had therefore shown himself to be a loyal supporter and is rewarded for this support and his advanced position in the retinue of 1388 is therefore a reflection of this relationship. It is of interest that Alderton has secured a royal pardon in 1398 and this reflects the support given to Arundel during the years of Appellant supremacy.[101] This information can be gathered from very little in terms of source evidence, and justifies the attention paid to the key sources.

It is also possible to draw evidence from other sources for the careers of other esquires, who may otherwise be obscure in the references. Robert Norton has a brief entry in *History of Parliament* which describes how he represented Warwick on five separate occasions, his final term being the Merciless Parliament of 1388.[102] The complete entry for Robert Norton follows:

> Norton was said to be 'of Warwick' when returned to his third Parliament and 'of Warwickshire' when he was granted a royal pardon in June 1398. To judge from his five elections to Parliament, he was of some local importance, but nothing else is known of him.

From this information, considering that he needed to secure a royal pardon in 1398[103] and also that his last election to Parliament was for the Merciless Parliament, it would seem that Norton may have connections to the Appellants and therefore may have been involved in the expeditions undertaken in their years of supremacy. In fact a Robert Norton served as an esquire in the retinue of Sir Thomas West in 1388.[104] *History of Parliament* has not noted this service, but this service fits with the other facts stated about Norton. He was a supporter of the Appellants, perhaps of the earl of Warwick, and was involved in the expedition of 1388 following the defeat of the king's favourite de Vere in the winter of the previous year. This association would explain his requirement to secure a royal pardon following the fall of the Appellants and may also go some way to explain the loss of local influence after 1388 when he is no longer elected to parliament. This would coincide with Richard's regaining of control at court. The information contained in the muster rolls can enhance our understanding of the information gained from other sources.

Sir Edward St John, who served with Arundel in the expedition of 1387,[105] was also connected to Arundel in his non-martial capacity. Interestingly, St John only served in the first half of the campaign, which included the successful defeat of the Flemish fleet. He is noted as being absent, from 29 April, during the period in which Arundel's fleet returned to England for refitting following the battle and brief harassing of Sluys. A Sir Edward St John is named as owing

---

101 C67/30 m. 2.
102 *HOP*, vol. iii, p. 852.
103 C67/30 m. 16.
104 E101/41/5 m. 7.
105 E101/40/33 m. 1, described as 'Vacat de xxix d'aprill'.

60 marks on the death of the earl of Arundel's father.[106] However, this could be this Sir Edward's father who is recorded as having died on 18 March 1386.[107] It is also probably his father who was a king's knight of Richard II.[108] Goodman names St John (junior) among loyal supporters of Arundel in his study of the Appellants. He shows that he was required to arrest those who refused to perform services for the earl together with his other retainer, Sir Edward Dallingridge.[109] In another parallel with the muster roll, St John and Dallingridge are separated by one man on the roll for the expedition of 1387. Again it is demonstrated that proximity on the roll can be mirrored by relationships in other walks of life. However, whereas Dallingridge went on to be a loyal supporter of the king, it is not clear from the available evidence how St John's career advanced.

A Sir John d'Arundell is involved in the expeditions of 1387 and 1388 as a retinue captain.[110] His retinue is listed on the muster rolls in fourth and fifth place respectively and his retinue increases from 70 to 90 men over the two expeditions. He seems to have other connections to Arundel, for on the death of the earl's father he is said to have been holding 8,486 marks on behalf of the earl.[111] Both his prominence in the retinues and also this connection to Arundel's father, would perhaps indicate a strong relationship between these two men. He can be identified as Sir John de Arundel of Somerset, Dorset and Wiltshire, who was retained as a king's knight of Richard II in 1386.[112] It would therefore appear that it was possible to be retained by the king and also serve with Arundel during the period of Appellant supremacy. We have not been able to find any later information regarding Sir John and therefore cannot comment on how his royal career may have been affected by this service.

Sir Payn Tiptoft is a knight whose career can be reconstructed to a greater than normal extent from the available sources. Tiptoft's service in the retinue of Arundel in 1378, 1387 and 1388 can be reconstructed from the muster roll evidence.[113] For a knight with such vintage of service with Arundel, one would expect to find other connections with the earl and this is indeed the case. *History of Parliament* describes how a minor second son manages to gain himself land and prestige in the service of a major magnate.[114] Tiptoft's first overseas experience seems to have been in the expedition of John of Gaunt in 1373. The

---

[106] L.F. Salzman, 'The Property of the Earl of Arundel', *Sussex Archaelogical Collections*, 91 (1953), pp. 32–52, p. 33.

[107] *CPR, 1385–1389*, p. 121.

[108] *Royal Household*, p. 286, retained in 1378.

[109] Goodman, *Loyal Conspiracy*, pp. 110–115.

[110] 1387: E101/40/33 m. 5; enrolled attorney, C76/71 m. 6. 1388: E101/41/5 m. 5.

[111] Salzman, 'Property of the Earl of Arundel', p. 34.

[112] *Royal Household*, p. 283, retained in 1386.

[113] 1378: E101/36/32 m. 3. Henry Tipetot is listed first among the esquires and this is perhaps a relation. 1387: E101/40/33 m. 1. 1388: E101/41/5 m. 1. Enrolled attorney, C76/73 m. 2. The version of his name Typpetoo and Tipetot is probably a reflection of his father's title, Lord Tybotot, *HOP*, vol. iv, p. 628.

[114] *HOP*, vol. iv, pp. 628 – 630. Represented Cambridgeshire on two occasions at Parliament in 1399 and 1404.

biography in *History of Parliament* argues that his first connection with Arundel was in 1387 with his position in his retinue. However, as I have shown, this connection can be began with military service in 1378 and continued into service in 1387 and 1388. *History of Parliament* places much stress on this relationship:

> By that time (1384) Tiptoft had in all probability already entered into the service of Richard Fitzalan, earl of Arundel, to whom he was to remain closely attached until Arundel's condemnation and execution for treason in 1397. In March 1387, by then a knight, he joined the large force which the earl was to command at sea, doing so as a member of the admiral's immediate entourage, and when, at the end of the year, his lord, in league with the duke of Gloucester and the earl of Warwick, rose in arms against the king's unpopular favourites, he was at their side.[115]

Arundel even put right his failure to gain a royal licence in order to grant to Tiptoft the manor of Beeston on the Norfolk coast for life, whilst in control of royal government in May 1388.[116] He was also later made a trustee of Arundel's manor of Kenninghall and enfeoffed of the Fitzalan lordships in the marches of Wales and of a number of other properties. He was named among Arundel's executors and was left two of his best horses and a silver goblet following the execution of the earl. *History of Parliament* goes on to describe Sir Payn's predicament following the earl's arrest in 1397.

> On 15th September, just a few days before Arundel was due to be tried and executed, a royal serjeant-at-arms was ordered to find him for interrogation by the King's Council. Then, on 3 April following he and 27 others were commanded, each under penalty of £200, to present themselves immediately before the council at Westminster 'to answer what shall be laid against them'. He was no doubt forced to pay a heavy fine to obtain the royal pardon issued to him at the end of the month.[117]

It is because of these events that *History of Parliament* assumes that he was involved in the battle against the king's favourite at Radcot Bridge in 1387. As a close associate of Arundel, this is indeed possible; however, it is not certain. Just being an associate of Arundel might have been dangerous at this time! However, Tiptoft only had a few years to wait until his fortunes again changed for the better. His son, John, had been a member of the future Henry IV's household prior to his exile. *History of Parliament* suggests that both men gave Henry active military support after his landing in England in 1399. Tiptoft even secured revenge for the earl's downfall by being a member of the parliament that deposed Richard and then acclaimed Henry as king. He did not however continue his association with the Fitzalan family following the deposition. He was

---

[115] *HOP*, vol. iv, p. 628: misses the references to 1378 and 1388 service, also no reference for his presence at Radcot Bridge in 1387 – this comment probably draws from the royal pardon which mentions service with the Appellants: C67/30 m. 2.

[116] *CPR, 1385–1389*, p. 440.

[117] *HOP*, vol. iv, p. 631.

one of just 12 men called upon to serve as knights of the king's chamber along with his son, who had been knighted on the eve of King Henry's coronation.[118] It was his son who mainly benefited from the new regime; Sir Payn has to content himself with his fees and livery at the household. He had to act for the king in his martial capacity and served on the Scottish expedition in 1400.[119] In August 1402, he was specially commissioned to raise an armed force to advance into Wales against Glyn Dwr's revolt.[120] This is another case of former colleagues being in conflict, as both Tiptoft and Glyn Dwr had served in Arundel's retinue in 1387.

Another interesting connection exists, as Tiptoft took the confession of a John Oke and John Veyse in his position as sheriff of Huntingdon in August 1405. These men claimed that they had collected money from clerics and laymen sympathetic to the Welsh rebellion and had taken this money to Owain Gyn Dwr.[121] Although none of their claims were proved, it is interesting to note that a John atte Oke serves as an esquire in the expedition of 1387[122] and thus may have come into contact with the future Welsh rebel who served in the expedition. Tiptoft also had to assist in the response to the Percy rebellion of 1403.

It is interesting to note further family connections within Arundel's retinue of 1388 when Tiptoft served alongside his brother-in-law, Sir John Wroth.[123] This service is missed in *History of Parliament* entry, which does not mention Sir John's relationship with Arundel.[124] *History of Parliament* mentions that Sir John Wroth secured a royal pardon in April 1398, but comments that this was 'presumably on formal grounds alone'.[125] However, this pardon was taken along with those others who felt it prudent to gain protection following Richard's attack on the Appellants and their followers. This pardon, together with the service in 1388, would indicate that Wroth was fully supportive of the Appellants and could also have been active during the Radcot Bridge campaign. This association does not appear to have harmed his personal standing with the crown, as he even appeared in the parliament of 1397 that condemned the Appellants to execution for treason.

Wroth prospered from 1397 onwards when he occupied a prominent place among the gentry of Middlesex as a commissioner, justice of the peace and shire knight. This is perhaps evidence of Richard securing loyalty from former associ-

---

[118] *Royal Household*, p. 287, knight of the chamber and lay officer of the household, of Cambridgeshire, retained in 1402 (1401). His son, Sir John Tiptoft, *Royal Household*, p. 287 (keeper 1406–1408), retained for life, knight of the chamber and lay officer of the household, of Cambridgeshire, retained in 1402 (1399).

[119] Brown, 'English Campaign in Scotland, 1400', pp. 40–54.

[120] *CPR, 1401–1405*, p. 138, Tideswell, 'commission to supervise and try all the fencible men of the county, directed to go to Shrewsbury to resist the malice of Owen Gyndourdy. Payn Tiptoet, "chivaler" and Thomas Hasilden in the county of Cambridge'.

[121] Ralph Griffiths, 'Some Secret Supporters of Owain Glyn Dwr?', *Bulletin of Historical Research*, vol. 37 (1964), pp. 77–100.

[122] E101/40/33 m. 13.

[123] E101/41/5 m. 1.

[124] *HOP*, vol. iv, pp. 909–910.

[125] C67/30 m. 27.

ates of the Appellants in the localities in order to increase his power base. It is also another example of men serving because of family connections. *History of Parliament* mentions a later association between Wroth and Tiptoft over the sum of 1,000 marks. It mentions that 'the nature of this transaction remains obscure, especially as Wroth did not have any other obvious dealings with his influential kinsmen'. However, as we can see, family connections were important, and probably led to Wroth's association with Arundel in 1388, thus showing that the printed sources sometimes fail to reveal the whole picture of relationships in this period. One particular comment in *History of Parliament* is curious in this regard: 'Very little is known about Wroth's private affairs, largely because he made no real attempt to exploit the wealth and connections at his disposal.' As we can see, he did exploit his connections in 1388, by supporting the earl of Arundel. Indeed, he felt it was necessary to purchase a royal pardon, following the earl's demise in 1397. The change of regime in 1399 again seems not to have affected Wroth in any particular way. He attended the Great Councils in 1401 and 1403 along with his brother in law and in March 1407 he became controller of the wool subsidy in the port of London.[126] Interestingly, his family estates passed to Sir John Tiptoft, son of Sir Payn, in 1413, following his daughter Elizabeth's death.

Goodman has identified that 19 of the 74 shire knights elected to the Merciless Parliament in 1388 can be connected to Arundel.[127] Can we identify any of the members of parliament from the Merciless Parliament in the campaigns of 1387–1388? This might indicate further links with the Appellants. In fact, thirteen soldiers can be identified from *History of Parliament* as serving in 1387–1388 namely: John Boys, Sir Hugh Browe, Robert Caldebrook,[128] Sir Edward Dallingridge, Sir John Dauntsey, John Keen,[129] Sir Richard Ludlow, Sir Oliver Mauleverer, John Mendham, John Northampton,[130] Robert Norton, Sir Robert Turberville[131] and Sir Robert Turk.[132] Of these men Goodman identifies Sir Hugh Browe, Sir Edward Dallingridge and Sir John Dauntsey as connected with the Appellants. Therefore a further ten members of parliament can be added to those already identified. This perhaps suggests that the Appellants had made an attempt to stack parliament in their favour. Of those sitting in the Merciless Parliament, however, only four were members of parliament for this parliament alone.[133] The other men had been member of parliament on at least one other occasion thus suggesting that many were experienced parliamentar-

---

126 Another connection can be identified, for in 1404 Sir Roger LeStrange acted as a feoffee for Sir John Wroth, *HOP*, vol. iv, p. 503. Both men served in the retinue of Arundel, LeStrange in 1387 and Wroth in 1388.
127 Goodman, *Loyal Conspiracy*, p. 45.
128 1388: E101/41/5 m. 14. *HOP*, vol. ii, p. 464.
129 1388: E101/41/5 m. 13. *HOP*, vol. iii, pp. 510–511.
130 1388: E101/41/5 m. 7. *HOP*, vol. iii, pp. 848–849.
131 1388: E101/41/5 m. 1.
132 The other members of parliament are discussed in other sections; for references and discussion see the index.
133 Boys, Mendham, Northampton and Turberville.

ians. Of these men four would require royal pardons in 1398,[134] and all but four of the men can definitely be connected to the Appellants or their associates.[135] Six of the men serve in the retinue of the earl of Arundel[136] and seven of the members of parliament only serve in 1388, thus following the Appellant dominance of proceedings at the Merciless Parliament. The presence of these members of parliament in the campaigns of 1387–1388 demonstrates a further connection to Arundel and as such this evidence supports that provided by Goodman. It does indeed suggest that an attempt was made to ensure the election to parliament of men sympathetic with the Appellant process against the king's favourites.

It can therefore be shown that a number of men serving in the campaigns of 1387 and 1388 have links with the earl of Arundel. Some of these links are very clear, such as landholding and previous military service. Others are connections via known associates. A good number of these men have also secured a royal pardon in 1398 in order to gain protection from prosecution because of their support for Arundel and the Appellants ten years earlier. Arundel was executed in 1397 and one might have expected his supporters to be similarly prosecuted. However, apart from Sir Thomas Mortimer and his esquire William Curtis, these supporters have been able to continue free of prosecution, despite their guilt by association which can be seen in the large number of pardons secured by the soldiers fighting on the Appellant led campaigns. It has also been shown that a healthy proportion of these men do not suffer a withdrawal of royal favour following 1388, despite the fact that they secure royal pardons in 1398. Some became king's knights, others served on the royal expeditions to Ireland in the 1390s. It is also possible to show these men prospering under the reign of Henry IV despite their years of service with Richard II. Partisanship during this period is therefore hard to define and it is no surprise to find soldiers who have previously served together fighting both for and against Henry IV at the battle of Shrewsbury in 1403. We have therefore shown that Arundel has drawn upon men whom he knew or had connections with, for his recruitment of his armies in 1387–1388.

Arundel's retinue in 1378

A number of the men discussed in the previous section have been identified as serving in the expedition of 1378 in Arundel's retinue. This demonstrates a relationship of at least ten years in the service of the earl of Arundel. How many other men serving in the campaigns of 1387–1388 were known to Arundel from service in this earlier campaign? The muster roll for 1378 has survived which

---

134 Boys, Browe, Norton and Turk.
135 The four without obvious relations with Appellants are Caldebrook, Keen, Mendham and Turberville.
136 Browe, 1387; Dallingridge, 1387; Dauntsey, 1387 and 1388; Ludlow, 1387 and 1388; Mendham, 1388; Turberville, 1388. Service only in 1388: Boys, Caldebrook, Keen, Mauleverer, Northampton, Norton and Turberville.

Table 23. Comparison with Arundel, 1378

Year	Title	First name	Surname	Position	Captain name
1378		John	ap Howell	Esquire	Arundel, Richard, earl of
1387		John	ap Hoell	Esquire	Arundel, Richard, earl of
1388		Johan	ap Howel le fitz	Esquire	Arundel, Richard, earl of
1378		Bambe	atte Brigg	Esquire	Arundel, Richard, earl of
1387		Lambert	atte Briggs	Esquire	Arundel, Richard, earl of
1388		Lambert	atte Brugges	Esquire	Arundel, Richard, earl of
1378		John	Bere	Esquire	Arundel, Richard, earl of
1387		John	Bere	Esquire	Arundel, Richard, earl of
1388		Johan	Bere	Esquire	Esmon Randulph
1378		Henry	Bolton	Esquire	Arundel, Richard, earl of
1388		Henry	Bolton	Esquire	Mons Gilbe Talbot
1378		John	Bonham	Esquire	Arundel, Richard, earl of
1388		Johan	Boneham	Esquire	Arundel, Richard, earl of
1378		John	Bortham	Esquire	Arundel, Richard, earl of
1388		Johan	Bortham	Esquire	Mons Thomas Ponynges
1378	Mons	Hugh	Browe	Knight	Arundel, Richard, earl of
1387	Mons	Hugh	Browe	Knight	Arundel, Richard, earl of
1388	Mons	Hugh	Browe	Captain	Mons Hugh Browe
1378		Ingram	Brunn	Esquire	Arundel, Richard, earl of
1388	Mons	Yngham	Broyn	Knight	Arundel, Richard, earl of
1378		William	Burton	Esquire	Arundel, Richard, earl of
1387		William	Burton	Esquire	Mons Hugh le Despencer
1388		William	Burton	Esquire	Mons Hugh le Despencer
1378		John	Buteler	Esquire	Arundel, Richard, earl of
1387		John	Butiller	Esquire	Mons Hugh le Despencer
1378		Richard	Chambleyn	Archer	Arundel, Richard, earl of
1387		Richard	Chambleyn	Archer	Arundel, Richard, earl of
1378	Mons	Renand	Cobeham, de	Knight	Arundel, Richard, earl of
1387	Mons	Reynald	Cobham, de	Captain	Mons Reynold de Cobham
1378		Thomas	Cooke de Slene	Archer	Arundel, Richard, earl of
1388		Thomas	Cook	Archer	Mons Johan Grymesby
1378		Robert	Cooke	Archer	Arundel, Richard, earl of
1388		Robert	Cook	Archer	Mons Henry Jugloos
1378		John	Crabbe	Archer	Arundel, Richard, earl of
1388		Johan	Crabbe	Archer	Le Counte Marshall
1378	Mons	John	Daundesey	Knight	Arundel, Richard, earl of
1388	Mons	Johan	Daundesey	Knight	Arundel, Richard, earl of
1378	Mons	John	Daundesey le fitz	Knight	Arundel, Richard, earl of
1388	Mons	Johan	Daundesey le fitz	Knight	Arundel, Richard, earl of
1378	Mons	John	Ffalleston	Knight	Arundel, Richard, earl of
1387	Mons	John	de Fallowesles	Knight	Arundel, Richard, earl of
1388	Sire		le Say	Baron	Arundel, Richard, earl of
1378		Thomas	Ffrer	Esquire	Arundel, Richard, earl of
1387		Thomas	Ffrere	Esquire	Arundel, Richard, earl of

1378		John	Hager	Archer	Arundel, Richard, earl of
1387		John	Hagge	Archer	Mons Richard Craddok
1378		John	Kyng	Archer	Arundel, Richard, earl of
1388		Johan	Kyng	Archer	Mons William Briene
1378		John	Kykested	Esquire	Arundel, Richard, earl of
1388		Johan	Kyvekestede	Esquire	Le Counte Marshall
1378		Roger	Lestrauge	Esquire	Arundel, Richard, earl of
1387	Mons	Roger	Lefozannge	Knight	Arundel, Richard, earl of
1378		Hamond	Lestrauge	Esquire	Arundel, Richard, earl of
1387		Hamond	Leftanges	Esquire	Arundel, Richard, earl of
1378		Richard	Lodelowe	Esquire	Arundel, Richard, earl of
1387	Mons	Richard	Ludelowe	Knight	Arundel, Richard, earl of
1388	Mons	Richard	Ludlowe	Knight	Arundel, Richard, earl of
1378		Roger	Manston	Esquire	Arundel, Richard, earl of
1387		Roger	Manston	Esquire	Le Counte de Devens
1378		William	Meller	Archer	Arundel, Richard, earl of
1387		William	Mellars	Archer	Mons Arnald Savage
1378		John	Nougell	Esquire	Arundel, Richard, earl of
1388		Johan	Noungle	Esquire	Mons Johan Bohun
1378		John	Parker	Archer	Arundel, Richard, earl of
1387		John	Parker	Archer	Arundel, Richard, earl of
1388		Johan	Parker	Archer	Arundel, Richard, earl of
1378		Hamond	Pesaell	Esquire	Arundel, Richard, earl of
1388	Mons	Hamond	Peshale	Knight	Arundel, Richard, earl of
1378		John	Pethe	Esquire	Arundel, Richard, earl of
1387		John	Petche	Esquire	Mons Gilbe Talbot
1378	Mons	Thomas	Ponyngs	Knight	Arundel, Richard, earl of
1388	Mons	Thomas	Ponyngs	Captain	Mons Thomas Ponynges
1378		John	Picard	Esquire	Arundel, Richard, earl of
1387		John	Pycard	Esquire	Mons Thomas Trenet
1388		Johan	Pycard	Esquire	Mons Johan Clanyng
1378		Janyn	de Sande	Esquire	Arundel, Richard, earl of
1388	Mons	Johan	Sandes	Captain	Mons Johan Sandes
1378		John	Seys	Archer	Arundel, Richard, earl of
1388		Johan	Seys	Archer	Richard Cryse
1378		John	Smale	Esquire	Arundel, Richard, earl of
1387		John	Smale	Esquire	Mons Thomas Ponynges
1388		Johan	Smale	Esquire	Mons Thomas Ponynges
1378		William	Stoke	Archer	Arundel, Richard, earl of
1388		William	Stoke	Archer	Le Counte Marshall
1378		Payn	Tipetot	Esquire	Arundel, Richard, earl of
1387	Mons	Payn	Typpetoo	Knight	Arundel, Richard, earl of
1388	Mons	Payn	Typtot	Knight	Arundel, Richard, earl of
1378		William	Well	Esquire	Arundel, Richard, earl of
1388		William	Welles	Esquire	Arundel, Richard, earl of
1378		Robert	Whitfeld	Esquire	Arundel, Richard, earl of
1387		Robert	Whitfeld	Esquire	Arundel, Richard, earl of

Year	Title	First name	Surname	Position	Captain name
1378		John	Wodeward	Archer	Arundel, Richard, earl of
1387		John	Wodeward	Archer	Mons Thomas Mortemer
1378		William	Wigindon	Esquire	Arundel, Richard, earl of
1387		William	Wygynden	Esquire	Mons Reynold de Cobham

allows a comparison to be made between those serving in these campaigns.[137] The comparison is aided by the use of a computer database. Table 23 shows the names of the men who can be identified as serving in 1378 and the campaigns of 1387–1388.

Table 23 demonstrates that we are able to identify 42 soldiers who fought with Arundel in 1378 and again in the campaigns of 1387–1388.[138] This accounts for 15% of Arundel's retinue in 1378. 11 soldiers serve in 1387 and 1388; 13 in 1387; 18 in 1388. The men who show this continuation of service can be found in all parts of the army with 11 archers, 19 esquires and 12 knights represented in the table. This is interesting as it demonstrates that nearly as many archers as knights can be shown to have continued their service with Arundel on expedition. Such information on the continued service of knights and esquires can sometimes be discovered from other sources. However, detailed information on the continued service of archers does not readily exist. This information therefore demonstrates that archers also showed their allegiance by serving for a particular lord over a number of campaigns. We have already discussed the careers of some of the men who serve on campaign in 1378 and 1387–1388, such as Sir Hugh Browe, Sir John Dauntsey and Sir Payn Tiptoft. The overall number of men who can also be seen to be continuing their service suggests that Arundel has recruited from his earlier retinue. This would perhaps be because he was aware of their martial skills and also because he felt he could depend upon their loyalty.

It is interesting to note that ten of these 42 men have decided to serve in all three of the expeditions led by the earl of Arundel. Therefore, just less than one quarter of these men have demonstrated their loyalty to the earl on three separate occasions. This would suggest that these men were probably connected to Arundel in some way other than in this military capacity. For men such as Sir Hugh Browe, these connections can indeed be demonstrated by reference to other sources. However for those who do not appear in these sources, this continuance of service is in itself, a possible indication that such a connection did exist. Seventeen of these soldiers, nearly half of the total, only serve in the

---

[137] E101/36/32.

[138] It is sometimes difficult to identify men demonstrating continuation of service because of more than one man of the same name serving in a campaign. This is the case in this table for Thomas Cook, archer, as two men with identical names serve in the campaign of 1388. 1378: E101/36/32 m. 1. 1388: E101/41/5 m. 10d, listed as Thomas Cook, archer, forty-eighth in the retinue of Sir John Grymesby; 1388: E101/40/39 m. 1, listed as Thomas Cook, archer, 129th in the retinue of Sir Thomas Percy. As the force captained by Percy was separate from the main expedition, I have selected Thomas Cook from the retinue of Sir John Grymesby for the purposes of the table.

retinue of the earl of Arundel, again suggesting a close relationship. Of the other soldiers, 24 men also serve under another retinue captain on at least one of the campaigns and two men, Sir Hugh Browe and Sir Reginald de Cobham captain their own retinues. These other soldiers are spread throughout the constituent retinues of the campaigns and include service in 20 other retinues. It may well have been that Arundel was ensuring that he had key men, whom he could trust, in a number of the other retinues. Alternatively, this continuation of service could be evidence of men serving for other reasons, such as professionalism, patriotism or serving with other friends and colleagues. When all of the service from these 42 soldiers is accumulated for 1378, 1387 and 1388, it accounts for 94 units of service. This number is not insignificant and it demonstrates that a commander would rely on people he knew and had served with before to make up a core of his recruited force.

The Welsh connection: case studies

It is difficult to judge where individual loyalties lie, not least as loyalties can be multifaceted. What other bands of loyalties can be discerned from careful study of the muster rolls and associated sources? From reading the muster rolls it is evident from the names that there is a sizeable element of Welsh-sounding names. If we look closely into the background of these individuals we find a group which have their own agenda by taking part which cannot be easily ascribed to one particular loyalty. The most senior of these figures is Owain Glyn Dwr, who led the famous Welsh revolt against Henry IV from 1400.[139] He is an esquire in Arundel's retinue in 1387 and is first in the list of esquires expected in 1388.[140] This later entry is, however, crossed out, as it appears he did not turn up for the expedition in 1388 as expected. He is accompanied in 1387 by his brother Tudor ap Gruffudd,[141] and one other interesting figure, Gronw ap Tudor[142] in Arundel's retinue. Gronw came to a particularly nasty end after being captured at the beginning of the revolt in 1400.[143]

Davies comments that there were other men in the retinue of Arundel whom Owain would have known:

> Two of the bannerets were powerful Shropshire neighbours: Fulk Fitzwarin of Whittington and Richard Talbot of Ellesmere, Blackmere and (eventually)

---

[139] See R.R. Davies, *The Revolt of Owain Glyn Dwr* (Oxford, 1997) for details of his career. Davies identifies his presence in 1387 and adds 'after 1387 disappears from view' – he points out correctly that he withdraws from the army, and is indeed 'crossed and crossed out' on the muster probably before embarkation, pp. 149–150.

[140] 1387: E101/40/33 m. 1. 1388: E101/41/5 m. 1. However, this entry is crossed at the side and crossed out.

[141] E101/40/33 m. 1d. Not listed next to his brother Owain, but is listed next to Gronw ap Tudour.

[142] E101/40/33 m. 1d. Listed next to Tudor de Glyndors.

[143] Davies, *Revolt of Owain*, p. 103; the four quarters of his body were sent to four border towns after he was captured in 1400 at the rebel attack on Ruthin.

Goodrich Castle. Among the knights was a distant family member also from Shropshire, Roger Lestrange of Knockin. Also in the ranks of the knights was Reginald Grey, heir to the lordship of Dyffryn Clwyd and Glyn Dwr's future deadly foe.[144]

Interestingly, Fulk Fitzwarin[145] and Richard Talbot's[146] relationship as neighbours is reflected in the muster roll for 1387 where they are listed next to one another in Arundel's retinue. Fitzwarin serves in both expeditions and is listed in a high position in Arundel's retinue for both years, suggesting a strong relationship. However we have not yet discovered any further links. Richard Talbot has a number of other links with Arundel which supports his position in his retinue. On three occasions he was appointed commissioner of the peace along with Arundel in Salisbury in 1388, 1390 and 1391.[147] He also seems to have been intent on going to Ireland on expedition in 1386 as he organised letters of protection; however these were revoked, as he did not partake in this trip.[148] This Richard Talbot, is most likely the Richard, Lord Talbot, kinsman of Arundel, described in *History of Parliament*'s entry for Hugh Browe[149] and also who married Arundel's niece as described in the entry for John Daras.[150]

Richard, Lord Talbot and Browe accompanied the king to Ireland in 1394.[151] Lord Talbot has an entry in *Complete Peerage*, which describes how Richard II knighted him at his coronation. He was born in 1361 and was thus twenty-six when he served in 1387. He served in Ireland, with Edmund earl of March in 1380–1381 and succeeded to his title on 24 April 1387. He was summoned to parliament from 17 December 1387 to 13 November 1393. He served on the royal expedition to Scotland in 1385. Talbot died in 1396, aged thirty-five, before his loyalties were tested by the deposition of Richard II.[152] It is clear that Lord Talbot had a number of connections, including that with Arundel, because of his position in Shropshire society. Many of these relationships can be seen to have been continued into service in the earl's retinue in 1387. He can be shown to have been heavily involved both in local government and also in royal expeditions as a member of the military community.[153]

Roger Lestrange is also connected with Arundel, other than from his inclu-

---

144 Davies, *Revolt of Owain*, p. 148.

145 1387: E101/40/33 m. 1, listed fifth in the retinue; enrolled protection, C76/71 m. 14; enrolled attorney, C76/71 m. 10. 1388: E101/41/5 m. 1, listed third in the retinue.

146 E101/40/33 m. 1, listed fourth in the retinue. Enrolled protection, C76/71 m. 14; enrolled attorney, C76/71 m. 10.

147 *CPR, 1385–1389*, p. 545; *CPR, 1388–1392*, pp. 344 and 524 6 Dec 1391.

148 *CPR, 1385–1389*, p. 189 (protection), p. 277 (revocation).

149 *HOP*, vol. ii, p. 385.

150 *Ibid.*, pp. 755–756.

151 *CPR, 1391–1396*, p. 489, protection with clause volumus for half a year for Hugh Browe, knight, going to Ireland on the king's service in the company of Richard, Lord Talbot.

152 For Richard, Lord Talbot, and family see *Complete Peerage*, vol. xii, pp. 616–620.

153 Richard, Lord Talbot, was the son of Gilbert, Lord Talbot (d. 1387) and father of Gilbert, Lord Talbot (b. 1383), and also father of John, Lord Talbot, future earl of Shrewsbury, see *Complete Peerage*, vol. xii, pp. 614–617.

sion in his retinue in 1387.[154] He obviously held a prominent position in Arundel's retinue in 1387 as he is listed first amongst the knights; it is therefore interesting to also find a John Lestrange in Arundel's retinue which accompanied John of Gaunt in his expedition in 1378 to France.[155] John Lestrange was the uncle of Roger Lestrange[156] and thus it can be seen that military service with Arundel has continued through this family. John also was further connected with Arundel, being appointed on two occasions as commissioner of the peace in Salisbury together with the earl of Arundel in 1390 and 1391.[157] Lestrange appeared at two parliaments as representative for Middlesex, and his entry in *History of Parliament*, although it does not identify the relationship with Arundel, identifies him as having a strong relationship with Richard II, established in the court of Edward III.[158] This relationship can be demonstrated when he was knighted prior to the royal expedition to Scotland in 1385, and he was made a king's knight by 1391.[159] He can also be shown to have a relationship with Sir Fulk Fitzwarin, with whom he served in 1387, listed seventh and fifth respectively. He was granted the marriage of Sir Fulk's widow, Elizabeth, in 1391; however she chose to marry Sir Hugh Courtenay, the brother of the earl of Devon, who also appears in the muster rolls for both 1387 and 1388.[160] Despite this setback, Lestrange prospered under the patronage of Richard II and in addition served with him in Ireland in 1394.[161] It is not clear how he prospered under Henry IV, although he did serve both his terms at parliament during his reign.

These three individuals present in the muster for 1387, along with Sir Reginald Grey and Owain Glyn Dwr, hold prominent positions in the retinue of Arundel as banneret, knight and esquire respectively. All these men are drawn from the Shropshire Welsh border and many connections with Arundel are evident from the other available sources. It would seem that Arundel therefore drew heavily for his support from this area, and that their positions of prominence in the retinue list was reflected in their personal relationships with the commander. Such evidence would lend credence to the assumption that position on the retinue list reflected the relationship of the individual with the retinue captain. It also shows that key figures in Arundel's retinue were well known to him and could therefore be counted upon as loyal supporters. This supports the evidence available from Arundel's Sussex holdings, where it could be seen that the earl drew heavily upon his tenantry there. From the evidence provided by the muster rolls for men from the Welsh borders, it appears that he would have drawn upon the service of men from all of his lands to support him in his expeditions.

Further details on Owain's career and loyalties are contained in the note by

---

[154] E101/40/33 m. 1.

[155] E101/36/32 m. 3.

[156] Davies, *Revolt of Owain*, p. 136. See *Complete Peerage*, vol. xii, part i, pp. 354–355.

[157] *CPR, 1388–1392*, pp. 344 and 524.

[158] *HOP*, vol. iv, pp. 503–504. Represented Middlesex in 1404 (October) and 1411.

[159] *Royal Household*, p. 286, retained in 1391.

[160] 1387: E101/40/33 m. 3. 1388: E101/41/5 m. 4.

[161] *CPR, 1391–1396*, p. 486 (protection).

Anthony Goodman, 'Owain Glyndwr before 1400'.[162] Goodman states that Owain served in Richard II's expedition to Scotland in 1385, as he testified to this in his deposition to the court of chivalry in 1386.[163] He probably served in the retinue of Sir Degory Sais.[164] There appear to have been links between Owain and Arundel, who were neighbouring landholders in the marches of Chirk and Oswestry, and thus this relationship would have developed into a military capacity and he is further identified as an esquire of Richard, earl of Arundel by two fifteenth-century chroniclers.[165] Goodman believes that Arundel would have retained the services of Owain after 1385, if he was not already retained before this. Goodman identifies the only definite evidence of a connection between Owain and Arundel as being the two muster rolls under discussion in this book. He notes the inclusion of 'Tudor de Glyndour' and 'Grono ap Tudour' in the muster roll of 1387. In addition, he also comments that Owain must have 'distinguished himself in the earl's eyes during the course of it, for in May 1388, when Earl Richard's retinue was mustered for overseas service, "Oweyn Glyndouredy" headed his esquires, but his name is crossed through in the lists'.[166] Goodman, therefore states that position in the retinue lists would indicate status within the retinue itself. He continues to argue that it would have been very likely that Owain indented to serve the earl both in peace and war and therefore would have joined with the earl in his defiance of the king at the battle of Radcot Bridge.

Goodman suggests that Owain was connected to both Henry IV and Thomas, Arundel's disinherited son. He comments that he may have joined with Henry in 1399 on his return to England. However, although Thomas was made earl of Arundel by the new king in his first parliament, Owain did not prosper under the new regime, and indeed lost out in a dispute with his neighbour, Reginald Grey, lord of Ruthin. Reginald had also served under Arundel in 1387 and was in the same retinue as Owain.[167] Grey was a strong supporter of Arundel and also of Henry IV; it would seem that the new king favoured his support over that of the Welsh esquire. Goodman suggests that it was these links with the critics of the crown, which failed to bring rewards on the establishment of a new regime, which drove Owain to revolt. The inclusion of Owain in the expedition of 1387 and intended presence on the muster roll for 1388, show how loyalties can change over a decade. In the years under discussion Owain and his supporters are fighting on a royal expedition of the king of England. He later leads a rebellion against the English crown, perhaps using tactics that he may have learned

---

[162] Anthony Goodman, 'Owain Glyndwr before 1400', *Welsh Historical Review*, 5 (1970–71), pp. 67–70.

[163] *Scrope v. Grosvenor*, vol. i, p. 254.

[164] E101/39/39 for identification in the retinue of 'howeyn Glyndourne and Tedyr Glynderne'. This is probably Oweyn and his brother Tudor in the muster roll of Degory Sais at Berwick-on-Tweed. Sais, 1385: Lewis, 'Last Medieval Summons', p. 17.

[165] *Eulogium Historiarum sive Temporis*, ed. F.S. Haydon, vol. iii (Rolls Series, 1863), p. 388; John Capgrave, *Liber de Illustribus Henricis*, ed. F.C. Hingeston (Rolls Series, 1858), p. 110.

[166] Goodman, 'Owain', p. 68.

[167] E101/40/33 m. 1. This identification is also made by Goodman, 'Owain', p. 70.

on royal expedition. In addition, as has been shown, some of the men he fought alongside in 1387 were later involved in the Royal response to his revolt. Thus brothers in arms would later have to oppose one another in battle. This demonstrates that soldiers could change their loyalties through the years and would fight against those who had once been their colleagues when required.

Sir Reginald Grey was a powerful figure in the marches of Wales, and was also a landholder in Cheshire, where Richard II had held a power base. It is not surprising that Henry IV chose to keep him happy. Grey was a man with much military experience, he was a deponent in the Scrope vs. Grosvenor controversy,[168] and also served on the Rheims campaign of 1359–60.[169] He fought in the campaign of 1387 and later accompanied Henry IV to Scotland in August 1400.[170] He also featured in his own case at the court of chivalry from 1408–1410 against Sir Edward Hastings, contesting the inheritance of the earl of Pembroke, who was killed in a tournament in 1389.[171] It is interesting to note that the first attack of the revolt of Owain Glyn Dwr was on the Grey town of Ruthin.[172] He seems to have prospered under the rule of the Appellants and he is also linked with another of the Appellants in 1388, as a commissioner of the peace in Bedford along with the Earl Marshal[173] and in July 1388 the estate of his son was ratified in Salisbury Cathedral.[174] Grey was a staunch supporter of Richard, earl of Arundel. In August 1394, Grey was one of Arundel's sureties for his good behaviour towards the king and was his feoffee in 1396.[175] It is not surprising that Grey accompanied Arundel in his retinue in 1387 and then quickly supported Henry IV in 1399. He did not appear in the retinue lists for 1388. However his position in Cheshire may have meant that he was better placed for keeping an eye on Arundel's position in England.

Grey was a figure who undoubtedly supported Arundel. The presence of such men in the expeditions would lend a political note to these campaigns. However, his allegiances are not so clearly defined and by 1397 he began to witness royal charters and was entrusted with the custody of the duke of Gloucester's heir during the Irish campaign of 1399.[176] He also seems to have campaigned with the king in Ireland in 1394, as he has taken out letters of

---

[168] *Scrope v. Grosvenor*, vol. i, p. 208.

[169] Ayton, *Knights and Warhorses*, p. 265.

[170] Davies, *Revolt of Owain*, p. 148; Brown, 'English Campaign in Scotland, 1400', p. 47n.

[171] Keen, 'English Military Experience and the Court of Chivalry', pp. 125–127.

[172] Davies, *Revolt of Owain*, p. 153. R.I. Jack, 'Owain Glyn Dwr and the Lordship of Ruthin', *Welsh History Review*, 2 (1965), pp. 303–322; R.I. Jack (ed), *The Grey of Ruthin Valor: The Valor of the English Lands of Edmund Grey, Earl of Kent, drawn up from ministers' accounts of 1467–8* (Sydney, 1965).

[173] *CPR, 1385–1389*, p. 545.

[174] *CPR, 1385–1389*, p. 478, 'ratification of the estate of Roger, son of Reginald Grey of Netherhavene in the Cathedral church of Salisbury'.

[175] *CCR, 1392–1396*, p. 368; *CCR, 1396–1399*, p. 72.

[176] C. Given-Wilson, 'Royal Charter Witness Lists 1327–1399', *Medieval Prosopography*, 11 (1991), pp. 35–93; H.T. Riley (ed.), *Annales Ricardi Secundi et Henrici Quarti*, in J. de Trokelowe *et al.*, *Chronica et Annales* (Rolls Series, 1866), p. 321; as cited in C. Given-Wilson, 'Richard II and the Higher Nobility', in *Richard II: The Art of Kingship*, ed. Anthony Goodman and James Gillespie (Oxford, 1998), p. 115.

attorney for such purpose.[177] Thus, when Richard was prosecuting his enemies, Grey had moved firmly into the royal camp. However, he was still quick to support Henry in 1399. This again shows how loyalties with the local gentry were easily changed depending upon the political circumstance and self-preservation.

Connections to Richard II: case studies

It is also possible to identify men in the muster rolls who are clearly supporters of Richard II and have still been willing to serve with the earl of Arundel during the period of Appellant supremacy. Sir Gilbert Talbot, a retinue captain in both 1387 and 1388,[178] appears to have been a full member of the English military community and a loyal follower of Richard II. He was retained as a king's knight in 1392.[179] His retinue in 1387 consisted of 73 soldiers and he has increased this to a retinue of 80 soldiers in 1388. His biography in *History of Parliament* gives further details of this individual's career. He was a member of parliament only once for Berkshire in 1386, was born *c.*1346 and died in 1399, thus in 1387 was forty-one years old.[180] He had a long military career, in his own words beginning at the age of thirteen, when he accompanied Edward III's army to France in 1359 in the retinue of John of Gaunt. In his deposition in October 1386, he stated that he was forty years of age and that he had been in arms for twenty-five years, since the age of just fifteen.[181] His final expedition was accompanying the king on his Irish campaign in 1394 at the age of forty-eight.[182] His military career therefore spanned thirty-five years in total and seems to have been a career in arms mirrored by many other such younger sons. His other travels included visits to Italy as part of the royal party involved with the marriage of Lionel, duke of Clarence in 1366 and 1367. In 1369, he again served with John of Gaunt on his chevauchée across Normandy. He appears to have been knighted by 1377 and served with a contingent of 38 soldiers with Thomas, earl of Buckingham. In 1383, he served on the border with Scotland in the force commanded by Gaunt. Indeed, Simon Walker has identified him as a retainer of

---

177 *CPR, 1391–1396*, pp. 474–475.

178 1387: E101/40/33 m. 12; enrolled protection, C76/71 m. 11. 1388: E101/41/5 m. 11d.

179 *Royal Household*, p. 286.

180 *HOP*, vol. iii, pp. 560–563. I am not entirely convinced by all of the description of the career of Sir Gilbert Talbot as relayed in *History of Parliament*. It may well be drawing upon the careers of three different men. The first man is Sir Gilbert Talbot of Richards Castle, Herefs, and Wadley, Berks. This is the man who served in the expedition of 1387. His career has possibly been enhanced by reference to the careers of Gilbert, Lord Talbot (1332–1387) and Gilbert, Lord Talbot (b. 1383), see *Complete Peerage*, vol. xii, pp. 614–616 and pp. 617–618. For instance, the above reference to Given-Wilson refers to Gilbert, Lord Talbot, snr and jnr as king's knights and therefore not this Sir Gilbert Talbot. I have, however, kept the framework suggested in *HOP* for this case study as it is clear that most of the biography refers to our Sir Gilbert Talbot.

181 *Scrope v. Grosvenor*, vol. i, p. 174, vol. ii, p. 397.

182 *CPR, 1391–1396*, p. 476 (attorney).

Gaunt between 1383 and 1387.[183] He returned to Scotland in Richard II's expedition of 1385, with a force of one knight, 4 esquires and 12 archers.[184] *History of Parliament* comments that, although Talbot served the king's uncles, he was first and foremost 'a king's knight'.[185]

How does this tie in with his actions during the years of Appellant supremacy? His very participation in both campaigns as retinue captain would suggest that he had no problem with serving with the king's opponents. Indeed his continued service over both years would suggest that he accepted the Appellants' authority which had been imposed by force at Radcot Bridge.[186] In addition to this show of loyalty to the Appellants, he also was appointed in March 1388 to take oaths from the influential men of the country that they would support Arundel and his fellow Appellants.[187] Another interesting link to the Appellants is his cousin, Sir Reginald Grey of Ruthin, who was a staunch ally of Arundel in Shropshire.[188] He was also connected to William Beauchamp of Warwick, the brother of the earl of Warwick, and other members of the expedition namely Sir Ivo Fitzwarin and Sir Thomas West.[189]

Ivo Fitzwarin served in 1387 in Arundel's retinue,[190] the same retinue as Fulk Fitzwarin, and was therefore probably related. Fulk Fitzwarin was a neighbour of Reginald Grey of Ruthin, and thus this shows that Talbot had further links with the Shropshire supporters of Arundel. Sir Thomas West served in the expeditions of 1387 and 1388.[191] In 1387 he is listed next to Ivo Fitzwarin on the muster roll, showing a further connection between these combatants.[192] However, although linked with Arundel from these expeditions, other personal connections between Talbot and the admiral have not been traced. Sir Gilbert Talbot's connections with the Appellants during the years of supremacy, did not affect his future advancement with the king. As *History of Parliament* points out, he was retained as a favoured 'King's knight' throughout the 1390s.[193] He also accompanied Richard II on his expedition to Ireland in 1394 and did not

---

183 Walker, *The Lancastrian Affinity*, p. 282, served overseas in 1373 and 1386.

184 Lewis, 'The Last Medieval Summons', p. 18.

185 *HOP*, vol. iii, p. 561.

186 *HOP* again recognises that he served in 1387 but not in 1388. It again also gives the reference for the 1387 muster roll as E101/41/5, which is the muster roll accompanying the expedition for 1388.

187 E101/402/20 m. 34d.

188 *Scrope v. Grosvenor*, vol. ii, p. 397.

189 *CPR, 1388–1392*, pp. 157–158; he is named with a group of other men as being granted a king's licence for a manor previously acquired without one. Among these men are William Beauchamp of Warwick, knight, Ivo Fitzwarin, knight, and Thomas West, knight.

190 E101/40/33 m. 1.

191 1387: E101/40/33 m. 1; enrolled protection, C76/71 m. 14; enrolled attorney, C76/71 m. 10. 1388: E101/41/5 m. 7; enrolled protection, C76/72 m. 6.

192 He may have served in Scotland with Richard II in 1385; Lewis lists a Sir Thomas West with a retinue of two esquires and three archers, but this was probably his father. *CPR, 1385–1388*, p. 242, Nov 21st 1386, 'pardon for acquisition of lands to Thomas West son and heir of Thomas West'; this is probably our Thomas West as his father had now passed away.

193 *CPR, 1391–1396*, p. 48, 'grant during the war with France, to the king's knight Gilbert Talbot'.

return to England until April 1395.[194] As he died in February 1399 it is not possible to judge his relationship with the king on his actions during the deposition. However, it does seem that he was a man deeply immersed in the military community and had a complicated web of connections with established military figures[195] and also other combatants on the expeditions. He had served with the king and his uncles, felt able to serve with Arundel as a retinue captain in 1387 and 1388, and even act for him by collecting oaths of loyalty in Berkshire. This service during these years of political instability has not harmed his chances of advancement with the crown. He was able to find continued favour as a king's knight and serve on the royal expedition to Ireland in 1394.

A couple of men with Ricardian links are also present on the expeditions and can be identified on the muster rolls, namely Sir William Lisle[196] and Sir George Nowers.[197] However, they both found it very easy to quickly find a new role within the reign of Henry IV and act as jurors on the trial that prosecuted those who rebelled against the newly installed king in the Epiphany Plot.[198] They had both also found it pertinent to secure a royal pardon in 1398.[199] Sir Peter Bessels was also a juror at the trial, but he had had less involvement with Richard II and gained his influence under the reign of Henry IV. Leland describes how Lisle could be one of two men from the same family, either uncle or nephew. Both men had a similar background in their service to Richard II and Leland argues it is the younger Lisle who is present on the jury. It is not clear from the muster roll which man went on campaign in 1388. Both men of this name have been retained as king's knights for Richard II and interestingly also for Henry IV.[200] This demonstrates how service in 1388 has not harmed their advancement under Richard II and their position was able to be confirmed under Henry IV. Sir George Nowers was a less prominent local knight and his appearance on the muster roll for 1387 adds to our knowledge of his background. Leland describes how he was linked to Sir Richard Abberbury, a Ricardian courtier. The appearance of these men in the jury of the Oxford Trial of 1400 demonstrates how loyalties were quickly formed and changed and how, perhaps, local relationships were more important that those formed with the royal court. These men found it very easy to move from service under one king to the next with a seamless transition. It is also interesting to note that three of these jurors

---

[194] *Ibid.*, pp. 476 and 536.

[195] For instance, Sir Matthew Gourney, the veteran soldier, was married to his niece, Philippa, *CPR, 1388–1392*, pp. 157–158.

[196] E101/41/5 m. 9.

[197] E101/40/33 m. 7.

[198] Leland, 'Oxford Trial', pp. 170–171, 173–174, 182.

[199] Lisle 'the younger', C67/30 m. 27. Nowers, C67/30 m. 17.

[200] Lisle 'the younger', Richard II: *Royal Household*, p. 283, knight of the Chamber and lay officer of the household, retained for life 1392. Henry IV: *Royal Household*, p. 289, retained 1401. Lisle 'the elder', Richard II: *Royal Household*, p. 285, retained for life 1397. Henry IV: *Royal Household*, p. 289, retained 1401.

[201] E101/41/5 m. 9.

were involved in the expeditions of 1387 and 1388, demonstrating that these campaigns were able to draw upon senior figures from the local gentry.

As has been discussed earlier, Sir Ralph Vernon who was a retinue captain in 1388[201] had a strong relationship with the king. Indeed Knighton states in his chronicle that Sir Ralph was, 'sent by the King to muster his forces to oppose the Appellants' prior to the battle of Radcot Bridge in December 1387.[202] It is therefore of great interest to note that in a matter of months, Sir Ralph is commanding a retinue under the command of the earl of Arundel, whom he had been mustering a force to oppose. Although he felt able to serve the opposition to Richard II at this point, he showed his old loyalties had not died and in fact was executed for his part in the revolt of 1403 against the new regime of Henry IV.[203]

Another such man with strong links to Richard II was Thomas, Lord Camoys who was discharged from Parliament in 1383, perhaps as suggested by Given-Wilson, because of his political support for Richard II[204] and then abjured from the royal court in 1387.[205] A number of courtiers were compelled to abjure the court as described by John Leland in his article, which comments on the alliances and careers of these fifteen people.[206] In the article Leland states that Thomas, Lord Camoys was loyal to Richard in the early part of his career, but after the Appellant crisis lost favour from Richard II. Leland comments that 'Richard seems to have missed an opportunity to hold the support of an able captain'.[207] However, this loss of favour could be due to Camoys taking up arms with the earl of Arundel on his expedition in 1388,[208] which is not noted by Leland. Not only did Camoys captain a retinue in this expedition, but at 135 soldiers, it was the fourth largest retinue out of the 41 retinues on campaign. As such, Camoys would have assumed quite a significant position on this expedition and this is again quite a turn around for someone who has been recently expelled from the court for his support of Richard II. As he did not return to the court circle, it would seem that Richard did not forget this change of allegiance. Indeed Camoys also secured a royal pardon in 1398, perhaps referring to his actions in 1387–1388.[209] He later regained his court influence under Henry IV and was listed, although not sworn in, amongst the jurors who were to try the rebels involved in the Epiphany Plot uprising of 1400. He was also famously to command part of the army at Agincourt.[210] It is possible to trace the service of Thomas Tryskebett, esquire, who serves in Camoys' retinue in 1388 and continues this service to the Agincourt campaign of 1415. This demonstrates a relationship with Camoys which has continued in a martial capacity over nearly

---

202 *Knighton's Chronicle*, p. 419.
203 *CPR, 1401–1405*, p. 353.
204 *Royal Household*, p. 247.
205 *Westminster Chronicle*, p. 231.
206 Leland, 'The Abjuration of 1388'. John, Lord Lovel, was also required to abjure the court and can be seen to be serving in 1388: E101/41/5 m. 3.
207 Leland, 'The Abjuration of 1388', p. 134.
208 E101/41/5 m. 6. Enrolled protection, C76/72 m. 6.
209 C67/30 m. 11, 18 August 1398.
210 Leland, 'The Abjuration of 1388', p. 134.

thirty years.[211] Both Sir Ralph Vernon and Thomas, Lord Camoys were supporters of Richard II who decided to fight with Arundel in 1388. However, later while Camoys found fame under Henry IV and V, Vernon met his death for rebelling against the new regime.

Another supporter of Richard II is the king's knight, Sir William Elmham.[212] He can be found on the muster rolls captaining a retinue in 1387 and serving in the retinue of Sir Thomas Percy in 1388. He was an important member of the military community and also served in the expedition of Bishop Dispencer in 1383, when he was a military advisor to the Bishop, and on the royal expedition to Scotland in 1385.[213] His fame was such that Froissart, when reporting the events of the expedition of 1388, refers to him by name.[214] He was close to Richard II as can be seen in the report of the Monk of Westminster, where the latter identifies Elmham as one of the knights who tortured the Carmelite friar who accused the Duke of Lancaster as plotting an attempt on the king's life in 1384. Indeed, the Monk describes Elmham as being heavily involved in this event.

> They now took him down and forced his feet and the whole length of his shins up to the knees to rest for some time on the fire, while Sir William Elmham sat so heavily astride his loins that he was deprived of all power to draw his feet back from the flames; with the result that through the scorching and burning of the fire a number of heat-cracks were plainly visible on his feet and shins until the day of his burial.[215]

Elmham was also involved in the events of the Appellant crisis and the Monk of Westminster describes how he was arrested on 1 January with eight other knights and three clerks who were sent to various fortresses for safekeeping. Elmham himself was sent to the custody of Nottingham Castle. The order in the *Calendar of Close Rolls* states that the men should not be allowed to speak to one another and should be deliberately split up.[216] The Merciless Parliament of 1388 passed the sentence of execution on a number of these knights including Sir Simon Burley, Sir John Beauchamp, Sir James Berners and Sir John Salisbury due to their support for Richard II.[217] Things were therefore not looking good for Sir William as he could perhaps expect the same judgement. However, the Monk of Westminster reports:

> On 30 May the three knights, William Elmham, Thomas Trivet, and Nicholas Dagworth, were released under mainprise from the Tower of London with the

---

[211] E101/41/5 m. 6; 1415: Harris Nicholas, *History of the Battle of Agincourt*, p. 343.

[212] *Royal Household*, p. 284, retained 1386.

[213] 1387; E101/40/33 m. 11. 1388: E101/40/39 m. 1. 1383: *Westminster Chronicle*, p. 45, as adviser to Bishop Despencer. 1385: Lewis, 'The Last Medieval Summons', p. 20.

[214] Froissart, *Chronicles*, p. 383.

[215] *Westminster Chronicle*, p. 75.

[216] *CCR, 1385–1389*, p. 394, order for custody and order to be brought to Westminster.

[217] *Westminster Chronicle*, pp. 331–332.

proviso that they were to appear in the next parliament to answer whatever charges the Lords Appellant wished to bring against them.[218]

The order of their release gives the knights extra time to report to the council, if they were unable to attend parliament due to being delayed 'upon the present expedition at sea in the King's wars'.[219] It is evident from this entry that Elmham was spared the fate of his colleagues because of his usefulness in the earl's overseas expedition, to which the order of release explicitly refers. As he had also served in 1387, the earl of Arundel had recent experience of his effectiveness on such a campaign. Elmham survived this attack upon the king's favourites, but how did he manage in the changeover to the new regime of Henry IV? One factor, which should also be considered, is that he had required a royal pardon in 1398. This is surprising considering the support he seems to have given to Richard II in these years.[220] From the records it would seem that his military fame was again appreciated and the new king immediately made him a king's knight in 1399.[221] The career of Elmham demonstrates that political life in the 1380s was dangerous and that he escaped with his life, probably because of his military skills that were well known to the king's enemies.

Yet again the career of one prominent member of the campaign, leads to information about another. Sir Thomas Trivet was arrested with Sir William Elmham in 1388 because of his relationship with Richard II and was also released under the same order.[222] He was also known to the Appellants having served under Arundel in the expedition of 1387 as a retinue captain, leading a force of 155 men, which was the fourth largest retinue in the campaign.[223] He was again a senior figure in the military community as is shown by the size of the retinue he captained in 1387. His career stretched back into the reign of Edward III and he captained a retinue in the expedition of Sir Robert Knollys to France in 1370, when he was around twenty years of age.[224]

In his own deposition to the court of chivalry, Trivet claimed he had commenced his career in arms in 1373. He served in Gascony with John of Gaunt in 1378 and also was lucky to survive the storm that wrecked the expedition of Sir John Arundel in 1379. He served with the earl of Buckingham in 1380.[225] In addition he was an advisor with Sir William Elmham on Bishop Despencer's Flanders campaign in 1383. During this campaign, Trivet was one of the captains who had surrendered captured towns to the enemy for a bribe. He survived the wrath of Parliament over his actions by throwing himself on the king's mercy.[226] He also served on the royal expedition to Scotland in 1385,

---

218 *Ibid.*, p. 339.
219 *CCR, 1385–1389*, p. 397, order for release.
220 C67/30 m. 28.
221 *Royal Household*, p. 288, retained 1399.
222 *CCR, 1385–1389*, p. 394, order for custody and order to be brought to Westminster; p. 397, order for release.
223 E101/40/33 m. 7; enrolled protection, C76/71 m. 14.
224 Sherborne, 'Indentured Retinues', p. 7.
225 *Scrope v. Grosvenor*, vol. i, p. 179, vol. ii, p. 413.
226 *Westminster Chronicle*, pp. 45, 47, 51–53.

leading a force of 39 men.[227] In addition, he had preceded the earl of Arundel as Admiral of the West from 22 February 1386 to 10 December 1386.[228] He had some success in this role as can be seen from the record of ships he had captured in the *Calendar of Patent Rolls*. It is also of interest that an order for the repair of Trivet's ship, *la Kateryne* of Sandewych, which was 'much battered in the king's service', was made on 27 November 1387 as he had promised further service. This order is recorded as being made by the authority of the Council.[229] This order is dated only ten days following the attempted ambush of the Appellant lords by Sir Thomas Trivet on 17 November, described below. This demonstrates that Trivet's experience as admiral was valuable to the Appellants.

Goodman suggests that Arundel's success in 1387 was as a result of copying the tactics of blockading the channel as practised by the previous admirals. Indeed, the fleet captured by Arundel in 1387 may have been artificially swollen because of this previous success.[230] Goodman does not mention the inclusion of Sir Thomas in the campaign, but it is clear that his experience and knowledge of the channel would have aided Arundel in his success of 1387. Sir Thomas was a king's knight from the beginning of Richard II's reign.[231] It is also evident why he was arrested in 1388, as he was a close supporter of the king. The Monk of Westminster describes how Richard absolved him in 1383 from his part in the debacle in Flanders. Trivet also had to restrain the king from attacking the archbishop of Canterbury in 1385. The monk also describes how in November 1387 'Sir Thomas Trivet had advised the king to take the field and unfurl his standard against the insurgents, a piece of advice which caused them intense displeasure'.[232]

Trivet had also laid ambushes for the Appellants in London and thus they were delayed for two hours in meeting with the king on 17 November. It is not surprising that he was held in custody at the beginning of 1388, but perhaps more of a surprise that he was released in order to serve with Arundel on his expedition. He had already served in the previous year and thus it is evident that the military experience that Trivet could offer was of great value to the Appellants, even though he had opposed them on behalf of the king. It is not clear that he served in 1388, as he cannot be identified in the muster rolls. However, Elmham served with Sir Thomas Percy in this expedition and this muster roll

---

[227] Lewis, 'Last Medieval Summons', p. 18.

[228] *Handbook of British Chronology*, p. 139.

[229] For reference for repair of his ship see *CPR, 1385–1389*, p. 395; for ship captures see p. 216, with one of the captured ships being granted to Sir Simon Burley; p. 266, grant of Spanish ship, captured by the admirals, *la Seint Marieship* of Santander, to Richard Crys, esquire, of Devon; also p. 315, where Richard Crys petitions for the return of the tackle (apparatus) of the ship as it had been removed. Richard Cryse was a retinue captain in both 1387 and 1388. 1387: E101/40/33 m. 19; enrolled protection, C76/71 m. 12. 1388: E101/41/5 m. 17. Goodman, *Loyal Conspiracy*, p. 129, suggests that Cryse may have served in this ship in the expedition of 1387.

[230] Goodman, *Loyal Conspiracy*, p. 129.

[231] *Royal Household*, p. 286, retained 1378.

[232] *Westminster Chronicle*, p. 213.

has been damaged by fire.[233] It may be that Sir Thomas Trivet was listed on the damaged roll. We cannot know whether Trivet would have survived the Appellant prosecution, as the Monk of Westminster describes his bizarre death in 1388: 'On 6 October, when Sir Thomas Trivet put his horse to the gallop over some newly ploughed land, his mount happened to stumble between the furrows, and fell with its weight on top of him, crushing him so badly that he lived barely nine hours more.'[234]

It is clear from the careers of Elmham and Trivet that being a member of the expeditions of 1387 and 1388 did not require political allegiance to the Appellant cause. Both these men were close to Richard II and were serving because of their military experience, which was appreciated by the Appellants who were pragmatic when choosing whom they would take on expedition. The service of both these men, who had also fought together in 1383 and 1385, demonstrates that military service was a shared experience and this can be shown throughout the ranks of the army from the most experienced knight to an archer about whom little else is known.

A strong supporter of Richard II as a regular attender at court and a member of the Royal Household, Sir John St John also served in the expedition of 1388 in the retinue of the Earl Marshal.[235] This involvement would make him vulnerable in the last years of Richard's reign, especially following the fall of the older Appellants and then the exile of Nottingham, the Earl Marshal, and Hereford. Sir John had a long and distinguished career serving three subsequent kings and was a member of parliament on four occasions.[236] St John's career is detailed in *History of Parliament* and is a prime example of a man who made the most of his prominent local position to ensure that his support was appreciated by the strongest power as the political landscape changed, and the following summary is taken from this source. St John was a near contemporary of Thomas Mowbray, earl of Nottingham, and struck up a close relationship following his being awarded temporary custody of St John's estates in 1381. *History of Parliament* does not note his service in the retinue of the Earl Marshal in 1388, but does note that he benefited from property confiscated from a victim of the Merciless Parliament. Following, this flirtation with the Appellants, St John was quickly back in Court, together with his patron, the junior Appellant, Nottingham. In 1389, he was involved in a tournament before the king at Woodstock, where he accidentally killed the young earl of Pembroke in a practice joust and thus unintentionally sparked the Grey v. Hastings case in the court of chivalry.[237] Richard II retained him as a knight of the body in 1393, for the annual fee of 40 marks, payable for life from the Exchequer.[238] It was in this capacity that he was

---

[233] E101/40/39, for damaged muster roll.
[234] *Westminster Chronicle*, p. 369.
[235] E101/41/5 m. 3.
[236] *HOP*, vol. iv, pp. 280–283.
[237] See Keen, 'English Military Experience and the Court of Chivalry', pp. 125–127, for discussion of this case. The dispute arose because of the untimely death of the young earl of Pembroke and concerned the rightful recipient of his inheritance.
[238] *Royal Household*, p. 286, retained for life in 1393.

involved in the Irish expedition of 1394 where he served with a personal retinue of four mounted archers. He served both the interests of Nottingham and the king's favourite, Thomas, Lord Despencer (later earl of Gloucester), who also fought in 1388,[239] in their Welsh Marcher lands. It was, however, following the banishment of Nottingham in October 1398, that St John's loyalty to the crown was called into question. *History of Parliament* notes that his name was omitted from a list submitted to the king of a continual council to govern the affairs of Nottingham whilst in exile. He was also required to take out letters of pardon following the downfall of the other Appellants the previous summer,[240] and joined Richard II on his expedition to Ireland in 1399. We can therefore infer from this that he must have taken an active supportive role in 1387–1388, which required him to be wary of the king's favour at this time. It is indeed possible that he may have been with the Earl Marshal in his retinue that came into conflict with the Cheshire forces of de Vere at Radcot Bridge.

It is not clear how St John coped with the return to England of Richard II in 1399; however it is likely that he was one of the many who deserted the king in his hour of need. Indeed, his concern following the exile of Mowbray, may have caused St John to welcome the new regime and he was immediately made a king's knight in 1399.[241] He was further helped in his alliance to the new regime following the death of the Earl Marshal in Venice in the same year. St John reached new positions of influence under Henry IV, and gained much experience combating the Welsh revolt of Glyn Dwr, where he was also associated with Henry, Prince of Wales. He was a knight of the prince's household and an annuitant from 1406.[242] He stayed loyal to the throne during the rebellion of Archbishop Scrope in 1405 when the young Earl Marshal was summarily executed without trial. His continued loyalty and connection with the Prince of Wales, placed him in a strong position on the accession of Henry V. He was made mayor of Bordeaux and served with the king on his expeditions in Normandy.[243]

Service with the king in Ireland, 1394 and 1399

As discussed in Chapter 1, Richard II personally led two expeditions to Ireland in 1394 and 1399. It would be of value to compare the men who served on these expeditions with those who served in 1387–1388. We can demonstrate how many men involved in the earlier campaigns advanced to serve the king in

---

[239] E101/41/5 m. 1.

[240] C67/30 m. 13.

[241] *Royal Household*, p. 290, retained in 1399.

[242] Griffiths, 'The Military Career and Affinity of Henry, Prince of Wales', pp. 173, 214, and *CPR, 1413–1416*, p. 95.

[243] Sir John St John had letters of protection because he was going to France, taken on 24 September 1413 at Westminster and also on 7 April 1422 at Southampton, where he is described as of Westpery, Northamptonshire, and as going to France in the retinue of the king, *Annual Report of the Deputy Keeper of the Public Records 44*, pp. 548, 637. I am grateful to Professor Anne Curry for these references.

person. This shows whether service in the campaigns in the years of Appellant supremacy had precluded men from service with the king in his campaigns in Ireland. The following table demonstrates service in Ireland and compares it with service in 1387–1388. Unfortunately, muster rolls for the Irish expeditions do not exist. Therefore, a full comparison between the forces cannot be carried out. However, a number of men have taken letters of protection and attorney for these campaigns and these can be found in the *Calendar of Patent Rolls*.[244] From this information, 293 named individuals can be identified as serving in the 1394 campaign and 306 named individuals can be found serving in the 1399 campaign. Table 24 demonstrates how many of these men can also be identified in the campaigns of 1387–1388.

Letters of protection and attorney only provide a glimpse of the military community which would have joined these expeditions and is also no guarantee that these men actually attended the campaigns. These sources do not always state whether a soldier would be serving as an esquire or archer or the retinue in which they were serving, but they do occasionally offer information about participants' residence and occupation. The evidence for service in 1394 is supplemented by the *vadia guerre* (pay rolls) for the retinue of Richard II on the Irish campaign.[245] This pay roll lists the soldiers who accompanied Richard II in 1394. It details how much they were paid and for how long they served. It also has information about how many esquires and archers each knight had with them on campaign. This evidence demonstrates that of 89 knights serving with Richard II, only 38 had taken letters of protection or attorney. This indicates that nearly 58% of the knights serving in this expedition had not secured letters of protection or attorney. The evidence thus provided in the *Calendar of Patent Rolls* only gives a small sample with which to compare service in 1387–1388. This source has been supplemented for the campaign of 1394 by knights identified in the pay rolls for the retinue of Richard II and such men are also included in Table 24. The numbers of soldiers identified by name as serving in 1394 therefore is increased by 51 knights to a total of 344 participants with which to compare continuation of service.[246]

The evidence presented demonstrates that 97 of the men who serve in 1387–1388 also serve in at least one of the king's Irish expeditions in 1394 and 1399. 64 of these men are found fighting with the king in 1394 and 49 in 1399. Of these men, 16 soldiers serve in both Irish expeditions. For 1394 this is 19% of the named soldiers who are identified as serving and for 1399 it is 16% of

---

[244] 1394: *CPR, 1391–1396*, pp. 474 (protection), 477 (attorney). 1399: *CPR, 1396–1399*, pp. 525 (protection), 530 (attorney).

[245] The knights present in the pay roll, E101/402/20 mm. 33ff, are listed in Mitchell, 'Some Aspects of the Knightly Household of Richard II', Appendix III, pp. 306–309. Saul, *Richard II*, p. 279, comments that these accounts in the wardrobe book demonstrate the force in the king's household numbered from 4,000 to 5,000 in size. He also comments that the overall size of the force was around 7,000–8,000 men.

[246] Table 24: those soldiers with letters of protection or attorney are listed with *CPR* in the reference column; those soldiers present in the pay roll for Richard II's retinue are listed with Mitchell in the reference column (Shelagh Mitchell, 'Some Aspects of the Knightly Household of Richard II' (D.Phil. thesis, London University, 1998)).

Table 24. Service with the king in Ireland in 1394 and 1399

Year	Title	First name	Surname	Rank	Captain name	Location	Ref
1387		William	Arderne	Esquire	Mons Reynold de Cobham		
1394		William	Ardern		Edward, earl of Rutland		*CPR*
1388	Mons	William	Arundell, D'	Knight	Arundel, Richard, earl of		
1394	Sir	William	Arundell	Knight	Richard II		*CPR*/Mitchell
1388		William	Barbour	Archer	Mons Thomas Percy		
1394		William	Barbour		Richard II	Teneby	*CPR*
1388	Le Sire		Bardolf	Baron	Le Counte Marshall		
1394	Sir	Thomas	Bardolf	Knight	Richard II	Wermegey	*CPR*/Mitchell
1399	Sir	Thomas	Bardolf, lord of Bardolff	Knight		Wirmegey	*CPR*
1387		Thomas	Barneburgh	Archer	Robert Geffard		
1388		Thomas	Barneburgh	Esquire	Mons Thomas West		
1394		Thomas	Barnebourghe	Esquire	Richard II		*CPR*
1387	Le Sire		Beamount, de	Captain	Le Sire de Beaumount		
1394	Lord	John	Beaumont, John Lord	Banneret	Richard II		Mitchell
1387		John	Bebey	Archer	Le Sire de Beaumount		
1399		John	Beby		Albemarle, Edward earl of	Cyston	*CPR*
1387		Piers	Besilles	Esquire	Mons Gilbe Talbot		
1388		Piers	Besiles	Esquire	Mons Gilbe Talbot		
1394	Sir	Peter	Besyls	Knight	Richard II		*CPR*/Mitchell
1387	Mons	John	Bohun, de	Banneret	Arundel, Richard, earl of		
1388	Mons	Johan	Bohun	Captain	Mons Johan Bohun		
1394	Sir	John	Bohun	Banneret	Richard II		Mitchell
1387	Mons	Thomas	Butiller	Knight	Arundel, Richard, earl of		
1394	Sir	Thomas	Boteler/Boteller	Knight	Richard II	Gloucester	*CPR*/Mitchell
1387		Raynad	Braybrok	Esquire	Le Counte de Devens		
1388		Reynald	Braybrok	Esquire	Mons Thomas Percy		
1394	Sir	Reginald	Braybroke	Knight	Richard II		*CPR*/Mitchell
1399	Sir	Reginald	Braybrok	Knight			*CPR*
1387		William	Breton	Esquire	Mons Reynold de Cobham		
1388		William	Breton	Esquire	Mons Thomas Ponynges		
1399		William	Breton	Esquire			*CPR*
1388	Mons	William	Briene	Captain	Mons William Briene		
1394	Sir	William	Briene alias Brian	Knight	Richard II		*CPR*/Mitchell

1387 Mons	Hugh	Browe	Knight	Arundel, Richard, earl of		
1388 Mons	Hugh	Browe	Captain	Mons Hugh Browe		
1394 Sir	Hugh	Browe	Knight	Richard, Lord Talbot		CPR
1388	Johan	Bysshop	Archer	Robert Geffard		
1399	John	Bisshop, the elder, 'goldbeter'			London	CPR
1388	Benet	Cely	Captain	Benet Cely		
1394 Sir	Benedict	Cely	Knight	earl of Huntingdon, the king's brother	Sussex	CPR
1388	William	Clifford	Esquire	Mons Thomas Percy		
1394 Sir	William	Clifford	Knight	Richard II		Mitchell
1399 Sir	William	Clifford	Knight			CPR
1387	James	Clifford	Esquire	Mons Thomas Trenet		
1394	James	Clifford	Esquire	Richard II		CPR
1387 Mons	Nich	Clifton	Captain	Mons Nichol Clyfton		
1388 Mons	Nicol	Clyfton	Captain	Mons Nichol Clyfton		
1394 Sir	Nicholas	Clifton	Knight	Richard II		Mitchell
1388	William	Clynton	Archer	Mons Thomas Ponynges		
1399	William	Clynton, de	Esquire	Richard II		CPR
1388	Robert	Cole	Archer	Mons Johan Grymesby		
1394	Robert	Cole			Stafford	CPR
1387	John	Cormewayle	Esquire	Arundel, Richard, earl of		
1388	Johan	Cornewaill	Esquire	Mons Thomas Camoys		
1399 Sir	John	Cornewaill	Knight			CPR
1387 Mons	Hugh	Courtenay	Knight	Le Counte de Devens		
1388 Mons	Hugh	Courteney	Knight	Le Counte de Devens		
1399 Sir	Hugh	Courtenay		Richard II		CPR
1387 Mons	Richard	Craddok	Captain	Mons Richard Craddok		
1394 Sir	Richard	Cradoc	Knight	Richard II		CPR/Mitchell
1399 Sir	Richard	Cradok	Knight			CPR
1388	William	Curteys	Archer	David Lacy		
1394	William	Curteys	Esquire	March, Roger, earl of		CPR
1387	Johan	Dalyngrigg	Esquire	Arundel, Richard, earl of		
1388	John	Dalingrugg	Esquire	Mons William Heron		
1399 Sir	John	Dalyngregge	Knight	Exeter, earl of		CPR
1387 Mons	William	Dangle	Knight	John Slegh		
1388 Mons	William	Dangle	Knight	Mons Gilbe Talbot		
1394 Sir	William	Dangle	Knight	Richard II		CPR/Mitchell

Year	Title	First name	Surname	Rank	Captain name	Location	Ref
1387	Mons	Robert	Denny	Knight	Mons William Elmham		
1388	Mons	Robert	Denny	Knight	Mons Thomas Camoys		
1394	Sir	Robert	Denny	Knight	Richard II		Mitchell
1387	Mons	Hugh	Despencer, le	Captain	Mons Hugh le Despencer		
1388	Mons	Hugh	Despencer, le	Captain	Mons Hugh le Despencer		
1388	Mons	Hugh	Despencer, le	Captain	Mons Hugh le Despencer		
1394	Sir	Hugh	Despencer, le	Knight	Richard II		*CPR*/Mitchell
1399	Sir	Hugh	Despencer, le				*CPR*
1388	Sire	Thomas	Despenser, le	Baron	Arundel, Richard, earl of		
1394	Lord	Thomas	Despenser, le, lord of Glomorgan and Morgan'	Baron	Thomas le Despencer		*CPR*
1399	earl	Thomas	Despenser, le, earl of Gloucester	Peer	Thomas le Despencer		*CPR*
1388		John	Drayton	Esquire	David Lacy		
1399	Sir	John	Drayton	Knight	Richard II		*CPR*/Mitchell
1388		Johan	Dymmok	Esquire	Arundel, Richard, earl of		
1399		Johan	Dymmok				*CPR*
1387	Mons	William	Elmham	Captain	Mons William Elmham		
1388	Mons	William	Elmham	Knight	Mons Thomas Percy		
1394	Sir	William	Elmham	Knight	Richard II		Mitchell
1387	You	You fitz	Waryn	Knight	Arundel, Richard, earl of		
1394	Sir	Ivo	Fitz Waryn	Knight	Richard II		Mitchell
1388		Johan	Fort	Esquire	Mons Johan Wogan		
1394		John	Fort	Esquire	Richard II		*CPR*
1399		John	Fort	Esquire			*CPR*
1387	Mons	Renand	Grey, de	Knight	Arundel, Richard, earl of		
1394	Sir	Reginald	Grey, de	Knight		Ruthin	*CPR*
1399	Sir	Reginald	Grey	Knight		Ruthin	*CPR*
1387		Thomas	Grene	Archer	Mons Hugh le Despencer		
1388		Thomas	Grene	Archer	Mons Hugh le Despencer		
1399		Thomas	Grene, alias de Grene	Esquire	Richard II		*CPR*

1387	Andrewe	Hake	Esquire	Arundel, Richard, earl of	Sussex
1388 Mons	Andrew	Hake	Captain	Mons Andrewe Hake	
1399 Sir	Andrew	Hake	Knight		CPR
1387	Esmon	Hales	Esquire	Mons Hugh Loterell	
1399	Edward	Hales	Esquire		CPR
1387	William	Hay	Esquire	Le Sire de Beaumount	
1388	William	Hay	Esquire	Mons Andrewe Hake	
1399	William	Hay	Esquire		CPR
1387 Mons	William	Heron	Knight	Mons Nichol Clyfton	
1388 Mons	William	Heron	Captain	Mons William Heron	
1394 Sir	William	Heron	Knight	Richard II	CPR
1387	William	Hert	Esquire	John Slegh	
1399	William	Hert, usher of the chamber			CPR
1388	Johan	Holand	Esquire	Arundel, Richard, earl of	
1399	Johan	Holand	Esquire	John, duke of Exeter Harlagh	CPR
1387	Thomas	Holand, de	Esquire	Arundel, Richard, earl of	
1394 Sir	Thomas	Holande, de	Knight	Richard II	CPR/Mitchell
1387	John	Holt	Esquire	Le Sire de Beaumount	
1399	John	Holt			CPR
1387	John	Hore	Esquire	Le Counte de Devens	
1394	John	Hore	Esquire	Raddington, Baldwin	CPR
1387 Mons	John	Howard	Knight	Arundel, Richard, earl of	
1394 Sir	John	Howard	Knight	Richard II	CPR/Mitchell
1399 Sir	John	Howard	Knight		CPR
1388	William	Knottynglee	Esquire	Mons Thomas West	
1394	William	Knottyngley, one of the yeoman of the Crown		Richard II	CPR
1387	Richard	Kyngeston	Esquire	Mons Hugh le Despencer	
1399	Richard	Kyngeston, clerk			CPR
1388	Johan	Kyrkeby	Esquire	Mons Johan Clanyng	
1394	John	Kirkeby, clerk			CPR
1388	William	Lane,	Archer	Le Counte de Devens	
1394	William	Lane, clerk		Richard II	CPR
1399	William	Lane, king's clerk			CPR
1387 Mons	Roger	Lefozannge	Knight	Arundel, Richard, earl of	
1394 Sir	Roger	Straunge	Knight	Richard II	CPR/Mitchell

Year	Title	First name	Surname	Rank	Captain name	Location	Ref
1387	Mons	Estrephne	LeScrop	Knight	Arundel, Richard, earl of		
1394	Sir	Stephen	LeScrope	Knight	Richard II		Mitchell
1387		John	Leyre	Esquire	Mons William Elmham		
1394		John	Leyre, clerk		Richard, Lord Talbot		*CPR*
1388		Johan	Litel	Archer	Mons Thomas Ponynges		
1394		John	Litill		Richard II	Bristol	*CPR*
1387	Mons	Hugh	Loterell	Captain	Mons Hugh Loterell		
1394	Sir	Hugh	Luterell/Lutrell	Knight	Richard II		*CPR*/Mitchell
1399	Sir	Hugh	Lutrell				*CPR*
1388	Mons	John	Lovell	Knight	Le Monsers W Sire de Welles		
1394	Sir	John	Lovell	Knight	Richard II		*CPR*/Mitchell
1399	Sir	John	Lovell		Richard II	Tychemerssh	*CPR*
1388	Mons	William	Lysle	Knight	Mons William Briene		
1394	Sir	William	Lisle, senior	Knight	Richard II		Mitchell
1394	Sir	William	Lisle, junior	Knight	Richard II		Mitchell
1387	Le Compte		Marechall	Baron	Arundel, Richard, earl of		
1394	earl	Thomas	of Nottingham, earl Marshall	Captain	earl Marshall		*CPR*
1388		Johan	Mareschall	Esquire	Le Counte Marshall		
1399		John	Marshall	Esquire			*CPR*
1388		William	Mareschall	Esquire	Mons William Heron		
1394		William	Mareschall		Nottingham, Thomas, earl of		*CPR*
1388		William	Maynell	Esquire	Arundel, Richard, earl of		
1394	Sir	William	Maynell	Knight	Richard II		Mitchell
1387		Johan	Merland	Esquire	Mons Hugh le Despencer		
1388		John	Merland	Esquire	Mons Hugh le Despencer		
1394		John	Merland	Esquire	Richard II		*CPR*
1388		Here	Mystelburgh	Knight	Mons Thomas West		
1394		Here	Mistilburgh	Knight	Richard II		Mitchell
1388		Robert	Morlee	Esquire	Le Counte Marshall		
1394	Sir	Robert	Morle	Knight	Richard II	Norfolk	*CPR*/Mitchell
1387	Mons	Thomas	Mortemer	Captain	Mons Thomas Mortemer		
1394	Sir	Thomas	de Mortuo Mari	Knight	Roger, earl of March		*CPR*
1388		Constanty	Mortunere	Esquire	Arundel, Richard, earl of		
1399		Constantine	de Mortuo Mari/ alias Mortmer		Thomas de Morley, lord of Morley	Norfolk	*CPR*

1388		Hugh	Mortymer	Esquire	Arundel, Richard, earl of		
1394		Hugh	de Mortuo Mari/Mortymer	Esquire	Thomas, lord le Despencer		*CPR*
1387	Mons	Robert	Mounteney	Captain	Mons Robert Mounteney		
1394	Sir	Robert	Mounteneye	Knight	Richard II		*CPR*/Mitchell
1387		John	Parker	Esquire	Mons Johan Darundell		
1388		Johan	Parker	Esquire	Mons Johan Darundell		
1394		John	Parker	Esquire	Richard II	Haveryng atte Boure	*CPR*
1387		John	Pek	Archer	Mons Reynold de Cobham		
1394		John	Pekke, clerk		Richard II		*CPR*
1388	Mons	Thomas	Percy	Captain	Mons Thomas Percy		
1394		Thomas	Percy		Richard II		Mitchell
1399		Thomas	Percy, earl of Worcester		Thomas Percy, earl of Worcester		*CPR*
1388		John	Philip	Esquire	Mons Henry Jugloos		
1399		John	Philip		Exeter, earl of		*CPR*
1388	Mons	Johan	Routhe	Knight	Arundel, Richard, earl of		
1394	Sir	John	Routhe	Knight	Richard II		Mitchell
1388		William	Savage	Archer	Richard Cryse		
1399		William	Savage		Exeter, earl of	Smerdale	*CPR*
1387		Richard	Savage	Esquire	Mons Thomas Mortemer		
1399		Richard	Savage	Esquire			*CPR*
1388		Robert	Scot	Esquire	Mons Hugh le Despencer		
1399		Robert	Scot		Albemarle, Edward earl of	Abbotysle	*CPR*
1388	Mons	Johan	Senitjohn	Knight	Le Counte Marshall		
1394	Sir	John	Seynt John	Knight	Richard II		*CPR*/Mitchell
1399	Sir	John	Seint Johan	Knight			*CPR*
1388		Johan	Shepeherd	Archer	Mons William Briene		
1394		John	Shepherd		earl Marshall		*CPR*
1388		Nicholas	Sketon	Archer	Mons William Briene		
1394		Nicholas	Skelton, king's serjeants-at-arms		Richard II		*CPR*
1399		Nicholas	de Skelton				*CPR*
1387		John	Sly	Captain	John Slegh		
1394		John	Slegh, king's butler	Esquire			*CPR*

Year	Title	First name	Surname	Rank	Captain name	Location	Ref
1388		Richard	Spencer	Esquire	Le Counte de Devens		
1399		Richard	Spenser				CPR
1388		Johan	Spencer	Esquire	Le Counte de Devens		
1399		John	Spencer				CPR
1387		Humfrey	Stafford	Esquire	Arundel, Richard, earl of		
1394	Sir	Humphrey	Stafford	Knight	Richard II		Mitchell
1388		Thomas	Stout	Esquire	Thomas atte Lee		
1399		Thomas	Stoute				CPR
1388	Mons	William	Sturmy	Knight	Le Counte de Devens		
1394	Sir	William	Esturmy	Knight	Richard II		CPR/Mitchell
1387		William	Sutton	Esquire	Mons Arnald Savage		
1394		William	Sutton	Esquire	Richard, Lord Talbot		CPR
1388		Robert	Sutton	Archer	Mons Thomas Percy		
1399		Robert	Sutton	Esquire	Thomas de Morley, lord of Morley	Cambridge	CPR
1387		Mitther	Swetenham	Archer	Arundel, Richard, earl of		
1394		Matthew	Swetenham		Richard II	Chester	CPR
1399		Matthew	Swetenham, yeoman of the Crown				CPR
1388		Thomas	Talbot	Esquire	Aleyn Seintjust		
1399	Sir	Thomas	Talbot	Knight			CPR
1387	Mons	Gilbert	Talbot	Captain	Mons Gilbe Talbot		
1388	Mons	Gilbe	Talbot	Captain	Mons Gilbe Talbot		
1394	Sir	Gilbert	Talbot	Knight			CPR
1388		Edward	Thorp	Esquire	Mons Hugh le Despencer		
1399	Sir	Edmund	Thorpe	Knight			CPR
1388		Johan	Toly	Esquire	Arundel, Richard, earl of		
1399		John	Toly		Thomas de Morley, lord of Morley	Crystissale, co. Essex	CPR
1387	Mons	Robert	Tourke	Knight	Mons Reynold de Cobham		
1394	Sir	Robert	Turk	Knight	Richard, Lord Talbot		CPR
1387	Mons	Thomas	West	Knight	Arundel, Richard, earl of		
1388	Mons	Thomas	West	Captain	Mons Thomas West		
1399	Sir	Thomas	West	Knight	Richard II		CPR
1388	Mons	Johan	Wylteshyre	Knight	Arundel, Richard, earl of		
1399	Sir	John	Wiltshire	Knight			CPR
1388		Johan	Wyndesore	Archer	Arundel, Richard, earl of		
1399		John	Wyndesore	Esquire			CPR

those named as serving in 1399. This demonstrates that just under a fifth of the men who campaigned in Ireland have also served in the campaigns of 1387–1388. It should be noted that the evidence for those serving in Ireland is not as extensive as that for 1387–1388 and therefore these results are based upon a limited sample. Nethertheless, the table demonstrates that a large number of men show continuance of service between the mainly naval campaigns of the earl of Arundel and the royal expeditions to Ireland with Richard II. This suggests that the men who fought in the later years of the fourteenth century were happy to serve in different locations and at land or at sea. It also demonstrates that service in the Appellant campaigns had not prevented a soldier from later gaining employment in a royal expedition.

It is also possible to identify two men who serve in both Arundel's campaigns in 1387–1388 and Richard II's Irish campaigns of 1394 and 1399. These men are Sir Reginald Braybrook[247] and Sir Hugh le Despencer[248] These men would therefore appear to have been important members of the military community. We have already discussed the career of Sir Hugh le Despencer, who indeed became the governor of the Prince of Wales, under the regime of Henry IV. Sir Reginald Braybrook deserves further discussion at this point. Sir Reginald benefits from a biography in *History of Parliament*, serving as member of parliament for Kent in 1404.[249] He was born *c*.1356 and was therefore around 30 years of age when he served as an esquire in the retinues of the earl of Devon and Sir Thomas Percy in 1387 and 1388 respectively. He was knighted between October 1389 and August 1390. As well as serving with Richard II in Ireland in 1394 and 1399 he was also retained as a king's knight in 1390–1391.[250] He was the nephew of Robert Braybrooke, bishop of London, and *History of Parliament* suggests it may have been through his influence that he entered the royal circle. It is clear that he reached a position of responsibility in the household of Richard II despite marrying Joan, grand daughter of John, Lord Cobham. Cobham was prosecuted in 1397 for his earlier support of the Appellants and banished to Guernsey. Perhaps his favour at court also stemmed from his father's earlier service with the Black Prince, which had included attendance at the battle of Poitiers. Henry IV did not retain Sir Reginald, but he did serve militarily at sea in 1404 and in Flanders with Thomas of Lancaster in 1405. He died as a result of a wound received in an attack on Sluys during this final campaign. Sir Reginald was therefore a man with considerable military experience which was appreciated by Richard II and later by Henry IV. It is clear that this level of continuance of service in royal expeditions by Despencer and Braybrooke would suggest that these men attended such expeditions in a professional manner.

---

[247] 1387: E101/40/33 m. 3. 1388: E101/40/39 m. 1. 1394: *CPR, 1391–1396*, p. 498 (attorney). 1399: *CPR 1396–1399*, p. 538 (protection).

[248] 1387: E101/40/33 m. 9; enrolled protection, C76/71 m. 14. 1388: E101/41/5 mm. 10 and 18; enrolled protection, C76/72 m. 7. 1394: *CPR, 1391–1396*, pp. 483 and 494 (protection), 498 (attorney). 1399: *CPR, 1396–1399*, pp. 541 and 552 (attorney).

[249] *HOP*, vol. ii, pp. 349–350. See also biographies of his father and brother, both Sir Gerald Braybrooke, *HOP*, vol. ii, pp. 343–349.

[250] Mitchell, 'Some Aspects of the Knightly Household of Richard II', p. 234.

Other men with royal connections have also served in the campaigns led by Arundel. The royal nature of the campaigns of 1394 and 1399 is demonstrated with participants described as holding positions in the king's household. William Hert, esquire, is described as usher of the chamber;[251] William Knottynglee, esquire, one of the yeomen of the crown;[252] and William Lane, archer, king's clerk.[253] It is interesting that these men have been able to enter the king's service even though they have also served in the campaigns of 1387–1388. William Hert required a royal pardon in 1398; thus he had not been completely exonerated for his earlier allegiance.[254] Perhaps his service in 1399 was to further demonstrate his loyalty to the king.

It is clear from this table that service in 1387–1388 with the earl of Arundel did not exclude a soldier from serving with the king on his Irish expeditions in 1394 and 1399. We can also see that members of the military community and men in the king's household also show continuance of service between these campaigns. Men such as Sir Thomas Percy, who prospered under Richard II as the earl of Worcester, and Sir John St John are further evidence of this continuance of service. Both these men were close to Richard II and thus have not been hampered in their advancement in royal service because of their earlier service with Arundel. Indeed, 48 of these 97 men are serving in the retinue of Richard II on these campaigns. Further, 31 of the men showing continuance of service can also be identified as king's knights of Richard II. This evidence would suggest that service with Arundel during 1387–1388 was not considered as being a political act. One could serve in these expeditions and still show allegiance to the king. They may have therefore served in 1387–1388 as continuation of royal service and as an act of patriotism. Although we have identified many Arundel loyalists in the campaigns, it is also evident that other men, without such loyalty also served and went on to demonstrate this in future military service with the king.

King's knights of Richard II and Henry IV

The retention of knights by the king was a method of creating a military affinity for service in war. However, following the crisis of 1387–1388, Richard II retained knights, not for service in war, but to spread his influence throughout the shires. A study of these king's knights has been undertaken by Professor Given-Wilson, who has also published a list of these knights in his *The Royal Household and the King's Affinity*.[255] It is possible to compare the men who were retained by Richard II and also by Henry IV with the men who served in

---

[251] 1387: E101/40/33 m. 18, described as 'vacat le xvi iour d'aprill'. He has therefore only served during the first part of the campaign. 1399: *CPR, 1396–1399*, p. 538.

[252] 1388: E101/41/5 m. 7. 1394: *CPR, 1391–1396*, p. 483 (protection).

[253] 1388: E101/41/5 m. 4d. 1394: *CPR, 1391–1396*, p. 473 (protection). 1399: *CPR, 1396–1399*, p. 522 (protection).

[254] C67/30 m. 1.

[255] *Royal Household*, Appendix V and VI, pp. 282–290. Saul, *Richard II*, pp. 265–269.

the campaigns of 1387–1388. This will show how many men who were loyal to Richard II also fought with the earl of Arundel. It will also show how many of these men were retained by Henry IV. Table 25 shows which of the combatants of the expeditions of 1387–1388 were retained by Richard II and Henry IV. It displays the date of retaining and the locality from which they were drawn. It also integrates information drawn from the recent study of king's knights by Dr Shelagh Mitchell.[256] This work has suggested that modern research on the 'king's knight' is based partially upon a misunderstanding of the printed sources. Through an analysis of the original sources, Mitchell argues that the king's knights of Richard II were actually members of his household and she has provided an additional listing of such knights. As such these king's knights would have an actual central role rather than being appointed purely for their local influence. Table 25 displays those knights listed by Given-Wilson and, where different, by Mitchell.[257]

Table 25 shows that 52 of the combatants were retained as king's knights by either Richard II or Henry IV. Of these, 42 knights were retained by Richard II and 20 knights by Henry IV. Ten knights have been retained by both kings. The men in this table were those with local authority and influence. Thus it can be seen that Richard II was more interested in how they could assist him in their localities than the fact that they had served with the earl of Arundel in 1387–1388. Henry IV has also drawn upon this group of men as can be demonstrated by the use of the same knights and also of other knights from within these campaigns. This evidence suggests that the campaign would have attracted men with local influence, who had already, or would be, retained as king's knights. These men may have been serving in these campaigns out of a sense of responsibility or patriotism to the realm and not because of allegiance to the Appellant cause. It is suggested that this group of men who wielded local influence and responsibility were the same men who would feel it was appropriate to serve in royal expeditions. It may have been that the nature of the campaign, set against the background of Appellant supremacy, was less important than the sense of service for duty.

It is of interest to note the date at which these men were retained by the kings. For Richard II it has been suggested that the majority of his retainers became so following his humiliation in 1387–1388.[258] This is reflected in Table 25. Of the 42 knights, 11 were retained prior to 1387 and 31 were retained subsequently. This demonstrates that over 70% of these men had served with Arundel before being taken on as a king's knight. In addition it demonstrates that a good number were already retained by the king and still served on an expedition led by his enemy. For Henry IV the dates of retention are also of interest as all the knights from these campaigns are retained before 1404: thus within the first five years of his reign. Indeed 15 of the 20 knights are retained within the first three

---

[256] Mitchell, 'Some Aspects of the Knightly Household of Richard II'. See pp. 233–237 for alphabetical listing of these knights. My thanks to Dr Shelagh Mitchell for providing me with an electronic version of her thesis.

[257] All references are to *Royal Household*, unless otherwise stated.

[258] Saul, *Richard II*, p. 266.

Table 25. King's knights, Richard II and Henry IV

Year	Title	First name	Surname	Rank	Captain name	Richard II*	Henry IV*
1387	Mons	Thomas	Adirbury	Knight	Le Sire de Beaumount	p. 283, Thomas Abberbury, king's knight, of Oxon/Berks, retained in 1386	
1388	Mons	William	Baron de Hylton	Captain	Mons William Baron de Hylton	p. 285, William de Hilton, life retainer, King's knight, of Durham/Westm'land, retained in 1386	
1387	Le Sire		Beamount	Captain	Le Sire de Beaumount	p. 284, John, lord Beaumont, life retainer, king's knight, of Leics/Lincs, retained in 1393	
1387		Thomas	Botiller	Esquire	Mons William Elmham	p. 284, Thomas Botiller, life retainer, king's knight, of Gloucs, retained in 1393	
1388		Thomas	Boteler	Esquire	Mons Arnald Savage		
1387	Mons	Hugh	Browe	Knight	Arundel, Richard, earl of		p. 288, Hugh Browe, life retainer, king's knight, of Cheshire/Rutland, retained 1400
1388	Mons	Hugh	Browe	Captain	Mons Hugh Browe		
1388	Mons	Wauter	Bytterley	Esquire	Mons Johan Darundell		p. 288, Walter Bytterley, king's knight of Salop, retained in 1400
1387	Mons	John	Calverlee, de	Captain	Mons John de Calverlee	p. 284, John de Calvely, life retainer, king's knight, of Cheshire/Leics, retained in 1394	
1388	Mons	Johan	Calvylegh	Knight	Le Counte Marshall		

* Page references are to *Royal Household*, unless otherwise stated.

Year		First name	Surname	Rank	Lord/Captain	Notes
1387		Robert	Chalons	Esquire	Le Counte de Devens	p. 287, Robert Chalons, knight of the chamber and lay officer of the household, of Devon, retained in 1402 (1399)
1388		William	Clifford	Esquire	Mons Thomas Percy	p. 288, William Clifford, king's knight, of Westm'land/Yorks, retained in 1399
1387	Mons	Nich	Clifton	Captain	Mons Nichol Clyfton	p. 284, Nicholas de Clifton, life retainer, king's knight, of Cheshire, retained in 1396
1388	Mons	Nicol	Clyfton	Captain	Mons Nichol Clyfton	
1388	Mons	Johan	Clyfton	Knight	Le Counte Marshall	p. 288, John Clyfton, king's knight, of Notts, retained in 1400
1387		John	Cornewayle	Esquire	Arundel, Richard, earl of	p. 288, John de Cornewall, king's knight, of Salop, retained in 1400
1388	Mons	Johan	Cornewaill	Esquire	Mons Thomas Camoys	p. 284, John de Cornewall, life retainer, king's knight, of Salop, retained in 1397
1387	Mons	Richard	Craddok	Captain	Mons Richard Craddok	p. 284, Richard Cradok, life retainer, king's knight, of Cheshire, retained in 1391
1388		Johan	Croft	Esquire	Mons Johan Wogan	p. 284, John de Croft, life retainer, king's knight, of Lancs, retained in 1398
1387	Mons	Edward	Dalyngrigg	Knight	Arundel, Richard, earl of	p. 284, Edward Dalyngridge, life retainer, king's knight, of Sussex, retained in 1389
1387		John	Dalyngrigg	Esquire	Arundel, Richard, earl of	p. 287, John Dalyngridge, knight of the chamber and lay officer of the household, of Sussex, retained in 1402 (1400)

Year	Title	First name	Surname	Rank	Captain name	Richard II	Henry IV
1387		William	Dangle	Knight	John Slegh	p. 284, William D'Angle, king's knight, Foreigner, retained in 1386	
1388	Mons	William	Dangle	Knight	Mons Gilbe Talbot		
1387	Mons	John	Darundel	Captain	Mons Johan Darundell	p.283, John de Arundel, king's Knight, of Somerset/Dorset/Wilts, retained in 1386	
1388	Mons	Johan	Darundell	Captain	Mons Johan Darundell		
1388	Mons	William	D'Arundell	Knight	Arundel, Richard, earl of	p. 282, William de Arundel, life retainer, knight of the chamber and lay officer of the household, of Sussex/Surrey, 1392	
1387	Mons	Hugh	Despenser, le	Captain	Mons Hugh le Despenser	p. 284, Hugh Despenser, life retainer, king's knight, of Northants, retained in 1391	p. 288, Hugh Despenser, life retainer, king's knight, of Northants, retained in 1399
1388	Mons	Hugh	Despencer, le	Captain	Mons Hugh le Despenser		
1388	Mons	Hugh	Despencer, le	Captain	Mons Hugh le Despenser		
1387	Mons	Ivo	FitzWaryn	Knight	Arundel, Richard, earl of	Saul, p. 266, CPR 1391–6, p. 577, Sir Ivo Fitzwaryn	
1388	Mons	William	Fulthorp	Esquire	Mons William Baron de Hylton		p. 288, William de Fulthorpe, king's knight, of Yorks, retained in 1400
1387	Mons	William	Godrych	Esquire	Mons Johan Darundell	p. 284, William Goderiche, king's knight, of ?Lincs, retained in 1394	
1387	Mons	Robert	Greneage	Knight	Le Counte de Devens	p. 285, Robert Greenacres, king's knight, retained in 1388	
1388	Mons	Robert	Grenenaw	Knight	Mons Rauf Vernon		
1387	Mons	Andrew	Hake	Esquire	Arundel, Richard, earl of	p. 285, Andrew Hake, king's knight, of ?Gloucs/?Sussex, retained in 1397	
1388	Mons	Andrewe	Hake	Captain	Mons Andrewe Hake		

1387	Mons	William	Heron	Knight	Mons Nichol Clyfton		p. 287, William Heron, Lord Say (steward 1402–4), knight of the chamber and lay officer of the household, of Northum'land/ Sussex, retained in 1402
1388	Mons	William	Heron	Captain	Mons William Heron		
1387	Mons	John	Howard	Knight	Arundel, Richard, earl of	p. 285, John Howard, life retainer, of Norfolk, retained 1394	
1387	Mons	Roger	Lefozannge	Knight	Arundel, Richard, earl of	p. 286, Roger Lestraunge, king's knight, of Salop, retained in 1391	
1387	Mons	Estrephne	LeScrop	Knight	Arundel, Richard, earl of	p. 283, Stephen Lescrope (under-chamberlain 1398–9), life retainer, knight of the chamber and lay officer of the household, of Yorks, retained in 1398 (1396)	p. 288, Stephen Lescrope, king's knight, of Yorks, retained in 1404
1388	Mons	John	Lovell	Knight	Le Monsers W Sire de Welles	p. 285, John, lord Lovell, life retainer, king's knight, of Wilts/Oxon, retained in 1386	
1388	Mons	William	Lysle	Knight	Mons William Briene	p. 282, William Lisle, 'the younger', life retainer, knight of the chamber and lay officer of the household, of Cambs/Oxon, retained in 1395 (1392) or p. 285, William Lisle, 'the elder', life retainer, king's knight, of Bedfords, retained in 1397	p. 289, William Lisle 'the younger', king's knight, of Cambs/Oxon, retained in 1401 or William Lisle 'the elder', life retainer, King's knight, of Bedfords, retained in 1401
1387	Mons	Robert	Mounteney	Captain	Mons Robert Mounteney		p. 288, Robert Mounteney, king's knight, of Suffolk, retained in 1402

Year	Title	First name	Surname	Rank	Captain name	Richard II	Henry IV
1388	Mons	Thomas	Percy	Captain	Mons Thomas Percy	p. 283, Thomas Percy (under-chamberlain 1390–93; steward 1393–99), knight of the chamber and lay officer of the household, of Yorks/diverse, retained in 1390 (1398)	p. 287, Thomas Percy (steward 1401–2), knight of the chamber and lay officer of the household, of Yorks/diverse, retained in 1401
1388	Mons	Hamond	Peshale	Knight	Arundel, Richard, earl of	p. 285, Adam Peshale, life retainer, king's knight, of Staffs/Salop, retained in 1390	
1388	Mons	William	Plupton	Knight	Mons Johan Grymesby	p. 285, William de Plumpton, life retainer, king's knight, of Yorks, retained in 1398	
1388	Mons	Michael	Pole, de la	Baron	Arundel, Richard, earl of	p. 285, Michael de la Pole, jnr, king's knight, of Yorks/Suffolk/diverse, retained 1386	
1388	Mons	Johan	Routhe	Knight	Arundel, Richard, earl of	p. 285, John de Routhe, life retainer, king's knight, of Yorks, retained in 1394	
1387	Mons	Arnald	Savage	Captain	Mons Arnald Savage	p. 283, Arnold Savage, life retainer, knight of the chamber and lay officer of the household, of Kent, retained in 1392 (1386)	p. 290, Arnold Savage, king's knight, of Kent, retained in 1403
1388	Mons	Arnald	Savage	Captain	Mons Arnald Savage		
1387	Mons	Edward	Seint John	Knight	Arundel, Richard, earl of	p. 286, Edward St. John, king's knight, of Sussex, retained in 1378	
1388	Mons	Johan	Senitjohn	Knight	Le Counte Marshall	p. 286, John St John, life retainer, king's knight, of Devon/Hereford, retained in 1393	p. 290, John St John, king's knight, of Devon/Hereford, retained in 1399

Year		First name	Surname	Rank		Notes
1387		Benet	Sely	Esquire	Arundel, Richard, earl of	p. 283, Benedict Sely, life retainer, knight of the chamber and lay officer of the household, of Sussex, retained in1395 (1391)
1388		Benet	Cely	Captain	Mons Benet Cely	
1387		Humfrey	Stafford	Esquire	Arundel, Richard, earl of	p. 290, Humphrey de Stafford, king's knight, of Dorset, retained in 1399
1388		Umfrey	Stafford	Esquire	Mons William Briene	p. 290, William Sturmy, king's knight, of Hants/Wilts, retained in 1401
1388	Mons	William	Strumy	Knight	Le Counte de Devens	p. 286, William Sturmy, life retainer, king's knight, of Hants/Wilts, retained in 1392
1387	Mons	Gilbert	Talbot	Captain	Mons Gilbe Talbot	p. 286, Gilbert, Lord Talbot, jnr, king's knight, of Hereford/Berks, retained in 1392
1388	Mons	Gilbe	Talbot	Captain	Mons Gilbe Talbot	
1387	Mons	Thomas	Trenet	Captain	Mons Thomas Trenet	p. 286, Thomas Tryvet, king's knight, of Somerset, retained 1378
1387	Mons	Payn	Typpetoo	Knight	Arundel, Richard, earl of	p. 287, Payn Tiptoft, knight of the chamber and lay officer of the household, of Cambs, retained in 1402 (1401)
1388	Mons	Payn	Typtot	Knight	Arundel, Richard, earl of	
1388		Johan	Veer, de	Esquire	Mons Johan Coupeland	p. 286, John de Veer, king's knight, Foreigner, retained in 1399
1387	Mons	John	Walssch	Knight	Le Sire de Beaumount	p. 286, John Walsh, king's knight, of Lincs, retained in 1384

years demonstrating that Henry IV was immediately drawing upon the same body of men in order to secure local influence. Saul argues that these men were retained for their social and political influence and not for any military purpose. What can be shown is that, even if this was the case, a number of these men were a part of the military community and had been involved in overseas expeditions. Thus local authority and military experience appear to be strongly linked. Men with such local power may also have felt a responsibility to support such campaigns in the king's name.

We would therefore expect the knights who had been retained by both kings to be both militarily experienced and locally connected. Who were these men? Both kings retained Sir William Clifford, esquire, who served with Sir Thomas Percy in 1388.[259] Clifford served in the king's household retinue in Ireland in 1394, and was knighted on the expedition on 26 October 1394. He also served in the Irish campaign in 1399.[260] He is described as from Westmorland/Yorkshire and has quickly been retained by Henry IV following his return from service with Richard II in Ireland in 1399. This swift transition suggests that Sir William was valuable to both kings. Indeed, Given-Wilson describes how Clifford was important to both Richard II and Henry IV because of his local influence in Westmorland. His main loyalty was to the earl of Northumberland and this probably explains his service with his brother, Sir Thomas Percy, in 1388. Sir William's career following the accession of Henry IV was extraordinary, rebelling with the earl of Northumberland in 1403, 1405 and 1408. Despite this inconsistency, he was continually pardoned and remained a king's knight. In 1408, the rebellion was led by his father-in-law, Thomas, Lord Bardolf, who was executed as a result. Lord Bardolf also served in 1388, thus indicating another family relationship within the muster rolls. Clifford demonstrates how continual disloyalty could be condoned by the king if an individual had more to offer. In Clifford's case this appears to have been his influence in Westmorland, where he was the head of the leading local family. Nevertheless, Henry's continued patience with Sir William is certainly enlightening.[261]

Sir Hugh le Despencer was another knight who was retained by both kings: Richard II in 1391 and Henry IV following his accession in 1399.[262] We have already discussed Sir Hugh's career in detail due to his long military career in the service of the king. He captained a retinue in 1387 and two retinues in 1388 and also served with Richard II in Ireland in 1394 and 1399.[263] It is clear that Sir Hugh would have been an asset to the crown due to this military experience. In fact, Henry IV put his experience to good use, appointing him governor to the

---

[259] 1388: E101/40/39 m. 1. Mitchell, 'Some Aspects of the Knightly Household of Richard II', p. 234, retained in 1394–1395. *Royal Household*, p. 288, retained in 1399.

[260] 1394: Mitchell, 'Some Aspects of the Knightly Household of Richard II', p. 308, citing E101/402/20 m. 36, knighted on 26 October 1394. 1399: *CPR, 1396–1399*, p. 552 (attorney).

[261] For Sir William's career see, *Royal Household*, pp. 228–229. My thanks to Dr Shelagh Mitchell for this reference.

[262] King's knight, Richard II: *Royal Household*, p. 284, retained for life in 1391. Henry IV: *Royal Household*, p. 288, retained for life in 1399.

[263] 1387: E101/40/33 m. 9; enrolled protection, C76/71 m. 14. 1388: E101/41/5 mm. 10 and 18; enrolled protection, C76/72 m. 7.

young Prince of Wales. Sir Hugh demonstrated that someone with his experience was an asset to a ruler and both Richard II and Henry IV retained him as a result of his experience. His attendance at campaign between 1387 and 1388, and capture in 1387, had not harmed his royal career.[264]

The identification of Sir Stephen Lescrope as the knight who served with Arundel in 1387[265] and also a king's knight of Richard II and Henry IV is more problematic.[266] The discussion is made clearer, although not solved, by reference to the 'History of the Family of Scrope', included in the Scrope v. Grosvenor controversy by Sir N. Harris Nicolas.[267] There are three Sir Stephen Lescropes who the participant in 1387 could arguably be, and it may well be that he is not the same man who was retained by Richard II and Henry IV. The man who was retained by Richard II and then Henry IV is most likely Sir Stephen Lescrope of Bolton. This Sir Stephen was the third son of Richard, Lord Scrope, who was contesting the famous Scrope vs. Grosvenor case in the court of chivalry in the 1380s.[268] In his biography by N. Harris Nicolas, he is described as beginning his military service with the duke of Lancaster in 1373 and was active in Scotland in 1384. He would have been aged around thirty-seven in 1387. He was with Richard II when he returned to Wales following the invasion of Henry, duke of Hereford, the future Henry IV, in 1399 and managed to survive a trial for treason in 1400. He went on to serve for Henry IV in Ireland, where he died in 1408.[269] His presence in the expedition of 1387 would be supported by the appearance of his brother, Sir Roger Lescrope in the following year of 1388, also serving in the retinue of the earl of Arundel.[270] Less is known about the career of Sir Roger; therefore his identification on the muster roll for 1388 adds to the knowledge of this individual.[271] It is pertinent to note that their elder brother was Sir William Lescrope who was created earl of Wiltshire in 1397, demonstrating that he was greatly favoured by Richard II. He was a major supporter of Richard II and was beheaded in Bristol following its capture by Henry in 1399.[272] It is therefore no surprise to see Sir Stephen serving Richard II, although it is maybe surprising that he was also retained by Henry IV, considering the fate of his elder brother.

The other candidates for identification as the member of the campaign in 1387 are drawn from the family of Lescrope of Masham. The most likely individual is Sir Stephen Lescrope, second Lord Scrope of Masham.[273] Evidence supporting his case includes the fact that he took a royal pardon in 1398, perhaps

---

264 For capture by the French in 1387 see *Knighton's Chronicle*, p. 391

265 E101/40/33 m. 1.

266 King's knight, Richard II: *Royal Household*, p. 283 (under-chamberlain 1398–1399), retained for life, knight of the Chamber and lay officer of the household in 1398 (1396). Henry IV: *Royal Household*, p. 288, retained in 1404.

267 *Scrope v. Grosvenor*, vol. ii.

268 For Lord Scrope of Bolton see *Complete Peerage*, vol. xi, pp. 539–541.

269 *Scrope v. Grosvenor*, vol. ii, pp. 45–52.

270 E101/41/5 m. 1.

271 *Scrope v. Grosvenor*, vol. ii, pp. 53–57.

272 *Ibid.*, vol. ii, pp. 39–45.

273 For Lord Scrope of Masham see *Complete Peerage*, vol. xi, p. 564.

to excuse his service in 1387–1388.[274] In addition, a Sir John Lescrope also serves in the earl of Arundel's retinue in 1387. Sir John can be identified as this Sir Stephen's brother, and thus would be another example of family members serving together on campaign.[275] This Sir Stephen had a long career, and was aged around fifty in 1387. He had fought with Edward III in France in 1360 and had also joined the crusade led by the king of Cyprus against Alexandria, made famous in *The Canterbury Tales*.[276] He fought with the Black Prince at the battle of Najera in 1367. He survived the transition to the regime of Henry IV unscathed and died in 1406.[277] The other candidate for the campaign on 1387 is this Sir Stephen's uncle, also Sir Stephen Scrope of Masham. He fought at Crécy in 1346 and thus would have been aged at the least in his fifties in 1387. It is not clear when he died and therefore this identification is probably the most doubtful.[278]

It is not possible to decide which Sir Stephen Lescrope fought with Arundel in 1387, as both men were members of the military community and could arguably have been involved in this campaign. Perhaps the case for Sir Stephen of Masham is stronger because of his need for a royal pardon and also the probability that he would serve alongside his brother. This is not a definite identification as Sir Stephen of Bolton may just as well have been serving with his kinsman, and his brother attending the campaign of the following year strengthens his case. We may never be able to make a full identification for this Sir Stephen Lescrope and thus his relationship with Richard II and Henry IV must remain in doubt.

Another difficulty is presented by the identification of Sir William Lisle the younger and Sir William Lisle the elder as king's knights of Richard II and Henry IV. Only one of these men serves in 1388, in the retinue of Sir William Briene.[279] We have previously discussed the career of one of these men, as Sir William Lisle was also a juror at the trial of the Epiphany Plot in 1400. In addition one of these men met with Froissart on his visit to England in 1395. It is not possible to say which of these men, uncle or nephew, participated in the expedition of 1388, however, as both were king's knights, we can surmise that both men were well connected to the royal circle. Our Sir William Lisle, is more likely to be identified as 'the younger'. He was a member of the royal household of Richard II, and he was therefore the knight who Froissart met on his visit to England. We have earlier commented that it may well have been Sir William who told Froissart about the expedition of 1388. This would therefore place Sir William Lisle 'the younger' in the expedition of 1388. The fact that Sir William Lisle 'the younger' also required a pardon in 1398 strengthens his case for inclu-

---

[274] C67/30 m. 13.
[275] *Scrope v. Grosvenor*, vol. ii, pp. 127–128.
[276] *The Riverside Chaucer*, p. 24, line 51, General Prologue to *The Canterbury Tales* by Geoffrey Chaucer. The first line of the description of the knight's career follows, 'At Alisaundre he was whan it was wonne'.
[277] *Scrope v. Grosvenor*, vol. ii, pp. 130–132.
[278] *Ibid.*, vol. ii, pp. 108–110.
[279] E101/41/5 m. 9, listed as Mons' William Lysle.

sion in this campaign.[280] Sir William had not suffered in his advancement under Richard II, even though he attended the Appellant-led campaign. He did, however, find it pertinent to secure a royal pardon in 1398, and thus had not completely exonerated himself for his earlier allegiance. He moved smoothly into the new regime, despite his position in the household of Richard II. Both Sir William and his uncle were therefore useful to both kings and he demonstrated that attendance at the expedition in 1388 did not disqualify one from advancing in the king's service.

Sir Thomas Percy can be identified as a king's knight of Richard II and Henry IV and also served with Arundel in 1388.[281] As noted in Chapter 2, although Percy was supposed to go to support John of Gaunt in Gascony, he actually sailed with Arundel on campaign.[282] The career of Percy, future earl of Worcester, was discussed in Chapter 3. He was a senior member of the military community, brother of the earl of Northumberland, uncle to Hotspur and a deponent at the Scrope v. Grosvenor case.[283] He was created earl of Worcester in 1397 by Richard II and had thus not been damaged by his support for the Appellants by his attendance at campaign in 1388. Although he was a king's knight of both Richard II and Henry IV, he would ultimately turn against both of them. He abandoned Richard in 1399 following the invasion by Henry, who had been supported by the earl of Northumberland. He then joined his brother and nephew in open rebellion in 1403, was defeated at the battle of Shrewsbury and executed a few days later. Percy was therefore a man who ultimately put family loyalties before loyalty to his sovereign.

Sir Arnald Savage attended both campaigns of 1387–1388 as retinue captain and was also a king's knight of Richard II and Henry IV. He had been retained by Richard II in 1386, therefore prior to the campaigns of 1387–1388. He was able to lead a retinue in both campaigns despite this connection with Richard II. His participation would suggest that men were able to serve as members of the military community and without any political consequence. He managed to prosper under the reign of Henry IV, despite being close to Richard II and became speaker of the House of Commons.[284]

A man whose career as a Richard II loyalist has been discussed was Sir John St John. He served in the expedition of 1387[285] and was a king's knight of

---

[280] C67/30 m. 27, listed as Lisle, William, kt. Junior.

[281] King's knight, Richard II: *Royal Household*, p. 283 (under-chamberlain 1390–1393; steward 1393–1399), knight of the Chamber and lay officer of the household, retained in 1390 (1398). Henry IV: *Royal Household*, p. 287 (steward 1401–1402), knight of the Chamber and lay officer of the household, retained in 1401.

[282] See E101/40/39 for the muster roll for the force of Sir Thomas de Percy in 1388. The muster roll is incomplete due to damage by fire with only the first 346 men detailed in 8 retinues surviving. Percy's retinue: E101/40/39 m. 1, listed as Mons' Thomas Percy: the retinue consisted of 152 soldiers, including 16 knights, 49 esquires and 86 archers.

[283] *Scrope v. Grosvenor*, vol. i, p. 50, vol. ii, p. 167.

[284] For his biography see, J.S. Roskell, 'Sir Arnald Savage of Bobbing: Speaker for the Commons in 1401 and 1404', *Archaelogia Cantiana*, lxx (1956), pp. 68–83.

[285] E101/41/5 m. 3.

Richard II and Henry IV.[286] Sir John had therefore managed to advance under Richard II despite his service in 1388. He served with Richard II in Ireland in 1394,[287] but still required a royal pardon in 1398 following the fall of the Appellants.[288] He served with Richard II in Ireland in 1399, but would appear to have abandoned his king as he was immediately created a king's knight of the new king, Henry IV in 1399.[289] Sir John therefore was a man whose military experience was an asset to a ruler and he managed to serve under three kings during his extensive career.

Finally Sir William Sturmy served in the retinue of the earl of Devon in 1388[290] and was also a king's knight of Richard II and Henry IV.[291] Saul identifies Sir William as being retained by Richard II in 1392 because of his influence, which stretched across many counties.[292] Sturmy has attracted biographical comment owing to his serving as Speaker of the Commons in 1404.[293] Sturmy held the bulk of his lands in Wiltshire, but also had substantial holdings in Devon and Hampshire. It was therefore through his Devon holding that he would have come into contact with the earl of Devon, and thus it is evident that this relationship resulted in his service in 1388. Sturmy's military experience would appear to begin with his service in 1388 and he continued his service with Richard II in Ireland in 1394.[294] His military experience was therefore not vast, although he probably served with Henry IV in Wales in 1402. Sturmy was important to the crown for his diplomatic skills and he first served Richard II by travelling to Rome in 1397 to negotiate with the rival popes in an attempt to end the schism in the Church. It was therefore probably for his diplomatic skills that he was retained by both kings. Indeed he travelled through Germany following Henry's accession attempting to gain recognition for the new regime. Amongst other official visits, he also visited Prussia to negotiate with the High Master of the Order of the Teutonic Knights, regarding an embargo which had been placed on the import of English cloth. As mentioned, he was Speaker of the Commons in 1404 and he also acted as Chief Steward of Queen Joan. *History of Parliament* comments that Sir William was 'perhaps the most important commoner in Wiltshire'. He served at Parliament on no less than

---

286 King's knight, Richard II: *Royal Household*, p. 286, retained for life in 1393. Henry IV: *Royal Household*, p. 290, retained in 1399.

287 *CPR, 1391–1396*, pp. 474 (protection) and 477 (attorney).

288 C67/30 m. 13.

289 *CPR, 1396–1399*, pp. 525 (protection), 530 and 552 (attorney).

290 E101/41/5 m. 4.

291 King's knight, Richard II: *Royal Household*, p. 286, retained for life in 1392. Henry IV: *Royal Household*, p. 290, retained in 1401.

292 Saul, *Richard II*, p. 266.

293 For accounts of his career see: *HOP*, vol. iv, pp. 520–524; J.S. Roskell, 'Sir William Sturmy'; J.S. Roskell, *Parliament and Politics in Late Medieval England* (3 vols, London 1981–83), vol. iii, pp. 91–105; J.S. Roskell, *The Commons and their Speakers in English Parliaments, 1376–1523* (Manchester, 1965). These accounts do not note Sir William's service in 1388.

294 *CPR, 1391–1396*, p. 487 (attorney), also E101/402/20 m. 34d, with one esquire and 3 or 4 mounted archers, cited in Mitchell, 'Some Aspects of the Knightly Household of Richard II', Appendix III, p. 307.

twelve occasions and also secured election for other members of his family and associates. Indeed, his growth in influence also brought him into conflict with his former retinue captain the earl of Devon in 1392.[295] It was therefore probably his local influence together with his value as a diplomat which made him so important to Richard II and Henry IV. Indeed he was even retained and served as an ambassador for Henry V. Sturmy demonstrates that it was possible to serve in successful reigns, despite any previous connections one may have demonstrated.

As has been seen, a substantial number of king's knights of Richard II and Henry IV were present in the campaigns of 1387–1388. These men were senior members of the military community, and the service in these years has not prevented some of them from rising to prominence in the service of Richard II. Indeed, this service does not appear to have harmed any of the careers of the men discussed above, even if they required a royal pardon in 1398. This evidence suggests that such service was seen as a part of their continuing military career and for these particular men was not necessarily politically motivated. The men whom Richard II retained as king's knights were those who were well connected in their local shires. This demonstrates that the men involved with local governance were also active in the military community. The retention of such men who had served the Appellants by Richard II and the continuation of this service under Henry IV, suggests that the loyalty of these men was important to the king. The men who served them both in peace and war were a commodity whose service was worth retaining, despite any previous loyalties they had shown.

Connections to Robert de Vere: case studies

It is interesting to note that the expeditions also involved supporters of the Appellants' enemies, including henchmen of the king's favourite, de Vere. One such man, Henry English, served as an esquire with the earl of Devon in the 1387 expedition.[296] However, English does not serve in the following year's expedition. The description in *History of Parliament* does not comment on this service, but does outline English's association with de Vere.[297] He was a trusted local official and was engaged in the administration of the estates of Edmund Mortimer, earl of March. He had entered the circle of de Vere by 1385 and was employed in positions of authority as the earl of Oxford gained prominence at the court of Richard II. *History of Parliament* describes how he lacked royal employment between 1386 and 1389 owing to his support of the Appellants' enemy. However, his involvement in the expedition of 1387 and also being appointed sheriff of Essex and Hertfordshire, four months prior to Richard's regaining power, demonstrates that he was able to swiftly distance himself from his former loyalty. Indeed his participation in 1387 may have indicated that he

---

295 *HOP*, vol. iv, pp. 521–522.
296 E101/40/33 m. 3.
297 *HOP*, vol. iii, pp. 27–29. He appeared as a member of parliament on five separate occasions from 1373 to 1390.

had been able to perceive the shift in the balance of power at this early stage and prior to Oxford's armed rising in support of the king.

Another loyal supporter of de Vere, Sir John Routh, has an entry in *History of Parliament*.[298] What is surprising is also to find him in the retinue of the earl of Arundel in 1388.[299] *History of Parliament* does not note this service, and this inclusion adds a different interpretation to his actions during the years of Appellant supremacy. *History of Parliament* identifies his service with Robert de Vere from 1385 and suggests that as the favourite progressed in the king's favour so did Routh's position of influence. The following section describes his actions during the period of Appellant supremacy:

> Routh may perhaps have been present on 20 Dec. at the battle of Radcot Bridge, which saw the complete rout of the half-hearted troops de Vere had raised in support of the king. Although he was not himself singled out for reprisals by the victorious Appellants, de Vere's flight to the continent and the attainder passed against him by the Merciless Parliament of 1388 placed him in an extremely vulnerable position, and he deemed it expedient to retire quietly to his estates in the north.

However, from the muster roll evidence, it can be seen that Routh did not retire quietly, but instead, joined with the Appellants in their expedition. This shows a startling lack of loyalty as he immediately joins the retinue of the earl of Arundel, who has recently vanquished his patron. He did not enter the king's household as one of his knights until 1394.[300] *History of Parliament* explains this by arguing that he could only gain influence as the power of the Appellants gradually weakened. However, perhaps this length of time before gaining the king's favour had more to do with him deserting the king's favourite so quickly in 1388. Richard seems to have mainly used Routh's influence locally and he does not seem to have been a member of the royal court. He did also smoothly progress into the service of the new regime and he remained a king's knight under Henry IV, Henry V and Henry VI. Routh does seem to have extremely good staying power and was able to offer his service to subsequent patrons, from de Vere to Arundel to Richard II and then to the Lancastrians. He was fittingly buried with the 'SS' collar of the Lancastrian livery. His monumental brass can be seen in Routh church in the East Riding of Yorkshire where he is presented in full plate armour.[301]

---

[298] *HOP*, vol. iv, pp. 239–241. He appeared at parliament twice in 1394 and 1404 (January).
[299] E101/41/5 m. 3; enrolled protection, C76/72 m. 6.
[300] *Royal Household*, p. 285, retained for life in 1394.
[301] Mill Stephenson, 'Monumental Brasses in the East Riding', *Yorkshire Archaeological Journal*, xii (1892–93), pp. 194–229, see pp. 222–225, with illustration of the brass.

The end of the reign

It would be pertinent to draw this chapter to a close by considering the available evidence for the actions of those who fought in 1387–1388 at the end of the reign of Richard II. We have already discussed the Irish campaign of 1399 where a number of men can be identified as demonstrating continuance of service from 1387–1388. Is it also possible to draw any information from sources regarding the armies raised following the invasion of Henry of Derby and also service with Henry IV in Scotland in 1400? We have already commented in the preceding case studies how a number of men were involved in the Epiphany Plot of 1400, and the subsequent trial; how men also served both for and against Henry at the battle of Shrewsbury in 1403; and how some men continued their service with Henry, Prince of Wales, in his fight against Owain Glyn Dwr. Is there any other analysis available which could allow us to make further comment?

Chris Given-Wilson has reconstructed the army with which the duke of York attempted to oppose the landing of Henry of Derby in 1399. He estimates that the regent of England made payments to around 3,300 men. This force did not put up a concerted effort to oppose Henry, other than an attempt led by the bishop of Norwich and Sir William Elmham, which ended in bloodless defeat.[302] When York met Henry at Berkeley Castle on 27 July 1399, he let him pass unopposed. Given-Wilson has put together nominal evidence for 79 soldiers, of which it can be shown that 15 men also served in 1387–1388.[303] This is in addition to the three men, Thomas Poynings, William Echyngham and Richard Hurst who have served in the campaigns of 1387–1388 and who were sent to resist the landing of the enemies of the king on 3 July 1399.[304] Table 26 summarises the service of these men in 1387–1388 and also their service with York in 1399.

The men who can be identified in the army with the duke of York in 1399 were therefore showing support to Richard II by opposing the landing of Henry in his attempt to claim his inheritance and the throne. As such therefore, they are demonstrating loyalty to Richard II. As these men also served in 1387–1388, they had either changed their allegiance in the meantime, or indeed participation in 1387–1388 was not seen as being politically motivated. Sir William Elmham, as mentioned, had attempted to put up some futile resistance. Elmham was also a king's knight and had been connected to Richard II since 1386. Elmham's service in the years of Appellant supremacy had called his loyal service into question and he felt it pertinent to secure a royal pardon in 1398. Despite his joining York's army in 1399, Elmham was quickly persuaded by the new regime

---

[302] Tuck, *Richard II and the English Nobility*, p. 216, citing Walsingham in *Annales Ricardi Secundi et Henrici Quarti*, p. 246.
[303] *Chronicles of the Revolution*, Appendix A: 'The duke of York's army, July 1399', pp. 247–251. He draws his evidence from payments recorded on the Exchequer issue roll and accounts from those who brought troops, citing E403/562, 12 July, and E101/42/12.
[304] *CPR, 1396–1399*, p. 596.

Table 26. Service with the duke of York, 1399

Year	Title	First name	Surname	Position	Captain name	Duke of York's army, July 1399*
1388		William	Barker	Archer	Mons Johan Wogan	p. 251, minor retinue, William Barket, of Ashwell, valet (joint captain with Hugh Heymes of Baldock, Robert Wyght of St Albans, valets), 57 archers, from Hertfordshire, 12 July–1 August.
1388		William	Blak	Archer	Aleyn Seintjust	p. 251, minor retinue, William Blake of Ruislip, valet, 19 archers, paid 5–28 July, from Middlesex.
1387	Mons	Jugrauy	Bruyn	Knight	Arundel, Richard, earl of	p. 250, minor retinue, Sir Ingelram de Bruyn, 1 man-at-arms, 26 archers, paid for 10 days, from Hampshire.
1388	Mons	Yngham	Broyn	Knight	Arundel, Richard, earl of	
1388		Wauter	Bytterley	Esquire	Mons Johan Darundell	p. 251, minor retinue, Sir Walter Bytterley, from Shropshire.
1388		Wauter	Clyfton	Archer	Mons Olyner Manlenerer	p. 251, minor retinue, Walter Clifton, valet, paid for 10 days, from Devon.
1387	Mons	William	Elmham	Captain	Mons William Elmham	p. 250, Sir William Elmham, 1 man-at-arms, 30 archers, 20 days.
1387		John	Gedeneye	Archer	Mons Johan Darundell	p. 251, minor retinue, John Gedeney, valet (joint captain with John Pertryng), with 38 archers, paid 5–28 July, from Middlesex.
1387		John	Halle	Esquire	Mons Arnald Savage	p. 251, minor retinue, John Hall, esquire, 1 archer, paid 12–29 July, from Middlesex.
1388	Mons	Robert	Massey	Captain	Mons Robert Massey	p. 251, minor retinue, Sir Robert Massy, sergeant-at-arms, 1 archer, paid for 20 days, from Cheshire.
1388		Johan	Mychel	Esquire	Arundel, Richard, earl of	p. 251, John Mitchell, sergeant-at-arms (unidentified).
1387		John	Norton	Esquire	Mons Robert Mounteney	p. 250, minor retinue, John Norton, esquire, 2 archers, paid for 10 days, from Hampshire.
1388	Mons	Michael	Pole, de la	Baron	Arundel, Richard, earl of	p. 250, Michael de la Pole, earl of Suffolk, 29 men-at-arms, 109 archers, paid 5–31 July.
1387		John	Preston	Esquire	Mons Reynold de Cobham	p. 251, minor retinue, John Person, esquire, (joint captain with John Hertewell) 5 archers for 20 days, from Northamptonshire.
1387	Mons	Robert	Tourke	Knight	Mons Reynold de Cobham	p. 250, Robert Turk, with Sheriff posse, from Herts: 1 man-at-arms and 10 archers, 12 July–1 August.
1388		Thomas	Wodyngfeld	Esquire	Thomas atte Lee	p. 251, Thomas Wodingfield, sergeant-at-arms, unidentified.

* Page references are to *Chronicles of the Revolution*, Appendix A.

and was made king's knight of Henry IV in 1399. Therefore Henry found it was useful to retain a man of Elmham's experience, and Elmham obviously had no qualms about showing his allegiance to the new regime.

Another man present in the army commanded by the duke of York, was Michael de la Pole, recently created earl of Suffolk. De la Pole was discussed in Chapter 3, and he can be shown to be another who did not suffer under the reign of Henry IV. His earldom was briefly removed, then restored by the new regime and he died at the siege of Harfleur in 1415. He had also required a pardon in 1398, and thus has a similar career to that of Sir William Elmham. Both men seemed to have begun by supporting Richard II; they then served in 1387–1388, for which they required a pardon in 1398; they joined York's army in 1399; but quickly showed support for the new regime following the deposition. This demonstrates that even being a member of the army opposing York in 1399, did not prevent one from prospering under the reign of Henry IV.

These are men who feature widely in the records; what can be shown by the careers of the other men who fought for Richard in 1399? Sir Ingelram Bruyn serves with the earl of Arundel in 1387 and 1388. His actual service with Arundel can be traced to 1378, when he campaigned in France as an esquire with the earl. His allegiance with Arundel was obviously called into question following the fall of the Appellants in 1397, and in order to secure his future, Bruyn took the precaution of a royal pardon in 1398.[305] He was still keen to show his loyalty to Richard II and thus joined the army in support of Richard in 1399. Sir Robert Turk served in the retinue of Sir Reginald de Cobham in 1387. He also served in Ireland in 1394 in the retinue of Richard, Lord Talbot.[306] Turk served as a member of parliament on seven different occasions, including representing Hertfordshire at the Merciless Parliament.[307] *History of Parliament* describes Turk's interesting career, which began as a merchant and member of the Fishmongers' Company in London and progressed to become a member of the landed gentry and active member of the local government and military community. Turk was fortunate with his second marriage, shortly after which his wife's father, mother and brother all died in quick succession. He took wholeheartedly to his new life, which included participation in royal campaigns. He campaigned with Sir Michael de la Pole in Brittany in 1378 and intended to campaign with the duke of Gloucester to Prussia in 1391. This appears to have been his only connection to the Appellants, but it is interesting to note that he required a royal pardon in 1398.[308] *History of Parliament* comments that this was taken as a matter of routine. The need for the pardon has not prevented him from joining the duke of York in support of Richard in 1399. Henry IV was happy to reappoint Turk as sheriff of Hertfordshire on the day of his accession.

---

305 1387: E101/40/33 m. 1. 1388: E101/41/5 m. 1. 1378: E101/36/32 m. 1. C67/30 m. 7.
306 1387: E101/40/33 m. 6; enrolled protection, C76/71 m. 12; enrolled attorney, C76/71 m. 10. 1394: *CPR, 1391–1396*, pp. 490 (protection), 509 (attorney).
307 *HOP*, vol. iv, pp. 673–675. He served as a member of parliament for Hertfordshire in 1378, 1382 (May), 1382 (October), 1384 (November), 1388 (February), 1388 (September), 1393.
308 C67/30 m. 18.

Therefore, perhaps the pardon evidence demonstrates that Turk was not a wholehearted supporter of Richard II.

Of the other men who serve in support of Richard II, Sir Walter Bytterley, king's knight of Richard II from 1395, became a king's knight of Henry IV in 1400 and thus has shown that his loyalty was immediately passed to the new regime;[309] John Preston, esquire, can be shown to have served in 1380 in the retinue of Sir William Windsor, and thus was a member of the military community;[310] Barker, Broun, Elmham, Hall, Holand, Mychel, Norton and Preston all secured pardons in 1398 and thus required protection for their earlier support of the Appellants;[311] John Holand was a deponent in the Scrope v. Grosvenor case.[312] Therefore these men do appear in the records, but do not show a common bond. However, it is of interest that eight of the men required pardons in 1398, and yet still serve on behalf of Richard II in the following year. This demonstrates that they may have served against the king earlier in the reign, but they now fully supported their king against the usurper. This army of York did not put up much of a fight and perhaps the lack of conviction of the participants can be partially explained by a number of these men already finding themselves on the wrong side of Richard II at the end of the reign. One further combatant from 1387, serving in the retinue of Sir William Elmham, was John Seymour, esquire.[313] Given-Wilson identifies him as an esquire of the household of Richard II and he showed his loyalty by attempting to rescue Richard at Lichfield when he was being transported to London in 1399.[314] His connection with Elmham demonstrates that those close to Richard had been happy to serve with Arundel in 1387 in what was in effect a royal expedition. This loyalty was shown despite both Elmham and Seymour requiring a royal pardon in 1398, most likely owing to adherence to the Appellants in 1387–1388.[315] Despite this, they were still willing to openly support Richard at his moment of need.

Given-Wilson has also reconstructed a list of men who accompanied Henry of Derby on his campaign through England in the summer of 1399. The evidence is drawn from those who received wages for their service and he has provided nominal information for 49 men who supported the usurper in his deposition of Richard II. Given-Wilson comments that more than half of those supporting Henry had been retainers of John of Gaunt. Table 27 shows the details of three men who serve with Henry in 1399 and also served in the campaigns of 1387–1388.

Of these three men, both Esmon Barry, esquire with the earl of Arundel in

---

[309] King's knight, Richard II: *Royal Household*, p. 284, retained for life in 1395. Henry IV: *Royal Household*, p. 288, Walter Bytterley, retained in 1400.

[310] E101/39/7 m. 3.

[311] Barker, C67/30 m. 6; Halle, C67/31 m. 12; Holand, C67/30 m. 13; Mychel, C67/30 m. 5; Norton, C67/30 m. 7; Preston, C67/30 m. 12.

[312] *Scrope v. Grosvenor*, vol. i, p. 279.

[313] E101/40/33 m. 11.

[314] *Royal Household*, p. 225.

[315] Seymour, C67/30 m. 12; Elmham, C67/30 m. 28.

Table 27. Service with Henry IV, 1399

Year	Title	First name	Surname	Position	Captain name	Bolingbroke 1399
1388		Esmon	Barry	Esquire	Arundel, Richard, earl of	p. 253, Edmund Barry, esquire, £10 from receiver of Norfolk.
1387		John	Berkley	Esquire	Le Sire de Beaumount	p. 253, Sir John Berkeley, £33, from receiver of Lancaster.
1388	Mons	Hugh	Husy	Knight	Mons William Heron	p. 253, Sir Hugh Husee, £12, from receiver of Bolingbroke.

* Page references are to *Chronicles of the Revolution*, Appendix B.

1388[316] and Sir Hugh Husy, knight with Sir William Heron in 1388,[317] were both indeed retainers of John of Gaunt. Barry had been retained between 1396 and 1399 and Husy had been retained between 1395 and 1399 and had served overseas with the duke of Lancaster in 1395.[318] Simon Walker describes how Barry was a Lancastrian retainer from East Anglia, who was retained as an investment for the future, rather than for his seniority at the time.[319] It should be added that Barry can also be identified as a deponent on behalf of Sir Edward Hastings during the Grey v. Hastings case in the court of chivalry in the early 1400s. In this case Barry testified that he had served with John of Gaunt on his Castilian expedition of 1386.[320] It can be seen that Barry was serving in a professional manner, as he joined the campaign in 1388, shortly after returning from Gaunt's Spanish adventure. Thus his service with the house of Lancaster can be traced back further than his official retention in 1396. John of Gaunt's 'investment' in Barry has proved worthwhile, as the latter supported his (Gaunt's) son Henry in his attempt on the throne. It is no surprise to see both Barry and Husy rushing to join with Henry considering their previous recent connection with his father. Indeed, their inclusion in the campaign in 1388 may indicate earlier support for Henry of Derby, who was a junior Appellant.

It would be interesting to make a comparison of the men serving in 1387–1388 and the campaign led by Henry IV to Scotland in the summer of 1400. Firstly, this will demonstrate continuance of service between these campaigns, providing nominal evidence of members of the military community and, secondly, will demonstrate how far Henry was able to draw upon this military experience in the first campaign of his reign. Henry's campaign has been detailed in an article by A.L. Brown.[321] He describes how the campaign was futile and how it was raised, unusually, by summoning all those who had a

316 E101/41/5 m. 1.
317 E101/41/5 m. 8.
318 Barry: Walker, *Lancastrian Affinity*, p. 263. Husy: *ibid.*, p. 272.
319 *Ibid.*, pp. 193n, 203.
320 Keen, 'English Military Experience and the Court of Chivalry', p. 139.
321 Brown, 'English Campaign in Scotland, 1400', pp. 40–54. See also Wylie, *History of England under Henry the Fourth*, pp. 119–140.

Table 28. Service in Scotland, 1400

Year	Title	First name	Surname	Position	Captain name	Scotland, 1400
1388		William	Asschenton	Esquire	Mons Thomas Percy	Morgan, p. 209, William de Assheton, In hundredo de Macclesfield
1388	Le Sire		Bardolf, de	Baron	Le Counte Marshall	p. 47n, Bardolf, 14 men-at-arms and 50 archers
1388		William	Brerton	Esquire	Mons Johan Bohun	Morgan, p. 209, William de Brerton, In hundredo de Northwico
1387		John	Dalyngrigg	Esquire	Arundel, Richard, earl of	p. 47, John Dalyngrigge, chamber knight
1388		Johan	Dalingrugg	Esquire	Mons William Heron	
1387	Mons	Renand	Grey, de	Knight	Arundel, Richard, earl of	p. 47n, Grey of Ruthin, 18 men-at-arms, 100 archers
1387		John	Hardyng	Esquire	Richard Shingulton	Morgan, p. 209, John Hardyng de Twemlow, In hundredo de Northwico
1388		Johan	Hardyng	Esquire	Richard Shingulton	
1387		John	Lee, del	Esquire	Mons Nichol Clyfton	Morgan, p. 209, John del Lee, In hundredo de Broxon
1388		Johan	Mychel	Esquire	Arundel, Richard, earl of	p. 50, John Michel, a serjeant-at-arms
1388	Mons	Michael	Pole, de la	Baron	Arundel, Richard, earl of	p. 47n, earl of Suffolk (with earl of Westmorland), led a retinue of 200 men-at-arms and 1,000 archers)
1387	Mons	Payn	Typpetoo	Knight	Arundel, Richard, earl of	p. 47, Payne Tiptoft, chamber knight
1388	Mons	Payn	Typtot	Knight	Arundel, Richard, earl of	
1388		Thomas	Vernon	Esquire	Mons Rauf Vernon	Morgan, p.209, Thomas le Vernon, In hundredo Wici Malbanki, 10 sagitt'

* Page References are to Brown, 'English Campaign in Scotland, 1400'; or, where so indicated to Morgan, *War and Society*.

personal bond with the king. By this method, over 13,000 men were mustered, which was one of the largest assembled in England in this period. Brown also investigates the wage payments for service and provides nominal evidence for 53 of these participants, but these are concentrated on the peers who attended and also men with positions in the royal household.[322] It is possible to compare continuance of service with these named participants. In addition, Philip Morgan has included a transcription of the Cheshire retinue who served in Scotland in 1400. Morgan suggests that these men served for Henry IV as part of their commitment to repay the money that had been granted to them for their loyal service to Richard II.[323] This evidence provides a further 64 names. In total

[322] Brown, 'English Campaign in Scotland, 1400', pp. 40, 45–46.
[323] Morgan, *War and Society*, pp. 209–210, transcribed from the source E101/42/29, Names of the leaders of certain soldiers from Cheshire to Scotland, 1 membrane.

therefore, we are able to make a comparison with just 117 named participants out of a total of 13,000. This will not therefore allow us to make a thorough analysis, but some themes may emerge. Table 28 demonstrates that just 11 men can be identified as serving both in 1387–1388 and also in the campaign into Scotland in 1400.

As can be seen from the table, five of the participants are identified from the Cheshire retinue and six are identified by Brown. Of these men, it can be seen that Sir Michael de la Pole, earl of Suffolk, has jointly commanded a large force of 200 men-at-arms and 1000 archers with the earl of Westmorland. This is despite his support for Richard II when he joined the duke of York to oppose the landing of Henry in the previous year. Both Sir Payn Tiptoft and Sir John Dallingridge have both been made Chamber knights of Henry IV. The career of Tiptoft has been described in the section regarding supporters of the earl of Arundel. He had not been a supporter of Richard II; and therefore did not have a problem in serving with the new regime. Sir Edward Dallingridge, Sir John's father, was a major supporter of Richard II; however his son has quickly joined with the new regime. What perhaps is also interesting is that John Mychel is described as 'serjeant at arms' in both 1399 in the royal army raised by the duke of York and in the campaign into Scotland in 1400. This demonstrates that Mychel has been able to keep his official position in the royal armies despite the changeover of regimes.

The inclusion of Thomas, Lord Bardolf, is also of interest. Bardolf served in the retinue of the Earl Marshal in 1388.[324] Bardolf has an entry in *Complete Peerage*, which mentions that he was born on 22 December 1369, and he was thus only nineteen years of age in 1388. Although he serves in 1400, *Complete Peerage* describes that just five years later, in 1405, he joined the earl of Northumberland in rebellion and fled to Scotland. He was declared a traitor and died at the battle of Bramham Moor, in Yorkshire, on 19 February 1408. As a result of his treason, his body was quartered and his head placed on the gates of Lincoln.[325] He therefore showed his loyalty at the beginning of the reign; however after a few years, paid with his life for opposing the new regime.

It is difficult to provide many significant conclusions from the information provided by those who demonstrated continuance of service from 1387–1388 to 1400. From the 13,000 who probably took part, only 11 men are identified from the available printed sources. These show that the force included men who were loyal to the new regime and who prospered under Henry IV. It also included a number of Cheshire esquires who were probably serving because of an enforced repayment of previous sums paid to them by Richard II. Finally, Lord Bardolf demonstrated that a man may serve because of compulsion, but his later actions demonstrate that he was not loyal to Henry IV. The numbers involved in this mobilisation mean that a very mixed group of men would have served in 1400. It is perhaps significant that around 10% of those identified by name also served in 1387–1388, demonstrating that such men would serve as a part of their continued military career.

Despite the limited printed sources, it is still possible to demonstrate continuance of service from 1387–1388 to the events of 1399–1400 for 28 men. This includes representatives of the nobility, knights, esquires and archers. They can be seen serving both with Richard II and also in the army supporting Henry IV in 1399 and on campaign in Scotland in 1400. This demonstrates that the men who served in 1387–1388 would be valued for this military experience. Their actions during the deposition, showing support for both Richard and Henry, demonstrate how difficult it is to make assumptions regarding military service. What perhaps is shown by the limited evidence is that men who fought in campaigns such as that of 1387–1388 would also become readily involved in other campaigns, whether they were for or against the reigning king. This is perhaps also demonstrated by the large number of pardons that have been taken by these combatants in 1398. Many of these men demonstrate a professional career and have served in other campaigns. In general, they have not suffered under the changeover to the new regime, perhaps indicating that nothing really changed for the ordinary soldier and participant in such campaigns. Such manpower was valued and there was always a demand for men with martial experience and skill.

Conclusion

The extensive evidence which has survived regarding the campaigns of 1387–1388 has allowed us to identify and sketch the careers of a selection of those who served on expeditions with Richard Fitzalan, earl of Arundel. The computer database has enabled the more efficient management of the available materials that give information on the large numbers of men involved in the campaigns. It has also facilitated comparisons with sources regarding other campaigns and has provided the ability to demonstrate continuity of service between 1387 and 1388. Therefore, as well as identifying individual continuity of service, we can now, in conclusion, make some general comments regarding patterns of service and relationships within armies in the later fourteenth century.

The muster roll evidence has allowed us to identify that, for the campaigns of 1387 and 1388, Richard, earl of Arundel, had to recruit over 6,000 soldiers. It can be shown that 473 men chose to serve with Arundel in both expeditions. This is a large body of men, representing 19% of the force in 1387 and 13% of the force in 1388, and suggests that a level of professionalism is evident. This is especially notable at the position of retinue captain, where 66% of the captains of 1388 had already served in 1387. By analysing the composition of the army, it can be shown that the ratio of man-at-arms to archer is consistent at 1 to 1.3 for both campaigns. This ratio is consistent throughout the retinue structure of the army, suggesting that the movement towards the ratios seen in the later campaigns of Henry V, such as 1 man-at-arms to 3 archers as demonstrated at Agincourt, had not yet begun.[1] In fact, they reflect the ratios seen in the other campaigns undertaken during the final years of the reign of Edward III.

From the muster roll evidence we have been able to build the careers of individuals by the use of both primary and secondary sources. This has enabled us to look at the questions we have posed throughout the book. Was the political background to the campaigns influential on the composition of the armies? How did service affect future favour under Richard II? Why did men serve on campaign?

Much has been written about motivation to serve since K.B. McFarlane stated that a soldier 'made no pretence of fighting for love of king or lord, still less for England or for glory, but for gain'.[2] It has been demonstrated that such motivating factors as patriotism, ties to a regional lord, friendship and kinship and also a sense of duty as a senior member of the local community were also important to the English soldier in the Hundred Years War. Although examples of men who 'made their fortune' can be demonstrated, these are perhaps only

---

[1] Anne Curry, 'English Armies in the Fifteenth Century', pp. 39–68, p. 45.
[2] McFarlane, *Nobility of Later Medieval England*, p. 21.

the minority of careers that can be developed using the source materials.[3] We have shown that examples can be found representing many different areas of interest and loyalty which can explain why men chose to fight in these particular expeditions.

The ability to link records has provided evidence highlighting the lives of the soldiers who served in the campaigns of 1387 and 1388. We have shown that 169 men hold land as tenants of the earl of Arundel in Sussex: this includes 11 knights, 65 esquires and 93 archers. In addition, 42 soldiers serve with the earl of Arundel in 1378, including 12 knights, 19 esquires and 11 archers. We have also identified 559 men who secure pardons between 1397 and 1398, probably because of their service with Arundel in 1387–1388. This represents records for 37 knights, 387 esquires and 313 archers. We have discovered 63 men who are witnesses at the Scrope v. Grosvenor and Grey v. Hastings cases at the court of chivalry, representing 25 knights, 26 esquires and 2 archers. Soldiers can be shown to have fought with Sir William de Windsor in 1380, with 49 records being linked, including 1 knight, 19 esquires and 29 archers. We can also show continuance of service with the campaigns led by Richard II to Ireland in 1394 and 1399 for 97 men, including 50 knights, 36 esquires and 11 archers. The evidence for loyalty demonstrated by king's knights provides further information regarding 52 knights. Finally, we have shown that 15 men serve with the duke of York in 1399, including 5 knights, 6 esquires and 4 archers whilst 3 men serve with Henry IV's invasion army, including 1 knight and 2 esquires. It is also possible to identify 11 men who serve in Scotland in 1400, including 4 knights and 7 esquires. Therefore, we have demonstrated that nominal evidence survives for all parts of the expeditionary armies in 1387 and 1388, supplying information which provides insights into continuance of service and the loyalties of soldiers during the reign of Richard II. Overall we have been able to find 1,060 nominal records providing additional evidence regarding the service of the soldiers present in the campaigns of 1387–1388. This has demonstrated that it is possible to find information to investigate the service of a large number of the combatants including being able to develop the pattern of service of knights, esquires and even the often obscure bowmen.

This nominal evidence has been used to provide case studies regarding links with Arundel and other senior figures and also to investigate the changing loyalties of the men who served on campaign. In this way we have been able to comment in detail upon the careers of 126 individuals. The nature of the surviving evidence has biased these case studies towards describing the careers of knights, as more information has survived regarding landholding and service in government for these individuals. Therefore, 70 of the case studies feature the careers of knights. Unfortunately, especially for archers, evidence does not survive in such quantities for the lower echelons of society. However, we have still been able to highlight the careers of 42 esquires and 14 archers.

We have shown that men served in the campaigns because they were members of the English military community. Indeed 22 (17%) of the case

---

[3] For an overview see Ayton, 'War and the English Gentry under Edward III', pp. 34–40.

studies describe men with extensive careers in the service of the English crown and 30 (24%) of the case studies show connections to Richard II. Men such as Sir William Elmham and Sir Thomas Trivet, who were close to Richard II, can be shown to have served on multiple royal expeditions. This type of service can also be shown for men who were less well connected. Thus, we find that the service of the esquire John Bathe can be seen to have been in continuation of a career in arms stretching back to 1369. The evidence of the court of chivalry is of great assistance when tracing a career in arms. We can also show, for instance, that the esquire William Plumstead and the archer Robert Fysshlake had extraordinarily rich careers in royal service. Plumstead had served in expeditions stretching back to 1370, whilst Fysshlake had served in royal armies in 1378, 1379 and 1380 and his travels had taken him to Jerusalem and the eastern Mediterranean. The presence of such men on campaign in 1387 and 1388 demonstrates that these men served because these were *royal* expeditions. The fact that they were carried out against a background of political uncertainty did not deter such men from continuing their careers in arms.

As would also be expected, a number of men who served can be linked to the leader of the expedition, Richard, earl of Arundel. It is of note that 70 (56%) of the case studies refer to a connection between the soldier and the earl of Arundel. This can especially be seen through connections of land tenure, especially in Sussex, where an estate survey exists with which to compare the muster rolls.[4] Through this comparison, as mentioned, 169 individuals can be found to hold land of, and also serve with, the earl of Arundel. The landholding of Arundel was concentrated in Shropshire and many connections can be identified here and in the Welsh marches. This explains the service of Owain Glyn Dwr in 1387 and his intended service in 1388. The relationship of soldiers with Arundel is also shown by the comparison with his retinue in the expedition of 1378.[5] It can be seen, as previously noted, that 42 men have served with Arundel in 1378 and in his campaigns of 1387–1388. This shows a martial relationship of ten years and suggests that their service in 1378 has enabled them to impress Arundel such that he has retained them for his later campaigns.

Men can also be seen to be serving with members of their family. This can be shown for men with the same surname listed next to one another on the muster rolls, such as the archers John Clone and Robert Clone in Arundel's retinue in 1388, listed 256th and 257th respectively. In addition, we can identify Sir Edmund Fitz Herbert serving with his nephew Sir Thomas West in Arundel's retinue in 1387, listed eleventh and sixteenth respectively. Local ties also seem to be important for the motivation for service in a military campaign. This can be explicitly seen for the esquires Wauter Haket and Richard Romyn. Both men are listed next to one another in the muster rolls for 1387 and 1388. This relationship can be shown to be close, both men being tenants of Arundel and neighbours to one another in the hundred of Bourne in Sussex. Ties of kinship can be demonstrated for a group of six men from Shropshire who serve with

---

4 *Two Estate Surveys.*
5 E101/35/32.

Arundel in 1387–1388 and can also be connected to one another in local society. These men, John Burley, Sir John Cornwall, John Daras, Sir Richard Ludlowe, Fulk Sprenghose and Thomas Whitton are therefore serving because they knew one another and also because of their position in local society. A number of these men are members of parliament and, together with other men who can be identified from *History of Parliament*, form a strong group within the muster rolls. This evidence suggests that men who were in the position to be members of parliament also felt a responsibility to serve in royal expeditions. The service of these men is perhaps evidence to show that they served out of a sense of duty because of their leading position in society.

The number of men who can be demonstrated to be connected to Arundel in the case studies perhaps suggests that attendance at the campaign was politically motivated. This argument is strengthened by the evidence available from the pardon rolls of 1397–1399, which are related to service with the Appellants and especially the battle of Radcot Bridge in December 1387. The comparison with the pardon rolls identifies over 500 men serving in the campaigns of Arundel in 1387–1388 who also secured a royal pardon at this time. Rather than suggesting that these men took pardons because of their service on campaign, it may in fact demonstrate a continuance of service against the royal forces of de Vere in December 1387. Despite this, it is also possible to find a number of men serving on campaign in 1387–1388, and also gaining favour in the service of Richard II. This relationship with Richard II may have been established prior to 1387. Indeed, as mentioned, eleven men can be found serving on campaign who were also king's knights before 1387. It also includes men such as Sir Thomas Percy and Sir Michael de la Pole who were later promoted to the peerage by Richard II.

Attendance at the campaigns of 1387 and 1388 does not appear to suggest any particular political motivation. The sources have demonstrated that men later continued their service in Ireland in 1394 and 1399. Some men supported the duke of York in his defence of the realm in 1399, whilst others supported Henry of Derby joining his invasion army. A number of men supported the Epiphany Plot in 1400, whilst their colleagues from 1387–1388 are to be found on the jury that prosecuted them. Representatives from 1387–1388 can be found on Henry IV's first campaign into Scotland in 1400, whilst others can be found fighting against the rebellion of Owain Glyn Dwr, another colleague in arms from the expeditions. Men from the campaigns of 1387–1388 can be found meeting their death fighting on both sides at the battle of Shrewsbury in 1403, and supporting or opposing the other revolts led by the earl of Northumberland. Men also demonstrate the power of survival throughout the reigns at the turn of the century and examples can be found of men, such as Thomas, Lord Camoys: he was abjured from the court in 1388 for his support of Richard II; captained a retinue under the command of the earl of Arundel on the expedition of 1388; took a royal pardon in 1398; and who commanded the left wing of the army at the battle of Agincourt in 1415. It is difficult to discover a theme concerning the loyalty shown by men who served in 1387–1388. It is possible to demonstrate that each individual reacted differently to the upheavals of 1386–1389 and the repercussions of 1397–1399. What perhaps can be concluded is that the fourteenth-century soldier was interested in the affairs of state, but perhaps was more interested in his own personal survival.

My research has demonstrated that careful examination of the surviving sources for the expeditions of 1387–1388, together with the analysis made available by the computer database, can extend the knowledge of the men who served in the expeditions of the earl of Arundel. The great bulk of soldiers, the ordinary esquire and archer, of the expeditionary armies in the Hundred Years War have mainly remained unnamed and uncharacterised. We have shown that by gathering together the source materials, for esquires and to a lesser extent for archers, portraits can be drawn to illustrate the careers of the lives of these previously neglected members of the English military community. We have found that reasons for service were diverse and included a professionalism of service, connections to the commander, connections to a retinue captain, family links, ties of locality and kinship – especially to their comrades in arms – participation in a royal expedition and loyalty to the king. In addition, a strong body of men who can be identified as serving also occupied a position of authority in the local and national community. These men could be members of parliament, sheriffs, justices of the peace and may also have been appointed to other local commissions. It would appear that men who were involved in such a way with local and central government also became involved in royal expeditions. It is not going too far to suggest that military service on royal expeditions was an expected duty for men of such local prominence and social status – expected not only by the king and the leaders of the armies, but also by them themselves as part of their patriotic and social duty. On the whole, therefore, this study has indicated that service on the campaigns of 1387 and 1388 was a patriotic act and not a political gesture, although we will never be able to enter into the minds of all of the participants and to know what precisely involvement in the campaigns meant for them.

Bibliography

Manuscript sources

Public Record Office
Accounts Various
E101/36/32. Muster rolls of the retinue of Richard, earl of Arundel. 6 ms. For expedition 1378.
E101/39/6. Rolls of the retinue of Sir William de Windsor. For expedition 1380.
E101/40/33. Roll of the retinue of Richard, earl of Arundel, and captains serving under him. 20 ms. For expedition 1387.
E101/40/34. Muster of the forces under Richard, earl of Arundel. 26 ms. For expedition 1387.
E101/40/35. Particulars of the account of Richard, earl of Arundel, Admiral of the Fleet. 1 m. For expedition 1387.
E101/40/36. Account of payments to mariners. 3 ms. For expedition 1387.
E101/40/39. Muster of the retinue of Thomas de Percy. 2 ms. For expedition 1388.
E101/40/40. Particulars of the account of Thomas Durant of mariners' wages. 4 ms. For expedition 1388.
E101/41/4. Particulars of the account of Richard, earl of Arundel, Admiral of the Fleet (with indenture). 2 ms. For expedition 1388.
E101/41/5. Muster roll. 21 ms. For expedition 1388.

Memoranda Rolls
E159/167. For expedition 1388.

Enrolled (Foreign) Accounts
E364/21. For expedition 1387.
E364/24. For expedition 1388.

Issue Rolls
E403/515. For expedition 1387.
E403/519. For expedition 1388.

Treaty (or French) Rolls
C76/71. For expedition 1387.
C76/72. For expedition 1388.

Supplementary Patent Rolls
C67/30. For regnal year 21, 22 June 1397 – 21 June 1398.
C67/31. For regnal year 22, 22 June 1398 – 21 June 1399.

Printed primary sources

Annual Report of the Deputy Keeper of the Public Records 44 (London, 1883)

Anonimalle Chronicle, 1333–81, ed. V.H. Galbraith (Manchester, 1927)

The Bondage and Travels of Johann Schiltberger, ed. J.B. Telfer, Hakluyt Series, 58 (London, 1879)

Calendar of Charter Rolls, 1341–1417 (London, 1916)

Calendar of Close Rolls, 1377–1399 (6 vols, London, 1914–27)

Calendar of Fine Rolls, 1377–1399 (3 vols, London, 1926–29)

Calendar of Inquisitions Post Mortem (London, 1906–74)

Calendar of Patent Rolls, 1377–1399 (6 vols, London, 1895–1909)

Carte, Thomas. *Catalogue des Rolles Gascons, Normans et François*, vol. xx (London and Paris, 1743)

The Chronicle of Adam Usk, 1377–1421, ed. and trans. C. Given-Wilson (Oxford, 1997)

Chronicles of the Revolution, 1397–1400, ed. C. Given-Wilson (Manchester, 1993)

Chronicon Adae de Usk, 1377–1421, ed. E.M. Thompson (1904)

Chronicon Angliae, ed. E.M. Thompson (Rolls Series, 1874)

Chronique de la Traison et Mort de Richart II, ed. and trans. Benjamin Williams (London, 1846)

Clough, Marie (ed.). *Two Estate Surveys of the Fitzalan Earls of Arundel* (Sussex Record Society, 1969)

Creton, J. 'French Metrical History on the Deposition of Richard II', ed. and trans. J. Webb, *Archaeologia*, xx (1824), pp. 1–441

Croniques de Franche, d'Engleterre, de Flanders, de Lille et especialement de Tournai, ed. A. Hocquet, Publications de la Société des bibliophiles belges, xxxviii (Mons, 1938)

Eulogium Historiarum sive Temporis, ed. F.S. Haydon, vol. iii (Rolls Series, 1863)

Expeditions to Prussia and the Holy Land made by Henry, Earl of Derby, in the Years 1390– and 1392–3, ed. L.T. Smith, Camden Society, new series, lii (London, 1894)

Froissart, J. *Chronicles*, ed. and trans. T. Johnes (2 vols, London, 1874)

Gesta Henrici Quinti. The Deeds of Henry the Fifth, ed. and trans. Frank Taylor and John S. Roskell (Oxford, 1975)

Hardy, Sir Thomas Duffus. *Syllabus to Rymer's Foedera*, vol. 2, *1377–1654* (1873)

Historia Vitae et Regni Ricardi Secundi, ed. G.B. Stow (1977)

Jack, R.I. (ed). *The Grey of Ruthin Valor: The Valor of the English Lands of Edmund Grey, Earl of Kent, drawn up from ministers' accounts of 1467–8* (Sydney, 1965)

John Capgrave, Liber de Illustribus Henricis, ed. F.C. Hingeston (Rolls Series, 1858)

Jones, Michael, and Simon Walker (eds). 'Private Indentures for Life Service in Peace and War 1278–1476', in *Camden Miscellany XXXII*, Camden Society, fifth series, vol. 3 (London, 1994)

Knighton's Chronicle 1337–1396, ed. and trans. G.H. Martin (Oxford, 1995)

Muratori, L. (ed.). 'Antonio Fiorentino – Chronica Volgare', *Rerum Italicarum Scriptores*, xxvii, part ii (Cita de Castella, 1900–23)

Philip de Mézières: Letter to Richard II: A Plea made in 1395 for Peace between England and France, ed. G.W. Coopland (Liverpool, 1975)

Riley, H.T. (ed.), *Annales Ricardi Secundi et Henrici Quarti*, in J. de Trokelowe *et Anon.*, *Chronica et Annales* (Rolls Series, 1866)

The Riverside Chaucer, ed. Larry D. Benson (Oxford, 3rd edn 1992)

Rotuli Parliamentorum (6 vols, London, 1767–77)

Rymer, T. *Foedera, Conventiones, Litterae etc.*, ed. A. Clarke, F. Holbrooke and J. Caley (4 vols, London, 1816–69)

The St Albans Chronicle: The Chronica Maiora of Thomas Walsingham, Volume 1, *1376–1396*, ed. John Taylor, Wendy R. Childs and Leslie Watkiss (Oxford, 2002)

The Scrope and Grosvenor Controversy, ed. N. Harris Nicolas (2 vols, London, 1832)

Walsingham, T. *Historia Anglicana*, ed. H.T. Riley (2 vols, Rolls Series, 1863–64)

The Westminster Chronicle, 1381–1394, ed. and trans. L.C. Hector and B.F. Harvey (Oxford, 1982)

The Works of Sir John Clanvowe, ed. V.J. Scattergood (Cambridge, 1975)

Secondary sources

Allmand, Christopher. *The Hundred Years War* (Cambridge, 1989)

Aston, Margaret. 'The Impeachment of Bishop Despencer', *Bulletin of the Institute of Historical Research*, vol. xxxviii, 98 (1965), pp. 127–148

Atiya, A.S. *The Crusade of Nicopolis* (London, 1934)

Atiya, A.S. *The Crusade in the Later Middle Ages* (London, 1938)

Ayton, Andrew, and Virginia Davis. 'The Hull Domesday Project', in Peter Denley and Deian Hopkin (eds), *History and Computing* (Manchester, 1987)

Ayton, Andrew. 'War and the English Gentry under Edward III', *History Today*, xlii, 3 (March 1992), pp. 34–40

Ayton, Andrew. *Knights and Warhorses: Military Service and the English Aristocracy under Edward III* (Woodbridge, 1994)

Ayton, Andrew. 'The English Army and the Normandy Campaign of 1346', in David Bates and Anne Curry (eds), *England and Normandy in the Middle Ages* (London, 1994), pp. 253–268

Ayton, Andrew. 'English Armies in the Fourteenth Century', in Anne Curry and Michael Hughes (eds), *Arms, Armies and Fortifications in the Hundred Years War* (Woodbridge, 1994), pp. 21–38

Ayton, Andrew. 'Knights, Esquires and Military Service: The Evidence of the Armorial Cases before the Court of Chivalry', in A. Ayton and J.L. Price (eds), *The Medieval Military Revolution: State, Society and Military Change in Medieval and Early Modern Europe* (New York, 1995), pp. 81–104

Ayton, Andrew. 'Edward III and the English Aristocracy at the Beginning of the Hundred Years War', in Matthew Strickland (ed.), *Armies, Chivalry and Warfare in Medieval Britain and France: Proceedings of the 1995 Harlaxton Symposium* (Stamford, 1998), pp. 173–206

Barron, C.M. 'The Tyranny of Richard II', *Bulletin of the Institute of Historical Research*, xli (1968), pp. 1–18

Bayley, C.C. 'The Campaign of 1375 and the Good Parliament', *English Historical Review*, lv (1940), pp. 370–383

Bell, Adrian R. 'England and the Crusade of Nicopolis', *Medieval Life*, issue 4 (Spring 1996), pp. 18–22

Bennett, Michael. *Community, Class and Careerism: Cheshire and Lancashire Society in the Age of Sir Gawain and the Green Knight* (Cambridge, 1983)

Bennett, Michael. *Richard II and the Revolution of 1399* (Stroud, 1999)

Brown, A.L. 'The English Campaign in Scotland, 1400', in H. Hearder and H.R. Loyn (eds), *British Government and Administration: Studies presented to S.R. Chrimes* (Cardiff, 1974), pp. 40–54

Clarke, M.V., and V.H. Galbraith. 'The Deposition of Richard II?', *Bulletin of the John Rylands Library*, 14 (1930), pp. 125–181

Cokayne, G.E. (ed.). *The Complete Peerage* (13 vols, London, 1910–57)

Crouch, D. *The Image of Aristocracy in Britain, 1000–1300* (London, 1992)

Curry, Anne. *The Hundred Years War* (London, 1993)

Curry, Anne, and Michael Hughes (eds). *Arms, Armies and Fortifications in the Hundred Years War* (Woodbridge, 1994)

Curry, Anne. 'English Armies in the Fifteenth Century', in Anne Curry and Michael Hughes (eds), *Arms, Armies and Fortifications in the Hundred Years War* (Woodbridge, 1994), pp. 39–68

Curry, Anne. 'The Organisation of Field Armies in Lancastrian Normandy', in Matthew Strickland (ed.), *Armies, Chivalry and Warfare in Medieval Britain and France: Proceedings of the 1995 Harlaxton Symposium* (Stamford, 1998), pp. 207–223

Curry, Anne. 'Richard II and the War with France', in Gwilym Dodd (ed.), *The Reign of Richard II* (Tempus, 2000), pp. 33–50

Curry, Anne. *The Battle of Agincourt: Sources and Interpretations* (Woodbridge, 2000)

Curry, Anne (ed.), *Agincourt 1415: Henry V, Sir Thomas Erpingham and the Triumph of the English Archers* (Stroud, 2000)

Curtis, E. *Richard II in Ireland* (Oxford, 1927)

Davies, R.R. *The Revolt of Owain Glyn Dwr* (Oxford, 1997)

Dictionary of National Biography (63 vols, London, 1885–1900)

Dodd, Gwilym (ed.), *The Reign of Richard II* (Tempus, 2000)

Eberle, Patricia J. 'Richard II and the Literary Arts', in Anthony Goodman and James Gillespie (eds), *Richard II: The Art of Kingship* (Oxford, 1999), pp. 231–254

Friel, Ian. 'Winds of Change? Ships and the Hundred Years War', in Anne Curry and Michael Hughes (eds), *Arms, Armies and Fortifications in the Hundred Years War* (Woodbridge, 1994), pp. 183–193

Fryde, E.B., D.E. Greenway, S. Porter and I. Roy (eds). *Handbook of British Chronology* (London, 3rd edn 1986)

Gillespie, James L. 'Thomas Mortimer and Thomas Molineaux: Radcot Bridge and the Appeal of 1397', *Albion*, vii (1975), pp. 161–73

Gillespie, James L. 'Richard II: King of Battles?', in James L. Gillespie (ed.), *The Age of Richard II* (Stroud, 1997), pp. 139–164

Gillespie, James L. (ed.), *The Age of Richard II* (Stroud, 1997)

Given-Wilson, C. *The Royal Household and the King's Affinity: Service, Politics and Finance, 1360 – 1413* (New Haven and London, 1986)

Given-Wilson, C. 'Royal Charter Witness Lists 1327–1399', *Medieval Prosopography*, 11 (1991), 35–93

Given-Wilson, C. 'Richard II and the Higher Nobility', in Anthony Goodman and James Gillespie (eds), *Richard II: The Art of Kingship* (Oxford, 1999)

Goodman, Anthony. 'Owain Glyndwr before 1400', *Welsh Historical Review*, 5 (1970–71), pp. 67–70

Goodman, Anthony. *The Loyal Conspiracy: The Lords Appellant under Richard II* (London, 1971)

Goodman, Anthony. 'The Military Subcontracts of Sir Hugh Hastings, 1380', *English Historical Review*, 95 (1980), pp. 114–120

Goodman, Anthony. *John of Gaunt: The Exercise of Princely Power in Fourteenth-Century Europe* (Harlow, 1992)

Goodman, Anthony, and Anthony Tuck (eds), *War and Border Societies in the Middle Ages* (London, 1992)

Goodman, Anthony, and James L. Gillespie (eds), *Richard II: The Art of Kingship* (Oxford, 1999)

Gransden, Antonia. *Historical Writing in England*, Vol. II, *c. 1307 to the Early Sixteenth Century* (London, 1982)

Griffiths, Ralph. 'Some Secret Supporters of Owain Glyn Dwr?', *Bulletin of the Institute of Historical Research*, vol. 37 (1964), pp. 77–100

Guide to the Contents of the Public Record Office, Volume 1 (London, 1963)

Harris Nicolas, N. *History of the Battle of Agincourt* (London, 1833 edn)

Harris Nicolas, N. *History of the Royal Navy* (London, 1847)

Harriss, G.L. *Cardinal Beaufort* (Oxford, 1988)

Hay, D. 'The Division of the Spoils of War in Fourteenth-Century England', *Transactions of the Royal Historical Society*, 5th series, iv (1954), pp. 91–109

Housley, Norman. 'The Bishop of Norwich's Crusade, May 1383', *History Today*, xxxiii (May 1983) pp. 15–20

Housley, Norman. *The Later Crusades, 1274–1580: From Lyons to Alcazar* (Oxford, 1992)

Jack, R.I. 'Owain Glyn Dwr and the Lordship of Ruthin', *Welsh History Review*, 2 (1965), pp. 303–322

Jamieson, Neil. 'The Recruitment of Northerners for Service in English Armies in France, 1415–50', in Dorothy L. Clayton, Richard G. Davies and Peter McNiven (eds), *Trade, Devotion and Governance: Papers in Later Medieval History* (Stroud, 1994), pp. 102–115

Johnson, Dorothy B. 'Richard II and the Submissions of Gaelic Ireland', *Irish Historical Studies*, xxii (1980), pp. 1–20

Johnson, Dorothy B. 'The Interim Years: Richard II and Ireland, 1395–1399', in J.F. Lydon (ed.), *England and Ireland in the Late Middle Ages: Essays in Honour of Jocelyn Otway-Ruthven* (Dublin, 1981)

Jones, Michael. *Ducal Brittany 1364–1399: Relations with England and France during the Reign of Duke John IV* (Oxford, 1970)

Jones, Michael. 'The Ransom of Jean de Bretagne, Count of Penthièvre: An Aspect of English Foreign Policy 1386–8', *Bulletin of the Institute of Historical Reseach*, xlv (1972), pp. 7–26

Jones, Terry. *Chaucer's Knight: The Portrait of a Medieval Mercenary* (London, 1980)

Keen, Maurice. 'English Military Experience and the Court of Chivalry: The Case of Grey v. Hastings', in P. Contamine, C. Giry-Deloison and M. Keen (eds), *Guerre et société en France, en Angleterre et en Bourgogne, XIVe–XVe siècle* (Lille, 1992), pp. 123–42

Keen, Maurice. 'Chaucer and Chivalry Re-visited', in Matthew Strickland (ed.), *Armies, Chivalry and Warfare in Medieval Britain and France: Proceedings of the 1995 Harlaxton Symposium* (Stamford, 1998), pp. 1–13

Leland, John L. 'The Abjuration of 1388', *Medieval Prosopography*, 15:1 (1994), pp. 115–138

Leland, John L. 'Unpardonable Sinners? Exclusions from the General Pardon of 1388', *Medieval Prosopography*, 17 (1996), pp. 181–195

Leland, John L. 'The Oxford Trial of 1400: Royal Politics and the County Gentry', in J.L. Gillespie (ed.), *The Age of Richard II* (Stroud, 1997)

Lewis, N.B. 'The Last Medieval Summons of the English Feudal Levy, 13 June 1385', *English Historical Review*, 73 (Jan. 1958), pp. 1–26

Lewis, N.B. 'The Feudal Summons of 1385', with a reply by J.J.N. Palmer, *English Historical Review*, 100 (1985), pp. 729–746

Lopez, F. *The English in Portugal 1367–87*, ed. D.W. Lomax and R.J. Oakley (Warminster, 1988)

Lydon, J.F. 'Richard II's Expeditions to Ireland', *Journal of the Royal Society of Antiquaries of Ireland*, xciii (1963), pp. 135–149

Lydon, J.F. *Ireland in the Later Middle Ages* (Dublin, 1973)

Mawdsley, E., N. Morgan, L. Richmond and R. Trainer (eds), *History and Computing, III. Historians, Computers and Data: Applications in Research and Teaching* (Manchester, 1990)

McFarlane, K.B. *Lancastrian Kings and Lollard Knights* (Oxford, 1972)

McFarlane, K.B. *The Nobility of Later Medieval England* (Oxford, 1973)

McKisack, May. *The Fourteenth Century, 1307–1399* (Oxford, 1959)

Morgan, Philip. *War and Society in Medieval Cheshire, 1277–1403* (Manchester, 1987)

Myres, J.N.L. 'The Campaign of Radcot Bridge in December 1387', *English Historical Review*, xlii (1927), pp. 20–33

Newhall, R.A. *Muster and Review. A Problem of English Military Administration, 1420–1440* (Cambridge, Mass., 1940)

Palmer, J.J.N. 'The Last Summons of the Feudal Army in England (1385)', *English Historical Review*, 83 (1968), pp. 771–775

Palmer, J.J.N. 'The Impeachment of Michael de la Pole in 1386', *Bulletin of the Institute of Historical Resarch*, xlii (1969), pp. 96–101

Palmer, J.J.N. *England, France and Christendom, 1377–99* (London, 1972)

Palmer, J.J.N. 'The Authorship, Date and Historical Value of the French Chronicles on the Lancastrian Revolution', *Bulletin of the John Rylands Library*, 61 (1978–79), Part 1, pp. 145–181, Part 2, pp. 398–421

Prestwich, Michael. *Armies and Warfare in the Middle Ages: The English Experience* (New Haven, 1996)

Prince, A.E. 'The Strength of English Armies in the Reign of Edward III', *English Historical Review*, xlvi (1931), pp. 353–371

Prince, A.E. 'The Indenture System under Edward III', in J.G. Edwards, V.H. Galbraith and E.F. Jacob (eds), *Historical Essays in Honour of James Tait* (Manchester, 1933), pp. 283–297

Rogers, Clifford J. *War Cruel and Sharp: English Strategy under Edward III, 1327–1360* (Woodbridge, 2000)

Roskell, J.S. 'Sir Arnald Savage of Bobbing: Speaker for the Commons in 1401 and 1404', *Archaelogia Cantiana*, lxx (1956), pp. 68–83

Roskell, J.S. 'Two Medieval Lincolnshire Speakers. Part 1 – Sir John Bussy of Hougham', *Lincolnshire Architectural and Archaelogical Society, Reports and Papers*, vol. 7, part 1 (1957), pp. 27–45

Roskell, J.S. *The Commons and their Speakers in English Parliaments, 1376–1523* (Manchester, 1965)

Roskell, J.S. 'Sir William Sturmy', in J.S. Roskell, *Parliament and Politics in Late Medieval England* (3 vols, London 1981–83), vol. iii, pp. 91–105

Roskell, J.S. *The Impeachment of Michael de la Pole, Earl of Suffolk, in 1386, in the Context of the Reign of Richard II* (Manchester, 1984)

Roskell, J.S., L. Clark and C. Rawcliffe (eds), *The History of Parliament: The House of Commons 1386–1421* (4 vols, Stroud, 1992)

Russell, P.E. *English Intervention in Spain and Portugal* (Oxford, 1955)

Salzman, L.F. 'The Property of the Earl of Arundel, 1397', *Sussex Archaeological Collections*, 91 (1953), pp. 32–52

Saul, Nigel. *Knights and Esquires: The Gloucestershire Gentry in the Fourteenth Century* (Oxford, 1981)

Saul, Nigel. *Scenes from Provincial Life: Knightly Families in Sussex, 1280–1400* (Oxford, 1986)

Saul, Nigel. *Richard II* (New Haven, 1997)

Sherborne, J.W. 'The Cost of English Warfare with France in the Later Fourteenth Century', *Bulletin of the Institute of Historical Research*, 50 (1977), pp. 135–50, reprinted in his *War, Politics and Culture in Fourteenth-Century England*, ed. A. Tuck (London, 1994), pp. 55–70

Sherborne, J.W. 'The English Navy: Shipping and Manpower, 1369–89', *Past and Present*, 37

(1967), pp. 163–75, reprinted in his *War, Politics and Culture in Fourteenth-Century England*, ed. A. Tuck (London, 1994), pp. 29–39

Sherborne, J.W. 'Indentured Retinues and the English Expeditions to France, 1369–1380', *English Historical Review*, lxxix (1964), pp. 718–46, reprinted in his *War, Politics and Culture in Fourteenth-Century England*, ed. A. Tuck (London, 1994), pp. 1–28

Sherborne, J.W. 'John of Gaunt, Edward III's Retinue and the French Campaign of 1369', in *Kings and Nobles in the Later Middle Ages*, ed. R.A. Griffiths and J. Sherborne (Gloucester, 1986), pp. 41–61, reprinted in his *War, Politics and Culture in Fourteenth-Century England*, ed. A. Tuck (London, 1994), pp. 77–98

Steel, Anthony. *Richard II* (Cambridge, 1962)

Strickland, Matthew (ed.). *Armies, Chivalry and Warfare in Medieval Britain and France: Proceedings of the 1995 Harlaxton Symposium* (Stamford, 1998)

Sumption, Jonathan. *The Hundred Years War, I: Trial by Battle* (London, 1990)

Sumption, Jonathan. *The Hundred Years War, II: Trial by Fire* (London, 1999)

Tipton, C.L. 'The English at Nicopolis', *Speculum*, xxxvii (1962), pp. 528–40

Tuck, Anthony. 'The Cambridge Parliament, 1388', *English Historical Review*, lxxxiv (1969), pp. 225–243

Tuck, Anthony. *Richard II and the English Nobility* (London, 1973)

The Victoria History of the Counties of England: Rutland, vol. ii (London, 1908–35)

The Victoria History of the Counties of England: Sussex, vol. ix (London, 1937)

Walker, Simon. 'Lancaster v. Dallingridge: A Franchisal Dispute in Fourteenth Century Sussex', *Sussex Archaeological Collections*, 121 (1983), pp. 87–94

Walker, Simon. 'Profit and Loss in the Hundred Years War: The Subcontracts of Sir John Strother, 1374', *Bulletin of the Institute of Historical Research*, 58 (1985), pp. 100–106

Walker, Simon. *The Lancastrian Affinity, 1361–1399* (Oxford, 1990)

Wylie, J.H. *History of England under Henry the Fourth* (4 vols, London, 1884–98)

Wylie, J.H., and W.T. Waugh. *The Reign of Henry the Fifth* (3 vols, Cambridge, 1914–29)

Unpublished theses

Ayton, Andrew. 'The Warhorse and Military Service under Edward III' (Ph.D. thesis, University of Hull, 1990)

Curry, Anne. 'Military Organization in Lancastrian Normandy, 1422–1450' (2 vols, Ph.D. thesis, Council for National Academic Awards 1985)

Griffiths, W.R.H. 'The Military Career and Affinity of Henry, Prince of Wales, 1399–1413' (M.Litt. thesis, Oxford University, 1980)

Mitchell, Shelagh. 'Some Aspects of the Knightly Household of Richard II' (D.Phil. thesis, London University, 1998)

Index

Warfare in History

The Battle of Hastings: Sources and Interpretations, *edited and introduced by Stephen Morillo*

Infantry Warfare in the Early Fourteenth Century: Discipline, Tactics, and Technology, *Kelly DeVries*

The Art of Warfare in Western Europe during the Middle Ages, from the Eighth Century to 1340 (second edition), *J.F. Verbruggen*

Knights and Peasants: The Hundred Years War in the French Countryside, *Nicholas Wright*

Society at War: The Experience of England and France during the Hundred Years War, *edited by Christopher Allmand*

The Circle of War in the Middle Ages: Essays on Medieval Military and Naval History, *edited by Donald J. Kagay and L.J. Andrew Villalon*

The Anglo-Scots Wars, 1513–1550: A Military History, *Gervase Phillips*

The Norwegian Invasion of England in 1066, *Kelly DeVries*

The Wars of Edward III: Sources and Interpretations, *edited and introduced by Clifford J. Rogers*

The Battle of Agincourt: Sources and Interpretations, *Anne Curry*

War Cruel and Sharp: English Strategy under Edward III, 1327–1360, *Clifford J. Rogers*

The Normans and their Adversaries at War: Essays in Memory of C. Warren Hollister, *edited by Richard P. Abels and Bernard S. Bachrach*

The Battle of the Golden Spurs (Courtrai, 11 July 1302): A Contribution to the History of Flanders' War of Liberation, *J.F. Verbruggen*

War at Sea in the Middle Ages and Renaissance, *edited by John B. Hattendorf and Richard W. Unger*

Swein Forkbeard's Invasions and the Danish Conquest of England, 991–1017, *Ian Howard*

Religion and the conduct of war, c.300–1017, *David S. Bachrach*

Warfare in Medieval Brabant, 1356–1406, *Sergio Boffa*

Renaissance Military Memoirs: War, History and Identity, *Yuval Harari*

The Place of War in English History, 1066–1214, *J.O. Prestwich, edited with an introduction by Michael Prestwich*